Of Good Comfort

Text copyright © 2016 remains with the author

All rights reserved. Except for any fair dealing permitted under the Copyright Act, no part of this book may be reproduced by any means without prior permission. Inquiries should be made to the publisher.

Creator: Pietsch, Stephen John, 1964- author.

Title: Of good comfort : Martin Luther's letters to the depressed and their significance for pastoral care today / Stephen Pietsch.

ISBN: 9781925486476 (paperback)
       9781925486483 (hardback)
       9781925486490 (ebook : epub)
       9781925486506 (ebook : Kindle)
       9781925486513 (ebook : PDF)

Notes: Includes bibliographical references and index.

Subjects: Luther, Martin, 1483-1546.
 Lutheran Church--Doctrines.
 Depression, Mental.

Dewey Number: 230.41

Cover design and Layout by Astrid Sengkey

Text Minion Pro Size 10 &11

Published by:

An imprint of the ATF Press Publishing
Group owned by ATF (Australia) Ltd.
PO Box 504
Hindmarsh, SA 5007
ABN 90 116 359 963
www.atfpress.com
Making a lasting difference

Of Good Comfort
Martin Luther's Letters to the Depressed and their Significance for Pastoral Care Today

Stephen Pietsch

ATF Theology
Adelaide
2016

Table of Contents

Acknowledgments	vii
Preface	ix
Introduction	ix
Why this research?	ix
Why Luther?	x
Why these letters?	xii
Researching Luther Today	xiv
Luther's Letters as Sources for Theology and Practice	xix
Chapter 1 A Strange World Strangely Familiar	1
Sadness and Madness in Sixteenth Century Germany	2
The Art of the Letter	8
The *Consolatio* Tradition	15
Luther as Comforter	19
Conclusion	24
Chapter 2 'True Joy and Comfort in Christ'	27
Luther's Letters to Those with Depressive Illness	27
Luther in Mid-To-Late Career	30
Luther's 'Rhetoric of the Heart'	31
Overviews	33
Chapter 3 Disagreeing Likeness	101
A Widening Discussion	102
Social Dimensions	109
The Medical Identity of Depression	114
Psychology and Counselling	120
The Re-emergence of Spirituality	125
Pastoral Care Attitudes and Approaches	131
Conclusion	136

Chapter 4 'Comforting the Melancholy' meets
'Counselling the Depressed' 137
   Reaching the Heart: Cognitive–Behavioural
   Insights for Pastoral Care of Persons with Depression 138
   Assailed by the Enemy: Interpreting Luther's
   Demonology of Depression 149
   All Things in Christ: Justification By Grace
   As Comfort For the Depressed 165
   In His Good Time: Suffering, Patience and the Cross 181
   The Comforting Word: Luther's Use of Scripture
   as Consolation for the Depressed 206
   Of Good Cheer: Luther's Practical Theology of Joy 222

Chapter 5 Of Good Comfort 239
   Three Types of Critical Encounter 239
   Conclusion 253

Appendix: Translations 255
1. Elisabeth (Mrs John) Agricola 255
2. Johann Agricola 256
3. Johann Agricola 257
4. Prince Joachim of Anhalt 258
5. Prince Joachim of Anhalt 259
6. Prince Joachim of Anhalt 260
7. Prince Joachim of Anhalt 262
8. Prince Joachim of Anhalt 262
9. Prince Joachim of Anhalt 264
10. Prince Joachim of Anhalt 265
11. Elizabeth von Canitz 266
12. Queen Maria of Hungary 267
13. Barbara Liβkirchen 269
14. John Schlaginhaufen 272
15. George Spalatin 273
16. Mrs Jonas von Stockhausen 276
17. Jonas von Stockhausen 277
18. Jerome Weller 280
19. Jerome Weller 282
20. Jerome Weller 284
21. Matthias Weller 286
Bibliography 289
Index 301

Acknowledgments

I gratefully acknowledge Professor Andrew Dutney and Rev Dr Maurice Schild who supervised me through the PhD research which has led to this book. The critical feedback given by Professors Robert Kolb and Neil Leroux was invaluable, especially during the writing phase of the project.

This work would not have been possible without the loving encouragement, patience and faith of my wife, Coralie Pietsch, and her extensive technical support. For their understanding and unconditional good will I acknowledge my two children, Bethany and Oliver.

For their scholarly advice and assistance with the translation of German and Latin texts, I thank Jeff Silcock, Elmore Leske, Fraser Pearce, Brian van Wageningen and Lois Zweck. For their extensive editorial and technical assistance I acknowledge Rolly Stahl, Pamela Mibus and Greg Lockwood. For their financial assistance and support, I acknowledge the University of Divinity.

I am indebted to all my colleagues, friends and students at Australian Lutheran College and to the staff of Löhe Memorial Library.

Preface

A much larger crisis in pastoral care provided the framework for the Reformation that evolved from Martin Luther's posting of his 95 Theses. These theses on the practice of indulgences addressed the implications for 'the care of souls' and pious living which grew out of the offer of complete remission of the penalties of sin at a price. In Luther's age material well-being was increasing for many people during the on-going recovery from the economic and social devastation caused by the Black Death in the mid-fourteenth century. Germans in the late fifteenth century were therefore increasingly able to invest more time and money in displays of piety and in dedicating their efforts to sacred works designed to please God.

At that time a crisis in the study of the physical heavens was also taking place. Astronomers like Johannes Regiomontanus and his teacher Georg Peuerbach were striving to crunch and juggle the numbers that measured nautical miles and stellar movements to make the Ptolemaic theory fit the facts. It took the imagination of Nikolaus Copernicus' creative mind to offer a view of the solar system from an entirely new perspective. In parallel fashion in the church, late medieval confessors and preachers were strenuously struggling to make grace easier to obtain by modifying and mollifying the demands of the system that required human performance of at least some works, particularly sacred or religious works, to qualify for saving grace. God's grace was necessary to enable the performance of those works that God would accept as sufficient for earning his favor, in time and for eternity. But troubled hearts found ever less satisfaction in this system.

Luther came to break the mold, to redefine what it means to be Christian and how to live in a relationship with God that bestows peace and joy in the midst of a world permeated with evils of one kind or another. Luther's own personality and his orientation in Ockhamist philosophy, with its emphasis on the almighty power of God, combined with his study of Scripture to give him a glimpse of the Christian life as different from his predecessors' worldview as Copernicus' perception of the physical heavens was different from Peuerbach's and Regiomontanus'.

Luther found that God initiates the relationship between himself and his people, and he does so as a person, a person who engages his human creatures in human speech. The God of Scripture is a God of conversation and community, Luther discovered. He has his demands of human beings, to be sure, the professor of Bible from Wittenberg knew. But he also comes as the Creator, who brought the worlds into being by speaking, to give a promise of new life in his own Incarnate self, Jesus of Nazareth. Luther's acute consciousness of all that goes wrong in life, both because we are perpetrators and because we are victims, enabled him to hear more clearly than most the voice of the psalmists and the apostles as they sang sweet melodies of comfort and consolation. He translated their singing into language that spoke this comfort in the midst of what sixteenth-century society labeled *melancholia* and what Luther perceived as *Anfechtungen*—the attacks of evil, both in personal—diabolical—form and in a host of other forms as well.

In this volume Stephen Pietsch builds a bridge across the centuries to enable twenty-first century readers to converse with a pastor who made combatting profound stress and vicious depression his mission – though Pietsch takes seriously warnings against too easy equations of psychological phenomena in cultures separated by a half millennium and countless cultural or societal developments. Pietsch's keen eye and ear assess the rhetorical forms so vital and critical for Luther's pastoral caring as he sketches and analyses how the Wittenberg professor delivered the comfort he found in David's poems and Paul's letters, in the promises of Jesus and the proclamation of the ancient prophets, to sixteenth-century contemporaries, sometimes friends, sometimes only epistolary acquaintances.

Luther's letters offer concrete examples of how Luther joined in the struggle of his correspondents against their own despair, sadness, worries, and fears. His 'letters of consolation' form casebooks exemplifying how with Scripture and prayer, empathy and sensitive understanding, Luther brought the comforting, supportive encouragement of the love of Jesus Christ to the struggling and despairing.

Pietsch's historically sensitive demonstration of contrasts as well as similarities between Luther's world and ours, between his terminology and that of modern psychology, between perceptions of what goes wrong in life then and now, enable readers to enjoy an exchange from a significantly different and hauntingly similar point for viewing the troubles and trauma of those who perceive that life has gone bad. This volume captures the way in which history can speak meaningfully to the present. Its readers will profit much from the author's work as well as Luther's insights and practice.

Robert Kolb
Concordia Seminary, Saint Louis
The third Sunday in Advent 2015

Introduction

Why this research?

Depression is a rapidly growing problem today, emerging more and more commonly in the lives of people from all walks of life. The frequent emergence of depressive illness in pastoral work is, therefore, no surprise. It is clear from the literature that depression is a silent plague in post-modern culture, and is rapidly taking on pandemic proportions. Conservative reckonings are that 25% of Australians will suffer serious clinical depression in their life time and the World Health Organization reports that it has become the greatest single cause of health disability in the world.[1]

Despite this, the Christian Church has not, on the whole, responded to depression (or mental illness in general) very actively during the twentieth century. Since the emergence of psychiatry in the late nineteenth century, with its clinical taxonomy and definitions, and its general rejection of spirituality and religion as forms of neurosis, the church has tended to back away from addressing the needs of the melancholy and depressed, leaving it to the 'new orthodoxy' of medical science, to be treated within that distinct and separate sphere.

As depression has, over the last decade, once again become an object of wider community concern and awareness, the church has a chance to re-engage, offering its ministry of healing and grace to those who deeply need them. But if we are to take up this task faithfully, theological-pastoral insight and reflection are sorely

---

1. 'Depression: A Global Public Health Concern', World Health Organization, accessed August 2013, http://www.who.int/mental_health/management/depression/who_paper_depression_wfmh_2012.pdf.

needed. Pastors and pastoral carers need to understand not only the medical and psycho-social aspects of depression, but also the theological, spiritual and pastoral dimensions. In fact, the whole church, as a community of Christ-like compassion, needs to grow in its awareness and understanding of depression in order to be ready to welcome and care for depressed people, using its unique spiritual gifts and resources, while working collaboratively with medical and mental health professionals.

There is something to be gained from mining contemporary theological and pastoral resources in this area, but much more to gain from listening to voices within the rich history and tradition of the church; spiritual teachers from earlier eras who had not only extensive knowledge of depressive illness, but precious experience in helping depression sufferers. One such voice is that of the sixteenth century theologian and reformer, Martin Luther. This study examines twenty-one of Luther's letters of consolation to depression sufferers to see how his theology and practice may enhance, or even transform, our own pastoral care for the many people in our churches and communities today who suffer the destructive effects of depression.

Why Luther?

Luther himself is arguably Christianity's most famous depressive. It is now part of the rich human portrait we have of him, especially from his letters and *Table Talk*. Luther's depression is comprehensively treated by a number of his twentieth century biographers[2] and has fascinated psychologists, psychotherapists, historians, playwrights and filmmakers alike. Perhaps this aspect of his life has found such a strong foothold in the modern imagination because it reflects to us the growing depressive crisis we are facing today, showing us the human contours of a sickness we recognise all too well.

However, quite apart from the popularist images and legends, the historical sources show that Luther definitely did suffer from a serious depressive illness of some kind. Besides the depressive episodes of his

---

2. John M Todd, *Luther, A Life* (New York: Crossroads, 1982), 23–5, 57–8, 290–91, 343–45. See also HG Haile, *Luther, A Biography* (London: Sheldon, 1980), 299–309. See also Martin Brecht, *Martin Luther, His Road to Reformation 1483–1521* (Minneapolis: Fortress, 1981), 76–81.

youth and the ongoing struggles with it in his early adulthood, Luther suffered a serious and prolonged depressive breakdown between June 1527 and August 1528. During this period he was wretchedly despondent and also suffered severe physical symptoms.[3] In August 1527 he wrote to Melanchthon,

> For the last week I have been cast into death and hell, my whole body so bruised that I tremble in all my members. I had almost lost Christ, and was thrown into the billows and buffeted by storms of despair so that I was tempted to blaspheme against God.[4]

Depressive moods and periods of deep melancholy also visited Luther in latter life, and he remained intensely interested in the nature and dynamics of the malady, not just for his own sake, but because it was a widespread and serious problem in the church and society of his era.[5]

When examined as a separate theme in Luther's writing, depression and melancholy turn out to be surprisingly significant, mentioned a number of times in different contexts, especially in his *Table Talk*.[6] He spoke often about it in very honest personal terms. Most importantly,

---

3. Haile, *Luther, A Biography*, 301–302. See also Mark D Thompson, 'Luther on Despair', in *The Consolations of Theology*, edited by Brian S Rosner (Grand Rapids: Eerdmans, 2008), 61.
4. Letter to Melanchthon, 2 August, 1527. WA BR IV, No.1126, 226:9–11.
5. Luther speaks a lot about his own depressive *Anfechtung* in his *Table Talk*. See especially WA TR I, No.122, 47–52; WA TR I, No.461, 199–201; WA TR III, No.3298, 257; WA TR III, No.3798, 623–25. See also Brecht, *Martin Luther: His Road to Reformation 1483–1521*, 80–81.
6. From the *Table Talk* recorded between 1530 and 1535 (a period during which he was very involved in helping other depressive people with their struggles), much can be gleaned about Luther's understanding and experience of depressive melancholy. Among other things, we see (as corroborated by his letters) that he embraced both spiritual and medical explanations of the illness. See especially WA TR I, No.122, 47–52; WA TR I, No.461, 199–201; WA TR I, No.491, 215–218; WA TR I, No.522, 243–244; WA TR I, No.832, 404–405; WA TR I, No. 977, 494–495; WA TR I, No.1227, 610–611; WA TR II, No.1286, 64; WA TR II, No.1349, 64; WA TR III, No.2889a, 51; WA TR III, No.2889b, 51–54; WA TR III, No.2959, ; WA TR III, No.3298a, 257; WA TR III, No.3298b, 257–259. Luther of course refers to depressive illness throughout the *Table Talk*. See also WA TR III, No.3798, 623–625; WA TR III, No.3823, 640; WA TR IV, No.5155, 686; WA TR VI, No.6618, 81–82 and WA TR VI, No.6896, 256.

he spoke about how he had learned to live with this illness and its effects in the context of Christian faith and hope.

In the years 1530–1535 he was involved in intensive pastoral care and comfort with friends, close associates and members of the nobility who suffered with the dreaded *Schwermut*. Boarding at the Cloister and sitting around Luther's dinner table during this period were Jerome Weller (the tutor of Luther's children) and Johannes Schlaginhaufen (a pastor who had been sacked from his parish). Both were receiving Luther's spiritual and personal support in the midst of serious bouts of depressive illness. In 1534 Luther was also involved in a close pastoral relationship with a neighbouring Prince, Joachim of Anhalt, who was also afflicted with serious melancholy (as we will see from the seven letters Luther wrote to him at this time).

It has been an eye-opener to see how contemporary Christian depression blogs are full of depressed Christians seeking to interpret and affirm their experience of depression by finding in Luther both a *fellow-sufferer* and *spiritual interpreter* of depression, who affirms that this illness is not a failure of faith but *part of* the faith journey, and may even be seen as a mark of growth towards spiritual maturity.

Depressive suffering played a significant role not only in the development of Luther's life and personality, but also in the forging of his theology. In the jaws of depression's acute *Anfechtung* he was forced to develop a realistic theology in which spiritual suffering and agony were taken seriously and understood as meaningful. In this way the experience of depression was critical to the growth of Luther's theology as a marker of the depths to which the human soul can sink and yet still not find itself beyond the reach of God's redemptive hand.

Why these letters?

The answer to this question is best given in the form of a brief narrative. In August, 2008, I became involved in pastoral counselling with three students who had been diagnosed with clinical depression. At around the same time I had begun to read Theodore Tappert's well-known *Luther: Letters of Spiritual Counsel*,[7] which had until that time been

---

7. Luther, Martin. *Luther: Letters of Spiritual Counsel*. Edited by Theodore G Tappert. Volume 18 of The Library of Christian Classics. Louisville, Ky.: Westminster John Knox Press, 1955. Hereafter, this book will be cited as follows: Tappert, *Luther:*

out of print and difficult to obtain. *I quickly noticed several* letters in it which were addressed to people who also appeared to have been struggling with depressive illnesses. When I showed these pastoral letters to my depressive students, thinking they might perhaps gain some spiritual encouragement from them, an extraordinary and unexpected thing happened. The students reported that they found these 500-year-old letters extremely helpful and comforting. In one case the student had begun to read and reread certain letters because he found them so helpful. I certainly had not expected quite this positive response.

As I discussed this with the students on a couple of occasions over the following weeks, it became clear that there was more than one layer to their unexpectedly strong 'resonance' with Luther's letters. The students had the feeling that Luther—a depression sufferer himself—knew personally and intimately the internal experience of depression and was able to describe it in terms they recognised. Moreover, they found Luther's spiritual understanding of the depression experience and his advice on how to deal with depressive thoughts and moods very insightful and effective.

What was going on here? These letters of Luther had been translated into English from sixteenth century Latin and German. They were first written in an historical and social context vastly different to today's. Yet they spoke to the life situations of these three students with an immediacy and power far greater than any help which I or other pastoral carers had been able to offer them.

Subsequent research showed that Luther's letters of consolation often had the same effect on their original readers, and that his letters of comfort to the melancholy in particular have been regarded over the centuries as among Luther's finest and most efficacious consolatory writing. He is, of course, well-known for his deep understanding of human nature and his powerful and affective use of language. One of the reasons his work continues to be assiduously read and researched today is his apparent ability to 'tune in' to the experience of human beings of almost any era. These letters to the depressed are a case in point, perhaps especially because of Luther's own deep struggle with

---

Letters of Spiritual Counsel. At some points I cite Tappert's own commentary on Luther's letters and at other points, Luther's letters themselves. This method of citation covers both possibilities.

depressive illness during his adult life, and his experiential wisdom on how to cope with it.

Further research unearthed several more letters of consolation to the depressed from Luther's pen, most of which were not yet translated into English. Twenty one such letters were finally identified, and became the body of primary sources for this study. It became clear that these letters, together with the other letters of consolation to the melancholy which came to light in the course of preliminary research, represented an opportunity to explore some important questions: What can be learned from Luther about the specifically theological and spiritual dynamics of depression? Do these remarkable letters show us how we might be better equipped to give spiritual comfort and consolation to Christians suffering depression today? This study sets out to explore these and other related possibilities.

Researching Luther Today

In this Luther decade, as we move towards the 500th anniversary of the Reformation in 2017, scholars and researchers are increasingly moving away from historical and theological issues like 'recovering the real Luther' or 'the young Luther'. The focus is shifting toward *receiving* and *interpreting* Luther for our post-modern world; making him a 'dialogue partner' as we engage theologically with contemporary global issues and crises, like ecumenism, poverty, religious violence, injustice and ecology.[8]

Oswald Bayer describes this mode of Luther reception as a *Vergegenwärtigung*, a 'realisation' of Luther's theology in our contemporary context, in which we enter into a real critical yet open conversation with Luther.[9]

---

8. A recent example of such scholarship is Christine Helmer and Bo Kristian Holm, editors, *Transformations in Luther's Theology: Historical and Contemporary Reflections* (Leipzig: Evangelishe Verlagsanstalt, 2012). See also Christine Helmer, 'Introduction: Luther Beyond Luther', in *The Global Luther, A Theologian for Modern Times*, edited by Christine Helmer (Fortress: Minneapolis, 2009), 1–10. See also Risto Saarinen and Jason Lavery, 'Introduction: The Future of Luther Studies', *Dialog* 47, no. 2 (Summer 2008): 91–2.
9. Oswald Bayer, *Martin Luther's Theology: A Contemporary Interpretations*, translated by Thomas H Trapp (Grand Rapids: Eerdmans, 2008), xix.

Mental health—especially the 'pandemic' of depression we are facing today—is definitely a *global crisis,* as indeed it was beginning to become in Luther's Renaissance world, where upheavals and changes of all kinds were rocking society, just as western culture today is rocked by significant social and cultural shifts.[10]

Contemporary Luther scholars, Bo Kristian Holm and Christine Helmer note, 'to read Luther is to transform him with the contemporary questions brought to his theology; to read him is to risk the transformation of one's own perception, biases and judgements.'[11] This book shares the same spirit of contemporary Luther research, asking new questions of Luther's theology which bring forth not only the well-known themes and insights, but also fresh dimensions which speak creatively to today's pastoral context.

Melancholia and Depression

If any such contemporary 'realisation' of Luther's theology and practice is to be attempted, there are some complex historiographical questions which must be addressed. How does the 'melancholia' of Luther's sixteenth century world equate with 'depression' today? Do we know they even refer to the same illness? If so, how can it be established that the recipients of Luther's letters were indeed suffering from this illness?

Prior to the early twentieth century, the clinically identified illness 'depression' did not exist. It was only in the beginnings of the psychiatric movement in the late nineteenth century that depression, as a distinct diagnosis, was differentiated from the wider group of illnesses of the mind and temperament that had previously come under the general heading of *melancholia.*

---

10. Dan Blazer, *The Age of Melancholy: 'Major Depression' and its Social Origins* (New York: Routledge, 2005). Blazer's superb work is a survey of depression's rise in western culture as a response to the changing margins of modernity and postmodernity, influenced by other global issues like two world wars, economic crises and technology.
11. Helmer and Holm, *Transformations in Luther's Theology,* 9. While I could not agree with some of the highly speculative approaches taken in this particular book, the point made by the editors here is a valid one.

It is clear from the literature[12] that there is substantial congruence between what Luther (living in the sixteenth century) called *melancholia* and what is today called clinical depression; however, this congruence is not uncomplicated. A tangled web of language, philosophy, spirituality, culture, science and art bears on this connection. Depressive and melancholic illness has always been socially and culturally constructed to a significant degree.[13] Historically, *melancholia* has moved backwards and forwards across many social and cultural streams through the centuries, and has 'cloaked itself in different colours' at different times, in different places. In the ancient world it was described within the conceptual framework of natural philosophy by Aristotle and Hippocrates, and later in medical terms by Galen and his medieval successors. In the Renaissance, humanists gave it spiritual, intellectual and artistic meanings and in nineteenth century romanticism it became heroic, nostalgic and noble. With the birth of modern medicine and psychiatry it has again come to be defined and understood as disease.

The established authority on this 'winding journey' of melancholy is Stanley Jackson's monumental 1986 historical survey,[14] describing how the broad melancholy tradition gradually gave way to the development of modern medical concepts and categories under the influence of the early founders of psychiatric medicine, chiefly Emil Kraepelin.[15]

This view of the historical movement from melancholia to depression has been widely well-established for many years now. It is simply assumed by many writers and indeed is seen as self-evident. However, it has been challenged more recently by psycho-historian, Jennifer Radden.[16] She does not reject the basic point that modern-

---

12. Stanley W Jackson's comprehensive work *Melancholia and Depression: From Hippocratic Times to Modern Times* (Newhaven: Yale University Press, 1990) establishes this basic connection carefully and thoroughly.
13. See Arthur Kleinman and Byron Good, editors, *Depression and Culture: Studies in the Anthropology and Cross-cultural Psychiatry of Affect and Disorder* (Berkley, University of California Press, 1985). See also Blazer, *The Age of Melancholy*, 19–39.
14. Jackson, *Melancholia and Depression*.
15. See a brief but excellent excerpt from Kraepelin's own writing on the early categories of depression and their medical diagnosis in Radden, *The Nature of Melancholy*, 259–80.
16. Radden, *Moody Minds Distempered*, 75–90.

day depression and past melancholia overlap significantly in terms of their core phenomenology and ontology. However, she makes the observation that this overlap is becoming less discernible as modern-day psychiatric medicine uses increasingly descriptivist methods and language for diagnosing and treating depression. The current handbook of psychiatrists, *The Diagnostic and Statistical Manual of Mental Disorders* (DSM V),[17] works with a strongly categorical epistemology in regard to mental illness, dealing with the immediate phenomenological descriptions of a patient's moods and behaviours. This approach relies on external signs observed by the psychiatrist. The patient's own consciousness, insights and experiences are devalued, as indeed are the various possible contributing causes present in the patient's life-situation. Radden claims that by ignoring the causal and subjective ontologies of patients' depressive illness, modern psychiatry has moved away from the holistic psychodynamic platform of understanding that depression has traditionally shared with melancholia.

Radden's objection to equating today's depression with past melancholia is, therefore, more a reaction against the descriptivist philosophy of modern psychiatry and its abstraction of the human experiences of depression. It is, at any rate, not a claim that depression, as people experience it today, is something substantially different from depressive melancholic states in past eras. Radden herself is able to see the striking commonalities as well as the complexities.

It is also true to say that Radden is comparing melancholia and depression as two fixed points in an historical continuum, taking Renaissance *melancholia* as the standard against which she measures the current psychiatric diagnosis of depression.

Radden's objection to a simple identification of past *melancholia* with present-day depression draws attention to the complex nature of the continuity between past and present. Her scholarship highlights one key point in particular: that *melancholia*-depression is a 'moving target', subject always to the ongoing changes in the social, cultural, religious and medical constructions of history.

Writing from an historical standpoint, HC Erik Midelfort, in his work on madness in sixteenth century Germany, adds another layer

---

17. *The Diagnostic and Statistical Manual of Mental Disorders: DSM-V*, 5th edition, edited by American Psychiatric Association (Washington: APA, 2013).

of depth to this picture.[18] He warns against the risks of jumping too quickly to 'translating' mental disorders from the sixteenth century into today's technical medical language. So much can be—and often is—'lost in translation' in this way. Nevertheless, the very point of seeking to understand the experience of people in other eras is that we may come to know it in some way within the frame of our own experience. Midelfort observes therefore, that things may be 'found in translation' too;[19] a point that encourages the contemporary researcher to go forwards, albeit aware of the complexities and challenges ahead. It is crucial therefore, to take a disciplined phenomenological approach to understanding *melancholia* in its own historical framework, in order to appreciate its depth and complexity, and only then seek points of contact and meaningful encounter with today's experience and language.

Jennifer Radden's other essays on melancholia and depression[20] offer helpful insights. Clearly, not all *melancholia* in previous eras was what we today call depression. *Melancholia* took in a wide variety of things: fleeting dark moods, anxiety disorders both severe and mild, psychoses, mania, neuroses, normal, abnormal and prolonged grief reactions, episodic bouts of sadness and long-term character traits, as well as what would today be regarded as major clinical depression.

In real terms, therefore, it is clear that there is a substantial (though by no means simple) congruence between the melancholic states suffered by Luther's correspondents and what we today call depression. Comparing today's diagnostic indications of clinical depression with the symptoms of people in earlier eras it is clear that depression was present in previous times. The experiences of sadness, despondency, lethargy, agitation, ahedonia, sleep disturbances, withdrawal, fear and suicidal thoughts surface repeatedly as the symptoms of *melancholia* in the writings of the Renaissance, as they do in the diagnostic checklists for clinical depression today. However, in the process of analysing sixteenth century sources, great care must be taken to distinguish the cases of *melancholia* in which such depressive symptoms are clearly present, and those in which they

---

18. HC Erik Midelfort, *A History of Madness in Sixteenth-Century Germany* (Stanford: Stanford University Press, 2000), 9-11.
19. Midelfort, *A History of Madness in Sixteenth-Century Germany*, 9-11..
20. Radden, *Moody Minds Distempered*, 37-56, 58-70, 97-110, 180-86,188-95.

are not. All twenty one letters examined in this book show that the recipients were suffering from primarily depressive symptoms, unlike some other letters in which Luther was responding to situations in which people were displaying signs of other types of mental illness.[21]

Luther's Letters as Sources for Theology and Practice

While it is specifically Luther's pastoral approach to depression which is under examination in this book, it must be acknowledged that there is a significant limiting factor. We do not have access to any first-hand responses from his addressees. We know from other historical accounts that people found Luther's letters very helpful,[22] and in some cases it appears that his addressees did write to him. However, Luther did not as a matter of course collect or keep the letters he received, and they have largely been lost. Apart from a few glimpses and fragments, we consequently have access to only one side of these pastoral encounters.[23]

This issue is, however, mitigated somewhat by the information we have concerning the circumstances surrounding the addressees and their needs, which has been gleaned from the many other letters and historical accounts of the time, and from Luther's letters themselves. Moreover, part of the formal epistolary form of the letter of consolation in the early Renaissance was the *narratio* section, in which the writer recounted the circumstances which had prompted his letter and the sources from which he has received his information.

---

21. For example, in May 1537 Luther wrote to his friend and colleague, Conrad Cordatus (WA BR VII, 79-80) to help him overcome his *hypochondria* (or as it has been renamed in the DSM 5, 'Illness Anxiety Disorder'). In another letter of August, 1536, Luther wrote to his friend, Francis Burkhardt (WA BR VII, 508-509), who was at that time vice-chancellor of Saxony, appealing for mercy on behalf of a certain Frau Kreutzbinder, an insane old woman who was 'accustomed to rage' and had attacked her neigbour with a spear.
22. Mennecke-Haustein, *Luthers Trostbriefe*, 11-13.
23. Although the letters themselves have been lost, we know that Johann Agricola, George Spalatin, Jerome Weller, Johann Schlaginhaufen and Joachim of Anhalt wrote to Luther mentioning their depression and melancholy, because Luther makes reference to receiving their correspondence in his letters to them. In the cases of Johann Schlaginhaufen and Jerome Weller, we have fragments in Luther's *Table Talk* that show his ongoing pastoral care of them in their depressive struggles.

In most of Luther's letters of consolation he adheres to this practice, naming the issue and explaining the context.

These boundaries and limitations notwithstanding, Luther's letters of comfort to the depressed provide us with something unique and precious: his direct personal pastoral address to the reader. From these letters we know what Luther's theology looks like when pastorally applied to the sufferings of life and the struggles of faith. These letters are individual pastoral counsel, employing a wide range of personal and affective expression. They are theology done in the context of interpersonal relationship. Luther's particular rhetorical style of writing—for the ear rather than the eye—means also that what we read in these letters is a kind of direct 'speech', which brings us not only 'close to the man' but 'close to the moment'.

Pastoral Care as the Primary Focus

While medical and psychological definitions and information about depression inform this book, they do not comprise the primary conceptual framework for it. This study is interested primarily in evaluating the validity and relevance for today of Luther's *pastoral* approach, concentrating on the theological and spiritual means of *Seelsorge* which he employs.

While contemporary human sciences will inevitably come into encounter with Luther and find points of contact, this encounter plays only an ancillary role. The aim is not to evaluate Luther's pastoral care of the depressed in clinical terms, but to concentrate on what may be learned in terms of Christian ecclesial pastoral care.

Christian pastoral care is carried out by the church and primarily employs the spiritual means of ministry. While it may utilise insights and methods from psychology, it is nevertheless not a form of *treatment for clinical therapeutic effect*, even though it seeks to sustain, help, counsel, guide, heal and bless. While these pastoral functions may indeed contribute to a person's recovery from depressive illness, they do so from within a theologically constructed rather than a scientifically established frame of reference.

It is important to state this priority clearly in view of the fact that, in contemporary western culture, depression is understood above all else as an *illness* requiring medical and psychological intervention.

This means that spiritual and pastoral care are often sidelined or 'lumped in with' medical care or psychological treatment, and the unique concerns and gifts of Christian pastoral care not clearly distinguished or understood.

The intent of this book is to return to addressing the long-forgotten theological and spiritual dimensions of depressive illness, drawing on the unique insight and experience of Luther. As we engage with his advice to his readers, which is born out of his own profound experience of depression, and his spiritual reflections upon it, we not only find that Luther is able to address us meaningfully today, but that his theology and pastoral counsel have potential to enhance and even transform our practice of Christian care and comfort with depression sufferers.

Chapter 1
A Strange World Strangely Familiar
Melancholy and Comfort in Early Modernity

> 'Lost, is it, buried? One more missing piece?
> But nothing's lost. Or else all is translation
> And every bit of us is lost in it...'
> James Merrill, 'Lost in Translation'
> From his *Divine Comedies*, 1976.

As a first step toward understanding and interpreting Luther's letters for our day, it is important to try to understand on its own terms the 'strangeness' of Luther's world, even if, in this brief overview, we cannot do justice to all its depth and complexity.

There are a host of external features in Luther's world which are strange to us: the hierarchical structures of society, the socio-political importance of religion and the church, the formal nature of relationships, the imperial and electoral political worlds, the conventions of literature, customs of communication, marriage, family life and much more.

However, the differences run much deeper, to the underlying linguistic, epistemological and spiritual constructs of life. Luther's early modern *Lebensgefühl* is far more in touch with the spiritual dimension of life than is ours; his pre-Enlightenment world was more charged with the supernatural and with the sense of wonder and fear which accompanied it. No Cartesian dualism had yet split feeling and intuition from reason and logic, and so Luther's way of thinking about issues is far more integrated and holistic than ours is. As Birgit Stolt observes, today we may understand more but we *feel* less; our affective and emotional selves are subordinated to our rationality. While our language today is suited to science, there is a 'peculiar helplessness' of expression in regard to questions of life, meaning and death.[1]

Yet, even as we become aware of the strangeness of Luther's world, we find that we warm to the people we meet there, because early modern human beings and their needs, fears, delights and hopes are quite recognisable to us. The fundamental experiences of life in sixteenth century Germany are not so different to our own as to be strange beyond our understanding and imagination. As Peter Matheson points out, while we cannot simply assume that Luther and the people of his era thought and acted just as we do, it is equally wrong-headed to view them as though they are 'strange animals in a zoo'.[2]

Sadness and Madness in Sixteenth Century Germany

The cultural, social and religious world of early sixteenth century Germany is complex and many-layered, situated as it is at the opening of early modernity, with the legacy of the Middle Ages still exerting considerable influence. Apart from the Reformation movement and its associated geo-political issues, Renaissance humanism had emerged in Germany and brought with it significant cultural and literary changes. Especially significant for this study is the new and growing interest in individual human experience and its meanings, especially in the light of early modern medical research and the possibility (for the wealthy at least) of seeking medical help from professional doctors and apothecaries.

On this backdrop, new social and cultural constructions began to emerge. The growth of education and the development of the printing press created a flow of ideas and images of human life that had not been known. The wide availability of pamphlets and tracts made all this accessible to more people than ever before.[3]

---

1. Brigit Stolt, 'Joy, Love and Trust—Basic Ingridients in Luther's Theology of Faoth of the Heart', Luther Colloquy Lectures, 31 October 2001, Institutue for Luther Studies at Lutheran Theological Seminary, Gettysburg. Acessed 6 July 2011. http:/www.holytrinitynewrochelle.otg/yourti84373.html..
2. Peter Matheson, *The Imaginative World of the Reformation* (Minneapolis: Fortress, 2001), 102.
3. 'How Luther Went Viral: Social media in the 16th Century', The Economist,

Along with intellectual and religious renewal, there were darker aspects: the rise of occultism and magical approaches to medical science, and the witch-craze. This period was also characterised by an increasing incidence of *melancholia* of many kinds in Germany (including *depressive melancholia*). Levack observes that it was regarded as the 'fountain of most other kinds of illness'.[4] It affected people at all levels of society, from the peasant population to mad and melancholy princes and noble women. Poverty and deprivation were associated with mental illness, but so was the wealthy idleness of the aristocracy, among whom melancholy was increasingly the 'fashionable illness'. This 'culture of melancholy' among the elite was legitimised by neo-galenic medicine and fed by sophisticated philosophical and spiritual discourse. Historians still speculate about why there seems to have been such an escalation in the prevalence of melancholic illness in the early Renaissance. The most popular explanation is that the Reformation brought with it great spiritual, political and social upheavals which rocked European society's already fragile psychological homeostasis. Angus Gowland has also shown that melancholy's rise at this time was due in part to the development of European intellectual culture and the increasing interest in the psychology and the growing consciousness of individual experience, and the passions of the soul. This growing self-reflection and self-awareness encouraged a focus on states of mind and the development of new 'vocabularies of discomfort',[5] so that melancholy became much more than an illness; it was in fact one of the 'fundamental axes of Renaissance culture.'[6]

Religious Despair and Melancholy

One of the legacies handed down to early modern Christians was the continuing fear of God's wrath and judgement. This brief life was a testing ground for eternity, where one accumulated merits before God in order to forestall the certain judgement to come. The plague's regular visits to German towns and cities meant that death literally

---

December 17, 2011, accessed January 4, 2012, http://www.economist.com/node/21541719.
4. Brian P Levack, *The Devil Within: Possession and Exorcism in the Christian West* (New York: Yale University Press, 2013), 117.
5. Midelfort, *A History of Madness*, 14.
6. Levack, *The Devil Within*, 117.

was 'around the corner'. Beyond death lay purgatory or hell–not just theoretical possibilities for the early modern Christian, but terrifying realities. Even for those who had embraced the reformation faith in Christ's free justification of sinners and the assurance of eternal life, these deeply rooted fears still gnawed at the subconscious. The struggle with sin and the unruly passions still brought 'terrors of conscience'. Luther himself was troubled by this right to the end of his life.[7]

Not far in the background here, especially for the pious and well-educated, was the medieval view of depressive sadness (*tristitia*) as a form of blasphemy. Since life was God's good gift, to despair of it was sinfully to reject and deny God's goodness. Awareness of this judgement added even more weight to the terrors of depressive illness, as we can see from some of Luther's consolatory letters, in which he takes pains to explain and reinterpret the theological meaning of his reader's suffering.[8]

A more specific type of depressive melancholic malady which emerged from educated religious consciousness at this time was the fear of being predestined to damnation. An already well-known depressive obsession in the Middle Ages, this malady was stirred again in the Reformation not only by Luther's theology, but also by Calvin's teaching on the matter. In the face of God's sovereign foreknowledge of who is elected to salvation and who is not, individuals must somehow find out for themselves to which realm they belong. Sometimes a highly scrupulous individual's ongoing struggle with sin and fear of divine condemnation seemed like evidence of being eternally lost. And sometimes it was more complicated: many wrestled with the suspicion that their persistent fear of not being predestined to salvation was perhaps itself also a blasphemous rejection of God's sovereign will.

---

7. In a table talk recorded by Veit Dietrich on February 19, 1533, Luther comments, 'My trial is this, that I think I do not have a gracious God. This is the law. It is the most severe sorrow, as Paul says, which kills…' (WA TR I, No.461, 200: 6–8).
8. For example, Luther's *letter to Queen Maria of Hungary*, 1531 (See Appendix).

Luther's Understanding of Depressive Melancholy

While no thorough or extensive study has yet been done of the concept of *melancholia* in Luther's writings, it is not hard to construct an indicative picture.[9] What emerges is the oft-remarked-upon tension: Luther sometimes appears surprisingly modern, in tune as he was with much of the humanist thinking and science of his day. At other times, his view of life and the world is typically medieval. His understanding of *melancholia* and depressive illness reflects this duality in response to the increasing complexity of his time, with its changing cultural margins and paradigms. Luther's view of *melancholia* also reflects the dimensions of his own spiritual and theological development. He was, like almost every scholar at that time, an adherent of galenic medicine, which saw depressive melancholia as the product of an imbalance in bodily humours: an excess of black bile which dried out the flesh and bones, and caused dark moods and misery.[10] Unlike some other great humanist scholars of his day (including his close friend Philipp Melanchthon),[11] Luther never wrote a treatise on *melancholia* or madness. However, as Erik Midelfort points out, he often commented on these things in ways which show significant insight into the humanist medical psychology of his day.[12] It is also clear that he approved of—and himself accepted—the latest medical treatments for the sickness.[13]

---

9. While he mentions melancholy throughout his writings (including his letters), Luther deals with it most extensively in his *Table Talk*. See Pietsch, 'Reflection on Depression in Luther's *Table Talk*'.
10. WA TR III, No. 3823, 640:13-21. In this fascinating vignette, Luther talks about why wild game is often dry and tasteless, explaining that the animals had been 'melancholy' and anxious from being chased and hunted, therefore their flesh was dry and unappetizing. Luther's reasoning here reflects quite a technical understanding of galenic theory about *melancholia* and its effects.
11. Melanchthon was very interested in humanist thought on the topic, and indeed wrote an important treatise on melancholia himself: Philipp Melanchthon, *De melancholia hypochondriaca positiones inaugurales* (Basileae : Typis Iohan. Iacobi Genathii, 1629) originally published 1529, E-rara, original copy owned by Universitätsbibliothek Basel, accessed October 2013, http://dx.doi.org/10.3931/e-rara-17563.
12. Midelfort, *A History of Madness*, 83.
13. In July 1527, Luther suffered a complete depressive breakdown and was attended by a local physician and medical professor at the University, Dr Augustinus Schurff, who applied medical treatment which reportedly brought the patient back from the brink of death. See Maurice Schild, 'Luther as Comforter', in

However, Luther's medieval demonology, fostered through his religious life and experience, was still a strong driving force in his life. Like most of his contemporaries, he saw behind the medical aetiologies and treatments of the illness the devil's malign supernatural interference, especially in the form of baseless guilt and shame, sad and downcast thoughts and fears.[14] It is evident that when he speaks and writes more personally to others in their struggles with depressive illness, he views it through the lens of his own spiritual battles, as a kind of directly experienced evil-work of the devil who is anti-life and anti-God.[15] In a table talk he even asserts that the devil is himself a melancholic madman who is lonely, jealous and depressed, and so wishes to make others so.[16]

Luther uses vocabulary that is more medically oriented, like *melancholia* or *Melancholie* alongside and sometimes synonymously with spiritually loaded terms, especially *tristitia*; a word with its own long history and broad semantic profile.[17] Not only was Luther underlining the connection of the melancholic medical condition to the spiritual problem of *trisitia*, but also signalling the underlying implications of depressive illness for the conscience and faith of the sufferer.

Luther also used madness and *melancholia* in the blistering religious rhetoric he unleashed on his theological enemies. For him, theological error was not just wrong-headed but truly dangerous to one's very soundness of mind, because it led to false beliefs that plunged the soul into self-delusion and trust in its own fantasies, as in the case of Thomas Müntzer.[18] He saw this spiritually induced insanity as the cause of the demented ravings of the enthusiasts and

---

Perspectives on Martin Luther: Papers from the Luther Symposium held at Luther Seminary, Adelaide, South Australia, 22-23 March, 1996, Commemorating the 450th Anniversary of the Reformer's Death, edited by MW Worthing (Adelaide: Open Book SA. 1996), 16.

14. Levack, *The Devil Within*. 119-21.
15. Pietsch, 'Reflection on Depression in Luther's *Table Talk*', 25-6.
16. WA TR I, No. 977, 494:7-8.
17. Luther prefers the word *tristitia*, which was his main Latin noun for referring to depressive feelings. It has stronger spiritual-affective nuances. He tends to use the word *melancholia* more when referring to the sickness as a bodily illness to be diagnosed and treated medically. See Pietsch, 'Reflection on Depression in Luther's *Table Talk*', 17 (footnote 39).
18. Midelfort, *A History of Madness*, 107.

heavenly prophets, whom he considered mad, and who, having lost their minds, had been infiltrated by the devil.[19] True doctrine, on the other hand, was obviously healthful. The Gospel led people to Christ and his Word instead of leaving them to 'drive themselves crazy' by trying to achieve salvation by their own works.[20]

Depression and 'Anfechtung'

It is often assumed in the wider Luther discussion that in his writings the word *Anfechtung* (literally 'being attacked') simply equates to his depressive illness and the spiritual anxieties associated with it.[21] While it is clear that sometimes this is certainly what he means by *Anfechtung*, the picture is not just that simple. The term has a much broader semantic range than one meaning, and can carry many different connotations (material, relational, medical, psychological, political and spiritual) depending on the time and context of its use. Early in Luther's career the word is associated with his experiences of deep fear and melancholy as a sinner before a righteous and unmerciful God. In his more-mature years, he uses the word *Anfechtung* to refer to other trials as well. The term took on a deeper theological dimension through its close association with *tentatio* and God's use of suffering in the life of the Christian.[22] The word itself has a broad and complex range of meanings and needs to be interpreted carefully, according to the way Luther uses it in various contexts.

The term *Anfechtung* appears in only three of the twenty-one letters examined in this study, each time referring directly to the depressive melancholy of the addressee.[23] These references all reflect the two related emphases characteristic of Luther's use of *Anfechtung*:

---

19. Midelfort, *A History of Madness*, 83–6. This was, of course, a common theme in the sixteenth century. Zwingli also used the rhetoric of madness, in his polemics against the Anabaptists. See Gowland, 'The Problem of Early Modern Melancholy', 106.
20. Midelfort, *A History of Madness*, 107.
21. Such assumptions are imprecise and all too common. See Stone, *Depression and Hope*, 27. See also Ritchie, "The Depressed Luther."
22. Luther uses the German *Anfechtung* and the Latin *tentatio* almost synonymously at times, or at least as close counterparts, to refer to the Christian's experience of spiritual trial and testing. See Stolt, *Laßt uns Fröhlich Springen*, 66–7.
23. Luther's *letter to Queen Maria of Hungary* of 1531 (See Appendix); The *letter to Prince Joachim of Anhalt*, June 23, 1534 (See Appendix) and the *letter to Matthias Weller* of October 7, 1524 (See Appendix). The specific circumstances surrounding these three letters will be dealt with in chapter 4.

a) the emotion of terror, despair and anguish and b) the sense of being assaulted or attacked by the devil.[24]

What we may take from Luther's use of *Anfechtung* to refer to depressive illness in these letters is that he saw the devil's attack behind depressive melancholic illness. Not only does Satan attack the body through physical pain and suffering, but also 'the heart' and conscience through despairing thoughts (*schwere Gedanken*) of being condemned in sin, and lost forever—a fear Luther knew only too well and encountered in other depression sufferers. Depressive *melancholia* is for Luther therefore, a form of *Anfechtung* that affects the whole person and is particularly harmful and dangerous.[25]

The Art of the Letter

One of the most important aspects of Luther's world for us to elucidate is the central role of epistolary culture. The letter was a technically refined tool for every kind of communication and contact. In Luther's time the conventions of letter-writing, which had filtered down from antiquity through the Middle Ages, were in the midst of significant change. Renaissance humanism, with its fondness for all things classical, reprised the ancient rhetorical forms of the letter from Greco-Roman literature.[26] These often-elaborate and poetic ancient forms were used as literary devices for philosophical discourse or teaching. Such letters or 'epistles' were not always restricted to the educated. They were sometimes addressed to the general public or to a defined audience, in which case they could be read aloud. At times, however, the letter as a 'personal message' was used as a rhetorical

---

24. This double-emphasis has been noted by scholarly analysis over many years, most notably by Horst Beintkar, *Die Überwindung der Anfechtung bei Luther: eine Studie zu seiner Theologie nach den Operationes in Psalmos 1519-21* (Berlin: Evangelische Verlagsanstalt, 1954). See also the summary by Stolt, *Laßt uns Fröhlich Springen*, 60-5.
25. As we will see, in these twenty-one letters Luther warns many of his readers about the danger of melancholic depression ruining one's physical health and strength, robbing one of youth and vitality as well as leading to spiritual despair and suicide.
26. Judith Rice Henderson, 'Humanism & Humanities: Erasmus's *Opus de conscribendis epistolis* in Sixteenth-Century Schools', in *Letter-Writing Manuals and Instruction from Antiquity to the Present*, edited by Carol Poster and Linda C Mitchell (Columbia: University of South Carolina Press, 2007), 141-76.

device, put on for public consumption. This is the epistolary form that was adapted by the writers of the New Testament epistles, and by the early church fathers in their pastoral letters to the churches. These too usually functioned as open or circular letters, and were copied several times in order to be used as resources for catechesis and preaching.

The medieval period had seen the development of more formularised and specialised forms of the letter, written according to strict guidelines which regulated both style and content. Several famous manuals on the art of the letter date from this period, and the production of such manuals continued apace into the early Renaissance.

Judith Rice Henderson observes that the proliferation of these manuals in early modern Germany was probably due in part to the Lutheran reform movement itself, since letter-writing became part of the emerging curriculum of the new schools that were being opened in various parts of Germany. In 1524 Luther appealed to the leaders of the free cities in Germany to found Christian schools,[27] in order to popularise humanist education among the middle classes, enabling them to read the Bible for themselves.

In Luther's day, the letter was again, in varying degrees, being used in its classical rhetorical formats, under the growing influence of humanism. It served a variety of functions: to argue theological or philosophical points; to serve as a political or diplomatic instrument; to give consolation and encouragement to groups and individuals; to make requests for help and to give advice or direction. In Luther's world, letters were generally considered, as Gábor Almási aptly puts it, 'publicly private'.[28] Some letters were conceived at the outset as rhetorical pieces to be read aloud to groups. However, even letters that began as 'private correspondence' frequently did not remain so.

---

27. *To the Councilmen of all cities in Germany that they establish schools*, 1524, (WA XV, 9–15).
28. Gábor Almási, 'Humanistic Letter-Writing', EGO European History Online, accessed May 2012, http://www.ieg-ego.eu/en/threads/european-networks/intellectual-and-academic-networks/gabor-almasi-humanistic-letter-writing, 3-4. While some letters functioned as prefaces or introductions to other written pieces, and were therefore published, personal letters were more often shared, sometimes copied and passed on from person to person. Of course, there were *some* letters that remained confidential, and were not shared more widely.

Our strong values concerning the privacy of correspondence today were certainly not known in the sixteenth century. Letters were often delivered by couriers or messengers who knew a lot about the circumstances of the writer, and who often had verbal messages to deliver as well.[29] People routinely shared their letters with one another and their contents were often effectively in the public domain.[30]

Among the educated classes, where alliances, friendships, associations, familial relationships, common interests or professional networks needed to be maintained and built up over distance, the letter was an indispensable tool. Far from being the 'throw away items' they have largely become today, letters were treated as valuable gifts, frequently kept and treasured. Almási observes:

> The nature of the letter as a gift, particularly in Early Modern Times, was further supported by the fact that letters frequently travelled together with more material gifts: books, species of artefacts, plants, seeds, pieces of collections, etc. The exchange of letters served not only the goal of knowledge distribution and the spread of information of all kinds, but was the principal instrument for the exchange of gestures.[31]

Luther's Use of Letters

There is probably no sixteenth century figure who has left as many letters for posterity as Luther: in excess of 2,600 separate pieces, spanning thirty-six years, filling no fewer than eighteen fat volumes. Written quickly –sometimes at lightning speed– and dispatched by postal courier or sent with travellers or friends, Luther's letters covered a broad range of issues: family needs, political matters, theological discussion, advocacy of various kinds, advice and spiritual counsel, as well as casual observations on life.

Especially in the case of important and authoritative writers, letters were much more than 'documents' in the modern sense; they carried the authority and presence of the writer, and were a means of

---

29. In one of the letters in this selection there is an example of this. Luther wrote to Johann Agricola in Eisleben in July 1527 about the depressive illness of Agricola's wife, Elisabeth (Appendix:302). In this letter Luther refers briefly to another matter which 'Stephanus [the courier] will explain to you . . . .'
30. Almási, 'Humanistic Letter-Writing', 3.
31. Almási, 'Humanistic Letter-Writing', 9.

being able to 'speak' to others across time and distance. As with other professionals and scholars, the letter was one of Luther's main tools of trade, facilitating his work in all the spheres in which he operated–as reformer, theologian, politician, friend and pastor.[32] The narrative of the whole early Reformation can be told from Luther's prolific correspondence–as indeed it has been.[33]

While Luther did not embrace German Renaissance humanism in all its dimensions, he did make considerable use of humanistic literary and rhetorical conventions and contributed to their development. Many of his writings exemplify these features, and indeed his succeeding generation regarded him as the 'German Cicero', the 'founder' of the rapidly developing German language.

Luther had no hesitation in using the popular forms of his day for his own purposes, mixing and matching from the rich palette of epistolary styles in use at the time. Almási observes that in the early modern period a common feature of letter-writing was a kind of 'rhetorical intimacy of address' that did not fit with the actual relationship between writer and addressee, who in many cases may never even have met in person or corresponded before. This 'familiar letter' form seems to have been a device to enable correspondents to cut through the formalities and procedures which had characterised medieval epistolary etiquette. Luther used this device with ease, as Almási shows from Luther's letter to Erasmus in March 1519.[34] There is more than one example of it among the consolatory letters included in the selection for this study.[35]

Such familiarity was, however, not appropriate for all situations. Luther also used the more formal epistolary conventions for his purposes. He could use the traditional *captatio benevolentiae* very effectively too. Luther's self-effacement and his praise of others

---

32. Almási, *Humanistic Letter-Writing*, 5.
33. Martin Brecht's three volume biography of Luther, *Martin Luther: His Road to Reformation 1483-1521* (Minneapolis: Fortress, 1985), *Martin Luther: Shaping and Defining the Reformation 1521-1532* (Minneapolis: Fortress, 1990), *Martin Luther: The Preservation of the Church, 1532-1546* (Minneapolis: Fortress, 1999), like most biographies leans heavily on Luther's letters as primary sources for his life and work, both for the historical content and its interpretation.
34. Almási, *Humanistic Letter-Writing*, 2.
35. Luther's *letters to Maria of Hungary* (See Appendix); *Jonas von Stockhausen* (See Appendix); *Matthias Weller* (See Appendix).

(particularly in letters to noble and royal personages) may seem overdone to our eyes, but it is important to understand that this was a fixed feature of epistolary etiquette in this era. Frequently in his opening greetings Luther makes self-deprecating comments while heaping accolades on his addressee, but in the next paragraph deftly moves to the issue at hand, and speaks with surprising frankness.[36] Luther was also comfortable with classical stoic styles of *argumentatio* and *consolatio*. He often (particularly in his *Trostbriefe*) used letters to develop exegetical-theological discourses on biblical texts.[37]

However, one of the most striking rhetorical schemas Luther used in his letters was not borrowed from the humanist conventions of his time but from scripture. In the years following 1521, Luther sent a series of *Trostbriefe* to evangelical Christian communities and congregations in Germany who were suffering persecution, in which he imitates the Pauline epistles of the New Testament. A letter he wrote to the congregation at Wittenberg in August 1521, while still in hiding at the Wartburg, shows how Luther identified his own situation with that of the imprisoned apostle Paul.[38] Feeling himself closely aligned with followers of the Reformation movement elsewhere in Germany who were suffering opposition, he took on himself the role of apostolic teacher and comforter, and in this group of letters the distinct rhetorical and literary character of the 'apostolic epistle' can be seen.[39]

Whatever conventions Luther adopted, he showed a superior mastery of language in the way he wove his own theological and pastoral content into the well-known constructions and forms, using

---

36. See Luther's *letter to Queen Maria of Hungary* (See Appendix) and his *first letter to Prince Joachim of Anhalt* (See Appendix).
37. See Luther's letter to John Hess, the evangelical pastor in Breslau, Silesia, on whether Christians should flee the plague: WA XXIII, 323-386 (Tappert, *Luther: Letters of Spiritual Counsel*, 230-244). This letter, though addressed to a particular person and community, became an open letter which was republished many times and read all over Germany.
38. WA VIII, 210:7-15.
39. Luther did not see himself as some 'new apostle', but rather as one standing in continuity with Paul's teaching and practice, as can be seen by the way he quotes and explains passages of comfort and paranesis from Paul's own epistles. See also Luther's letter from February 1524, 'To the Christians of Miltenberg', WA XV, 54-78 (Tappert, *Luther: Letters of Spiritual Counsel*, 199-208). See also Timothy J Wengert, 'Martin Luther's Movement Toward an Apostolic Self-awareness as Reflected in His Early Letters', in *Lutherjahrbuch* 61 (1994): 71-92.

subtle as well as radical variations of style and approach. Working creatively with the tradition, he made expert use of the affective impact of the rhetorical language and forms at his disposal. He could convey much in how he chose his terms of address, formal framework and terminology, often making well-used epistolary formulae ring with new meaning, sincerity and conviction[40] As Birgit Stolt observes: with Luther's written texts the reader feels the power of his personality and presence. The rhetorical force of his words, even in the midst of formal discourse, can be direct and conversational.[41] Handling weighty issues with great deftness and, at times, even lightness, he gets to the heart of the matter in a few words. Using a mixture of formal and unexpectedly informal language, he moves easily backwards and forwards between personal and more public issues, keeping the reader guessing about what is coming next.[42]

Like other letters of this era, Luther's letters were never—at least not in the modern sense—really private. More often than not they became highly public, as they were copied and later, printed. Luther routinely assumed that his letters would be read by others, and read the letters of others himself. Lyndal Roper suggests that letters in Luther's time functioned rather like email does today, being readily forwarded and semi-public. This was accentuated by the new technology of print, which allowed Luther to use his letters—once published and widely available—to quickly enhance his popular support among the nobles, churchmen and academy of his time, by appealing to the public 'over the heads' of his apparent addressees. Somewhat cynically, Roper contends that the letter became one of the Reformation's most successful propagandist genres. She cites Luther's many prefatory letters to treatises and pamphlets written by others as Luther's way of giving his approval and support to those whose views he liked, thus increasing his propagandist reach.[43]

---

40. Mennecke-Haustein, *Luthers Trostbriefe*, 17.
41. Stolt, 'Joy, Love and Trust'
42. See, for example, some of Luther's *letters to Spalatin*: WA BR I, No.99, 214–15 and WA BR II, No.410, 337–338 as examples.
43. Lyndal Roper, '"To His Most Learned and Dearest Friend"': Reading Luther's Letter', in *German History*, 28, No 3 (September 2010). Luther's political use of letters is undeniable, however, such were the political tactics and games of the day. Luther was not the only one who had access to print or who used it to win support and criticise his opponents.

There is plenty of evidence therefore to suggest that when reading Luther's letters, we should not too quickly assume that we are being granted privileged access into correspondence disclosing his most intimate and personal thoughts. However, it may also be contended that in the case of many of the letters which were later copied and published, Luther's own personal thoughts are *exactly* what we find.[44] This is a unique feature of his pastoral practice; in laying his life (including his own weaknesses and struggles) open to others, he allowed others access to his inner struggles so that they might see God's help and comfort at work in the suffering of a human being who was like them. In the case of many of Luther's *Trostbriefe*—which were assiduously copied and passed to others—the outcome was that great benefit and comfort flowed beyond the addressee to other sufferers.

Taking into account the complexities involved in understanding Luther's intentions, his letters still reveal his character better and more fully than any other documents from his pen. His reputation for harsh invective and polemical crudeness has often led to simplistic caricatures which do no justice to the depth and range of Luther's personality. His letters reveal him to be not only a frank, choleric person of strong views, but also a person capable of great insight, wit, subtlety, deep compassion, humility, loyalty, empathy and personal warmth, who took time to care for the troubled, and who valued and maintained deep friendships.[45]

---

44. This is especially the case in his *Trostbriefe*. See his *letter to Barbara Lißkirchen* in 1531, in which Luther speaks about his own struggle with the doctrine of predestination (See Appendix), or his letter to Peter Beskendorf in 1535, in which Luther reflects on his spiritual coldness and struggles with praying (WA XXVIII, 351–73).

45. Luther's letters to his friends, Melanchthon, Spalatin and Bugenhagen demonstrate his consistent love and concern for those whom he considered his allies, brothers and confidants. A beautiful example of this is his *letter to Spalatin* in August 1544 (See Appendix), in which Luther comforts his old friend after he has made a serious pastoral mistake which precipitated his falling into a deep depression. The depth and quality of this friendship is shown by the way Luther is able to be both honest and compassionate, calling his friend to let go of his shame and guilt and live in the forgiveness of God. See also Lyndal Roper, 'Martin Luther's Body: The "Stout Doctor" and His Biographers', *The American Historical Review* 115, no. 2 (April 2010): 379–80.

The *Consolatio* Tradition

In order to understand the pastoral theology and practice of Luther in his letters to people with depressive illness, it is important to see how he was profoundly shaped by another important strand of the western cultural tradition: *consolatio* (the art of comforting and consoling those in affliction). This tradition of pastoral care fell largely into obscurity in the modern period, but in early Renaissance Europe it was a major theme in ecclesiastical life and personal spirituality. In its most general sense *consolatio* was a broad literary genre encompassing various forms of rhetorical speech and literature: orations, essays, poems, personal letters and public epistles. This strand of the Christian tradition is entwined with the classical epistolary genre sketched above, and the two function together in a complementary manner in the consolatory letters of the early modern period, including the letters of Luther. As with the conventions of letter-writing, so with *consolatio*, Luther shaped the received forms in his own way.

The Roots of the Tradition

Dating back to the fifth century BC, *consolatio* developed and grew during the Greco-Roman period, where it took on its classical philosophical character, chiefly through the influence of stoicism. Rhetorical consolatory speeches were made at funerals to comfort the mourners, and it was the duty of friends to send consolatory letters to the bereaved and afflicted. These expressions were sometimes highly personal and affective, and served to affirm and respond to the emotions of grief and suffering. Letters of consolation functioned in a semi-public way, serving to bring the empathy of the community in touch with the sufferer. *Consolatio* was, however, not primarily about outpourings of emotion but sought to ease the pain of loss and suffering by offering comforting 'arguments' or rationalisations. Typically, these comforts ran along stoic lines. In the case of bereavement, for instance, a common *argumentatio* was that death must come to all, young or old, and all who are born must likewise leave this life, so to accept living is to accept dying.

The *consolatio* genre, with its rhetorical forms and conventions, was readily taken over into Christian literature and life, influencing pastoral care practice, pastoral letters and epistles from the earliest times of the church. It is clear that strong elements of this are visible in Paul's epistles,[46] and it is certainly evident in early Christian literature.[47]

The tradition was embellished considerably by the church of the Middle Ages. It was seen as the vocation and office of all Christians (laity and clergy) to comfort others with works and words of loving mercy and empathy.[48] This *officium consolandi* was developed in an especially rich way in monastic communities, where an intensive form of religious community life had its own spiritual trials and suffering which required special spiritual consolations.[49]

Structure and Form

Christian *consolatio*, in its various rhetorical forms (oratorical or literary), is generally structured around seven basic elements which may expand or contract, or be reordered and reiterated, depending on context and specific content:

1. *Salutatio* (address and greeting)
2. *Exordium* (opening words)
3. *Narratio* (occasion and circumstances)
4. *Argumentatio* (the consolation itself-explanation and propositions)
5. *Remedia* (outcomes, means and/or actions which bring comfort and help)
6. *Exhortatio* (encouragement to particular attitudes, actions or habits)
7. *Conclusio* (prayer, blessing, commendation to God and/or good wishes)

---

46. Paul A Holloway, *Consolation in Philippians: Philosophical Sources and Rhetorical Strategy* (New York: Cambridge University Press, 2001).
47. JHD. Scourfield, 'The De Mortalitate of Cyprian: Consolation and Context', *Vigiliae Christianae* 50/1 (1996): 12–41. See also Hummel, *Clothed in Nothingness*, 8.
48. Part of Luther's view of consolation is the necessity of *Mitleid*–suffering with the person, Galatians 2:6. See Luther's *letter to Jerome Weller* from August 1530 (See Appendix).
49. Luther bears testimony to the profound value and importance of this system of pastoral care in his own life in the monastery in his repeated praise of the pastoral care he received from his confessor, Johann von Staupitz. See his table talk from 1531, WA TR I, No.122, 47–52 and his *letter to Jerome Weller* from the Coburg in July 1530 (See Appendix). It is clear that Luther's own deep commitment to and proficiency in pastoral care and counsel were shaped by this monastic model.

These seven basic elements can be seen, to varying degrees, in all late medieval and early modern consolatory writings. They can be clearly identified in all of Luther's consolatory writings too, but are particularly visible in his consolatory letters, in which the structure and progression are relatively unclouded by the length, repetition and complexity of other forms.

Luther's Reshaping of Consolatio

It is important to note that Luther received the tradition of Christian *consolatio* positively, and like much other theology and teaching that came down from the early church fathers, he held it in high regard. He also valued the medieval tradition of *consolatio* and its emphasis on the *officium humanitaris*—the duty of offering humanitarian help and mercy to those in distress. In so doing he also honoured the classical tradition of consolation as a function of friendship.

But more than this, Luther wanted to lift up the duty of all Christians of all classes to comfort others as the *mandatum Christi*—a task commanded by Christ and related directly to his work. This duty is shared by all Christians, lay and ordained, and is part of loving and suffering with the neighbour, as Paul commands in Romans 12:15.

Luther's Augustinian monastic formation was steeped in this principle of mutual love and *consolation*. It was out of this monastic culture that Luther developed his strong theology of *Seelsorge* as the 'mutual consolation and conversation of the brethren', a fundamental dimension of pastoral care in the church. This office of consolation, says Luther, is the vocation and work of every Christian, since comforting one another is one of the foundational means through which the Gospel of grace comes to people in order to strengthen their faith in the hour of trial.

Luther's understanding and use of *consolatio* was shaped by the theological and literary masters he had studied. There had of course been many contributors. The foremost name associated with the development of *consolatio* in the medieval period is that of French mystic and theologian, Jean Gerson (1363–1429), nicknamed *Doctor Consolatorius* (Doctor of consolation) by his contemporaries.[50]

---

50. This section of the chapter owes much to the masterly analysis of Gerson's influence on Luther's *Trostbriefe* in Mennecke-Haustein's *Luthers Trostbriefe*, 141–59.

Gerson was seen very much as a 'church Father' by German spiritual writers in the fifteenth and sixteenth centuries, including Luther. His consolatory tracts built elaborate cognitive–behavioural methodologies of consolation and comfort which are psychologically sophisticated, even by today's standards.[51] His emphasis is always on the superior function of reason (*ratio*) as the arbiter and moderator of all the affects, and the means by which negative thoughts and feelings may be controlled. In this way, Gerson follows the ancient stoic strategy of *consolatio*: coping with suffering, affliction or loss depends on how effectively one can place it within a larger rational framework and in so doing, objectify it and distance oneself from it emotionally.

Gerson's influence on Luther's views of depressive illness and how to remedy it can be seen quite clearly: the strong understanding of melancholy moods and depressive suffering as the devil's attack; making fun of, and showing contempt for, the devil rather than being afraid of him; the importance of embracing life's external gifts of joy–food, laughter, wine and music–and the use of cognitive and diversional strategies to counter depressive moods.[52] Luther was also attracted to Gerson because of the down–to–earth nature of his advice, which made it helpful not only for the wealthy and educated but for the worker and the peasant.

However, Luther's reshaping of Gerson's legacy was significant. Rhetorical analysis of Luther's writing in his letters of consolation shows that he was a master at taking the familiar and common conventions of consolatory rhetoric and remodelling them, sometimes quite radically, for his own purposes.

---

51. Luther was particularly influenced by two of Gerson's tracts which were widely read at the time: Johannes Gerson, 'Contra nimis strictam et scrupulosam conscientiam', (*Against an excessively strict and scrupulous conscience*) and 'Contra foedem tentationem blasphemiæ', (*Against the vile afflictions of blasphemy*) both found in *Opera Omnia, novo ordine digesta et in quinque tomos distribute*, reprinted, edited by Louis Ellies Du Pin (Hildesheim: Georg Olms Verlag, 1987), 3:241–46.
52. Luther refers incorrectly to a work by Gerson: 'De Cogitationibus Blasphemiae', almost certainly meaning 'Contra foedem tentationem blasphemiæ'(see footnote 83), in two letters in the selection. He refers to the strategy of treating melancholy thoughts with contempt, like the 'hissing of geese' or like the irritating trivial carping of a 'nitpicking critic" (*Leuseknicker*). See Luther's *letter to Jonas von Stockhausen* of 27 November 1532 (See Appendix) and the *letter to Jerome Weller* of 9 June 1530 (See Appendix).

Gerson and others had followed the lead of classical *consolatio* in offering comfort by means of *argumentatio* aimed at ameliorating the pain of suffering and placing it in some better light by means of comparison, rationalising or psychologising, using the sufferer's own feelings, actions and above all, reason. While borrowing from Gerson, Luther reshaped his approach considerably. He centred his comfort not in any internal 'self-talk' of the sufferer, but always around Christ and the *external* word of the Gospel. The themes of Christian consolation so often found in prior eras, such as patience, forbearance, resistance to temptation, and hope were recast in a new image by Luther: the image of Christ, both crucified and victorious over all enemies. In Luther's consolation it is the forgiveness, assurance and hope of Christ given to believers in the external word that takes over the role of human *ratio* in Gerson's model of *consolatio*.

Gerson's psychology of consolation was founded upon a *duplex voluntas* in which reason, acting as the superior faculty, mastered the negative passions and emotions of the human soul, in a dualistic fashion. In this way the distressed person may employ her own human strengths and resources in countering all that is sinful or painful.[53]

In his consolatory writings, Luther sought rather to integrate and draw together reason and affect with Christ and the Gospel as the consoling and mediating force. This is noticeable in the consolatory letters to the depressed, in which reason and affect are both defiantly turned around to become weapons against depressive moods, with the external *promissio* of Christ as the source of power and confidence to do so.

Luther as Comforter

As we have seen, Luther developed the various strands of the pastoral care and consolation tradition he had received, re-centring his theology and practice around the Gospel, mediated via the external word of Christ. Over the span of his career, his writing reflects the mature integration of this theology, as it was molded by his own journey of faith, marriage, family life, conflict, betrayal, suffering, grief, depression and old age.

---

53. Mennecke-Haustein, *Luthers Trostbriefe*, 141–59.

Throughout his career Luther understood theology not as a speculative or theoretical *scientia*, but as the servant of the church and its work of saving and comforting lost souls. As Gerhard Ebeling reflects, for Luther theology and pastoral care are so closely intermeshed that one without the other is unthinkable.[54]

Particularly in his later years, as the reform movement required less continual involvement and intervention from him, Luther saw himself not primarily as a reformer but as a teacher and pastor. Besides sharing the duty of all Christians to comfort others, he understood that it was also his duty to console and comfort others by virtue of his office as a pastor whose *particular vocation* it was to bring the scriptural word of comfort (*Trost*) to the suffering.[55]

As a comforter, Luther was also responding to the suffering of people living in the conditions of sixteenth century Germany, both rich and poor. The conditions of life in sixteenth century Germany were wretched, to say the least. It is not hard to see how religious despair and depression could become widespread among people who often saw themselves on the road to an eternal continuation of the pain and suffering of this life. This world was a place of intense and immediate realities: extremes of climate, sickness, high infant mortality, spiritual fear, *melancholia*, etc. Life and death, joy and sorrow were close neighbours. It was therefore also a world of strong emotions and affective responses: on the background of immanent sorrow and suffering, joy (*Fröhlichkeit*) was also experienced and expressed more intensely. This is indicated by the broad semantic field of affect and emotion (*Gefühlswortschatz*) of the time, in which there are so many words for expressing both positive and negative feelings and states of being. Luther's pastoral comfort responds to this context: he uses strongly emotive language and an intensity of feeling in his metaphors and images. He seeks to comfort not only the intellect but also the affects, especially the emotions.[56]

---

54. Gerhard Ebeling, *Luthers Seelsorge: Theologie in der Vielfalt der Lebenssituationen an seinen Briefen dargestellt* (Tübingen: JCB. Mohr (Paul Siebeck), 1997), 7–8.
55. Luther practises this in his proclamation of the word, and his giving of absolution and blessing in his letters. See Luther's *letter to Matthias Weller* of 7 October 1534 (See 325–326), where Luther speaks to his reader not merely as a friend but as a pastor, proclaiming the word in God's name and with his authority.
56. Stolt, *Laßt uns Fröhlich Springen*, 96–7.

Birgit Stolt observes that in all Luther's *Trostschriften, Trost* is the opposing force to *Anfechtung*. Just as in *Anfechtung* the image of an aggressive enemy (the devil) is implicit, so in Luther's concept of *Trost* a caring comforter is implied; a '*tröstlicher und freundlicher Gott*' who does not exact judgement in order to punish, but cares and comforts the believing sufferer. Luther saw comforting the suffering as leading them in spiritual battle against the devil who sought to draw them into fear and despair.

This comfort involves more than intellectualising. It requires affective and emotional defiance and opposition towards the enemy (*Trotz*) on the basis of faith in Christ. This is expressed in Luther's sometimes strong-and to our ears perhaps harsh-tone with those he comforts, where he calls them to fight against the devil's attack. We find often in Luther's writing what could be called his characteristic 'comfort-commands': 'seid getrost' or 'seid fröhlich', in which he calls his addressee to exercise their faith in Christ, through which their *Anfechtung* is turned back on the enemy who flees in the face of such confidence.[57]

Given its potential as a source of comfort, it is hardly surprising that the teaching of justification by grace was greeted with such eagerness in the opening years of the Reformation, despite opposition and persecution.[58] Between 1518 and 1530, Luther received many requests for letters and tracts of comfort from people seeking the help and reassurance of the Gospel in their suffering.[59] This custom was popular in early sixteenth century Germany as a means of finding solace and hope from outside one's own situation. Luther and his

---

57. Among the letters in this study, there are several examples of this, for example Luther's *letters to Prince Joachim of Anhalt* of 1534 (See Appendix).
58. Aided by the social media of the day, the Reformation faith gained an enthusiastic following, first in Germany, then throughout Europe. As Luther's teaching began to be discussed and his published pamphlets flew through Europe, large numbers of people became inquirers and adherents of the new evangelical faith, from crowned heads like King Christian of Denmark, Queen Maria of Hungary, Prince Georg of Anhalt to commoners, scholars, students and many others. This movement is described in 'How Luther Went Viral', The Economist.
59. A notable example is his *Sermon on preparing for death*, 1519 (WA II, 685–697) which was requested by the Electoral Authorities of Saxony. Luther received many other requests around this time, some of which he rejected, directing petitioners to existing consolatory works. See Mennecke-Haustein, *Luthers Trostbriefe*, 28–9.

wider circle of reformers at Wittenberg were continuously involved in providing such letters of comfort in response to requests from various people, especially kings, princes and other nobility.[60] People were hungry for the word of a gracious and loving God who could offer forgiveness, hope and succour, instead of the threats of a righteous and demanding judge who was impossible to please.

For Luther and the people of his time, however, the human struggle was not just with fears of the afterlife, but with the evil forces of chaos and destruction in this life. Luther's consolations directly address the temporal plight of human beings who are caught in the cosmic battle between God and the forces of hell, the devil and the world. The comfort of salvation in Christ was therefore not only offered as relief for those fearing purgatory or eternal punishment, but as strength and encouragement in the immediate troubles of this life.

Luther's Trostschriften

The tracts, essays and letters of consolation which Luther wrote, particularly early in his career, have together come to be known as his *Trostschriften*. As is so often the case with Luther's writings, however, it is unclear how to determine which pieces belong in this group, since so many of Luther's writings which are not explicitly consolatory in their outward literary form are nevertheless full of consolatory content. Besides the handful of writings that obviously qualify as *Trostschriften*, many of his sermons, lectures, table talks and other treatises could also be included.

Among this indeterminate group of writings, there are some pieces which are unambiguously and explicitly consolatory in both their form and content, and which have programmatic importance in Luther's pastoral and theological development.[61]

---

60. The three princes of Anhalt–Georg, Johann and Joachim–are an example. Between 1532 and 1535 they requested and received consolatory letters not only from Luther but from the other Wittenberg reformers as well. See Mennecke-Haustein, *Luthers Trostbriefe*, 239–41.
61. Some may include other writings besides the following; however, the most influential four are: *14 Consolations*, 1519 (WA VI, 99–134); *The Sermon on Preparing for Death*, 1519 (WA II, 685–679); *The Consolation for a Person in Great Affliction*, 1521 (WA VII, 779–90) and *Four Consolatory Psalms*, 1524, written for Queen Maria of Hungary (WA IXX, 542–51).

Of these, by far the most significant, especially in connection with the twenty-one letters under examination in this study, is the *Tessaradecas* or *Fourteen Consolations* of 1519.[62] Written at the request of Elector Frederick the wise of Saxony to comfort him in his struggle with illness, it deals with the way in which suffering may be placed into proper perspective in the life of the Christian. The idea of fourteen consolations was drawn from the fifteenth century tradition of *Die Vierzehnheiligen* (the fourteen holy helpers), a group of saints believed to have appeared to a shepherd in Bavaria. On the site of the appearances a basilica was later built, which became the object of pilgrimage for those seeking cures and other miracles. Luther used this well-known legend to shape his rhetorical structure of seven blessings and seven ills which lie within us, before us, behind us, to our right, to our left, below us and above us. With this allegorical construction, Luther effects a literary 'altar screen' with two corresponding panels, for the believer to contemplate the seven different dimensions of evil and blessing in life. The intent is to show the relative insignificance of the sufferings we must bear in this life (especially compared with what we truly deserve as sinners) as preparation for contemplating life's blessings. This enables the believer to see, from an even more beatific perspective, how small and light are the sufferings Christians must now cope with, in light of the gifts and blessings God showers upon his people, both now and in eternity. Jane Strohl comments:

> The powerful theological and pastoral insight Luther offers in the Fourteen Consolations is the realisation that what is perceived as evil can be transformed into blessing, that sufferings of all kinds, and most especially death become for believers signs of God's love and means of Christ's grace.[63]

This is a fundamental insight into Luther's consolation of the afflicted, and is developed in a variety of ways as Luther applies it to situations of human suffering in his *Trostschriften*, and more specifically his *Trostbriefe*.[64]

---

62. WA VI, 99–134.
63. Jane E Strohl, 'Luther's Fourteen Consolations', in *The Pastoral Luther: Essays on Martin Luther's Practical Theology*, edited by Timothy J Wengert (Grand Rapids: Eerdmans, 2009), 324.
64. Some notable examples from the selection of letters under examination in this project: The *letter to Queen Maria of Hungary* of 1531 (See Appendix); the *letters*

Luther's Trostbriefe

A sub-category of Luther's *Trostschriften* is the group of letters known as the *Trostbriefe* (letters of consolation). Once again it is difficult to make a definitive list here, but there are generally acknowledged to be about 100 such letters,[65] distinguished by their having been written expressly to address particular situations of suffering or pastoral need.

About 1524 Luther moved away from writing larger scale consolatory tracts and essays (*Trostschriften*) towards these shorter consolatory letters (*Trostbriefe*), addressed to specific and individual situations. With the close of the initial phase of the Reformation and the growing influence of the Protestant territorial princes in Germany there was no longer the same need for Luther's direct pastoral intervention to support and strengthen their resolve.

Luther's *Trostbriefe* have drawn more attention and interest than any other letters he wrote, both during Luther's own lifetime and in the subsequent centuries. They are acknowledged as exceptional not just on a theological-pastoral level, but as masterpieces of German literary innovation and excellence, and as major contributions to the epistolary culture of the early modern period.

Conclusion

Luther's *Trostbriefe* grew out of his consciousness of suffering, which shaped his developing theology, particularly as he reached his mature years, influenced by the literary traditions of *consolatio* and letter–writing as promoted by German humanism. The particular letters under examination in this book—letters of consolation addressed to those suffering with depressive illness—were shaped by his own theoretical knowledge and personal experience of depressive melancholic suffering, as it was formed and understood within the cultural, medical and religious context of his life and work.

This world of Luther, far away from us as it is, is not a complete mystery. It is strange to us in so far as we, in our era, can never

---

to Prince Joachim of Anhalt of 1534 (See Appendix) and the *letters to Jerome Weller* of 1530 (See Appendix).

65. The best and most carefully constructed list available has been compiled in Mennecke-Haustein, *Luthers Trostbriefe*, 277–81. This list includes 102 items.

completely apprehend the imagination or experience of its inhabitants. Yet those people of the sixteenth century were humans more like than unlike us. Through personal documents like these twenty one letters, these strangers have left open 'doorways and windows' which we may see into and at which we may evesdrop. And if we care to look and listen well, we may come to know them, not a as unfamiliar but familiar persons.

Chapter 2
'True Joy and Consolation in Christ'
Luther's Twenty-one Letters of Consolation to the Melancholy

> *'Christ is ours—yes, in every way ours, just as we long for him. And even if he makes himself an obstacle to reason, no matter.'*
> Luther to Prince Joachim of Anhalt, June 1534.

Having sketched the wider historical background of the context in which Luther wrote his letters of consolation, we turn to the twenty-one letters themselves. In the overviews of the letters which follow, we explore their historical, literary and rhetorical features, and their theological and pastoral content.

These overviews are crucial since any valid reception of Luther's letters in today's context depends on understanding them properly within their own. This needed phenomenological depth can come only from probing the individual human situations we find in these letters and noting the means which Luther uses to pastorally address them. Reformation social historian, Peter Matheson makes the point that this kind of detailed grounding in the personal and specific is vital for such a study because it puts us in contact with the actual texture of life as it was lived.[1]

Luther's Letters to Those with Depressive Illness

While it may be tempting to see these letters as 'literary artefacts', it is important to keep in mind that every one of them was written to a real living, suffering person. Luther reached out to touch their life—situations in the form of written personal address. As far as historical resources allow, this chapter describes these personal life-situations,

---

1. Matheson, *The Imaginative World of Reformation*, 1–3, 105.

noting the circumstances which led up to or contributed to their struggles with depressive illness.

Fifteen of the letters in the selection are written to people Luther already knew personally or with whom he was in some way acquainted. These letters were written on the basis of an existing and often warm relationship between writer and addressee,[2] and are appreciably different in tone to the remaining six which were written to persons whom Luther did not know. These are somewhat more formal in their structure and style.[3]

Unavoidably, the quality and completeness of the overviews provided is not uniform. Reformation history has tended to draw heavily on Luther's own 'ego-documents', particularly his letters. It has consequently centred around Luther himself and his career.[4] This means that unless the addressee was a member of Luther's *Lebenskreis* and had some continuing association with him, the information we have is often limited to the few details which come to light through their brief association with Luther. In some cases therefore, we have access only to a restricted snapshot of the addressees' lives.

In four cases there is more than one letter from Luther to the same addressee, which allows us a slightly fuller understanding of the person's situation and the progress of the illness and recovery. In the overviews which follow, where there are two or more letters to the same addressee, they will be discussed in terms of the overall picture which emerges from the letters together.[5] However, where appropriate, the unique features of individual letters are also noted.

So as to support the legitimate place of each letter within the selection, particular attention has been paid here to the indications of

---

2. The *letters to Johann and Elizabeth Agricola, Johann Schlaginhaufen* (Appendix) and *Jerome Weller* are good examples.
3. The *letters to Jonas von Stockhausen and his wife* (See Appendix) and *Matthias Weller* (See Appendix) are examples of more formal consolatory letters, adhering closely to the conventional style.
4. Roper, 'To His Most Learned and Dearest Friend', 283–84.
5. The investigation of these four 'mini-series' of letters has provided an unexpected depth of texture and human detail, unfolding the underlying narratives behind the documents. This has increased our understanding of the situations into which Luther was writing, and therefore our understanding of 'what he was saying' in his letters.

depressive illness which appear in the letters themselves, and in the other historical data associated with them.

To my knowledge no one else has assembled a collection of Luther's *Trostbriefe* addressed specifically to persons suffering with depressive melancholia. Certainly no one has done so in order to analyse the common themes and reflect on what may be learned for pastoral care today.

According to Ute Mennecke-Haustein, the selection of letters assembled for this study includes those widely considered to be the most interesting and original of the 102 *Trostbriefe* we have from Luther's pen. They stand out not only for their literary-rhetorical innovation, but also for their unique depth of theological and pastoral insight.[6]

One of the suprises which has emerged during this study is the extent to which Luther has used his rhetorical skills as a writer, to create intricate layers of comfort and encouragement. These letters are not just immediately helpful on the first reading, but offer deeper insights and perceptions as they are reread and reflected upon over time. This 'dimensionality' is not merely intellectual but also affective, drawing in the reader's total life-experience and self-understanding as a person in the world and before God.

Luther often concludes his *argumentatio* with strings of biblical quotes, which may at first appear to function simply as scriptural back-up for his consolatory constructions. On closer examination, however, it emerges that these strings of biblical references are no mere 'footnotes', but carefully assembled chain-commentaries on the life of faith, unfolding yet deeper mysteries and counsels of God's grace.[7]

---

6. I was surprised to find that Mennecke-Haustein's book on Luther's consolatory letters contained, as a small sampling of the letters singled out for closer analysis, fourteen of the twenty-one letters selected for this project. It is a coincidence that Ute Mennecke-Haustein and I were independently led to substantially the same small grouping of Luther's consolatory letters by quite divergent interests; in her case the linguistic-literary and in my case the theological-pastoral. While her analyses of these letters are loaded towards linguistic concerns, she does also touch on theological and pastoral issues, and her observations are helpful.
7. Some notable examples in this selection of *letters are those to Queen Maria of Hungary* (Appendix) and *Barbara Lißkirchen* (See Appendix).

In this way, and through many other modes of expression, Luther harnesses his own experiences of depressive illness together with theological reflection on God's justifying and comforting grace, in order to connect directly with the depressive experience of his readers, bringing hope and light into their darkness.

Luther in Mid–To–Late Career

These personal letters, written in his mid-to-late career (by which time he was a husband and father) increasingly show that Luther had become more emotionally attuned and relational as a person, having experienced not only spiritual *Anfechtung*, but also the love of marriage and the strong and tender emotions of fatherhood.[8] He demonstrates a deepening awareness of ordinary life-struggles and personal problems, and an appreciation of family dynamics and relationships in their many dimensions.[9]

Luther's theological emphases also began to change as he came into this mid-to-late life period. After the first frenetic beginnings of the Reformation, issues of the evangelical church's preservation and nurture became more important to him. Luther's life settled down somewhat into a less harassed and insecure existence, especially after the Diet of Augsburg in 1530. He was able to concentrate more on his work at the university, and take part in family life. It is in this mature mid-to-late career period that all of the twenty-one letters in the selection for this study were written, the earliest of them in 1527 and the latest in 1544.

---

8. Stolt, 'Luther's Faith of "The Heart"', 145. See also Stolt, 'Joy, Love and Trust', 9–11. The experience of fatherhood particularly shaped Luther's appreciation of God as a Father who shows us unconditional grace. Reflecting on his own love for his infant son he muses: 'In what way have you earned it? Why must I love you so? Peeing and shitting in your nappy, weeping and filling the whole house with your cries? Still I must be full of loving care for you!' (WA TR I, No.1004, 505:8–10). See also Stolt, *Laßt uns Fröhlich Springen*, 247–49.
9. Interestingly, Neil Leroux, in his book on Luther's comfort of the dying and bereaved, selected twenty letters from this same period in Luther's life, during which his life-experience helped him develop his consolatory theology and practice. See Neil R Leroux, *Martin Luther as Comforter, Writings on Death* (Boston: Brill, 2007), 187–188.

Luther's 'Rhetoric of the Heart'

The phrase 'rhetoric of the heart' was coined by Luther scholar, Birgit Stolt, to describe the powerful language Luther uses in all his writing, particularly in relation to his German translation of the Bible.[10] However, it becomes clear that this characterisation also applies to much of Luther's writing in the twenty-one letters in this selection, which is highly affective (not to say emotive) and persuasive. As Stolt observes, because Luther wrote so much from deep personal conviction, there is an *aural* quality to his writing. He is 'present' in his writing and we, his readers 'hear him speaking' directly to us. To him, for whom the primary faculty of spiritual reception was hearing, 'writing' meant 'talking'. Language was only truly alive when presented in spoken form. Stolt suggests that Luther was one of those who heard the spoken word in his 'inner ear' as he was writing, and this is why his writing still resonates with the experiential immediacy of personal encounter. This description fits closely with most of the twenty-one letters in this study, in which Luther's writing is highly conversational, and rings with a strong aural immediacy. Despite the 500 year gap between his writing and our reading, today's reader can still hear his voice and be impacted by his speech, and most interestingly, may receive and respond to the writer at the cognitive-affective level.

As Matheson comments, Luther's genius as pastor lay in the simplicity with which he was consistently able to go straight to the heart of things, avoiding the peripheral issues and fussy details that lead away from the core of the matter.[11] These twenty-one letters almost all exemplify this incisive simplicity. Luther's writing has an uncomplicated directness, deftness and accuracy to it. His imaginative use of language creates in the reader and hearer vivid impressions and images. This 'ageless' language of lived human experience communicates powerfully to the 'heart', that is, to the core of the whole person, encompassing mind, will, conscience, imagination and emotions.

Birgit Stolt points out that when reading Luther, it is important to recognise that, while he describes the experience of emotion using

---

10. Stolt, *Martin Luthers Rhetorik*, 42–60.
11. Matheson, *The Imaginative World of Reformation*, 122.

words and expressions we still recognise today, his sixteenth century *Gefühlswelt* was far more intensive than ours. Life experience was charged with a greater emotional current because of the immediacy of illness, death and eternity. When read against this background, we see that there is an emotional honesty and transparency in these letters that accounts for their powerful affect–even on *our* 'greyed out' post–modern emotional senses.

Much is often made of Luther's tendency to 'go over the top' when making a point, using language lavishly and sometimes immoderately. It may be shocking to some to discover that there are even such moments in some of these consolatory letters, where Luther wants to jolt his reader into reality or action.[12] This was in fact a feature of rhetorical speech in that era generally. However, it is more noticeable in Luther's case because of the choleric personality of the man, and because he was purposely subverting the language of theological and spiritual discourse.[13] Luther was not a systematic writer who was concerned primarily with consistency and accuracy of details. He has sometimes been described as an 'artist' or 'prophet' who responded theologically and experientially to the situation that confronted him. His speech was always *calculated for effect,* to speak the living word into the present moment.

For all the warmth and immediacy of Luther's rhetoric of the heart, however, we must remember that he is, as Risto Saarinen puts it, wearing a particular 'mask'[14] as he writes these letters. He is a man of the sixteenth century, a time when one's own individuality was less important than the particular role one had been given to play. The 'mask' he wears as he writes these letters is that of the *consolator,* the one who brings comfort and help in the midst of trials. This is the

---

12. For example, Luther's letter to Jonas von Stockhausen in November 1532 in which he advises his reader to tell the devil: 'lick my arse' (See Appendix). See footnote 70.
13. Vitor Westhelle, 'Communication and the Transgression of Language in Martin Luther', in *The Pastoral Luther: Essays on Martin Luther's Practical Theology*, edited by Timothy J Wengert (Grand Rapids: Eerdmans, 2009), 59–84. See also Harold Ristau, *Understanding Martin Luther's Demonological Rhetoric in His Treatise Against the Heavenly Prophets (1525): How What Luther Speaks is Essential to What Luther Says* (Lewiston: E Mellen, 2010).
14. Risto Saarinen, 'Luther the Urban Legend', in *The Global Luther: A Theologian for Modern Times*, edited by Christine Helmer (Minneapolis: Fortress, 2009), 30–1.

rhetorical *dispositio* he had taken up, and we need to relate to him in this role and not too easily suppose that we are seeing disclosed in this correspondence some 'private' or 'out of the public eye' Luther. The man is there, of course, but he is presenting himself 'in role' and this is how we need to read him.

Today's reader of Luther must be mindful of the 500 years that have in fact passed since he put pen to paper. He lived in a very different world, and there is a significant journey of careful analysis and interpretation to be undertaken in order to avoid anachronistic assumptions and misunderstandings.

Overviews

Three Letters to Johann and Elizabeth Agricola (See Appendix 255–258)

- June 10 1527 (WA BR.IV. No.1112, 210–211)
- Early July 1527[15] (WA BR.IV. No.1111, 210)
- July 1527 (WA BR.IV. No.1119, 219–220)

Elizabeth and Johann Agricola were good friends of the Luther family in 1527 when these letters were written. Johann was for many years a close and trusted theological ally and associate of Luther, who sent him to Frankfurt in 1525 to establish evangelical worship there. He later returned to Eisleben where he served as a teacher and preacher, until he became involved in a bitter theological controversy with Luther in 1540, after which time both he and his teaching were rejected by the Wittenberg reformers.[16]

At the time of this correspondence, the Agricolas were living in Eisleben and Luther was still on good terms with Johann. In fact from the intimate and friendly tone of all three letters, Luther seems to have been very close to both Elizabeth and Johann. This is indicated

---

15. Otto Clemen, editor of Luther's *Briefe* in the Weimar Edition, suggests (WA BR IV, 209) that the date of writing was June 10 (the same day he wrote to Elizabeth herself); however, Tappert's dating (sometime in early July) seems to fit in better with the events and circumstances described in the three letters themselves.
16. Johann Agricola's significant role in the Reformation, especially his later involvement in the antinomian controversy, is its own complex story and not relevant to this study.

in the way he addresses Elizabeth by her Christian name, and speaks about her in the third person in the same familiar way. Luther's willingness to take Elizabeth into his own home and family circle in order to help her recover from her malady also shows the close nature of the friendship.

To summarise the narrative behind these three letters, as far as we can piece it together, Luther's first interaction with Elizabeth Agricola regarding her depressive problems was in the *first* letter, written on June 10 1527 in which he counsels and encourages her regarding her despondency. In a *second* letter, this time to Johann, probably written a few days later, Luther suggested that Elizabeth come to stay in Wittenberg for a while with Luther and his family, in order to 'breathe again the air to which she is accustomed', and to rest and receive Luther's pastoral care and comfort. This invitation was accepted, and Elizabeth spent some days in Wittenberg with the Luther family sometime in late June.[17] The duration of this visit is not known; however, the *third* letter, which Luther wrote to Johann in early July, indicates that Elizabeth had already arrived in Wittenberg and been there long enough for Luther to assess her state, make a spiritual diagnosis of her problems and give some suggestions as to how she might be helped. It is not known how successful Luther was in his attempts to alleviate Elizabeth's depressive suffering in 1527. Nor is it known what the longer-term outcome of her illness was, although it seems quite likely that, had her illness continued, there would be some trace of an ongoing ministry of consolation on Luther's part, which there is not.

We turn now to an overview of the letters themselves, concentrating on the first and third letters in this group, since the second letter is, strictly speaking, only included in the selection because it helps to string together the narrative progression of events. It does not contain any material that contributes to our understanding of Elizabeth Agricola's illness or of Luther's consolation.[18]

---

17. The exact dating of this visit is impossible to determine because Luther's letter to Johann about his wife's illness is undated. The time-frame offered here is based on the observation that other historical records show that Elizabeth Agricola was not with the Luthers in Wittenberg at the time of Luther's own serious renal and urinary illness, around July 6. See Brecht, *Martin Luther, 1521-1532*, 492.
18. The brief letter is undated, and is not in any sense a formal letter of consolation. It contains only practical information. Some of it appears to refer obliquely to

The indications of Elizabeth Agricola's depressive illness are most pronounced in the **first letter**, from Luther to Elizabeth herself, where he refers to her being fearful (*kleinmütig*) and anxious (*zage*).[19] Brecht suggests the possibility that her depression was more of a situational response to a recent miscarriage. This is a reasonable speculation, though unsupported by other data.[20]

The letter is brief and does not carry all the distinguishing marks of *consolatio*. There is a warm opening address, which indicates the closeness of Luther's friendship with the Agricolas and his strong concern for Elizabeth in her suffering. Luther's use of the adjective '*liebe*' twice in the opening greetings is significant, especially the second occurrence where he addresses his reader as 'my dear [or perhaps more accurately, *beloved*] friend'.[21] A brief *narratio* follows in which Luther makes a point of mentioning Elizabeth's husband, Johann. The rest of the letter is made up of an extended *exhortatio-argumentatio*. Luther's words indicate that this depression had led Elizabeth to feeling that God had forsaken her. His interesting statement that it is Elizabeth's 'flesh and blood' that has led her to this false perception underlines that this feeling of God-forsakenness arises as a response to the physical and affective experience of the depressive illness which, though false, evidently *feels* very real. Luther advises that she should discover for herself that Christ *is* with her to comfort her, by praying to him and finding that he indeed hears and

---

a previous conversation between Luther and Agricola and is not clear to the 'outside' reader.

19. This early high German word is related to the contemporary German words *zagen* (to be apprehensive or timid) and *Zaghaft* (anxiety or fearfulness).
20. Brecht, *Martin Luther 1521-1532*, 205. Circumstantially, there are pointers to this possibility, although they are ultimately ambiguous. Luther speaks of her weakness of *body* and soul and reassures her that Christ is near her in her 'ills', which tends to indicate that at some point there was clearly a bodily component to her health problem. He later tells her husband, Johann, that her illness is not primarily a bodily one, as he had seemed to expect, but a malady of her conscience requiring spiritual comfort. Interestingly, it has always been a common response of women who 'have miscarried' to feel guilty and ashamed, as if miscarriages are automatically assumed to be due to mistakes or misconduct on the mother's part.
21. In his *Open Letter on Translating* of 1530 (WA XXX ii, 632-636), Luther makes a lot of the word 'liebe' as a word in the German language that expresses strong and deep feeling. See also Eric W Gritsch, 'Luther as Bible Translator', in *The Cambridge Companion to Martin Luther*, edited by Donald K McKim (Cambridge: Cambridge University Press, 2003), 67-8.

answers her prayer. Luther grounds this advice in the objective external Word of God, which testifies to Christ's love for, and commitment to, Elizabeth, shown by his readiness to suffer for her–and far more than she could or would suffer for herself or for him.[22] The body of the letter closes with a characteristic *exhortatio* that is found throughout Luther's *Trostbriefe*, 'now be of good comfort' (*So sei nu getrost*).[23] This is not the equivalent of 'so cheer up', as we might say today, but rather part of a carefully constructed rhetorical formulation of consolation–an exhortation made on the basis of something real and powerful: Christ's love for the sufferer, his suffering on her behalf, and his willingness to answer her prayers.

This letter to Elizabeth closes with a carefully crafted three-part rhetorical *conclusio*, which rings with deep compassion and sincerity. Firstly, Luther promises to pray for Elizabeth in future. This promise is then immediately made good in the next phrase by his prayer for God to strengthen Elizabeth in her weakness of body and soul. This prayer and the whole letter then closes with a blessing, or more properly, a commendation: 'with this I commit you to God's keeping'.

Luther voices here in his *conclusio* the assumption that Elizabeth's illness is one of 'body and soul', indicating that at this stage, he understands the illness to be a type of melancholic despondency related to physical illness.

However, in Luther's **third letter,** addressed once again to Johann, written in early July, the reader finds that this assumption has been overturned. Elizabeth had been with him in Wittenberg, perhaps for some days, and he had changed his assessment of her situation. Luther writes, 'her illness has, as you see, more to do with the soul than the body'. He then goes on to advise that, in his opinion, medical intervention (an option obviously being considered by Johann Agricola) was not what was needed, but rather *spiritual* healing. Neither the medicines of the *apothecaries*[24] nor the 'poultices of

---

22. This same formulation also appears in Luther's 1531 letter to the depressive Queen Maria of Hungary (See Appendix). Luther's point is that the natural human assumption we make is that our suffering shows God's indifference to us. The truth is the 'mirror-reverse': that *Christ's* greater and deeper suffering shows how much he loves us, and is prepared to suffer *with* and *for* us.
23. This formulation is distinct but not completely different from what is found in other letters: 'Sei fröhlich' (be of good cheer).
24. During the fifteenth and sixteenth century in Europe these early pharmacists

Hippocrates'[25] will help; only 'the efficacious plasters of Scripture and the Word of God'. Luther's diagnosis is drawn from his observation that it is Elizabeth's conscience, not her body, which is the seat of the sickness.[26] He sees the aetiology of her depressive illness as more spiritual than physical, and therefore judges that she needs the 'therapy of the Word'.[27]

The last section of Luther's letter to Johann Agricola concerning his wife is not easily understood. He reflects that Elizabeth, like his own Katie, tended to think that the Word of God was not for her, but only for her husband. This could be read as a typical cheeky 'sideswipe' at wives always knowing better than their husbands—the kind of quip Luther made about Katie on occasions.[28]

However, Luther spends too much time and care making this point for it to be a humorous one-liner. He appears rather to be talking about a serious issue. The problem appears to be that these

---

developed their science and trade, and were popularised by the development of medical science. In Wittenberg itself, Lucas Cranach operated such an *apothecary* shop. They prepared medicines of various kinds for the treatment of internal illnesses (such as *purgatives* and *emetics)* and skin complaints (ointments and balms etc).

25. Medical treatment given by physicians of the Renaissance was still largely based on the ancient *Hippocratic* model of medical science, as interpreted by Galen. It involved several different strategies, one of which was the use of various salves or poultices–ointments made from natural and manufactured substances which were rubbed or bandaged onto the skin.

26. Gerhard Ebeling gives a salient reminder that Luther's understanding of Elisabeth Agricola's sickness as 'spiritual' should not be understood according to the common category 'spiritual' used today in the *psychological* sense. In early Renaissance Germany physical sickness was not (as so often today) seen as neatly separate from emotional, psychological and spiritual sickness in a dualistic sense, but intertwined with it. While there is a clear understanding of the different aspects of illness, there is no dualistic separation of *physical* and *spiritual* as we are used to in modernist western culture. Luther is talking here about the aetiology of Elizabeth Agricola's illness, trying to discern its root cause so that it can be effectively dealt with. See Ebeling, *Luthers Seelsorge*, 374.

27. Luther uses this medical practice as a metaphor for the Word of God, which is powerful medicine for the soul, applied, notably, *from outside*. Plasters and poultices were extensively used in sixteenth century European medical practice. Medical compounds, often aqueous herbal preparations, were applied to the skin and bandaged over.

28. See Luther's letters to his wife, of February 7 and 10 1546 in Tappert, *Luther: Letters of Spiritual Counsel*, 105-08.

wives thought that their need to hear God's word was obviated by their being married to teachers of it. Luther reflects, 'Yet it is the way of our wives to think that the Word is not relevent to them but only to us, their husbands, who are their defenders and guardians'.[29] Whatever the underlying nature of this issue, Luther exhorts Agricola to impress on Elizabeth that when the Word of God is taught it has 'something to say to *her*'. He ends this paragraph on a sombre note: 'Our wives must watch out in case, when they do need to make use of the Word, they find, to their sorrow, that it is too difficult.'[30]

Luther's respectful concern for Elizabeth Agricola seems to reflect something of his attitude towards changing gender politics in the early Renaissance. In medieval and early modern Europe, women still usually occupied a subservient role in society, finding respectability and status through marriage and motherhood rather than through individual achievement or significance. Carolyn Schneider observes[31] that during this period women were also still seen as *spiritually weaker* than men, having played a significant role in the fall of humanity through Eve, who was directly tempted by the devil, unlike Adam who only followed her lead. Accordingly it was popularly supposed that melancholy and other spiritual ailments affected women more than men.[32] This makes it all the more noticeable

---

29. The scope of this overview does not allow us to explore this question or build a case either way, especially given the long and lively debate and large body of Reformation social history literature on the topic of Luther's view of women. It should, however, be noted that other letters to women in this selection show Luther's conviction that women *are* called to participate actively in the spiritual life, especially in reading Scripture and prayer. See the letters to Barbara Lißkirchen and Queen Maria of Hungary. See also Albrecht Classen and Tanya Amber Settle, 'Women in Martin Luther's Life and Theology', in *German Studies Review* 14/2 (May 1991): 252–54.
30. This statement in Luther's letter to Johann Agricola finds a striking point of contact in Luther's own struggle to get Katie to read the scriptures. In 1534, when the current German translation of the Bible was completed, he wanted his beloved wife to read it so much that he promised to pay her 50 gilders if she did. See Eduard Kopp, 'Tough and Valiant: Luther's "Herr Katie"', *Luther 2017, 500 Jahre Reformation*, accessed July 2013, http://www.luther2017.de/node/21600.
31. Carolyn Schneider, *I am a Christian, The Nun, the Devil and Martin Luther* (Minneapolis: Fortress, 2010), 105–6.
32. Carolyn Schneider, *I am a Christian*, 105, points out that depressive disorders still affect more women than men to the present day, citing the often quoted figures, that about twice as many women suffer with depression as men.

that Luther addresses Elizabeth Agricola not only with courtesy but with respect, as a *friend* in her own right, treating her depressive state as a spiritual illness rather than some kind of moral weakness, just as he does with males suffering the same malady. Perhaps as one who experienced depressive illness firsthand himself, he was inclined to be less patronising to women suffering in the same way.

Seven Letters to Prince Joachim of Anhalt (Appendix:258–266)

- May 23 1534 (WA BR VII, No.2113, 65–67)
- June 9 1534 (WA BR.VII. No.2116, 70)
- June 12 1534 (WA BR VII. No.2119, 73–74)
- June 13 1534 (WA BR VII. No.2120, 75)
- June 23 1534 (WA BR VII. No.2121, 76–77)
- June 26 1534 (WA BR VII. No.2122, 78–79)
- December 25 1535 (WA BR.VII. No.2279, 335–336)

This is the largest group of letters from Luther to a single addressee in the selection, and provides the most detailed picture we have of a pastoral situation in which Luther rendered care and comfort to a depression sufferer. It is possible to put together the basic elements of the narrative, chiefly from Luther's letters to Joachim, but also from those written by others who were close to the situation.[33] These seven letters afford a special opportunity to see Luther at work as *Seelsorger* in a long and demanding case of depressive illness. It is therefore appropriate to devote some considerable space to them here.

The first six letters listed above belong together as parts in an intricate narrative written in response to Prince Joachim's depressive-melancholic crisis which began in late May and continued until early August 1534. These six letters will be discussed separately from the seventh (written on Christmas Day 1535)[34] which was written 18 months after the May–August crisis of 1534. While this later letter

---

33. The three princes, Georg, Johann and Joachim were all corresponding at this time not only with Luther, but with other Wittenberg reformers, especially, Melanchthon, Bugenhagen and Jonas. The correspondence of Georg Helt, the tutor to the three princes, also contains information about Joachim's illness around this period. This wider correspondence is clearly summarised by Mennecke-Haustein: *Luthers Trostbriefe*, 239-40.
34. The dating of this letter is questioned by some scholars, however December 25 1535 is the most widely favoured option.

was also written to comfort the prince in a period of melancholy, some time had passed since the earlier crisis, and the nature and context of Joachim's depressive fears and anxieties had changed somewhat.[35]

There is a complex historical background to the situation in which these letters were written. Around 1532 lively contact began between the Wittenberg reformers and the house of Anhalt in Dessau (the neigboring territory to the east of Electoral Saxony) which had hitherto remained loyal to Rome. This contact involved the three brothers, Princes Johann, Georg and Joachim. They had become interested in the evangelical faith only since the death of their strict Roman Catholic mother in 1530. The driving force in this exploration was the second brother, Prince Georg 'The Pious'. Having received a theological education, he was deeply impressed by Luther's writings. He based his growing commitment to the Reformation faith on his own careful reading of scripture and other sources.[36]

In 1532, Luther sent his trusted and capable friend Nicolaus Hausmann[37] to serve as court chaplain to the three princes, and to strengthen the valuable fledgling alliance with Anhalt–Dessau. In the following year, 1533, the three brothers endured considerable opposition to their embrace of the evangelical faith from their Roman Catholic neighbours.[38] Hausmann at this time requested that Luther support the princes in their Lutheran convictions by writing them letters of encouragement, which he did. They were also supported at

---

35. As will become clear in the overview of this letter, Joachim's depressive thoughts were no longer fixed on the loss of his Roman Catholic piety and the general acceptance of evangelical doctrines, but seem instead to have fixed on the particular notion that, as a sinner, he had betrayed Christ.
36. Mennecke-Haustein: *Luthers Trostbriefe*, 239. The turning point for him seems to have been the publication of the Augsburg Confession in 1530, which provided him with a firm expression of the doctrines of the evangelical faith.
37. A trusted and able theologian and pastor, Hausmann was one of Luther's first and closest supporters, and had been sent already to Schneeberg in the Hartz mountains in 1520 to initiate evangelical worship there. He emerges in a lot of Luther's correspondence as a stalwart and reliable pastor and ambassador for the Reformation faith.
38. In October 1533 Duke George (of neighbouring Ducal Saxony) and Elector Joachim of Brandenburg, along with Archbishop Albrecht of Mainz, came to Dessau to exert pressure on the three princes of Anhalt to remain loyal to the Roman Church. By this time, however, the determination had been made and Anhalt was already under the banner of the Reformation. See Brecht, *Luther 1532-1546*, 26-7.

this time by their respected tutor, Georg Helt, who had also converted to the Reformation faith.[39]

The Reformation was publicly introduced in Dessau on Maundy Thursday 1534, with the distribution of the Lord's Supper under both kinds. Georg had by this time become a strong evangelical, and Johann seems also to have given his complete assent and support. However, it appears that Joachim was the last of the three brothers to wholeheartedly take on board Luther's Reformation teaching.[40] Around this time he received letters of comfort from the other Wittenberg reformers—Melanchthon, Bugenhagen and Jonas—who all made a point of how God-pleasing and praiseworthy it was that the evangelical faith had been introduced to Dessau.[41]

It hardly seems a coincidence that all this took place just a few weeks before Joachim's lapse into severe depressive melancholia.[42] Born in 1509 and the youngest of the three brothers, Joachim was strongly influenced by the strict penitential piety of his mother, and the ascetic tendencies of his older brother Georg. Shy, nervous and reclusive by nature, Joachim was also struggling to find his feet in the public and political realms. In 1534 he was only twenty-five years old, and while well-schooled in the formal sense, was still very sheltered and inexperienced in the realities of public and political life. The conversion of his two brothers and the introduction of the evangelical faith to Dessau can only have been a significant upheaval

---

39. Luther enlisted the support and participation of Melanchthon, Jonas and Bugenhagen in winning the princes over as loyal supporters, which they did by writing letters of comfort and encouragement.
40. As we will see, at various points in his letters of comfort Luther explained important points of evangelical teaching, particularly as they applied to the troubled conscience, and it is clear that Joachim suffered with doubts about the doctrine of the forgiveness of his sins, a common spiritual struggle of people with depressive illness.
41. Anhalt-Dessau was a close, important and influential ally in the battle to win the German territories and free cities over to the evangelical cause. A significant amount of effort was expended by Luther and his associates in Wittenberg in establishing the Princes of Anhalt in the evangelical faith, including letters of comfort and visits to Joachim, without whose acceptance of the Reformation faith the alliance could not be complete and strong.
42. Luther's first letter of comfort is dated May 23, about a month after Easter. Also in the correspondence of the court tutor, Georg Helt, written between May and July 1534, Joachim's illness is mentioned several times.

for the young prince. For a young man with such a sensitive nature, these major changes (requiring the overturning of his entire faith and spirituality) could be quite enough to trigger depressive illness, or at least contribute significantly to it.[43]

This is perhaps why, in his letters, Luther is reticent about mentioning the introduction of the Reformation to Dessau, sticking instead for the most part to attending to the prince's own personal situation.

It is therefore not the case, as one might conclude from a cursory reading of these letters (especially the later ones), that Luther wrote to Joachim on the basis of an already strong friendship. On the contrary, he was writing as one seeking to gain the prince's trust and confidence in a tense and difficult situation, in which the politics of family, state and church hovered like shadows in the background, together with Joachim's religious fears and mental health problems.

The six letters Luther wrote to Joachim in the midst of this depressive crisis of 1534 show how gently he handled this situation, and how he quickly realised (especially after spending some time in Dessau with the prince in early June) that this pious, serious and tortured young man needed to escape the penitential chains of his ascetic upbringing and learn the freedom of the Gospel, along with the skills and habits of enjoying life in the body and savouring God's gifts with a good conscience.

Luther initially addressed Prince Joachim with heightened formal courtesy, taking up the issue of the prince's illness with deliberate delicacy and caution. He relaxed this formality as the relationship was steadily established, and he felt free to speak more directly (yet always respectfully) to the prince about his illness and how to fight it.[44]

---

43. The portrait of Joachim which emerges from the historical sources (chiefly these seven letters of consolation from Luther) is one of a young man of somewhat fragile mental health. The challenge to his whole world view precipitated by the introduction of the evangelical faith to Anhalt-Dessau would have been a significant spiritual and psychological upheaval.

44. As Luther often did with people outside his intellectual circle, he chose to write all of these letters of comfort to Prince Joachim in German. This was not because Joachim was not fluent in Latin. He'd had an excellent and well-rounded humanist education. It is more likely that Luther was taking advantage of the superior expressive range of German as Joachim's 'heart language', in his reaching out to the young prince whom he was hoping to influence, not so much at the intellectual as at the *affective and emotional* level.

There are strong indications of Joachim's depressive illness in Luther's letters themselves, as well as in correspondence written by others around the time of the crisis in May to July 1534.[45] In the first letter of comfort written on May 23, Luther himself proposes (and later in the letter, twice assumes) that the prince is suffering from *melancholia* and *schwere Gemüte* (heavy moods). This suggestion seems 'strangely specific' in view of the fact that Luther himself had not yet, as far as we can tell, met or spoken with Joachim. In the opening *narratio* of this letter, Luther mentions that Nicolaus Hausmann had told him that the prince was 'a little weak'. Perhaps Hausmann (who had by this time been with the three princes in Dessau for some time as court chaplain) had briefed Luther more fully than Luther let on. Another possibility is that Georg and Johann had expressed their concern to Hausmann and had asked him to involve Luther to see if *he* could help in Joachim's increasingly desperate crisis. Around this time, Princes Georg and Johann were both also in contact with other Wittenberg reformers, so it is likely (according to the custom of the time) that information about Joachim's health and state of mind was shared through these channels, and came to Luther's notice in this way. What precisely had happened behind the scenes is, of course, impossible to determine.

In the remaining five letters from 1534, Luther does not refer to the exact nature of Joachim's illness again by name. He mentions it only indirectly, though it is clear from his statements that melancholia was still troubling Joachim.

We see from Luther's fourth letter during this 1534 crisis, on 13 June, that after a brief recovery, Joachim's symptoms had suddenly become more serious. In addition to his depressed moods, he had developed a fever from which he had not yet fully recovered when Luther wrote to him again ten days later on June 23. What connection existed between this onset of fever and Joachim's depressive moods is unclear.[46]

The course and duration of Joachim's depressive illness in 1534 is unknown. Luther's last known letter of comfort to Joachim from this period, sent on June 26, shows that Joachim's heavy and depressed

---

45. The correspondence of Georg Helt, tutor to the three princes. See Menecke-Haustein *Luthers Trostbriefe*, 239.
46. It is a feature of the period that melancholic depressions were often accompanied by fever, as in the case of Joachim, Luther himself, and also Melanchthon in 1540.

moods had not yet ceased. Luther went and stayed with the prince in Dessau from mid-July until the beginning of August, in order to comfort him and aid his recovery.[47] How much longer this bout of illness continued is impossible to say.[48]

The **first letter** of May 23 is characterised by the courtesy and care mentioned above. In her analysis Mennecke-Haustein observes that Luther totally discards the conventional approaches to consolation by openly suggesting a diagnosis of the prince's illness and its cause: 'I have often noticed that almost all the members of Your Grace's family have reserved, quiet, and serious natures,[49] and this has led me to think that Your Grace's illness may well be caused by melancholy and depression'. It is interesting to note that this is actually the only instance in Luther's letters of consolation where he refers to the addressee's illness using the word *melancholia*. Mennecke-Haustein notes that Luther prefers the Latin *tristitia* (with its spiritual and affective overtones)[50] and uses it as a synonym for *melancholia*–a word which, for him, seems to be associated more with Galen's *medical* understanding of the illness as an imbalance of the body's humours.[51] Why then does Luther depart from his usual semantic usage *here*?

It is possible that he is suggesting that Joachim's problems are at least partly somatic, inferring that a doctor's services are needed. The fact that he couples the word *melancholia* with a further descriptor (*schwere Gemüte*), denoting not the physical or medical aspect of the illness but rather the mood and state of mind caused by it, supports this explanation. *Melancholia* may well have been a more acceptable word for the prince himself, having been educated in the humanist

---

47. Brecht, *Martin Luther 1523–1546*, 27.
48. The fact that no further letters of comfort were written by Luther after his return to Wittenberg, together with the fact that Joachim's illness is not mentioned after this time by others in the court of Dessau, in their correspondence (as it had been previously), would tend to suggest that this episode of depressive illness lifted in early August, or at least became less severe and more manageable.
49. See footnote 54 below.
50. Mennecke-Haustein, *Luthers Trostbriefe*, 242. Luther did not normally use the Latin word *tristitia* when writing in German. In his German letters of consolation he refers to depressive and melancholic illness using a range of different words.
51. WA TR III, No.3298a, 257–258; WA TR III, No.3823, 640; WA TR I, No.977, 494 and WA TR I, No.1227, 610. Luther's use of the word *melancholia* in the *Table Talk* tends to run towards this medical understanding. See Pietsch, 'Reflection on Depression in Luther's *Table Talk*', 26–7.

milieu where this was increasingly accepted as the affliction of the noble, sensitive and refined.

Luther's explanation of the underlying cause of Joachim's *melancholia* is also important. He delicately suggests in this letter what he elsewhere says bluntly: that the ascetic way of life is toxic to the human body and soul.[52] This ascetic spirituality was a strong tradition in Joachim's family background.[53] The scrupulous, reclusive and introspective way of life into which Joachim had been brought up was, in Luther's view, the immediate cause of his present sickness.

With careful deference, Luther then begins a more conventional *argumentatio* and *exhortatio* by recommending to the prince that he seek the external consolation of joyful and active pursuits such as hunting and riding and enjoying the company of friends. Luther connects this counsel to the fact that the prince is a *young* man, whose youth will be quickly ruined if he continues with his present lifestyle. He supports his point with Ecclesiastes 11:9. His own experience of his youth being ruined by the ascetic solitude and misery of life as a monk certainly influenced him at this point: 'No one realizes how much harm it does a young person to avoid enjoyment and fall into being lonely and depressed'.

It is at this point that Luther applies to the prince's situation the evangelical teaching of the Christian's freedom, reassuring Joachim that pleasure, merry-making and fun are not inherently sinful or impious, but good gifts from God which may be used with thanksgiving and a good conscience; indeed God is pleased when we do so since this is the purpose for which he created us.

Luther's last *argumentatio* and *exhortatio* dig down one level deeper to the root of Joachim's sickness: a misplaced conviction that

---

52. He says this more strongly later in the letter, where he describes melancholy and solitude as 'poisonous'. This integrated understanding of mental, spiritual and somatic forms of illness is a hallmark of Luther's pre-modern thinking. There is no dualistic separation of the bodily and non-material. A person's state of mind and spirit can indeed make them physically sick and, on the other hand, bodily sickness may well be expected to affect the mental and spiritual faculties.
53. Joachim's great uncle, Prince William of Anhalt became a begging friar and his two paternal aunts became nuns. Mennecke-Haustein, *Luthers Trostbriefe*, 244, suggests strongly also that Joachim's mother, Margarethe, was a proponent of this strict quasi-monastic penitential form of Catholicism, and had greatly influenced her sons' upbringing through it.

sadness and misery are virtuous and God-pleasing. This intentional cultivation of penitential 'mourning' was part of the monastic life with which Luther was all too familiar. Inherent in this piety is the idea of earning merit by renouncing *all* joys of the world.[54] At this point the teaching of justification by grace comes into view as an alternative framework of the Christian life, as Luther explains to Joachim: 'participation in proper and honorable pleasures with good and God-fearing people-even if the talk and joking might sometimes go too far- is God-pleasing.'[55]

When living in a state of grace through Christ's forgiveness, the believer is liberated from the scruples of the conscience, and is able—and in fact *commanded*—to rejoice in receiving and using God's material and creaturely gifts. This emphasis on God's gift and command of joy is the chief theme of this first letter, and recurs in the subsequent five letters.

Luther has set up the *argumentatio* and *exhortatio* elements in a particular way: they are dynamically woven together rather than separated and ordered according to strict logic, with *exhortatio* following *argumentatio*. This has the effect of creating a suggestive, almost 'cajoling' tone. Close together throughout the text we find again and again the words *fröhlich, freuen and Freude,* as Luther not only *speaks about* joy but also seeks to *elicit it* from his reader on the basis of God's goodness and grace. Birgit Stolt notes how difficult it is to properly translate these German words today, since in the sixteenth century *freuen* or *fröhlich* had far stronger meaning than today: to dance, sing and even leap with delight. Luther exhorts the prince to be joyful not only on account of life's good and pleasurable gifts but also of Christ's forgiveness through which the believer is set free from sin and death in order to live a joy-filled life. Assuming dominical authority for his words, Luther writes:

---

54. This tradition, summed up in the dictum '*monachus debet esse tristis*' (a monk is obligated to be sad) had its roots in fifteenth century French Benedictine spirituality, but was widespread in Christian piety by Luther's time.
55. Luther may well also be protecting himself against accusations of libertine and wicked behaviour, which could well have been levelled at him by others who may read the letter, for example, the anti-Reformation neighbours of Anhalt Dessau, Duke George and Elector Joachim.

So, be joyful, both inwardly in Christ himself and outwardly in his gifts and good things. This is what he wants. This is why he is with us. This is why he provides his gifts—that we may use and enjoy them, and that we may praise, love, and thank him forever and ever.

In a brief but powerfully worded conclusion, Luther reinforces his points about God's will: that the Christian be joyful, even in the midst of suffering–particularly then, in fact! This underlines the point that Luther is not 'cheering the prince up' as we might try to do today, with a good humoured 'slap on the shoulder'. He is saying '*Take* delight and pleasure in life and God's gifts; *act joyfully* even if you might not *feel* joyful, indeed in *defiance* of your feelings'. He points out that old age, with its burdens, will soon bring enough cause for real sadness and melancholy.[56] A formal but warm commendation closes the letter.

In this first letter Luther artfully manages to address the prince, whom he does not know, with consideration, courtesy and respect, yet also manages to take up the issue at hand rather directly. Throughout the letter, Luther's tone is deferential and polite, yet he touches on personal and sensitive areas of Joachim's life.

The **second letter**, of June 9 1534 was written immediately on Luther's arrival back in Wittenberg following a trip to Dessau to visit the court and to comfort Joachim in his ongoing despondency. The letter was evidently sent back to Joachim with the armed escort that had been deployed by the prince to accompany Luther and Melanchthon (who was accompanying Luther) back to Wittenberg.

The letter has an 'incidental' character, as if Luther were using the opportunity afforded by this formal note of thanks to remind the

---

56. Luther's comments here and earlier in the letter, where he refers to youth as the time of life for activity, enjoyment and fun, and old age as a time when people are weighed down by illness and melancholy, reflect his awareness of the tradition of Constantinus Africanus' *De Melancholia* (written around 1020). Constantinus, a North African Muslim-turned–Christian, who translated into Latin ancient Arab texts on medicine and philosophy, has a lot to say about melancholy's effects on youth and vigour. In his works on melancholia, he prescribes a healthy diet and exercise for the young, in order to stave off brooding moodiness which leads to depression. See Constantinus Africanus, *De melancholia libri duo*, Europeana, original copy owned by Bodleian Libraries, Oxford University, http://www.europeana.eu/portal/record/92093/5B63F3F89D5D8FE6D1F9066ECE3A986D81A97BA5.html.

prince of consolations he had been given during Luther's visit. Luther reports that his thoughts and prayers during the journey home have been for Joachim, in connection with which he refers to praying the *Our Father* several times as an intercessory prayer on the prince's behalf. This use of the Lord's Prayer is common in Luther's letters of comfort. From one perspective, it could be seen as the remnant of the medieval practice of saying the 'Our Father' for others as a source of merit, but, given Luther's theology at this point of his career, this could hardly be what he has in mind here. It is quite possible that Luther is using the Lord's Prayer as an evangelical pattern of intercession for others; this flows naturally from his teaching about it in both the small and large catechisms, where he sees it as the primer for all prayer.[57]

In this letter Luther turns his attention more fully towards the prince's illness and thus also more formally takes up the task of consolation, albeit briefly. We have here again the threefold exhortation to be cheerful, picking up the theme of the last letter, and perhaps also a key-note of Luther's pastoral conversation with the prince at court.

He employs a highly conversational rhetorical device, reporting to the prince the conversation between himself and Melanchthon concerning Joachim's illness, which took place during or soon after the return journey to Wittenberg: 'Phillip M has since pointed out to me how Your Grace has never been especially unwell, until just recently, to which I said, "Then it's no wonder that His Grace has so easily become anxious; he is unaccustomed to it". By means of this report, the prince is allowed to be 'a fly on the wall', listening in on a private discussion about himself and hearing Luther's own private thoughts on the matter. Besides underlining the genuine concern that the two reformers had for the prince, this allows Luther to lead into the point he really wishes to make concerning Joachim's own attitude

---

57. Luther's spiritual comfort to Joachim in these six letters of 1534 takes up a number of themes that are reflected in the Lord's Prayer: God as loving Father who knows how to help and teach his children, God's provision, help and salvation in times of hard testing, the forgiveness of sins, etc. This opens up the insight that a key aspect of Luther's counsel to Joachim is catechesis in the basics of evangelical Christian faith.

to the problem, and it is in the next paragraph that this real *consolatio* is delivered.

Luther goes on to explain that God is doing the prince a service by getting him used to the experience of suffering. He uses the metaphor of God having taken Joachim 'to school in order to teach him how to suffer a good hiding',[58] that he may become accustomed to the rod. This way the rod will continue to be a rod and will not become an executioner's sword (*Henkerschwert*). The disciplinary image is used in a light-hearted and almost jovial tone, suggesting that this experience of suffering is just part of Joachim's schooling—his growth towards maturity. It is not some terrible terminal illness but a lesson on taking life's sufferings as God's good teaching. Luther concludes this section with an exhortation that has a decidedly paternal ring to it, showing the fathering role he had by then increasingly come to play in Joachim's life during this period: 'Come your Grace, my Lord and prince, be cheerful and remember that other brothers are suffering too, as St Peter says,[59] and perhaps more than you are. For Christ says "Because I live, you also will live".'[60]

Luther shows his commitment to Joachim's ongoing pastoral care by promising, here near the end of this letter, to visit the prince again in the near future. However, given the religious-political situation in Saxony in 1534, this might also be interpreted as a further opportunity to cement the political-theological bonds between the house of Anhalt-Dessau and Wittenberg. In any case, it seems that Luther's presence as a pastoral comforter is desired by the prince.[61]

---

58. Luther uses an old German expression: 'to suffer a good schilling's worth' (a sound hiding), to further place Joachim's troubles in perspective as part of God's 'school-masterly discipline' for spiritual growth.
59. 1 Pt 5:9. Luther's gentle reminder to Joachim here, that he is not the 'centre of the universe' and that others have it tougher than he does, fits together with the suggestion Luther puts forward earlier in the letter, that Joachim's character is being formed by God's loving discipline.
60. Jn 14:19. This verse is quoted in conjunction with the previous one. Christ who suffered *far more than* all, and *for the sake of* all—Joachim included—has made suffering and death redundant for those who trust in him. He suffered, died and was raised, and all Christians follow in these steps.
61. At various points in these six letters of consolation Luther is responding to requests from the prince for Luther to visit him in Dessau again. As we will see, Luther's pet joke was that he must 'feed his publisher a bit' (like a pet) so that he could be free to visit. The tone of Luther's reassurances at various points implies

This is the first letter in which Luther begins his private joke with Joachim concerning his publishers, who in this case are characterised as 'pets' who need to be 'fed' regularly in order to keep them happy. Rounding off the jocularity in the last paragraph is the promise that next time Luther comes to visit he will bring Bugenhagen with him.

The letter closes with the third reference to joy, in a commendation which is grammatically a little ambiguous: '*Und hiemit fröhlich Gott befohlen!*' It is not completely clear whether Luther is joyfully commending Joachim to God (the expected meaning), or whether he is commending Joachim to God joyful.

The **third letter** was written on June 12, only three days after the previous one, before Luther had been able to visit Dessau again. Luther is following up a positive report he had received–that Joachim was recovering well–by writing a cheerful and affirmative letter in order to build further on the positive effects of the prince's progress.

Luther continues the theme of joy and good cheer, and once again mentions his continuing prayers for Joachim, along with those of Joachim's brother, Georg, who was at that time provost (dean) of the Magdeburg Cathedral. Apart from these brief references, the letter does not contain any spiritual consolatory *argumentatio*, nor any scriptural allusions or quotes, but rather develops an approach which Luther had begun to hint at in his previous letter: the use of humour. This third letter is full of good–natured banter and joking, mostly at the expense of others. Luther is following up here on his comments in the previous letter, that enjoyment and fun are not to be avoided as sins, but embraced as God's gifts.

In 'playing the joker', Luther was also taking up an established tradition of humour and laughter as a treatment for depressive moods, by playing a role to which he was well–suited: *homo facetus*,[62] the witty, urbane and clever conversationalist who cheers his companions, 'takes them out of themselves' and gets them chuckling.

Continuing his joke from the end of the previous letter, Luther again mentions his 'publisher bosses' (*herrn drucker*) whom he must

---

that the prince's requests were quite insistent.

62. Gerd Dicke, 'Homo Facetus: vom Mittelalter eines Humanistischen Ideals', in *Humanismus in der Deutschen Literatur des Mittelalters und der Frühen Neuzeit : XVIII. Anglo-German Colloquium, Hofgeismar 2003*, edited by Nicola McLelland, Stefanie Schmitt, Hans–Jochen Schiewer (Tübingen: Niemeyer, 2008), 299–332.

'feed a little' before he can get some peace in order to visit Joachim again in Dessau. What then follows is a sustained joke in which Luther talks about his next visit to Dessau and who he will bring with him, using various comedic nicknames and metaphors. The sense of this section is grammatically unclear, and while we are able to gain some appreciation of the humorous images, there is no way of understanding at every point Luther's meaning and to whom he is referring.[63] He writes about bringing with him the '*pomer*' (Johannes Bugenhagen) so that he might see '*der pomerschen*' (possibly a nickname for Joachim's sister-in-law, Princess Margarethe, the wife of Prince Johann, who was also from Pomerania) and '*Hamester*' ('hamster', obviously a pet name or nickname for somebody else). There is a humorous reference to Bugenhagen and Margaretha (who had become good friends) looking 'so happily married', which can only be a joke based on the impression that they were, as we might say of two friends today, 'like an old married couple'. Luther's exact meaning is unclear, largely because we as readers stand outside this 'circle of friends' who had their own set of 'in-jokes' and nicknames.[64]

At this point Luther obviously intended to close the letter with the usual good wishes and prayers. Instead he added a humorous postscript about Franz Burkhardt, a close friend to Joachim and frequent visitor to the court at Dessau, who was at that time evidently visiting the prince. This ironic jibe at Burkhardt pokes fun at the latter's high opinion of his own chess-playing skills, but it is clear that here the game of chess is representative of life. Luther talks about Burkhardt's ability to play the game, moving his pieces around the board, then quips at the end, 'But the queen is his master in the game, and perhaps elsewhere too! He understands that the best.'[65]

---

63. Neither Otto Clemen's commentary (WA BR VII, 74-75) nor Mennecke-Haustein's analysis (*Luthers Trostbriefe*, 252-53) offer what I consider a clear or convincing interpretation of Luther's text here.
64. This humour is on the coarse or 'burlesque' side, with a hint of cartoonish carnival comedy about it. Also, referring to Princess Margarethe as *die pomersche* was probably pushing the bounds of respectfulness and good taste in a sixteenth century German royal court. The fact that Luther seems confident of getting away with it would indicate that with his first letter and subsequent visit to Dessau, he had been able to establish not just favourable, but quite open and friendly relations with the prince, and had gained his confidence to a significant extent.
65. Possibly a reference to Burkhardt being inept at dealing with women (Mennecke-

Luther is doing more here than merely 'having a laugh'. He is, in a real sense, coaching and leading the prince in how to have fun and enjoy a joke. One gets the impression that he had been able to do this in person during his recent visit, and that the jokes in this letter refer to humorous conversations the prince had enjoyed with Luther at that time.

The **fourth letter**, written on June 13, can hardly be termed a letter at all. It is rather a brief note, hastily written by Luther for Dr Augustinus Schurf [66] to take with him to Dessau, as he responded to an urgent call for medical help from Prince Joachim after a sudden deterioration in his condition.[67] Dr Schurf, who had no doubt briefed Luther on the situation, was in such a hurry that Luther was hardly able to dash off these few lines before the doctor departed.

It is evident that Luther feels a genuine concern for the young prince, in whose life he has already come to play a paternal role. No doubt partially because of time restraints, but also simply as a natural expression of care, he takes the unusual step of reversing the formal terms of address, playing up his own relationship with the prince, while assigning the prince's own titles and honours second place, beginning his address with the words '*My* gracious and beloved Prince and Lord'.

Though written hastily, this note is nevertheless full of signs that Luther was thinking pastorally, carefully assessing what was of greatest importance and what counsel the prince needed in his dire distress. His choice of comfort is telling: 'Christ our saviour will help your grace, should the moment [*stündlin:* literally, that 'little hour'[68]] come.

Haustein's hypothesis). Once again, the modern reader is not included in the 'wink and nod' that Luther is sharing with the prince in these lines, which appears to be based on private jokes they have shared in relation to Burkhardt.

66. Dr Augustine Schurf was Luther's friend and a respected professor of medicine at the University of Wittenberg. He acted also as a consulting physician to Luther, his family and other members of Luther's circle, including Prince Joachim. He is not to be confused with his brother, the lawyer and politician, *Jerome* Schurf, who was also well-known to Luther, having accompanied him as his legal advisor to the Diet of Worms in 1521.

67. There is no indication here of how precisely the prince's illness had worsened, but in the fifth letter (written ten days later) reference is made to the persistent fever which had compounded the prince's melancholy and depressive moods. It is clear that this deterioration in Joachim's health was seen as potentially fatal.

68. In German this expression was, and still is, often used to refer to the 'the hour of

Then his promises will not fail you'. In the face of death's approach, Luther, who is not able to be present to give Joachim his comfort and aid, tells the prince that should his time come, Christ himself will be present as the prince's helper and comforter. Then Christ himself would show that his promises (the Gospel promises of forgiveness, peace of conscience and eternal life, in which Joachim had trouble placing his trust) were not false, but true. We see here how *in extremis*, Luther reduces his *consciatio* to its christological core. In these few lines where there is space for only the truest and most essential word of comfort, Luther turns the prince's eyes to Christ alone, who at death's threshold comforts and helps those who believe in him.

This christological core of Luther's pastoral theology illuminates the rest of Luther's counsel and comfort to Joachim in these six letters: his numerous greetings wishing the prince grace and peace, his prayers for the prince's comfort and healing, his exhortations to joy in the face of depressive misery, and his commendation of the prince to God's grace and care at the close of his letters (including this one). This brief urgent word of assurance helps us to appreciate that Luther's comfort for Joachim, like all true Christian comfort, is also actually *Christ's* own gracious *consolatio*.[69]

It becomes apparent at the end of this letter that Joachim has recently written to Luther requesting him to visit, since Luther writes, 'I wish as soon as I have fed my publisher a little, to do as your grace has written, and as I have promised'.

The **fifth letter**, written on June 23, some ten days after Dr Schurf's mercy dash to Prince Joachim's bedside in Dessau, is quite different in nature from the previous two. There is little joking, nor is there the kind of urgency found in the previous letter of June 13, but rather measured and carefully constructed pastoral consolation. While it was still written under time pressure,[70] it is longer than the previous

---

death'.
69. As Johannes Schilling and Martin Treu have both also noted, this Christ-centrality in Luther's pastoral approach, where he is 'both the subject and content of pastoral care', is one of the key features of all Luther's *Seelsorge*. See Johannes Schilling, 'Gegen Lebensüberdruß und Todessehnsucht, Zwei Trostbriefe Martin Luthers', *Zeitschrift der Luther-Gesellschaft,* 81 (2010): 2. See also Treu, 'Trost bei Luther', 91–106.
70. Evidently, Luther and the Wittenberg reformers were under considerable pressure, working on proofs of the German Bible which was about to go to print.

short note and conforms more closely to the traditional consolation letter format, making use of the *argumentatio* and *exhortatio* forms.[71]

While it is difficult to ascertain the exact situation, by this time it seems that the most acute phase of Joachim's health crisis had passed and he was no longer close to death. The fever, however, was persistent despite medical treatment and the prayers of Joachim's many consolers and intercessors. In this letter Luther seeks to reassure the Prince that God has indeed heard his prayers and will act to restore him to health in his own time and way.[72]

The extended opening address is once more heavily personalised, so much so that it dispenses with *all* mention of Joachim's royal titles and honours.[73] The pastoral relationship between Luther and Joachim had become close quite quickly, especially, it seems, during Luther's recent visit. It appears that the young prince had become something more than an esteemed royal personage to Luther. Luther's own increasingly familiar and paternal tone of speech and his willingness to invest not only time, but also personal energy into Joachim's pastoral care, suggest that he saw the prince as something of a 'spiritual son'. Perhaps Luther saw in this young man (who was dogged by exaggerated spiritual guilt and melancholy) shades of

---

This is almost certainly the project to which Luther refers in his letters to Joachim in 1534, where he writes about having to 'feed his publisher' a little in order to get some peace.

71. This said, it is also clear that Luther has not conformed in a strict or comprehensive way to the *consolatio* letter format, but taken the elements which are useful to him. For example, he dispenses here completely with the standard *narratio* section, which would normally come at the beginning of a letter, outlining the circumstances and causes which have led to the sender writing the letter.

72. Luther's consolation in this letter responds to this issue with a directness and care which almost create the impression that Luther has a letter from the prince lying open in front of him and is answering Joachim's questions about why God has not alleviated his illness. See Mennecke-Haustein, *Luthers Trostbriefe*, 255.

73. This prolonged address, which makes little immediate sense when read as the introduction to the letter which follows, was in all likelihood not the letter's opening address but rather what Luther wrote either on the folded letter or envelope after he had completed it and was preparing it for the courier. This makes much better sense of Luther's reference to himself as a 'poor comforter and paraclete', since in the middle section of the letter he actually discusses Rm 8:26–27, which speaks about the role of the Holy Spirit as paraclete, especially in relation to his helping Christians to pray.

himself as a young monk struggling with his own depressed and burdened conscience, and seeking help from *his* spiritual father.[74]

Luther takes up the issue of the delay in Joachim's recovery by putting forward two related *argumentationes*: firstly, that God has knowledge of how to help us which is superior to ours, and secondly, that God's timing is therefore also superior. The comfort to be drawn from these two points is that God's redemptive actions in the world often take place *sub contrario*:[75] almighty God's help is right and good for us, even though it may not seem so to us at every point. Faith leads us to trust and be patient, believing that God hears our prayers and is answering them according to his perfect will.

Luther explains his consolation using three highly persuasive illustrations. He refers at some length to the narrative of the Israelites waiting for God to save them from slavery in Egypt (Exodus 3–14). Though at times they despaired of God's help, they rejoiced all the more at his redemption when it finally arrived, which was 'even more glorious' than they had hoped, since God dealt Pharaoh's army a fatal blow. In this way he–at the last moment–not only saved Israel but also assured their future freedom and safety. The insight which Luther brings to Joachim from this deft summary of the biblical narrative is that God's 'delaying' was, and should be seen as, *part of* his saving action.[76]

Luther uses two other illustrations, both from everyday life: the father who knows what is good for the child better than the child does and so acts as he sees fit for the child's good, and the doctor whose superior medical knowledge and desire to help leads him, for

---

74. It is ironic that many of the counsels Luther gave to young Prince Joachim in his depressive struggles are similar to the comfort he himself received as a young monk from his own confessor and mentor, Johann von Staupitz. See his *letter to Spalatin* of August 1544 (See Appendix). Luther's highly affective language to the prince in his letters of 1534 reflects his deepening emotional awareness that resulted from having his own children. See Birgit Stolt, "Martin Luther on God as Father", in *Lutheran Quarterly*, 8/4 (1994): 385–95.
75. Gerhard Forde's astute observation on this is that since all human beings are by nature theologians of glory, God, in his mercy, deals more with us *sub contrario*, using suffering and affliction, so that we cannot distort and overthrow his work in us. See Gerhard O Forde, *On Being a Theologian of the Cross, Reflections on Luther's Heidelberg Disputation, 1518* (Grand Rapids: Eerdmans, 1997), 31–2.
76. Mennecke-Haustein, *Luthers Trostbriefe*, 256.

the patient's own good, to sometimes ignore the patient's requests and desires.

Luther supports these *argumentationes* further by quoting (more or less) Ephesians 3:20: 'God will do far more than we could ever think or wish'; and Romans 8:26–27, which shows how God helps us in our weakness since we ourselves do not know what to pray for.[77]

Mennecke-Haustein neatly summarises the heart of Luther's pastoral theology in this letter:

> Luther wants to convey to the prince the very uncomfortable consolation that something may be beneficial for a person, but he may still experience it as something bad, and that God's grace can also work where a person feels only that he is experiencing God's anger.[78]

After carefully building the case, Luther then applies it to the prince's situation, asserting that since they have all been praying according to God's will and command, they can be sure that God already has the prince's ills in hand and plans to help him 'even more powerfully' than Joachim himself can imagine. Indeed at the end of this paragraph Luther says that God may use this situation to do more for the prince than merely restore his physical health; inferring perhaps that this trial may, by God's grace, bring about in Joachim some growth of faith, spiritual maturity and awareness.

Once again we find the same point coming through: Luther is trying to help Joachim, whose eyes have been fixed solely on his own personal suffering, to see that God's will and gracious purposes embrace and reach far beyond his perception and indeed, far beyond his individual situation, working 'more powerfully' than human reason can conceive.

---

77. Luther recasts these verses from Romans 8, which actually speak about the *Holy Spirit's* (not the Father's) role in helping Christians pray, probably because he wants to make the verse fit in better with the illustration he is about to use: the father helping his child. He wrote 'On this point we can learn from what the apostle Paul says in Romans 8: we truly do not know how we should pray, but he, as a true father, knows and sees how we should pray, and he acts according to his knowledge, and not according to how we pray.'
78. Mennecke-Haustein *Luthers Trostbriefe*, 256, translated by Brian van Wageningen (2011).

The *exhortatio* is brief but forceful, coming just before the closing section of the letter. Luther writes, 'Therefore, let your Grace be of good comfort. Christ is ours-yes in every way ours, just as we long for him. And even if he makes himself an obstacle to reason, no matter'. The prince needs to be patient, go on praying together with his friends and comforters, and wait for God's greater work and fuller consolation to be revealed.

Once again, Luther closes on a slightly humorous note, with his intentions to visit the prince in Dessau soon, once he has fed his 'pests' [79] a little (provided more written material for his printer).

The commendation at the end of this letter is brief and the reader may easily miss the highly significant phrase Luther uses: 'Christ our Lord himself is with your Grace; that is certain. To His grace and protection I commend you'. These words recall the urgent words of comfort Luther gave Joachim in the previous hastily-written note that Dr Schurf took with him on his emergency visit to Joachim's bedside: 'Christ our Saviour will help your Grace'. Here again, as he closes this letter, Luther reminds the prince of Christ's constant gracious presence with him, which saw him through his brush with death just a few days earlier, and on which he can count at all times.[80]

The **sixth Letter**, written on June 26, is the last that Luther wrote to Prince Joachim during his depressive crisis in 1534. It seems to have become Luther's practice, by this time, to dispense with the formal courtly greetings and addresses that marked his early letters. As always he opens this letter with a form of the apostolic greeting used by Paul at the beginning of *his* epistles. In most of these six letters from 1534, he shortens the greeting to 'Grace and peace'. Here, however, he extends and shapes it in a particular way. Once again he specifically mentions Christ Jesus; this time describing him as 'our dear Lord and comforting saviour'. This mention of Christ himself

---

79. '*meine Plager*' The reference is a joke at his own expense, in which he indirectly compares himself with Pharaoh, who also had to suffer *viel Plage* (many plagues), as Luther has mentioned in the middle section of this letter.
80. To us such comfort may sound very ordinary, even 'standard'. For Joachim, however, the notion of Jesus Christ as a loving intimate presence in his life would have been something new and radical. The penitential piety of his upbringing pictured Christ purely as a just and angry judge, before whom the penitent sinner stood in fear. Luther's application of the Gospel to Joachim's life was then effectively a complete overturning of his image of God.

as the prince's personal comforter ties this letter to the previous two, in which Luther has attempted to draw Joachim into the knowledge and experience of Christ's saving presence in the midst of his illness.

This letter was sent only three days after the previous–and longer–letter of consolation, and it seems that while the prince is no longer quite as weak as he had been, improvement is still slow. He must have regained some strength, however, in order to be well enough to entertain the prospect of guests and to participate in social contact.

This short letter was, as Luther himself explains in the brief *narratio* at the beginning, not motivated by any particular concern or issue, but an opportunity to greet and make contact with the prince by sending a letter with Francis Burkhardt, who was just at that time leaving to visit the prince in Dessau. It is not directed towards the goal of consoling the prince in any substantial way, as with the extensive *spiritual* consolations offered in the previous letter. Luther is rather preparing Prince Joachim for the forthcoming visit of their mutual friend, Burkhardt, whose job it is to divert the prince and lead him once more into the *external* consolations of good conversation, singing, playing music and other cheering and light-hearted pursuits.

Luther does, however, signal to Joachim this *transition* in his 'treatment'. In the fourth paragraph Luther briefly mentions and reminds the prince of some of the consolatory themes from his previous letter. In the fifth paragraph he speaks about the way in which earthly external consolations (such as music, conversation, games and humour) work together with spiritual consolation (such as prayer and scripture) to help people suffering with melancholy. He uses two biblical examples (Elisha[81] and David[82]) to show how music awakens (*erwecken*)[83] the heart to glorify and delight in God and his gifts.

This letter gives us a glimpse of the way in which early modern culture, in line with emerging humanistic thought, viewed the company of particular people as a kind of 'therapy' for the depressed. Such people were seen to be blessed with the gift 'for taking others out of themselves' or 'diverting' them, and were always in demand

---

81. 2 Kgs 3:15.
82. Ps 57:8.
83. Luther uses this verb twice in this letter, drawing on its many shades of meaning: to wake from sleep, to arouse, uplift and enliven.

as friends and companions.[84] In Luther's third letter in this series (written June 12) we noted how Luther himself takes on this role of *homo facetus*; now it is Burkhardt's turn to visit Dessau in order to serve as the prince's 'master of amusements'.

The tone of this letter is once again light-hearted, optimistic and hopeful, written to help set the mood for Burkhardt's visit. Luther's now-customary closing joke about the demands of his printers this time creates the comical image of Luther harnessed up with bit and bridle, like a horse ready to be ridden.

The **seventh** and last letter in the selection from Luther to Prince Joachim was written almost 18 months after the prince's 1534 depressive crisis, on Christmas Day, 1535. It is ostensibly a letter of Christmas greeting, but in terms of its content and tone, is really more of a *Trostbrief*, incorporating many consolatory elements.

Joachim is still suffering from bouts of melancholy. The crisis of 1534 seems to have passed, since there is no mention of it after early August. The problems which occasioned *this* letter seem to indicate a new depressive episode, this time manifesting slightly different symptoms.[85] It is clear from the letter itself that Joachim is in need of comfort in the midst of 'doubt' and 'despondency' (*Zweifel* and *Traurigkeit*), though not any longer on account of the actual evangelical doctrines themselves, as in 1534. It appears that this time his melancholy had fixated on a different spiritual issue, as indicated in the concluding paragraph of Luther's *argumentatio*: 'Your grace has not yet betrayed or crucified the dear Lord. Even if your Grace had, Christ nevertheless remains gracious. He prayed even for those who crucified him.' While it is dangerous to speculate too freely here, it is not 'stretching the bow too far', knowing Joachim's history of exaggerated religious scrupulosity, to imagine how he may well have negatively fixated on the notion of himself as a sinner being a 'betrayer' and 'crucifier' of Christ.[86] This is the issue that seems already to be in

---

84. In his *Table Talk* Luther mentions another of his acquaintances, a certain Christoff Grosz, whose 'human wit was able to gladden the hearts of depressed persons' (WA TR I, No.2965a and 2965b, 122:4-5, 7-17). Such people were the 'diversional therapists' of their time, and their company was always in demand.
85. A comprehensive understanding of Joachim's mental health history around this time is not possible; however, it is clear that after a period of substantial or perhaps even complete respite from the severe depressive symptoms of 1534, the problem had re-emerged.
86. This rhetorical way of speaking about the serious spiritual nature of sin before

focus earlier on in the letter, where Luther writes: 'What can distress us–apart from, perhaps, our sins and bad conscience? Yet Christ has removed these from us, even while we sin daily.'

Luther's unfolding of the Gospel in the main body of the letter (the *argumentatio*) is a compact but masterful piece of evangelical *consolatio*. He speaks about Christmas as the comforting and peace-filled feast of the incarnation,[87] which God undertook in Christ to comfort and bring peace and good will to all people. Though the devil seeks to slay us, in the light of God's decisive incarnational act, what can he do to us?[88] Yes, we may be weak and feel vulnerable, but 'Weak we must be, and are willing to be in order that Christ's strength may dwell in us.'[89] John T Pless reflects on Luther's words here: 'In weakness God puts his power to save on display. From the lowliness of the manger to the humiliation of the cross right down to the pits of Joachim's depression, God comes to save.'[90]

In the opening sentence of the *argumentatio* Luther mentions the creed and Gospel, and makes reference to Joachim by this stage being 'well-instructed' about 'that which is the truth, as opposed to the lies of the devil and the pope'. While Joachim, along with his brothers Georg and Johann, would have been instructed in the evangelical faith at various times from 1532 onwards by their Lutheran court preacher, Nicholaus Hausmann, and their tutor, Georg Helt (who had also converted to the Reformation faith), there is something about the emphatic nature of Luther's phrase ('*Stehet aber die Lehre und der Glaube wohl an*') which evokes the question of whether

---

God may have been used in a sermon or spiritual treatise that Joachim had heard or read, and triggered an obsessive negative response. This pattern of spiritual negativity, in which a powerful phrase or metaphor dominates a person's consciousness, is common among depression sufferers today, particularly people of strong faith. See Stephen J Pietsch, 'Depression and the Soul: a Cook's Tour' (paper presented for the opening lecture of Australian Lutheran College, Adelaide, Australia, February 8, 2010), accessed July 2012, http://www.alc.edu.au/assets/education/about/academic-publications/opening-lecture/2010-depression-and-the-soul.pdf.

87. Lk 2:14: 'Glory to God in the highest and on earth, peace, good will toward men.'
88. Luther paraphrases 1 John 4:14: 'Greater than the devil is he that is in us.'
89. 2 Cor 12:9: 'Christ's strength is made perfect in weakness.'
90. John T Pless, "The Comfort of the Incarnation: A Christmas Letter from Martin Luther", *The Lutheran Witness* 126, no. 11 (December 2007), accessed January 8, 2012, http://witness.lcms.org/pages/wPage.asp?ContentID=206&IssueID=17.

Prince Joachim had recently undergone some more *formal process* of catechesis, perhaps focussing on the creed and teachings of the Faith. While in terms of historical evidence there is little else to suggest precisely *this* possibility, Brecht observes that the association between Joachim's depressive illness and the introduction to Anhalt-Dessau of the evangelical faith meant that the task of counselling Joachim in his melancholy may have quite naturally entailed teaching him the faith of the Gospel and its main doctrines.[91]

It could therefore be said that in many ways Luther's consolation of Joachim through his struggle with depressive melancholia (both during and after the 1534 crisis) was not just pastoral care and counsel but also *catechesis*. While it is quite clear that Joachim accepted, and later conscientiously defended, the Reformation faith, it is nonetheless a pity that we do not have any of the correspondence that he wrote to Luther in which we might find some personal expression of the prince's own faith and spiritual growth during this period.

From Luther's side, there is a strong indication that he saw the prince's struggle with depression in 1534 as educational in the second of the six letters he sent during this period. Here he tells Joachim that God is 'taking him to school' and that he is receiving 'a good hiding'. The prince learned the teaching of the Gospel in the context of acute depressive suffering, as he received the Christ-centred consolation of Luther and others. This catechetical understanding of Luther's pastoral care and counsel with Joachim is also suggested by Luther's question in the second paragraph here in this seventh letter: 'if we stand firm in the Faith and the teaching, what does it matter if hell and all the devils fall upon us?' Like Luther himself, Joachim learned the Gospel not at the level of intellectual assent, but through *experiencing its comfort* in the midst of deep *affective* pain and distress.

Considering these **seven letters together** briefly at this point, by way of summary, will allow us to see the main contours of Luther's overall consolation of Prince Joachim. What can be drawn from this special extended case study?

It is important to note again here that these letters show us only Luther's side of this intensive pastoral relationship, which was itself part of a wider pastoral association between Joachim and the larger group of Wittenberg reformers. Keeping this in mind, we can see

---

91. Brecht, *Martin Luther, 1532–1546*, 27–8.

that, as Luther was comforting and counselling the prince, he was at the same time catechising him in the evangelical faith, proclaiming and modelling to him the forgiveness of sins through Christ and the freedom of the Christian, using many different explanations, biblical texts and examples. This comfort of the Gospel, centred on the person of Christ and his promises, came as a voice of love and acceptance which radically contradicted Joachim's highly penitential piety, centred wholly on the image of Christ as a righteous and just judge. The life into which Luther sought to lead Joachim was a life of joyful trust and peace, flowing from a cleansed and relieved conscience; a life in which the Christian is free to enjoy the creaturely gifts of this life in good faith. Music, humour, exercise, conversation and friendship were all part of the richness that Luther tried to help Joachim to discover. Luther teaches clearly here that the joy of this faith and hope is the means by which God sustains the believer in times of affliction, when the sufferer needs to be patient and wait for God's help. In these times God is testing, teaching and strengthening the soul.

In these various consolations, which are integrated and interwoven in many ways throughout the seven letters, Luther drew on past traditions and ancient wisdom, molding them to the teaching of justification by grace. Luther built a strong (perhaps even paternal) mentor relationship with Prince Joachim, leading and coaching him in the practical spiritual life-skills he needed to deal with his depressive illness. Very noticeable is the way in which Luther, himself under considerable pressure at the time, allowed himself to be drawn into the inconvenience and mess of Joachim's crisis. He understood from his own experience the need to maintain active contact, and to speak and act with truth, compassion and patience.

Letter to Elsa von Canitz (Appendix: 266ff)

- August 27 1527 (WA BR IV, No.1133, 236–237)

Like so many other minor characters in the early Reformation in Saxony, we know little about Elsa von Canitz until she enters the story in April 1523. She was known to Luther since she had been one of the group of twelve nuns who fled from the Marienthron Cistercian

Convent in Nimbschen (near Grimma in Ducal Saxony) on April 4 (the eve of Easter Sunday).[92]

The daring escape involved a town councillor from Torgau, Leonhard Koppe, who regularly delivered supplies to the Convent at Nimbschen. Luther had hatched a plot with Koppe to smuggle the nuns out of the convent in his covered wagon, disguising the undertaking as a delivery of herring barrels. Three of the twelve escapees found shelter with nearby relatives, but Koppe brought the remaining nine to Wittenberg, where Luther arranged for them to lodge in private homes.

Sharing the wagon to Wittenberg with Elsa von Canitz that night were some significant persons: Magdelena von Staupitz (sister of Luther's confessor, Johann von Staupitz) and one Katarina von Bora (who Luther had no idea would later become his wife). Luther endeavoured to oversee the resettlement of these nuns. He had plans to help some of them marry, and tried to find situations for others which would give them security and protection.[93]

It is not known where Elsa von Canitz was or what she was doing during the four years between her escape from Nimbschen in April 1523 and August 1527 when Luther wrote her this letter, when she was at that time 'visiting' in Eicha, near Leipzig. It is clear that the letter's primary purpose was not consolatory, but administrative. Luther invites (or rather summons) her to come to Wittenberg, where he wants to 'use' her as a teacher in the girls' school. He advises her that he has asked her aunt, Hanna von Plausig (in whose home Elsa von Canitz was a guest) to 'send' her to Luther for a while. Following this announcement, Luther then writes, 'I now ask you not to decline my invitation'.

Luther goes on to address the issue of his reader's depressive illness (*schwere Gedanken*), offering a couple of fragments of comfort. There is a genuinely empathetic tone to Luther's words in this paragraph, at the end of which he says, 'If you come I shall talk to you further about this'. It is hard to read between the lines here, but perhaps part of Luther's wish for Elsa von Canitz to come to Wittenberg (and live in his home) may have been that he felt he could help her recover from her melancholy and move on with her life, just as he had hosted others

---

92. Brecht, *Martin Luther, 1521–1532*, 100–01.
93. Brecht, *Martin Luther, 1521–1532*, 101.

(Johann Schlaginhaufen, Jerome Weller and Elizabeth Agricola) and helped them with their depression.

However, Elsa von Canitz did decline to come to Wittenberg. It is not known whether she reacted unfavourably to Luther's less-than-gracious request or whether she feared the plague which was rampant in Wittenberg at that time. A more likely possibility is that her depression was of a severity that she felt unable to face the stress of a new situation and the demands of teaching.

As he so often does, in this letter Luther characterises this illness as the devil's attack, and tries to reassure his reader that it is a sign that she truly is one of Christ's people, since he himself (together with all his prophets and apostles) had also to suffer such attacks. He tells her to be confident and of good comfort (*seid getrost*), knowing that her Father will remove this rod from her in his own good time.

Letter to Queen Maria of Hungary (Appendix: 267ff)

- 1531 (WA BR VI, No.1866, 194–197)

Queen Maria of Hungary was born in 1505, a Habsburg. She was the daughter of Phillip (the handsome) and Johanna (the mad); younger sister of Emperor Charles V and King Ferdinand of Austria. Known prior to her marriage as 'Maria of Austria', she became Queen Consort of Hungary and Bohemia in 1522, when she was married to King Louis II of Hungary. With the death of Louis in 1526 at the battle of Mohacs, Maria was still childless, and Louis' realms passed to her family, the Habsburgs, whose political interests she had been carefully promoting as Louis' Queen.[94]

At this time Maria persuaded an assembly of Hungarian nobles at Pressburg to elect her brother, Ferdinand of Austria, as their king. Her royal influence in Hungary, where she had won a loyal and admiring following, was greatly enhanced by her strong sympathies towards Luther and the Reformation movement, since she was surrounded by people who shared her criticisms of the Roman Catholic church as expressed by the reformers.[95] It seems likely that she was influenced

---

94. Gernot Heiss, 'Mary Queen of Hungary and Bohemia', in *Oxford Encyclopedia of the Reformation, edited by* Hans J Hillerbrand (Oxford: Oxford University Press, 1996), 3:28–9.
95. Queen Maria was reading Luther's writings prior to 1525, and is said to have

in this regard by her Lutheran brother-in-law, King Christian II of Denmark. Tappert suggests that it was at Christian's prompting that Luther wrote to this high and well-connected Habsburg lady[96] in 1526, dedicating to her a meditation on four psalms[97] to encourage her spiritual growth and her understanding of the Gospel. However, before he could complete this book, Maria's husband (the staunchly Catholic Louis II) was killed in battle, and Luther altered his devotional piece to be more of a book of comfort to the Queen in her grief. He wrote a dedicatory letter as the preface to this treatise, which is full of Christian comfort and catechesis.[98]

Luther also harboured hopes that the Queen might accept the Hungarian evangelical preacher Conrad Cordatus (one of Luther's students who was, at that time, at Wittenberg) as an evangelical chaplain and teacher; however, it became clear that Maria was unwilling to take this step.[99]

Her influence in Hungary as Queen Consort came to an end in 1531 when she was appointed Regent in the Netherlands. Her Lutheran sympathies may have made her too much of a risk in Hungary, where the reform movement was becoming popular. Though this deprived her of the opportunity to further develop her leadership and influence in Hungary, she distinguished herself in the Netherlands with her wisdom and moderation. She seems to have periodically suffered from bouts of depressive melancholia, possibly an illness she inherited from her mother, Joanna, known as 'the mad'.[100] Despite considerable problems in the economy of the

---

written two Protestant hymns. She was in contact with Luther through her court chaplain, John Henckel, and addressed several theological questions to him, seeking clarification on points of church doctrine and practice.

96. Tappert, *Luther, Letters of Spiritual Counsel*, 56.
97. *Vier Trüstliche Psalmen* was dedicated as a book of comfort for Queen Maria. It gave Brief meditative verse-by-verse commentaries on Pss 37, 62, 94 and 109 (WA IXX, 542-551).
98. Published in Tappert, *Luther, Letters of Spiritual Counsel*, 56-8.
99. Brecht, *Martin Luther, 1521-1532*, 346.
100. Historical sources disagree considerably about Joanna and her madness. Mental illness was indeed present in her family background. The general consensus is that, like so many other royals of the period, she suffered from some kind of depressive disorder. The romantic literary tradition of her wild and obsessive grief-fuelled insanity over her husband's death is known to be mostly fiction. The political theory that she was labelled 'mad' and locked

Netherlands, she succeeded in raising money for the empire's wars. She remained in the Netherlands until 1556, the year of her brother Charles' abdication from the imperial throne, and retired with him to Spain.

Her political competence and skills as a leader and diplomat show that Maria was a person of considerable strength and character, not to say a certain toughness of mind. She took an active part in politics from an early age. She was a patron of the arts and architecture, and a fan of the great Flemish masters, and of Titian. She loved hunting and music, and the intellectual views and ideas of her time. She was an admirer of Erasmus' writing as well as Luther's, and cultivated strong contacts with them both.[101]

Maria's growing sympathy with Luther's teaching was a source of alarm to her Roman Catholic Habsburg relations (especially her brother Ferdinand, an ardent anti-Lutheran).[102] However, at critical points in her life she showed that her ultimate loyalty was to the Hapsburgs and their powerful position in European politics. In 1556, when she retired to the Spanish court with her brother Charles, it was clear that she had abandoned the Reformation cause, and she remained a Catholic until her death.

This letter of 1531 is complex and carefully woven, warm but restrained and respectful in tone. Maria of Hungary was not a person to be easily charmed by lavish words of praise. Luther, still trying to win the Queen to the Reformation faith, appears to realise that he is dealing with a seasoned Habsburg politician who knows how to 'cut to the chase'. While carefully observing due courtesy, he concentrates above all on providing well-developed and affective consolation.

Following a brief *exordium-narratio*, in which he states the occasion of his writing and explains how he has come to know about the Queen's illness, there is the opening *exhortatio*, phrased in unusually deferential terms: 'Therefore this is my humble request and warning, your Grace: resist as much as possible your own thoughts,

---

up because she became an obstacle to her father's authority in Spain is also an over-simplification. See Bethany Aram's excellent book, *Juana the Mad: Sovereignty and Dynasty in Renaissance Europe* (Baltimore: Johns Hopkins University Press, 2005).

101. Heiss, 'Mary of Hungary and Bohemia'.
102. Brecht, *Martin Luther, 1521-1532*, 346.

which actually are not your own, but most certainly those which the devil has exaggerated'.

Luther makes several interconnected points by way of *argumentatio*. In each case these are followed by *exhortationes* or appeals. The core theme is that she needs to reject and disown her depressed thoughts and turn her attention to Christ and his grace. Luther begins and ends the main body of the letter with this point, using it as an *inclusio*, in order to redouble its impact.

In the middle section of the letter, we have significant clues about the particular cognitive–affective issues involved in Maria's depression. She is troubled by the burden of past sins on her conscience, and sees God as an angry and punitive judge, who is punishing her by taking away the beloved things in her life. Luther juxtaposes this image of an angry and punitive God who is happy to see sinners suffer with the 'beloved son' who willingly undergoes great *suffering for the sake of* humanity. As in other letters, Luther reflects to Maria the exact opposite mirror–image of her distorted spiritual thinking. God does not mercilessly will our suffering or death, but through his Son, suffers and dies on our behalf, bearing more than we can ever realise or understand. This helps us place our experience of life's suffering into proper perspective, both in relation to Christ's immense suffering for us, and the eternal peace and joy he has thereby won for us:

> If we think about it, this suffering which his beloved son has taken all on himself, for our sake, is so great that we should our own suffering as insignificant by comparison. So compared to the gall and vinegar which he suffered, our present suffering should only be considered fine wine and malvaiser.[103]

This makes sense when held alongside the events of Maria's life at the time. Written in 1531, this letter coincides with Maria's departure from Hungary to take up her duties as Regent in the Netherlands. It seems likely that it was her sense of loss at leaving not only a kingdom but also a position of leadership and a home that triggered her depressive bout. In Hungary she had begun to form her own political identity

---

103. A fine wine imported from Southern Europe, popular in the courts of Europe at that time and still made today under the name *Malmsey*.

and shape the life and future of the nation, using her political skills. She had also been free to explore her interests in the Reformation and its theology, whereas she had now been clearly told by her brothers, Charles and Ferdinand that in the Netherlands she must support absolutely the Habsburg Roman Catholic line.[104] In this way her career as a leader and politician had been substantially limited. This observation is supported by more than one passage in the letter, but particularly where Luther begins his second *argumentatio:*

> What does it matter then, if body and life, father and mother, brothers, kingdom, crown, honour, wealth and anything else one could mention pass away? For if God's grace remains ours, then God is our father and his Son is our brother, and his heaven and creation is our inheritance, and all the angels and saints are our brothers, cousins and sisters. So even if we lose everything, we have, after all, lost less than a halfpenny's worth, even if we have no kingdom, heaven or earth, we still have God himself and eternal life!
> So I now ask God the Father himself if he, by his dear Holy Spirit, would write on Your Grace's heart what is so richly found in the scriptures, and keep you thinking about this; and more, I pray that it will go much deeper, *into* your heart, deeper even than your own life and the things Your Grace holds dear on this earth.

Maria's depressive symptoms become clear from Luther's pastoral response. He mentions her depressed and melancholy thoughts (*schwere und traurige Gedanken*) and, as so often in his advice to people suffering in this way, repeats his counsel to 'allow them no room', lest they gain a foothold and take over.[105]

He concludes with a series of Psalm quotations and caps off his consolation with Philippians 3:2: 'the peace and comfort we have in God will overcome all things'. This is no piling up of texts for the sake of sheer 'weight of numbers', but a carefully assembled 'barget' of texts that combines to reveal the mystery that God delights in the prayers of the suffering and hurries to help and comfort them. This grouping

---

104. Heiss, 'Mary of Hungary and Bohemia'.
105. Luther is once again using Gerson's diversional strategy for fighting depressive thoughts, in which the sufferer actively ignores them and does something else in order to occupy the mind with different content.

of biblical texts is Luther's commentary on the lived experience of faith in the midst of depressive despair.[106]

A brief commendation closes the letter.

Luther's clear intention in this letter is not only to comfort Maria in her depression, but to do so by teaching and proclaiming the Gospel to her in the way that she needs to hear it in her life-situation, with its particular thoughts and feelings. His comfort is based squarely on justification by grace through the all-atoning and transforming suffering of Christ. He takes the opportunity to place before Maria his sacramental theology, tying these comforts in with baptism, the Lord's Supper and the gift of a clear conscience before God.

Letter to Barbara Lißkirchen (Appendix: 313–315)

- April 30 1531 (WA BR VI. No.1811, 86–88)

As in some other letters, the addressee of this missive, Barbara Lißkirchen, appears as a relatively minor figure in Luther's circle of acquaintances, and it is likely that he never met her in person. She was a sister of the Weller brothers (Peter, Jerome and Matthias) who were all known to Luther.[107] She married George Lißkirchen of Freiberg in 1525.[108] She was evidently conscientious about spiritual matters and seems to have been a strong supporter of evangelical reforms, even though her ideas may sometimes have been outside the bounds of good ecclesiastical order and practice. She petitioned Luther to allow her to celebrate the Lord's Supper with bread and wine in her own home in 1535; a request Luther refused on theological and pastoral grounds.[109]

---

106. Luther's quotations from Psalms 147, 51 and 50 together with Phil 3:21, create affective intensity at the end of this letter, as one hears scripture speak, first with God's gracious invitations to the sufferer and then with the authoritative assurance, 'the peace and comfort you have in God will overcome all things'.
107. Peter Weller lodged with Luther in his student days in Wittenberg, as did Jerome, who was tutor to Luther's children. Luther counselled both Jerome and Matthias during their serious bouts of depressive illness. His letters of consolation are included in the selection of letters in this study, and are outlined later in this chapter.
108. See Tappert's commentary: Tappert, *Luther, Letters of Spiritual Counsel*, 115.
109. Brecht, *Martin Luther, 1532–1546*, 72.

Despite the sketchiness of our knowledge about Barbara Lißkirchen's life, her name appears in many indexes. This letter of comfort Luther wrote to her has become significant in Luther studies as an important text for understanding Luther's theological development in the area of divine election and predestination. The letter also belongs to a noteworthy body of letters which Luther wrote to women. It gives interesting clues about his attitude towards, and treatment of, women, which have been noted by researchers looking at Luther from the perspective of women's studies and feminist theology.[110]

Luther's letter to Barbara Lißkirchen appears in the current study, however, for a different reason. We are looking into how Luther counselled this woman in her deep struggle with dark and troubling thoughts about divine election, and whether her doubts about her own salvation indicated that she had been predestined for damnation.

It could be argued that this letter should, strictly speaking, be omitted from the collection under examination in this book. There are not as many obvious indications of depressive illness as appear in other letters. Clearly, Barbara Lißkirchen's primary *presenting* issue is her anxiety concerning the doctrine of election, not a general or pervasive depression or melancholy. Moreover, the most telling key words that would indicate depressive melancholia (*melancholia, Schwermut, tristitia, betrübt*) that are found in other letters, do not appear here.

On what basis, therefore, has the letter been retained in the selection? While there is not as much *prima facie* linguistic indication of depressive illness, there are other important clues. There is the strong family history of depressive melancholia. Barbara Lißkirchen is the sister of two brothers who both very clearly suffered from depressive illness, and she herself presented with a mood disturbance of some kind. Like other Lutherans of this period, she has become

---

110. Schneider, *I am a Christian*, 106. See also Richard Marius, *Martin Luther: The Christian Between God and Death* (Cambridge: Harvard University Press, 1999), 119. See also Timothy George, *Reading Scripture with the Reformers* (Downers Grove: Intervarsity Press, 2011), 162.

'deeply troubled' (*hoch bekümmert*) with the fear that she was predestined to damnation.

Therefore, within this specific historical context of a positive family history of depressive illness, and the common melancholy fixation on divine election and predestination, the less conclusive linguistic indications of depressive illness in this letter take on greater significance. The word *Gedanken*, used seven times in this letter, is a marker for cognitive and affective depressive symptoms in Luther's letters to the depressed, and elsewhere, where he speaks about his own or others' struggles with melancholy.[111] On the basis of these factors combined, this letter has been retained in the selection and treated as a letter of comfort to a sufferer of depressive melancholia.

As with depressive illnesses today, it is the sufferer's thoughts (and the associated feelings and attitudes)[112] that become distorted and catastrophised. It is therefore hardly surprising that for people with such depressive tendencies, the ambiguities of the church's teachings on divine election were a common focus for depressive anxiety. In the aftermath of the Roman penitential system, in which people relied on a predictable 'economy of salvation' even though it was loaded against them, the difficulties of gaining a clear understanding of scripture's teaching on election at times cast people again into spiritual uncertainty and fear.

Luther's view is that delving into this matter with a depressed person who is vulnerable to such distorted and negative thinking leads nowhere, and it is better not to enter on that path at all. Pastorally, the

---

111. See his letters in this selection to *Jonas von Stockhausen* (Appendix:319–320) and *Queen Maria of Hungary* (See Appendix). See also WA TR I, No.461, 199–201:10 and WA TR I, No 832, 404:25,27,28. When speaking about melancholy and depression, Luther typically uses certain adjectives *traurige Gedanken* or *schwere Gedanken* or *cogitationes tristitiae*. Here the word *Gedanken* appears without such adjectives, but Luther's subsequent description of these 'thoughts' afflicting Barbara Liβkirchen is consistent with those suffered by others who were clearly battling depressive melancholy.
112. It is clear that, for Luther, these words *Gedanken* and *cogitationes* are not indicative only of rational functioning, but also include the individual's entire interior affective personal experience: feelings, imagination, fears, desires etc. See WA TR I, No.491, 215. See also Pietsch, 'Reflection on Depression in Luther's *Table Talk*', 56–7.

more one enters into debates and speculation in this area of Christian teaching with depressed people, the shakier ground one is on. He handles Barbara Lißkirchen's morbid fears by counselling her to reject the thoughts themselves as the devil's deceptions, giving alternative input for her meditation: scripture and its promises and assurances of salvation to all who believe and trust in Christ.

As is so often the case with Luther, it is the context of pastoral practice which brings questions of teaching and doctrine into clearer focus. Although this letter is often cited as one of Luther's profound expressions of his teaching on election, there is little here in the way of extended commentary or theological argument on that issue. He does not enter into any lengthy explanation or discourse about the teaching on divine election itself but rather appeals to simple biblical images, promises and teachings, put simply and clearly. In this sense, the letter is a piece of true 'practical theology', illustrating that Christian teaching finds its profoundest and clearest expression in the context of the lived experience of the human soul.

Although much could be said about Luther's expression of his theology of divine election in this letter, the purpose of this study is to explore the way in which he uses it to comfort and encourage his reader, and so the overview offered here is limited accordingly.

Following the *salutatio*, Luther immediately begins a brief and to–the–point *narratio*, in which he explains that his knowledge of Barbara Lißkirchen's troubles with eternal election has come from her brother Jerome, and that he sympathises with her suffering. There is a sense of purpose and urgency here, born of Luther's desire to help his reader with an *Anfechtung* he knows only too well himself. This section of the letter ends with a blessing: 'may Christ our Lord save you. Amen.' Luther's palpable compassion comes from his conviction that he knows the suffering and agony that are caused by such fears. He says 'I myself was brought to the very edge of eternal death by it'. While acknowledging the difficulty of dealing with such an issue by letter, he sets out to do his best to relate how God had helped and was still helping him.

The lengthy *argumentatio-exhortatio* section which follows is made up of four numbered paragraphs, in which Luther unfolds his insights into this malady and his advice on how to deal with it. These four unfolding arguments weave their different threads into an integrated whole:

1. The need to reject the evil thoughts as the promptings of the devil, as per the clear witness of scripture.
2. The will of God that humans do not delve into things that are not clearly revealed to them by the word.
3. The believer's need to focus on the commandments of God, especially the first in which God says 'I am *your* God', since he has given us this command and promise to busy ourselves with, not his eternal counsels.
4. The highest command of all is to hold before our eyes the Father's dear Son, Jesus Christ the Lord. He alone is our true 'mirror' (*Spiegel*) in which we see how much God the Father loves us.

All of these four themes, developed in each of the four paragraphs, create the powerful impression of a highly-constructed yet simple and consistent pastoral counsel,[113] as does Luther's assertion in the summary paragraph immediately following:

> In this way, this way I say, can one learn the right art of dealing with predestination. This way, it will it be clear that you believe in Christ. And If you believe, then you are called. And if you are called, then you are most certainly predestinated. Do not let this mirror and throne of grace be torn away from the eyes of your heart.

The lengthy *conclusio* reiterates a lot of what has already been said, using different images. There is, however, one new element here: a gentle but nevertheless solemn warning. It is hinted at in the previous *argumentatio* section, where Luther directs his reader away from her anxious speculations to the first commandment. In this final section of the letter, Luther goes further:

> The wretched devil, who is the enemy of God and Christ, tries to use such thoughts (which are against the first commandment) to tear us away from Christ and God and to make us think about ourselves and our own worries. If we do

---

113. This elegant rhetorical device, using an unfolding four-part construction, is more about effect than logic. Luther's purpose is to produce a 'weight of assurance' and give clear and concrete directions and strategies for his reader to use in her situation. A full and in-depth rhetorical analysis is provided by Mennecke-Haustein, *Luthers Trostbriefe*, 195–206.

this, we take upon ourselves the role of God, which is to care for us and be our God. In paradise the devil wanted to make Adam equal with God so that he would be his own god and care for himself, robbing God of his divine work of caring for him. The result was Adam's terrible fall.

In the following paragraph Luther sharpens his point even more by referring to the folly of delving into things which God has not commanded or revealed as the very arrogance that led the devil to fall into the abyss of hell.

Luther also indicates that he is writing to Barbara Lißkirchen's brother, Jerome Weller, from whom he learned of her illness, asking him to reinforce the advice he has given.[114]

The final blessing is one of the most beautiful in any of Luther's letters of consolation: 'May our dear Lord Jesus show you his hands and his side and greet you with a friendly heart, and may you see and hear only him until you find your joy in him. Amen'. This biblical metaphor at once changes the tone of solemnity so evident in the preceding paragraph, placing the reader into a vivid imaginative context. Suddenly we are with the disciples in the upper room. Thomas, like Barbara Lißkirchen, has been struggling with his doubts until Christ himself shows his wounds: the signs of his atonement for all sinners, and the evidence that it truly is him, risen, and bringing joy and hope (John 20:27).[115]

Letter to Johann Schlaginhaufen (Appendix: 272ff)

- December 12 1533 (WA BR XVIII, No.4353, 561)

Little is known about Johann Schlaginhaufen's early life besides his birth in 1498 at Neunburg in the Palatinate. He was an evangelical

---

114. See Tappert, *Luther: Letters of Spiritual Counsel*, 117 (footnote 31). This letter to Jerome Weller has not been preserved.
115. Another dimension implicit in this biblical allusion ties it to the advice of Luther to meditate on the first commandment—*I am the Lord your God. You shall have no other gods*. In the verse following John 20:27, where Jesus shows Thomas his hands and side, Thomas responds with the confession 'My Lord and *my God*' (Jn 20:28). Thus Luther, in his one-line allusion to Jn 20:27, only begins the scene, and invites the reader to play it out in their own memory and imagination. As he often does, Luther here plants seeds that will grow and bear fruit for the reader as she reads and rereads the letter and meditates more deeply on it.

pastor who served in various places in Saxony between c.1530 and his death in 1560. Working initially as the pastor in the village of Werdau, near Zwickau in Saxony, he was called back to serve as pastor at Zahna, near Wittenberg, in 1532.

It was here that his life and ministry were seriously injured by controversy when he was suddenly and for no apparent reason, dismissed from his parish in Zahna by Wittenberg's head Bailiff, Hans Metzch.[116] At this time he became a lodger in Luther's home, and one of the important recorders of the *Table Talk*, which dealt often with the topic of melancholy.[117]

Sometime in early 1533 Schlaginhaufen was rehabilitated and found a new place in the Saxon church. He was appointed as the pastor at Köthen in East Saxony, where he was living when Luther wrote him this letter.

Schlaginhaufen was an energetic champion of the Reformation in Saxony. He worked hard in Anhalt-Köthen to establish evangelical preaching and worship, following the practices he saw modelled in Wittenberg. He was loyally supported by Prince Wolfgang of Anhalt-Köthen, who rewarded him with a piece of land in Köthen, and took

---

116. Several apparently arbitrary dismissals happened during the second visitation of parishes in Saxony by senior clergy and officials in 1530-1532. The visitation's purpose was to help maintain good standards of Christian life and teaching among the new evangelical congregations, and to maintain the proper payment of pastors. However, it appears that political agenda were sometimes pursued via this process, and it was not always well done. Following Schlaginhaufen's dismissal by Wittenberg's head bailiff, Hans Metzch (the reasons for which were never recorded), Luther championed his cause, and tried to intervene on his behalf, but his good offices were rudely rejected. He was so infuriated that he threatened to leave Saxony himself. See Brecht, *Martin Luther, 1532-1546*, 6-7. Luther had something of a 'running battle' with Hans Metzch, who more than once seems to have taken the opportunity to get back at Luther for twice excluding him from the Lord's Supper for being physically abusive to his wife.
117. See Brecht, *Martin Luther, 1521-1532*, 6 and Tappert, *Luther: Letters of Spiritual Counsel*, 87-8. Luther's letters to both Schlaginhaufen and Weller about their depression give the impression that behind them lie other conversations. Luther biographer, HG Haile has reconstructed from Luther's *Table Talk* the 'counselling' dialogues between Luther and Schlaginhaufen, whom he nicknamed 'Herr Turbicide'. This exercise is revealing. It shows Schlaginhaufen's depressive moods even more clearly, and also the extent to which Luther interpreted his friend's struggles as attacks of the devil. See Haile, *Luther, A Biography*, 187-92.

him to Smalkald when he travelled there to sign the Smalkald articles in 1537. Sometime in the early 1540s Schlaginhaufen was appointed superintendent of the churches in Köthen and its surrounding lands, a post in which he served until his death in 1560.[118]

Tappert observes that Schlaginhaufen was a man of 'mercurial temperament', who complained on many occasions of spiritual trials and temptations, and tended to fluctuate markedly between cheerfulness and depression.[119] It is clear that he turned to Luther often for solace and help, especially following his crisis in Zahna. The contents of this letter give the impression that Schlaginhaufen had developed a dependency on Luther. He recorded table talks in which Luther comforted him in his frequent depressions and doubts. His own words of commentary on these recorded conversations give a clear picture of a severely depressed person.[120] Luther also gives a strong indication of Schlaginhaufen's history of depression in this letter of December 1533, where he says he is saddened to hear that his friend is still sometimes depressed (*betrübt*).

Luther begins with warm personal greetings, which bind him to the reader. The *salutatio* which begins this letter, however, is more effusive than usual. Carefully listing Schlaginhaufen's position and recognising his faithful service to the Word of God, Luther addresses him finally as 'my dear brother'. He then makes a point of thanking him for the medlars[121] Schlaginhaufen had sent him–another personal touch. The reason for this heightened personal warmth becomes clearer in the main body of the letter.

The rest of the letter–an *exhortatio* and *argumentatio* combined–is brief, but powerfully worded; appealing to Schlaginhaufen to trust in Christ and his love, on the basis of Christ having shed his blood for

---

118. Biographical details from Franz Kindscher, 'Johann Schlaginhaufen', in *Allgemeine Deutsche Biographie* (Leipzig: Duncker & Humbolt, 1890), 31:329–36.
119. See Tappert's commentary: Tappert, *Luther: Letters of Spiritual Counsel*, 91.
120. See a table talk recorded by Sclaginhaufen himself in December 1531:Tappert, *Luther: Letters of Spiritual Counsel*, 87–8.
121. A large persimmon–like fruit native to Germany, which was widely grown and eaten in the sixteenth century, and still growing in gardens in Germany today. They are highly acidic until they are ripe and extremely soft, which is traditionally when they are eaten.

him. In this main body of the letter, Luther seems to gently move his friend away from turning to *him*, in order to help him place his faith and reliance in *Christ*:

> Dear friend, honor this good, faithful Man. And believe that he favours and loves you more than Dr. Luther or any other Christian. What you expect from us, expect even more from him. For what we do, we do at his bidding, but what he who bids us does, he does naturally from his own goodness.

Perhaps in order to sharpen the impact of these words, Luther ends the letter quickly at this point, with a friendly but brief commendation.

Letter to George Spalatin (Appendix: 273–276)

- August 21 1544 (WA BR X, No.2041, 638–640)

George Spalatin was born Georg Burkhardt in 1484 at Spalt, near Nuremberg, and assumed the Latinised name *Spalatinus*, following the humanist trend of the time. A brilliant young scholar and linguist, Spalatin quickly rose through the ranks, becoming a teacher in the monastery at Georgenthal, where he was ordained a priest in 1508. In the following year, promoted by his mentor Conrad Mutianus, he was employed by the Elector of Saxony, Frederick III (the Wise) as a tutor to his nephew. He distinguished himself quickly in this post, and was rewarded by being named a canon of the Altenburg Diocese. He was soon after made private secretary and chaplain to the Elector, handling all his public and private correspondence. Spalatin became Frederick's trusted confidential advisor and remained with the Elector until his death in 1525.

Being close to Elector Frederick, Spalatin became aquainted with Luther almost from the beginning of the Reformation. He formally converted to Luther's teachings around the time of the Diet of Worms (1521). Although ordained, Spalatin never had a great interest in theology, but was attracted to humanist literature and the classical languages. However, right from the beginning of their twenty-seven–year association, it seems that Luther had a profound effect on Spalatin, and became his close counsellor and friend. Lyndal Roper goes so far as to assert that this was one of the key relationships that made the Reformation possible.[122]

Because of his position at court and his proximity to both Frederick and Luther, Spalatin was involved in some way with almost all the important early developments of the Reformation movement.[123] He often translated and read Luther's writings to the Elector. He accompanied Frederick to the Diet of Augsburg in 1518 and Worms in 1521, and drafted much of the diplomatic paperwork for the difficult negotiations and communications with Rome and Saxony's neighbouring states.

After Elector Frederick's death, Spalatin moved away from the Court of Saxony to take up residence as canon in Altenburg (a position he had formally held since 1512). There he was involved in promoting the evangelical cause and engaged in visitation programs for the schools of Saxony. During his latter years in Altenburg, as an older man, Spalatin became somewhat unstable and volatile in his moods, and often fell out with his colleagues and the Altenburg council. Luther was forced to intervene twice in such conflicts, and was able to convince Spalatin's community to tolerate the eccentricities of his old age.

Over the years of their long friendship, Spalatin and Luther exchanged many letters. Spalatin's letters have been lost, but being a diligent and organised secretary he kept all of Luther's correspondence, which is among the most helpful and enlightening historical documentation from the early Reformation.

This letter of August 21, 1544 is possibly the gem of the selection for this study. Much more could be said by way of analysis here, but space dictates that only the main points be covered.[124]

This consolation was prompted by Spalatin's descent into a deep and persistent depression[125] following a serious mistake he had

---

122. Roper, 'To His Most Learned and Dearest Friend', 283–95.
123. Roper, 'To His Most Learned and Dearest Friend', 288. Roper goes so far as to say that Luther, Spalatin and Frederick the Wise formed a powerful 'triangle' within which the early Reformation was nurtured and protected.
124. For a more comprehensive analysis see Stephen J Pietsch, 'Luther Comforts a Depressed Pastor: Luther's Letter of Consolation to George Spalatin–Analysis and Reflection', *Lutheran Theological Journal* 35, no. 3 (December 2011): 144–148.
125. The text of Luther's letter makes it very clear that Spalatin's illness is a severe

made in giving spiritual advice. He had allowed a local pastor to marry the stepmother of his deceased wife. Luther overruled this decision, maintaining that the marriage was improper and had to be dissolved. Spalatin's shame and humiliation led quickly to a complete breakdown, and he refused to be comforted. This ordeal weakened him and he died a few months later in early 1545.

The letter is long and comprehensive, employing the traditional *consolatio* format in an intentional manner. It is written in a high rhetorical style, yet is nevertheless the letter of an intimate friend, bold in its honesty and tender in its compassion. Some readers of this letter are surprised by the judgements Luther makes and the bluntness of his statements. It is important in this regard to understand the deep and long-term friendship between these two men, which had matured over twenty-five years of working together, sometimes in tense and difficult situations. They knew one another's strengths and weaknesses and had forged a bond of mutual love and respect. As can be seen in this letter, there was a mature trust and understanding in this friendship. So Luther's strong statements are not based on assumptions or hearsay, but on a deep understanding of his reader. Luther's love for his old friend is apparent not only in his tender comfort and appeals for Spalatin to accept forgiveness and move on with life, but also in his willingness to say clearly where his old friend had gone wrong.

Although Spalatin was a professed Christian and believer in the Gospel, as a passionate humanist he was still optimistic about human nature; and he highly valued language, reason and philosophy. What Luther does in this letter is represent—in the face of this humanist mindset-the cause of theology, the central doctrine of sin and grace, law and gospel. He makes use of irony and sarcasm in his *argumentatio* in order to help Spalatin understand what it is to be a 'real sinner' in need of Christ, as a *real* saviour.[126] He observes that Spalatin actually has little real experience of battling against sin, a bad conscience and the law. Luther exposes the point that Spalatin's

---

case of depressive despondency (*tristitia*) which he likens to his own illness.
126. Luther refers to the telling-off he received from Staupitz, in which he told Luther that he thought he was only a *peccator fictus* (a painted sinner) who only needed a *salvator fictus* (painted saviour).

depression is the 'other side' of his proud desire to justify himself and retain his spiritual autonomy:

> Or it must be that until now, you have been only a trifling sinner, aware of having committed only the tiniest peccadillos. Therefore I beg you, join us truly great and hardboiled sinners so that you do not diminish Christ for us, who is not a saviour for imaginary or trivial sins but rather for real sins–not only small ones but great ones–yes even the worst, and for all sins committed by all people.

Luther's *exhortatio* towards the end of the letter stands out among all his letters of consolation as a most moving and powerful enactment of the Gospel:

> Imagine that I am St Peter who stretches out his hand and says to you 'In the name of Jesus Christ, rise and walk.'[127] In this way, my dear Spalatin, listen and believe everything which Christ is saying to you through me, for I am not mistaken (of this I am certain) and I am not speaking Satan's lies. Rather, Christ is speaking through me and is commanding you to trust this brother of yours, with whom you share the one faith.

Here Luther draws his reader into a highly imaginative visualisation (one might almost say *meditation*) on the text. His choice of passage for this *exhortatio* is also highly significant. The man whom Peter and John meet in Acts 3:1–10 is a cripple from birth who is begging for alms in the temple—a telling portrayal of the spiritual reality of Spalatin's situation. He too needs to recognise his identity as a crippled beggar to whom Christ, through Luther, is stretching out a saving hand.[128] This is typical of Luther's view of the Word of God as a concrete bodily event, involving not just the mind, but also physical touch and healing.

As with Luther's consolations to Prince Joachim of Anhalt, so here we see the deeply christological nature of Luther's comfort for the suffering. As a fellow-Christian and a pastor, Luther sees his words of comfort as those of Christ himself, and therefore commands Spalatin to hear and listen to him in Christ's name.

---

127. Acts 3:6.
128. Pietsch, 'Luther Comforts a Depressed Pastor', 149.

Rich in biblical quotes and references to God's mercy and images of God's healing,[129] this letter of consolation is a clear example of Luther's understanding of the forgiveness of sins as the true heart of Christian consolation and comfort.

Two Letters to Jonas and Mrs Jonas von Stockhausen (Appendix: 280–285)

- November 17, 1532 (WA BR VI, No.1974, 386–388) To Jonas von Stockhausen)
- November 27 1532 (WA BR VI, No.1975, 388–389) To Mrs Jonas von Stockhausen

The first of these two letters, to von Stockhausen himself, is one of the most well-known and written about of Luther's letters of consolation over the last twenty years. It deals not only with depressive illness but also with the associated issue of *Lebensüberdruß (weariness of life)* leading to thoughts of suicide. What Luther says about it here has therefore captured the attention of some contemporary theological and pastoral writers. There is important material here for understanding Luther's pastoral care in such a situation, in which the depressive spiral has led to a desperate and dangerous crisis.[130]

This letter is also noteworthy because it is one of the most linguistically pleasing and artful of Luther's letters of consolation. It is a tight and efficient piece of writing, yet rhetorically potent, demonstrating Luther's ability to alter the epistolary format to fit his particular pastoral aims without, in the process, giving up a rigorous and clear structure.

---

129. 2 Cor 7:10; 2 Kgs 21:2–15; Rm 8:23; John 3:16; Ps 118:13; Acts 3:6; Joel 2:13; 1 Jn 3:8; Ps 147:11; Ps 34:18 and Ps 51:17. Luther aligns these scripture verses with his own appeals all the way through this letter, perhaps hoping that he may awaken Spalatin's memory and awareness of God's grace. Each verse adds power to the single dominant appeal of this letter: receive God's free mercy and forgiveness and live!
130. Suicide in the medieval and early modern eras was considered the most desperate of acts, and was subject to general (in some places, unconditional) condemnation. Luther's own engagements with this issue reflect a more open and gracious view, though he does respond to pastoral situations of suicide in various ways. See Gerhard Krause, 'Luthers Stellung zum Selsbtmord: Ein Kapitel seiner Lehre und Praxis der Seelsorge', *Luther* 36 (1965): 51–71. See also Leroux, *Luther as Comforter*, 202–3.

Depressive illness is strongly implied by the suicidal thoughts and weariness of living (*Überdruß des Lebens*) being experienced by the addressee. In the Middle Ages and early modern Europe, this common state (also referred to as *taedium vitae*) was strongly associated with melancholic–depressive sickness. It was considered one of the natural results of *tristitia*, which was linked directly to suicidal intentions as a result of an even deeper state of hopelessness and sadness: *desperatio*.[131] This stage of depressive illness was seen as a moment of terrible physical and spiritual danger, in which a person may at any moment commit the ultimate perverse act of 'self-murder'(*Selbstmord*).

Once again, in this case Luther was writing a pastoral letter to somebody he did not know. By way of *narratio*, he says simply that 'good friends' have let him know of von Stockhausen's situation. It is not clear whether Luther wrote these letters on his own initiative after hearing about such a dire crisis (as a concerned Christian who felt able to help), or whether the letters were requested on behalf of von Stockhausen and his wife by the mutual good friends whom Luther mentions. Here again, our knowledge of the addressees is limited because the von Stockhausens simply do not appear elsewhere in the early Reformation story.

Jonas von Stockhausen's station in life at that time was an important and responsible one. In the early sixteenth century, it was customary that a city or town might ask a neighbouring nobleman to serve as 'captain of the guard' or 'sheriff', who, together with a body of mounted knights, would police and protect the community. Jonas von Stockhausen served the neighbouring town of Nordhausen in Thuringia as 'captain' (*Hauptmann*) for eleven years, between 1521 and 1532, when he asked to be relieved of his duties because of illness.[132]

While urgent in content and tone, the letter itself is rather formal in style, and follows the *consolatio* structure closely, beginning with the opening *salutatio*, *narratio* and *exhortatio*, then moving on to a tightly structured two-part *argumentatio* before a closing *exhortatio*, prayer and commendation.

---

131. Mennecke-Haustein, *Luthers Trostbriefe*, 230.
132. See Tappert's commentary: Tappert, *Luther: Letters of Spiritual Counsel*, 88–9.

The body of the letter begins with an *exhortatio* of such strength and seriousness that it is better described as a *warning*. It is clear that Luther considers his addressee to be so disoriented and deeply lost in his depressive confusion that he must, rhetorically speaking, 'shout' to get his attention. He tells von Stockhausen that it is 'high time' he stopped following his own thoughts and started listening to those who are free of the depressive *Anfechtung*; in other words, to those whose thinking and perception are more reliable than his own. This command is intensified by a striking and powerful metaphor: 'Bind your ears tightly to our mouth'. The physical image evoked here is of the sufferer shutting out the negative and destructive voices plaguing him by cupping his ear to the mouth of the comforter, so excluding all voices but his. The point of this image is that, having *heard* true Christian comfort through the *ears*, it will then go to the *heart*. For Luther, this word *spoken and heard* is the most powerful instrument of spiritual affect. He writes here as if speaking, and speaks so powerfully that he seems almost personally present in order to seize his addressee's attention. The final phrase in this opening *exhortatio* shows, however, that Luther's own speaking is not the point here: 'This is how God will strengthen and comfort you: by means of our words'.

Luther's *argumentatio* against his reader's wish to end his own life is comprised of two related points: firstly, that human beings must obey God's will; and secondly, that God gives and disposes of life as *he* sees fit. He supports these points by giving positive examples of saints bearing with the unpleasantness of life according to God's will, showing how Elijah (1 Kgs 19:4), Jonah (Jonah 4:3), other prophets (Jer 20:14) and even Jesus (Jhn 7:6) were sick of this life, but fought their weariness of life, remaining obedient to God, whose will it was that they go on living.

In the following extended *exhortatio* Luther goes on to tell his reader that he must therefore set his will and mind against devilish thoughts of suicide by whatever means he can. He uses two highly-charged images which portray the deadly danger of the reader's situation. He tells von Stockhausen to imagine himself bound in chains, from which he must break free through great sweat and strain. He then uses the image of the devil's poisonous darts (Ephesians 6:16) as a metaphor for despairing suicidal thoughts, which must be torn out of his flesh by force. As Luther goes on here, building to a rhetorical crescendo, it emerges that it is against his *own flesh* that von Stockhausen must wage warlike resistance, defying his own wishes and feelings. Yet it is not ultimately himself that he must resist, but the devil, who has planted and goes on promoting his deadly suggestions.

In this section as elsewhere in the letter, Luther creates the sense of a 'call to arms'. He uses the militaristic language, images and values of von Stockhausen's own profession as a captain of the guard: armed conflict, resistance, battle-wounds, self-discipline, resolve and strength in the face of fierce enemies. He addresses his reader as a man of decisive action who has weathered many a 'sticky situation' and knows how to 'grit his teeth' (an expression Luther actually uses in the letter) and get on with it. In the background here is Luther's interpretation of von Stockhausen's vocation as captain of the guard in Nordhausen, a role that required him to 'carry the sword' on God's behalf so that he might keep peace and order in the face of demonic and chaotic forces.

However, in the next paragraph this advice is followed by counsel which may initially seem to completely contradict what has just been said. Luther here puts forward Gerson's strategy of contempt[133] against melancholy: 'Do not struggle against your thoughts at all, but ignore them and act as if you do not feel them'. He speaks of treating depressive thoughts with utter disrespect by not attending to them, turning rather to consciously give attention to something else entirely. The devil, who is the planter and cultivator of this misery, is to be treated with abuse and derision: 'Dear devil, if you can't do better than that, then lick my arse. I have no time for you now.'[134]

It becomes clear that within Luther's logical framework, this strategy of ignoring and despising the devil and his depressive thoughts

---

133. As we noted in an earlier chapter, Luther mentions Gerson here by name, referring to his strategy of treating melancholy thoughts with dismissive disdain, as if they were the 'hissing of geese' (menacing but empty threats) and the 'carping of the *Leuseknicker* (nit-picker)' who nags and complains about unimportant trivia.
134. My own translation. Tappert's rather more sanitised translation (*Letters*, 89) misses the point of Luther's strong language here. It may seem strange that such coarse words are found in a letter of consolation; however, Luther's very point is that this is an extreme situation of spiritual attack in which the use of extreme language against the enemy is needed!

is not really contradictory to his earlier advice to fight against them, but just another way to characterise the same determined resistance towards them. No doubt both images and attitudes may be helpful to the person struggling with depressive thoughts at one time or another.

This *exhortatio*, comprising the latter third of the letter, builds to a powerful and impassioned climax as Luther uses various devices to intensify his appeals. He builds the pathos and impact of his words, piling image upon image, redoubling his use of modal verbs, shortening his sentences, making use of metre and alliteration.

The closing prayer and commendation are extended, and speak of Christ's triumph and victory over the devil in von Stockhausen's heart. Luther uses an unusual and striking turn of phrase at the end of this sentence: 'May he bring us all joy through the help he gives you and the miracle he does in you.' This underlines the fact that von Stockhausen has sunk very far into his depressive state and that, at this point, nothing less than God's miraculous intervention is required for his recovery. However, it does also create a theological *inclusio* as the letter comes to a close with the same point that is made in the opening *exhortation*: that whatever may be said by the human comforter and whatever efforts may be made by the sufferer, ultimately it is Christ himself who performs the miracle of healing, and he alone who can prevail over illness, the devil and all affliction.

The brief **letter to Jonas von Stockhausen's wife**, written the same day as the letter to von Stockhausen himself (November 27 1532), is not in any formal rhetorical sense a letter of consolation but more a brief letter of instruction, even though there are a couple of elements of the consolatory format here, as we will note. Since Luther did not know this couple personally, he is probably unaware of his addressee's Christian name, and so the letter begins on a note of slightly awkward formality. Luther refers twice during the letter (perhaps by way of apology) to its brevity, which tends to create the same tone of urgency as the letter to von Stockhausen himself.

Following the opening address and Pauline greeting, Luther moves immediately into a brief theological explanation of the affliction which she and her husband are now suffering. Because they love Christ, the devil has singled them out for attack, yet they must, and can, bear the suffering with God's love and help. Luther gives a kind of brief 'digest' of biblical verses to round off his word of comfort, put together from John 15:19, 16:33 and Psalm 116:15. The picture created by this combination of Scriptural verses reflects the same 'battle lines' that Luther draws up in his letter to Jonas himself: the devil hates those who love and serve Christ, and so wages war on them. They can endure, however, supported by the knowledge that Christ's decisive victory has already been won and will be made manifest. At the same time, this functions rhetorically as a 'call to arms' (as we found in the letter to Jonas) and an assurance of Christ's ever-present help.

What follows is a series of instructions on how to help her husband in the crisis he faces. Luther tells his reader not to leave him alone for a moment for 'solitude is utter poison to him', allowing him to sink into his depression and become vulnerable to the devil's suggestions. Luther advises that she should not leave anything lying around with which he might harm himself.

He then gives a brief description of how von Stockhausen's wife might employ external consolations in order to divert her husband: conversation, curiosities, stories, laughter and joking. It is interesting that Luther includes in this bracket of advice the suggestion that even if the patient becomes angry and argumentative, that is preferable to his being quiet and pensive, since he is at least responding to external stimuli. The closing commendation reiterates the assurances of the opening.[135]

Three Letters to Jerome Weller (Appendix:277–325)

- June 19 1530 (WA BR V, No.1593, 373–375)
- July 1530 (WA BR V, No.1670, 518–520)
- August 15 1530 (WA BR V, No.1684, 546–547)

Born in 1499, Jerome Weller was from an educated and noble Saxon family.[136] After his father died when Jerome was just 10, he was sent to live with an uncle in Naumberg where he studied at the cathedral school. He began his studies at Wittenberg in 1517 and graduated two years later with his bachelor's degree. Unfortunately, financial constraints prevented Weller from continuing his studies at this time,

---

135. Luther quotes Zechariah 2:8 as a closing blessing.
136. According to descendants of Jerome Weller, now resident in the US, Jerome was himself a genealogist and traced his family's origins back to the time of Charlemagne. The family's castle and lands were at Molsdorf in Thuringia.

and he went to Zwickau to earn a living as a teacher. With the financial assistance of relatives, he returned to study law in Wittenberg in 1525. It was at this time that he heard a sermon by Luther which made a powerful impression on him and soon after he switched to studying theology. He lived in Luther's home and worked as tutor to his children for eight years, between 1527 and 1535. Although Weller was shy and a melancholic type of personality throughout his life, his depression first emerged as a serious impediment during his time in Wittenberg in June 1530. Luther's brief descriptions of Weller's symptoms and moods in these three letters between June and August point strongly to severe depressive illness.

During 1530 Luther was away from home for an extended period, from April to October, lodging at the Coburg while Elector Johann attended the Diet of Augsburg.[137] He therefore had to try to help Weller as best he could by letter.[138] These three letters from Luther to Weller during this time are among a larger body of Luther's correspondence from this period referred to as the 'Coburg letters'.[139]

After he returned to Wittenberg in October, Luther devoted considerable time to Weller's pastoral care and supported him as he continued to struggle with his severe *melancholia*. This became a difficult and tiring task for Luther, as Weller's depression persisted. As is often the case today with people suffering with depressive illness, Weller seemed, on the one hand, to often feel lonely and fearful, yet

---

137. It was feared that if Luther appeared in Augsburg with Elector Johann and the other Wittenberg theologians, Emperor Charles (or his agents) would seize the opportunity to charge him with heresy and have him executed. However, Elector John wanted Luther close enough that if his counsel needed to be sought during the diet, he could be reached more quickly. Veste Coburg, a possession of Elector Johann within striking distance of Augsburg, was the ideal place for Luther to be secreted during the diet, which took six months. See Brecht, *Martin Luther, 1521–1532*, 373–79.
138. During this lengthy time away from home, Luther was almost cut off from direct contact with the outside world, apart from the visits of his friend Veit Dietrich, who relayed information, messages and letters from Wittenberg and Augsburg. Luther depended greatly on these letters. See Brecht, *Martin Luther, 1521–1532*, 374–75.
139. Luther wrote a great many letters to others during this time, seeking to stay in touch with the world outside. The originals of these three letters to Jerome were unfortunately lost and the second letter has been transmitted only in summary form. See Mennecke-Haustein, *Luthers Trostbriefe*, 182.

on the other hand, found it hard to face others or participate in social situations.

As mentioned briefly above, it was around this same period (1530–1535) that Luther's other depressive friend, Johann Schlaginhaufen also lodged with the Luther family for an extended period. Both he and Weller were involved in recording Luther's table talks, especially those in which he spoke about his own struggles with depression and melancholy, and how to battle it. This period of Luther's life, during which he was heavily focussed on depressive illness in his table conversation, is the chief reason we have so many of Luther's own accounts of his depressive *Anfechtung* in the monastery, providing insights into the young Luther's internal struggles and crises.

As already noted, three of Jerome's six siblings also had contact with Luther, and two of them also struggled with depressive illness and received letters of consolation from Luther.[140] Brecht's observation that Jerome's depression was an inherited or familial illness therefore seems well-founded.[141]

It seems that Weller's depressive illness abated at some point after 1530, or at least eased to the point where it became manageable enough for him to lead a more normal life. In 1535, as part of his doctoral program of studies, he had to overcome his lack of confidence in order to preach in the Wittenberg Castle Church, although with significant help from Luther in preparing his sermons. In that same year he was married in Wittenberg and received his doctorate from the university there.

Weller moved to Freiberg in 1539, where (thanks partly to the lobbying of his friend Nicklaus Hausmann) he took up a prestigious post as Rector at the *Hochschule*. He became an eminent and respected churchman in his latter years, and was often consulted regarding doctrinal disputes and problems. He died on March 20 1572, after a prolonged period of illness.

---

140. These were his sister, Barbara (whose struggles have been described already in this chapter, in the overview dealing with Luther's letter of consolation to her) and his brother, Matthias (a brilliant musician and, for some years, organist at the cathedral in Freiberg, and secretary in the chancellery of Duke Henry of Saxony), whose depressive illness will be dealt with in the overview of Luther's letter of consolation to him, in the next section of this chapter.
141. Brecht, *Martin Luther 1521–1532*, 378.

The three letters written to Jerome Weller from the Coburg in 1530 show a broad thematic unity, all holding in common the understanding of Weller's depressive illness as *tristitia* (sadness, depression, despondency).[142]

There is also a kind of natural 'psychological' progression in these three letters. The first concentrates on the need to resist melancholy thoughts. The second focusses on the reasons for God allowing such temptations. The third summarises the content of the first two and gives a word of counsel and advice that Weller should re-evaluate how he is handling his depression.

The **first of the three letters**, written from the Coburg on June 19 1530, opens with congenial greetings. Luther refers to two letters he has previously received from Weller which pleased him. It is possible that Weller was writing to Luther for his own reasons, though it seems more likely that the letters were primarily written to report the progress of Luther's four-year-old son,[143] Hans, who had recently started his schooling under Weller's tutelage. Luther expresses his happiness at the news (reported particularly in the second letter) that Hans was settling down well to his school work.[144]

Overall, Luther's counsel for Weller's melancholy in this letter is, at this early stage of the illness, more general and pragmatic (along the lines of Gerson's advice) rather than overtly spiritual.[145] His advice

---

142. *Tristitia* (Luther's standard Latin noun for depressive illness) and its various cognates appear all through these letters. In the first letter, Luther speaks about Jerome suffering from a *spiritus tristis*—a spirit of sadness, meaning an ongoing state of pervasive affective depression and melancholy. Luther's use of this word does not carry with it the medieval idea that *tristitia* is a sin per se. Luther, on the back of his own struggle with this issue, sees *tristitia* rather as a spiritual *sickness* frequently caused by influences outside the individual.
143. Weller, it seems, had not mentioned his depressive illness to Luther in these letters, since Luther refers, at the beginning of his brief *narratio*, to having learned of it from *Magister Vitus* (Veit Dietrich).
144. Another letter written by Luther from the Coburg that same day (June 19) was to his little son, Hans. This letter describes a lovely garden where, if they do their lessons and say their prayers, children are allowed to play, dance, shoot crossbows, ride on ponies with golden reins and silver saddles, and pick sweet fruits to eat straight from the trees. See Tappert, *Luther: Letters of Spiritual Counsel*, 144. Luther took time to write this letter to his son in the midst of great tension and anxiety about the outcome of the Diet of Augsburg.
145. Even though Luther uses five sayings from scripture (Proverbs 17:22; Eccl 11:9; Eccl 30:23; 2 Cor 7:10b and Mk 12:27) to summarise his point, they all

assumes that Weller's depression has not yet taken hold and become a self-perpetuating pattern. Luther gives a sustained *argumentatio* about choosing to repel and drive away melancholy thoughts rather than to entertain and indulge them. He quotes practical wisdom from Proverbs, Ecclesiastes and Ecclesiasticus (backed up by 1 Corinthians 7:10) about how bad it is for both body and soul, and about how it damages one's youth.

Following on from this, Luther asserts that Jerome's depression is an attack of the devil. To emphasise this he uses a rhetorical device to drive his argument home: a *gradatio* of three pairs of opposites, climaxing with words from Christ himself, which stamp Luther's argument with divine authority: 'these evil and sad thoughts of yours are not from God but from the devil. That's because God is not a God of sadness but a God of consolation and joy, just as Christ himself says, "God is not a God of the dead but of the living".[146] Melancholy thoughts are therefore to be despised and rejected.

In line with this sensible and pragmatic approach, and with Jerome's humanist interest in the classics, Luther also quotes Virgil, who advises not to yield to trouble, but 'rather go more boldly'.[147]

Sad thoughts should not be scrutinised or followed up, but passed by. Luther uses a striking image from Gerson here to describe how this works cognitively and experientially, which is vivid to anyone who has grown up on a farm with poultry. He says that one should treat depressive thoughts as one treats the menacing hiss of a goose, who will only give chase if one turns and shows fear or provocation. If one ignores the goose and walks past, its bluff is called. Likewise, if one is depressed, then sad and negative thoughts will come and seek

---

tend to focus on the traditional wisdom teaching for how to live a full and joyful life, rather than on matters of sin, grace and the conscience. Luther does refer briefly to the spiritual themes which are developed more fully in other depression letters. However, in this letter they play a supporting rather than central role in his *consolatio*.

146. Mk 12:27.
147. '*tu ne cede malis, sed contra audentior ito*', from Virgil *The Aeneid*, Book VI, Chapter 4, Line 95, *romansonline*, trans. Theodore C. Williams, accessed September 2013, http://www.romansonline.com/Src_Frame.asp?DocID=Vrg_ae06_04.

to take control. However, there is a choice to be made here by the individual, who has freedom to say no.[148]

Luther presses the point here, possibly because he understands that for most people, this strategy is counter-intuitive. One usually deals with problems by readily engaging with them in order to think them through and find a solution, or arrive at a more positive and hopeful outlook. Depressive thoughts are different: if allowed in and entertained, they lead one further into sorrow, confusion and despair, which take hold and overcome the sufferer. Luther uses three colourful examples to illustrate his point further. This passage of the letter shows his own profound experiential understanding of depression and its cognitive-affective dynamics.

In a brief closing *exhortatio* he advises Weller to 'play with others' and to do 'other joyful things'. There is a closing warning that sad and melancholy thoughts should not be mistaken for useful or godly sorrow over sin, which is brief and gives way to joy at God's forgiveness. Depressed thoughts must be seen for what they truly are: an attack of the devil that lead not to clarity of conscience and peace, but only to 'a mess of worries and useless thoughts concerning God'.

The letter comes to a slightly awkward and abrupt end. Probably Luther was pressed for time. He sends hasty closing greetings to others in Wittenberg,[149] and commends little Hans again to Weller's teaching (in so doing, perhaps also reminding Jerome to address himself to life and its duties and activities). However, the closing commendation is not a generic one, but a blessing tailored to Weller's situation.

Luther's **second and longer letter** of consolation to Jerome from the Coburg is thought to have been sent sometime in July 1530.[150] It

---

148. Luther is once again drawing on the wisdom of Jean Gerson. From a contemporary perspective, cognitively-based strategies such as this work better with some kinds of depression than others and at some stages in the illness better than others. With a person who is deeply and severely depressed, the decision to take control of their thinking may be very hard, even impossible.
149. It is not known who Luther means by 'the other Brother to whom I began to write'. *Oinotomos* is a Latinised form of the surname *Schneidewein*, here almost certainly referring to Weller's and Luther's common friend, Johannes Schneidewein, a student who also lived in Luther's household.
150. Clemen's introduction ('WA BR V, 518) suggests that the letter could not have been written later than sometime in July since Luther, busy and away from home, is still able to recall his words to Weller on June 19 (and indeed this second letter almost reads like a continuation of that previous one), whereas

is more indicative of Luther's stage of development and the growing emphases on defying the devil in this pastoral and theological approach.

Judging by Luther's slightly more urgent tone and the more specific advice he gives, news has come to him (perhaps in the form of a letter from Jerome himself)[151] that the depression is getting worse rather than better.

In the incomplete form in which we have the letter, there is only the brief greeting at the beginning before Luther resumes his *argumentatio*, so very little is known about what the immediate context of the letter may have been. The letter is more loosely structured; Luther moves backwards and forwards, revisiting and expanding his content.

This letter deals more with the spiritual dynamics of Jerome's depression than the first one, especially those of the devil's spiritual attack, possibly in view of the depression's strength and persistence.

Luther cannot resist a crack at his theological adversaries, noting that they are 'smug and happy' because the devil does not need to attack those who already belong to him. Real Christians on the other hand, are always under spiritual attack, and should rejoice because their suffering shows they belong to Christ.

Luther responds to Jerome's fear that he will break down and give way completely to despair by diagnosing it as a 'wile of the devil' who chips away at his victims, hoping to wear them down and prevail over them. He once again advises Weller not to allow himself to dwell on his 'deadly thoughts' but rather to despise and mock the devil by resisting them and turning his attention elsewhere, to joking and playing games.

Luther returns to the point that, though the devil tries to use depression for his own deadly ends, it nevertheless serves a different purpose within the wider framework of *God's* counsels. He uses a turn-of-phrase here which also appears in his *Sermon on cross and*

---

     by August 15, he has lost the thread of what he had previously written to Jerome concerning his depression.

151. In the second paragraph, Luther refers to Jerome's own description of his feelings: 'You say . . . ' implying that, in some way, Jerome had communicated directly with Luther about his illness.

suffering (also written during his time at the Coburg in 1530).[152] He tells Jerome that his depressive sufferings are 'more necessary for him … than food and drink'.[153]

He substantiates this assertion using two unusually detailed intimate stories about himself. He first relates how Staupitz counselled him in the midst of his depressions in the monastery: God was preparing him for greatness through his suffering. The second, shorter anecdote reports the words of a man Luther once comforted on the loss of his son: 'Wait and see, Martin, you will become a great man'. The point of these stories was to encourage Jerome to look forward in faith, believing that God had great things in store for him:[154]

> And so it turned out. I was made a great doctor (I can appropriately say this about myself) though at the time when I suffered this trial I never would have believed that possible. I have no doubt that this will happen to you too. You will become a great man.

Luther then moves to an extended *argumentatio* concerning the necessity to resist *tristitia* by enjoying the company of other men, drinking, joking and jesting, and even committing a sin in defiance of the devil, and not becoming neurotically guilty about it. He advocates claiming the full freedom of faith to live joyfully and without undue scrupulosity as a means of sticking it to the devil.

Using one of his favourite rhetorical devices, Luther sketches out a little drama with the devil coming to point out the reader's sins, telling him that he deserves death and hell. The justified sinner's defiant speech is already prepared:

> I admit that I deserve death and hell. So what? Does this mean that I will be condemned to eternal damnation? In no way,

---

152. *Sermon on Cross and Suffering* 1530, WA XXXII, 37:2-4.
153. In his *Sermon on Cross and Suffering* Luther makes his point at greater length, shedding further light on what he means by this phrase in his letter to Jerome. He is saying that God nurtures and builds up the soul through suffering, to prepare a person for the role they will play later in his kingdom. Just as food and drink strengthen the body, so the soul is strengthened in faith and hope through being tested and hardened by *tentatio*.
154. In 1535, Weller did achieve a significant degree of success when he was awarded his doctorate, and later became an eminent and respected teacher and theologian.

because I know who suffered and made satisfaction for me. His name is Jesus Christ, the Son of God. Where he is, there will I also be.

The customary *conclusio* and blessing at the end are missing, almost certainly because of the letter's incompleteness.

The **third and final letter** is different again to the previous two. As Luther himself says at the beginning of the letter, in many ways it re-presents, in a slightly different and abbreviated form, the core arguments in the first two letters. There is, however, a new element introduced: the unity of the body of believers and the common sharing of one another's suffering as brothers of Christ. Luther personalises this in a direct and striking way in the first paragraph: 'just as I suffer for you, so you suffer for me . . .' The reason that all Christians must share in one another's suffering in Christ is that they all have a common enemy who hates and persecutes them. This theme, which appears at various points throughout the letter, is stated most powerfully in the sentence: 'We are all bearing this with you, and we are all suffering *in* you'. When one member of the body suffers, all the members, in an immediate sense, suffer not only with but *in* that hurting brother or sister. This reflects Luther's deeply incarnational and experiential understanding of the *officium consolandi*, in which *all* Christians repeatedly and continually comfort one another, applying the same comfort of the Gospel in various ways in different situations.

In regard to this common sharing and bearing of suffering, Luther says that Jerome must learn to 'reappraise' the situation because he has not yet learned that he can draw strength from his fellow believers, and they from him.

It is hard to know how to interpret Luther's reference to the commandment, 'You shall not kill', in this consolation against depression, closely followed as it is by a reference to 'depressed and death-bearing thoughts' (*tristes et mortiferas cogitationes*). After this twofold reference (first to killing and then to thoughts of death) he then goes on to quote Psalm 30:5 and Ezekiel 18:23, which emphasise that life and not death is God's will and desire for people. Bearing in mind the seriousness of Weller's despondency it seems clear that Luther is delivering here a more specific warning against suicidal thoughts and intentions, which often accompany acute despressive illness.

The second-to-last paragraph appears to return to the core argument from the first letter (the need to put melancholy thoughts aside), but it has been modified significantly. Whereas in the first letter Luther stressed the point that one must resist and shrug off melancholy thoughts, here he says: 'I know that it is not within our power to eliminate these thoughts just whenever we wish.' By this time Jerome's depression has been going on for some time and has clearly taken hold more deeply. Luther shows considerable insight and understanding about the nature and progress of the illness here by softening his earlier statements; realising that his approach now needs to accommodate the reality that this depression has become more serious, and that Jerome is not, at this point, as able to resist his melancholy moods and patterns of thinking and feeling by using diversional strategies.

Luther's *conclusio* to this letter carries both a sweet and sour note. In a characteristically deft phrase: '*Sed Dominus Iesus aderit tibi, fortis lucator et invictus triumphator, Amen.*'[155] he creates a vivid image of Christ wrestling and struggling (with the devil) on behalf of his servant, Jerome, and ultimately triumphing over his illness. Here is the heart of Luther's comfort for the depressed: Jesus, the one who wrestles in the darkness on our behalf and triumphs over our enemies for us, when we have lost all our fight.

The *sour* note here comes as, according to custom, Luther gives the place of the letter's writing, but with the words *Ex Eremo* (out of the wilderness).[156] This shows Luther's frustration and tiredness, not only with Jerome's persistent depression, but with his isolation from Wittenberg and the matters to which he needs to attend there, including the welfare of his family. From May onward, this confinement at the Coburg also began to cause him to feel bored, frustrated and anxious.[157]

As he closes the letter, Luther adds the rider: '*Utinam gratias queam referre aliquando!*' ('Would that someday I shall be able to give thanks!'). Thanks for what exactly? This is a lonely and stressful

---

155. 'But the Lord Jesus, our strong wrestler and invincible victor be with you.'
156. These words are loaded with biblical images of solitude, suffering and testing, recalling Israel's wandering in the wilderness and Jesus' forty days of being sorely tested in the desert.
157. Brecht, *Martin Luther, 1521-1532*, 374.

period for Luther, and perhaps there are many things being hinted at here: not only Jerome's recovery from the dreaded melancholy, but also the prospect of Luther's reunion with his own wife and children, whom he greatly missed. In this enigmatic sentence, perhaps he is also voicing his anxieties and hopes for the Diet of Augsburg and its outcome. The letter closes without any blessing or commendation, and is not signed.

Letter to Matthias Weller (Appendix:286–287)

- October 7 1534 (WA BR VII, No.2139, 104–106)

Matthias Weller (1507–1563) was the younger brother of the better-known Jerome. Of the four Weller siblings associated with Luther,[158] least is known about Matthias, who seems to have been a quiet and retiring person, similar in temperament to Jerome. It is clear that he was a talented and admired musician in the court of Duke Henry of Saxony, and organist in the Freiberg Cathedral church.

This letter is an excellent example of Luther's general epistolary and consolatory style, and of his consolation to *depressed* persons in particular. It follows the traditional *consolatio* structure very clearly, but nevertheless expresses Luther's new and fresh approach to comforting the troubled.

The letter begins with a warm personal address which would normally indicate that Luther is on friendly terms with the reader, although nothing is known of a close friendship between the two and it is likely that they never actually met in person. This may be indicative of the 'familiar letter' epistolary style in which the writer addressed the reader as if a close bond existed between the two even though one did not. Alternatively, it is possible that friendship and good will is being extended here by Luther, both on account of his close association with Matthias' brother, Jerome, and also because of his desire to be especially positive, warm and encouraging as he comforts the severely depressed young man.

Luther's brief *narratio* not only lays out the facts as they have been presented to him by Jerome, but recognises the seriousness

---

158. As we have observed before, his brother, Peter and his sister Barbara were also known to Luther.

of Matthias' situation; that he is *deeply distressed* (*fast bekümmert*) and suffering the *Anfechtung* of *Traurigkeit* (the attack of depressive despondency).

The *argumentatio* which follows expresses two well-known and oft-repeated themes: 'depressive thoughts are of the devil', and one can 'be joyful in the Lord'. The most significant theme of consolation here, however, is the Christian 'office of consolation' (*officium consolandi*). As outlined above, this theme is also developed in one of Luther's letters of consolation to Matthias' brother, Jerome. However, here in this letter a different dimension comes to the fore. Luther uses short, forceful phrases to underline his point that Matthias needs to listen to others and what they have to say. Their words of comfort are not mere human words, but are spoken by God's command and so carry *God's* comfort. It is therefore God's will that the suffering should receive such words as 'from God himself'. For Luther, this office of consolation is no mere human rhetorical form or convention that has been *taken into* Christian life and practice, but a divinely-instituted and mandated work. As it witnesses to the Word and the Gospel it is a form of proclamation, and has an authority and power to which human comforts cannot come close. He follows up this assertion with a 'bouquet' of six biblical citations, which give this letter of consolation a new and unique weight of diginity.[159]

In this section of the letter, Luther therefore also stresses the importance of the affective connection between *hearing* and *believing*. He says that it is God's will that comfort be received 'with a believing heart', and therefore *orders* Matthias, 'Do not follow your own thoughts ... Listen then to what we are saying to you in God's name.'[160]

---

159. 1 Thess 5:14; Isa 40:8–9; Deut 28:47; Matt 6:25; 1 Pt 5:7 and Ps 55:22. Together these passages reinforce the dual point Luther has just made. They not only exhort the reader to trust in God's help and rejoice in his promises, but show that those who close their ears to the bearer of God's word of comfort are refusing help from God himself.

160. Here Luther looks at the *officium consolandi* from the *receiver's* end, stressing that just as Christians have a duty to comfort one another, they also have a responsibility to listen and receive others' consolation, and not stubbornly or proudly refuse it. It is often the case with highly capable and intellectually independent people that depression turns 'their best weapons against them'. Their very faculty of mind that is usually employed to overcome and resolve troubles 'turns rogue' and becomes destructive, captive as it is to the deeper mood disorder which shapes and drives the affective and cognitive functions.

The command to rejoice, which Luther repeats so often in his counsel to the depressed, is in this situation pastorally focussed towards Matthias Weller's particular musical gifts. The *exhortatio* which follows on from the fourth paragraph picks up this point strongly. Luther cites the biblical examples of David and Elisha[161] playing music in order to soothe and help troubled souls, telling Matthias to play his regal[162] and sing until his sad thoughts vanish.

This is not some kind of pragmatic strategy of self-distraction, but has its background in the long tradition of music as a unique and mysterious gift that has the ability not just to drown out sorrow, but to penetrate the heart and brighten the mood of a sad person. Luther presses his advice about playing and singing music on Matthias because of his own conviction that music does indeed have a healing effect. Luther also gives direction here about what Matthias could play. He suggests liturgical music: the canticles of praise, *Te Deum Laudamus* and *Benedictus*. Clearly, Luther has in mind that Matthias use music not merely as 'diversional therapy', but as a divine gift which acts spiritually upon his affects through the playing and singing of praise.[163]

In the final paragraph Luther revisits and restates earlier themes, though this time he adopts a more playful tone. As we have seen elsewhere, this making light of the reader's heavy thoughts is one of Luther's strategies for placing them in their proper perspective and unmasking them as false, and ultimately powerless. He reiterates the need to despise and ignore the devil's attacks. He creates the comical image of 'wacking the devil in the snout' and refers to Gerson's folk-

---

A depressed person who is accustomed to independent thinking and problem solving is often quite stubborn and resistant to putting aside their own perceptions and thoughts (irrational and destructive though they are) in favour of trusting others' guidance.

161. 2 Kgs 3:14–15.
162. A small table-top harmonium-like instrument, enclosing pipes in a wooden case, with keys on one side and bellows on the other.
163. There is a long tradition of using music for therapeutic purposes, dating back to the Pythagorians' understanding that it was a key means of exciting the soul and enabling *catharsis*. Galen also viewed music as the most effective way to counter depressive moods because of its ability to soothe the emotions. Music therapy for depression today draws on this same long tradition. See Günter Bandmann, *Melancholie und Musik, Ikonographische Studien* (Opladen: Westdeutscher Verlag, 1960), 20–1.

story of the nagging wife who is eventually exhausted and gives up, because her husband simply ignores her and merrily plays his flute.[164]

Luther once again reminds his reader to listen to others since God is speaking to him through them with the authority and power of his word, which is comfort indeed. The final blessings take up this same point from a different direction, reminding Matthias that Luther is writing this letter of comfort because God has told him these things and *he* must be obedient in passing them on. The unspoken implication is that if Matthias trusts in God, he too should obey by taking Luther's words to his heart.

Conclusion

What impresses the contemporary reader most about these letters is the way Luther brings together the theological, literary and rhetorcial resources at his disposal, reshaping and 'reorchestrating' them to serve his consolatory purposes. Moreover, as he does this, he responds pastorally to the needs of each inidividual addressee, employing his 'redesigned tools' in different ways, according to the context. True, he uses the same *argumentatio* and *exhortatio* for different recipients, but they are never employed in exactly the same way; they are fitted to each individual and their needs. The effect is powerful. Mennecke-Haustein describes Luther's writing in his *Trostbriefe* with the words, 'in the style of a miracle-worker,'[165] and indeed one of those who received a letter of consolation from Luther (Friedrich Myconius) claimed that the letter, which he received as he lay dying, brought him 'back from the dead'!ptember[166]

In these twenty one letters we see a true example of *practical theology*—the biblical teaching of law and gospel brought into true-life encounter with human suffering and need. People awaited Luther's letters of comfort with great anticipation, and they were often exchanged, copied and eventually published, the earliest edition

---

164. Mennecke-Haustein, *Luthers Trostbriefe*, 218.
165. Mennecke-Haustein, *Luthers Trostbriefe*, 11.
166. WA BR IX, No.3566, 301–303. Luther wrote to Myconius in January 1541, who was suffering from serious pulmonary illness. Later, after he had recovered, Myconius wrote to his friend, George Rörer: 'When I read it [the letter] I could not think but that I heard Christ say to me "Lazarus, arise"' (quoted by Tappert, *Luther: Letters of Spiritual Counsel*, 47–9).

being issued shortly after Luther's death. Their ongoing value is attested by the fact that five centuries later, Christians are still doing the same thing with them, as they are re-published and re-read by a new generation.

Chapter 3
'Disagreeing Likeness'
Depression's Contemporary Contexts and Paradigms

'There is in all melancholy a 'similitudo dissimilis', like mens' faces, a disagreeing likeness...'.

Robert Burton, *The Anatomy of Melancholy.* 1676

It is one thing to survey the cultural, religious, psychological and medical dimensions of depressive illness to which Luther's consolation was responding, but quite another to understand the complex facets of depression in today's global context. It is rightly observed by many that these are two different worlds, and yet as they are placed side by side, it becomes clear that they are not 'worlds apart'. The experiences of depressive illness, as described by depressive melancholics in previous eras, including Luther's, are strikingly like those recounted by depression suffers today.

Likewise, today's remedies and responses in many ways parallel those of earlier ages. Medicine, naturopathy, psychology, Christian and other spiritualities are all brought to bear as interventions for depression today, just a Constantinus Africanus, Galen, Paracelsus, Gerson and Luther applied them in their medieval and renaissance societies.

As observed in our historical exploration of depressive *melancholia*, depressive illness is today characterised by its presence right across the cultural, literary, religious, scientific and socio-economic strata of society. Despite modern advances in medical and psychological treatments, it continues to be a common feature of human experience; quite recognisable across various communities and eras, yet notoriously 'changeling' in the forms of its presentation.

A Widening Discussion

Shifting Paradigms

Since the major shift that took place during the nineteenth century, from a wider and more culturally integrated view of *melancholia* to the dominant medical-scientific construction of depression that held sway through the twentieth century, there has been still another movement in the way western communities are understanding and responding to depressive illness in these post-modern times. While medical and psychological approaches are still highly significant, there is a widening discussion taking place which shows a shift away from the dualism, rationalism and empiricism of the past century, and a greater openness towards human narrative, affect, experience and spirituality. This discussion is happening among people who suffer from the illness and among those who live with and care for them. People from many different helping backgrounds are taking part, representing various types of therapies and interventions, and those who are interested in pastoral care and spirituality of various kinds.

This discussion is a healthy and promising development which is happening in many different sections of the community. It is going on at the level of scholarly debate through books and journal articles, conferences and forums of various kinds. Popular news media and magazines carry depression news and stories consistently. Through online blogs, forums and chat lines, depression sufferers themselves share their situations with each other, making personal connections and discussing issues of mutual interest such as the effectiveness of different medications, helpful strategies for coping, perspectives on suffering, spirituality and relationships.

This broader discussion is reflected in the Australian community through the *beyondblue* materials on depression and anxiety. Through its comprehensive program, this national depression initiative continues to have a significant impact on the depression awareness of Australians. It has improved both the level of understanding about the illness itself, and the level of help-seeking by people who are experiencing symptoms.

Beyondblue has responded to this widening conversation and growing diversity by providing accurate and helpful information from as many different viewpoints, on as many different 'complementary and lifestyle interventions' for depression as possible. Its resource bank includes not only the various medical and psychological interventions, but also approaches that have usually been considered 'alternative', such as aromatherapy, music therapy, meditation, massage and prayer.

On the wider scene, natural therapies like herbalism and homeopathy, together with simple lifestyle issues like sleep, exercise, diet and nutrition, family relationships, sex and finance are all now part of the discussion. Australian radio personality, Tamra Mercieca[1] is an example of how depression sufferers are seeking a broader approach to the illness, and are prepared to try different things and open themselves to a wide range of options.

In conversations with depression sufferers it becomes clear that people often have begun to research, explore and reflect on what is happening in the *whole* of their lives, and on how they are living them. This reflection may cover medical care and drug treatment, but takes in a wider range of issues too, including habits, routines and influences that affect daily wellbeing on the physical, emotional, relational and spiritual levels.

Feminist Perspectives

Within the wider discussion, feminist perspectives are important for understanding the significant gender issues around depressive illness in western culture today. Recent feminist scholarship of various types has shown something crucially important in this respect: that, at many different levels, the issues involved in depressive illness for women are markedly different to those of men and require different approaches to treatment.[2]

The evolution of feminist thought from the 1960s and 1970s has moved the discussion of depression among women on from issues of career and equal opportunity toward the deeper and more complex

---

1. Tamra Mercieca, *The Upside of Down*.
2. Kira Cochrane, 'Why Do So Many Women Have Depression?' *The Guardian*, April 29, 2010, accessed August 2013, http://www.theguardian.com/society/2010/apr/29/women-depression-allison-pearson.

issues of cultural and familial roles, unearthing some of the deep social structures which affect depression as suffered by women.[3]

Depression has often been described in feminist writing as a 'gendered problem', since statistically it has always affected more women than men. It is this issue more than any other that has (directly and indirectly) occupied feminist thought and writing on depression. Many theories have been put forward to explain the disparity, but there does not seem to be any strong consensus about its cause.

Previous eras took the higher rate of depressive illness among women to mean that women were psychologically weaker than men and therefore more prone to mental defects. Renaissance melancholy is depicted in art as a bored, distracted and indolent woman.[4] Nineteenth century Victorian society saw women as inherently unreliable and prone to hysteria due to the mood fluctuations associated with their menstrual cycle. Female expressions of rebellion against the social order or assertions of personal freedom were viewed as madness. Most of the psychiatric photographic studies and drawings of melancholics from the period seem to be of women subjects. These stereotypes continued to be powerful for a long time, well into the 1960s, and were perpetuated by psychiatric practice. Valium (Diazepam), a new drug on the scene around this time, was prescribed to women so frequently that it became known as 'mother's little helper', after the song by the Rolling Stones.[5]

It is not surprising, then, that early feminists were quick to denounce such stereotypes and to criticise the psychiatric profession of the time. Jean Baker Miller, a psychoanalyst, psychiatrist, and exponent of cultural feminism, claimed that widespread depressive illness among women was caused by a loss of cultural roles. Responding to the demands of society by conforming to gendered social roles, women mourned the loss of needed freedom and identity. In Miller's view,

---

3. Janet M Stoppard, *Understanding Depression: Feminist Social Constructionist Approaches* (London: Routledge, 2000).
4. The famous examples are the engraving, *Melancholia 1*, created in 1514 by Albrecht Dürer, and Lukas Cranach the Elder's *Melancholy: An Allegory* of 1531. See Ty Alyea, 'Angst and Paralysis: Visualizing Melancholia from Albrecht Durer to Lars Von Trier', *VIZ.*, February 10, 2012, accessed August 2013, http://viz.dwrl.utexas.edu/content/angst-and-paralysis-visualizing-melancholia-albrecht-durer-lars-von-trier.
5. 'Mother's Little Helper by The Rolling Stones', Song Facts, accessed September 2013, http://www.songfacts.com/detail.php?id=460.

the oppressive affiliations and loyalties that depress women grew out of patriarchal male expectations.[6]

While a higher rate of *melancholia* and depression among women has been documented over many centuries, the relative rate of depression among women continues to rise steeply today, which has drawn some to wonder whether the feminist movement has not, in recent decades, made things worse rather than better. Dorothy Rowe suggests that by sandwiching women between their professional lives and the valuable roles of wife and mother (both demanding vocations in life), our culture has made the psychological pressures on women today unbearable. Having a career does not obviate the expectation for a woman (or perhaps her own desire) to also be an attentive and engaged mother.[7]

The more recent research of feminist psychologist Janet Stoppard has drawn on feminist scholarship in order to explore underlying social constructions of depression among women from a cultural and psychosocial perspective.[8] She has shown that it is a complex and multi-layered issue, in which social roles undoubtedly play a significant part. Stoppard's research looks at the way in which depression affects women over the course of life, and notes the specificity of female depressive illness and its relation to peculiar types of stress and adversity in women's lives. She identifies the 'girl-poisoning culture' of western society, the stress of conflicting expectations on women to be 'good mothers' and the issues for women around depression and aging.

It is interesting to note the number of women writers who have recently broken the 'stigmatic silence' about women suffering depression, and lifted the lid on their own specifically-female experiences of the illness. Stephanie Merritt,[9] Gwyneth Lewis,[10] Sally

---

6. Jean Baker Miller, *Toward a new Psychology of Women*, second edition (Boston: Beacon Press, 1986).
7. Dorothy Rowe was interviewed and quoted by Kira Cochrane, for her article about novelist Allison Pearson. See Cochrane, 'Why Do So Many Women Have Depression?'
8. Stoppard, *Understanding Depression: Feminist Social Constructionist Approaches.*
9. Stephanie Merritt, *The Devil Within: A Memoir of Depression* (London: Vermillion, 2009).
10. Gwyneth Lewis, *Sunbathing in the Rain: A Cheerful Book About Depression* (London: Haper Perenniel, 2006).

Brampton[11] and Daphne Merkin[12] have all contributed to the de-shaming of depression and of the women who suffer from it. These precious glimpses into women's experiences open a new horizon in depression studies today.

Narrative, Autobiography and Poetry

Through the profusion of depression narrative, biography and autobiography that has been published recently, there has been a definite re-valuing of the personal and subjective aspects of the illness. The experience of the person-of affect, sensation and emotion-has returned to the public arena, after having been all but banished by the strict objectivity of medical science and the increasingly descriptivist approach of psychiatry.[13] Among the many notable examples here is Andrew Solomon's *The Noonday Demon: An Atlas of Depression*,[14] in which the author reflects deeply on his own experiences from almost 'every point on the compass', talking not only about medical treatment but also historical, social, political, religious and spiritual aspects. As a knowledgeable yet humble fellow traveller, he offers his own observations and responses for readers to weigh against their own.

As in the romantic period of melancholy in the eighteenth and nineteenth centuries, one of the most healing forms of therapy for some depression sufferers today is to read or listen to the memoirs and poetry of writers who have been able to give authentic voice to their own depression. As others have observed, to feel understood from the inner world of experience is one of the things that can truly relieve the loneliness of depression. Arguably, the two most powerful examples of this today are Australian poet, Les Murray[15] and Welsh

---

11. Sally Brampton, *Shoot the Damn Dog: A Memoir of Depression* (London: Bloomsbury, 2008).
12. Daphne Merkin, 'A Journey Through Darkness', *New York Times Magazine*, May 6, 2009, accessed October 2013, http://www.nytimes.com/2009/05/10/magazine/10Depression-t.html.
13. For an historical and methodological analysis of this point see Radden, *The Nature of Melancholy*, 32-4.
14. Andrew Solomon, *The Noonday Demon: An Atlas of Depression* (New York: Scribner, 2001).
15. Les Murray, *Killing The Black Dog: A Memoir of Depression* (New York: Farrar, Strauss & Giroux, 2011). To view a podcast of Les Murray speaking

poet, Gwyneth Lewis,[16] who have both written autobiographical prose and poetry on their experience of depressive illness.

The Continuing 'Melancholy Tradition'

I believe that we find ourselves today at an historical vantage point where we see our era making its own contribution to the understanding of the ancient human phenomena of melancholy and depression. While valuable and helpful, this contribution is not definitive, superior or complete, but merely 'one among others' that have been offered for their time–and perhaps not even the best one at that.

Contemporary experience bears out the famous statement of Robert Burton in the seventeenth century about this illness's symptoms showing a 'disagreeing likeness (*similitudo dissimilis*), like men's faces'.[17] The melancholy–depression experience defies efforts to precisely categorise or tame it, even the efforts of modern psychiatry, with its constant refining and reviewing of categories. However, the mysterious paradox is that, as in past eras where this complexity and uncertainty was also present, so also today depression sufferers share a great commonality of personal experience, and draw strength from this shared experiential knowledge of depression as a universally recognisable human journey.

We are not witnessing the final exposé of 'what depression is', 'how it works' and 'how to remedy it', but rather the continuation of the ancient melancholy tradition. We too are participants in this unfolding multi-structured narrative through which we find ourselves in conversation with Aristotle, Hippocrates, Avicenna, Paracelsus, Luther, Kraepelin and many other characters in the story past, along with today's protagonists: medical science, psychology, spirituality and sociology.

---

about his depression and reading his poems on depression, see Les Murray, 'Les Murray on Killing the Black Dog (p1)', YouTube video, 23:44, posted by 'themonthlyvideo', May 2, 2013, accessed September 2013, http://www.youtube.com/watch?v=IYTRZniglVY.

16. Her autobiographical work is Lewis, Sunbathing in the rain. Her poems on depression are published in Gwyneth Lewis, Keeping Mum: Voices from Therapy (Highgreen: Bloodaxe Books, 2003).

17. Robert Burton, *The Anatomy of Melancholy*, First published 1621, 1932 ed., edited by Holbrook Jackson (New York: New York Review Books, 2001), 397.

Depression and Happiness

From this vantage point, some writers today have begun to critique the culture of entitlement and the mythology of 'happiness' in western culture, as if suffering (and in particular, mental suffering) is or ought to be escapable through the apparently-endless range of available distractions and pleasures. An alternative attitude which is quickly gaining allies is that depression is in many ways the natural and necessary counterpoint of joy and pleasure, the deep ravines that are inevitably juxtaposed to life's mountain peaks, part of the natural economy of human life.

> Melancholy is at the bottom of everything, just as at the end of all rivers is the sea. Can it be otherwise in a world where nothing lasts, where all that we have loved or shall love must die? . . . The gloom of an eternal mourning enwraps, more or less closely, every serious and thoughtful soul, as night enwraps the universe.[18]

Andrew Solomon, writing from his deep personal experience of depression, reflects:

> It is possible (though for the time being unlikely) that, through chemical manipulation, we might locate, control and eliminate the brain's circuitry of suffering. I hope we will never do it. To take it away would be to flatten out experience, to impinge on a complexity more valuable than any of its component parts are agonising.[19]

Reprising Freud's metaphor of mourning to reframe depression, Darian Leader talks about the way in which treatment for depression can be driven by the desire to take the quickest route to no pain, rather than the best route to healing. A healthy life requires its seasons of mourning and sorrow, and what we really need is to attend to, rather than run away from, them.[20]

---

18. Henri-Frédéric Amiel, *Amiel's Journal: The Journal In time of Henri-Frédéric Amiel*, second edition, translated by Mary A Ward (London: Macmillan and Company, 1893), 182.
19. Solomon, *The Noonday Demon*, 38.
20. Darian Leader, *The New Black: Mourning, Melancholia, and Depression* (London: Penguin, 2008).

Social Dimensions

Sociological Constructions of Depression

As it has woven its way in and out of the fabric of cultures and societies over the centuries, depression's 'colours have been set off differently'. The many variables at work in any one social context will interact uniquely with the illness. Cross-cultural studies have shown how differently depressive illness can present in different cultural and social settings.[21]

In sixteenth century Germany depressive *melancholia* was a socially accepted reality, depicted in art and openly spoken and written about. Its later social station at the height of the Renaissance was quite intellectually glamorous. In later nineteenth century Europe, it was a female form of madness. In the twentieth century depression has been objectified and medicalised. Its sufferers have become 'patients' who need treatment and are frequently socially stigmatised as 'mentally ill'. Today new social and community efforts to build awareness and de-mystify depression are working to break down the aura of medical pathology and nurture greater social acceptance and empathy.[22]

This changing face of depression is what has made, and continues to make, it so maddeningly difficult to understand and treat. Given the immense and rapid social transformations we have experienced in the western world in the last fifty years, it is no wonder that depressive illness has been in such a state of accelerated flux.

Social Effects of Modernity and Postmodernity

The growth of personal autonomy and individual self-consciousness during the modern era created the necessity for persons to find

---

21. For a rich and fascinating survey of this issue see Kleinman and Good, *Culture and Depression*.
22. beyondblue have adopted the strategy of actively listening to people speaking out about their illness in order to inform and focus their programs. See Bonnie Vincent, 'The Power of blueVoices', *Health Voices* 5 (October 2009): 10-11, accessed October 2013, https://www.chf.org.au/pdfs/hvo/hvo-2009-5-power-bluevoices.pdf. See also the beyondblue Ambassador's Program, in which high profile Australians speak about their illness and encourage others to seek assistance: "Ambassadors," *beyondblue*, accessed October 2013, http://www.beyondblue.org.au/connect-with-others/ambassadors.

meaning and hope within, rather than through, connection and community. The social agenda of continuous linear progress in society, driven by education, science and technology, leaves little room in the social mainstream for those who find themselves unable to move on and keep up. Dan Blazer[23] points out how all this has led towards social isolation and disconnection, those conditions in which depressive illness thrives. Modern psychiatry has functioned as an arm of the modernist scientific machine, tasked with restoring people to healthy functionality so that they may re-join the story of human progress.

More recently, postmodernity has responded to the void of hope left by the failure of science and technology. It has cynically rejected objective truth and certainty, including any substantive platform on which hope could be reconstructed. Blazer's comprehensive analysis of why depression is a growing problem in western countries today relates to the way in which postmodernity has caused eight identifiable losses: the loss of story, the loss of language, the loss of self, the loss of unity, the loss of trust, the loss of orientation, the loss of meaning and finally, a loss of existence or nihilism.[24]

David Karp, in his searing social analysis of depression in western society, describes the way in which depression is fed by the hopelessness of this postmodern vision:

> In an emerging postmodern world, the construction and maintenance of an integrated self becomes deeply problematic because the social structures necessary to anchor the self have themselves become unstable and ephemeral . . . as a person with depression I am inclined to embrace such an unrelievedly negative view.[25]

This decline in the stability of social and family roles and relationships in the last decades has certainly contributed to the growth of depression, along with other illnesses.[26] In Australia these trends have

---

23. Blazer, *The Age of Melancholy*, 140–2.
24. Blazer, *The Age of Melancholy*, 144–58.
25. David A Karp, *Speaking of Sadness, Depression, Disconnection and the Meanings of Illness* (New York: Oxford University Press, 1996), 186.
26. Danielle German and Carl A Latkin, 'Social Stability and Health: Exploring Multidimensional Social Disadvantage', *Journal of Urban Health* 89, no. 1 (2012):

been highly visible. Andrew Leigh, in his alarming book, *Disconnected* (published in 2009), shows how Australians are more isolated and lonely than ever.[27] More than one in five Australians live alone,[28] and probably do not know their neighbours or have many social networks through which they can find friendship and community.[29]

Limitless Self-Realisation?

A recent book by Liah Greenfeld has put forward the insightful proposal that today's culture of limitless self-fulfillment is actually contributing to the epidemic of depression and other mental illness. More than ever before, we are expected to reach our potential, to be the authors of our own unique and significant destinies. Greenfeld suggests that while this may be liberating for some, it places others under an unbearable psychic strain. In schools and workplaces people are constantly exposed to the need for self-management, self-improvement, appraisal and progress. For many, argues Greenfeld, this pressure is simply too much. Not everybody is able to embrace the task of continually pushing out the boundaries of achievement and extending personal limits. These people find themselves strangers in their own culture, left with no choice but to attempt life-styles that will make them mentally ill.[30]

Cultural and Social Stigma

The stigmatisation of illness, disability or other differentness is a complex social phenomenon. At its heart is fear of those who may be unsafe or unpredictable. With depression and mental illness, this fear is associated with the incongruity of irrationality in a culture which

---

19-35, accessed October 2013, http://www.ncbi.nlm.nih.gov/pmc/articles/PMC3284598/.
27. Andrew Leigh, *Disconnected* (Sydney: University of New South Wales Press, 2010).
28. See David de Vaus and Sue Richardson, 'Living Alone in Australia: Trends in Sole Living and Characteristics of Those Who Live Alone', *Australian Policy Online*, November 18, 2009, accessed August, 2013, http://www.apo.au/research/living-alone-australia-trends-sole-living-and-characteristics-those-who-live-alone.
29. Leigh, *Disconnected*, 86-177.
30. Liah Greenfeld, *Mind, Modernity, Madness: The Impact of Culture on Human Experience* (New York: Harvard University Press, 2013).

depends on cohesive rational systems for its stability. A person who is 'not in their right mind' threatens chaos by their very presence, or acts as an obstacle to others' 'normal' lives.[31]

The result is that in our 'correct' culture, where people with bodily disablements of any kind must be respected and treated with dignity, the media still trivialise and humiliate the mentally ill with terms like 'psycho', 'crazy' and 'nutcase', and perpetuate the comic stereotypes of mental illness.[32]

The other major ingredient in the stigmatisation of depression is the extreme difficulty for people in understanding what it is, apart from any direct experience of it. Sometimes this is simply the result of careless ignorance, but even with those who have a knowledge of the illness from others' descriptions, and who may be theoretically empathetic, there is little true understanding. In a world where things that are real can be seen and explained, depression–as an experience – is invisible, indescribable and often inexplicable.[33]

The stigma of mental illness attached to depression developed markedly in western culture during the twentieth century, and has been very persistent. The shame associated with depression perceived as weakness of character, moral failure or laziness is damaging enough but, as David Karp notes, with depression the most critical assaults come from within. The problem is then fed both externally and internally.[34]

The culture of denial and secrecy around depression in some social groups is often due to the illness being stigmatised in this dual fashion. Karp's qualitative studies with depression sufferers show how the social non-acceptance of others and the feelings of shame and humiliation feed one another.[35]

---

31. Mental health agencies and support groups still struggle with this deeply ingrained fear. See, for example, 'Stigma of Mental Illness Still Widespread', Cape Fear Healthy Minds.org, accessed August 2013, http://www.capefearhealthyminds.org/library.cgi?article=1115920904.
32. Amy Simpson, *Troubled Minds: Mental Illness and the Church's Mission* (Downers Grove: IVP Books, 2013), 144.
33. Lewis Wolpert, 'Stigma of Depression—a Personal View', *British Medical Bulletin* 57, no. 1 (March 2001): 221-224. I have frequently noted this issue in church communities, where people who are prepared to empathise find it hard to recognize or understand the suffering of depression.
34. Karp, *Speaking of Sadness*, 46-7.
35. Karp, *Speaking of Sadness*, 47.

The *beyondblue* initiative in Australia has adopted a strategy through which celebrities and national heroes who suffer with depression 'come out' publicly, acting as ambassadors or 'blue voices' who share their experiences of the illness. This has shown itself to be a powerful way to give hope to others.[36]

Economic impacts

Several studies over the last decades have shown that in western nations there is an increasing economic burden being carried by businesses and workplaces because of depression. Currently, depression is globally the second-highest ranking cause of disability for those aged between 15 and 44. As well as the impact on the bottom line, businesses feel the impact of depression through diminished morale and relationship problems.[37]

Depression manifests in the workplace as absenteeism, 'presenteeism' (not being able to 'fire up' and be productive at work), and erratic work performance. Kerrie Eyers and Gordon Parker indicate the extent of the hidden problem of depression in the workplace, and the degree to which it affects the efficient working of businesses. Six million workdays are lost per year through depression-related absenteeism in Australia, and it is estimated that the cost of lost productivity caused by untreated depression in the general working population per year is $10,000 per worker and $25,000 for a senior executive or professional. Depressive illness is therefore, now a major issue for employers, who need to develop policies and strategies in order to manage its effects on the workplace and its productivity.

The Medical Identity of Depression

A Long Medical Pedigree

Although psycho-historians often speak about 'premedical' and 'medical' views of melancholy and depression, there seems to have been some kind of medical engagement with this illness from the

---

36. As noted above (footnote 47), *beyondblue*'s strategy of using depression sufferers to publicly share their own experiences of depression, to give hope to others, and reduce their shame and embarrassment. See 'Ambassadors', *beyondblue*.
37. Kerrie Eyers and Gordon Parker, *Tackling Depression at Work: A Practical Guide for Employees and Managers* (Sydney: Allen & Unwin, 2010), 2–10.

earliest times, in the sense that there have always been attempts to understand, treat and even cure it. The medical understanding and treatment of melancholy and depression therefore has deep roots. In order to properly understand and appreciate the nature of contemporary medical treatment (and its attitudes and approaches) it is important to take some space for a brief historical excursus.

The medical treatment of melancholic–depressive illness is recorded in ancient Egypt around 1550 BC.[38] In the Greek world, the complex humoral theory of *melancholia* developed by Galen in the second century AD can be traced back to Hippocrates and Aristotle in the fourth century BC. This model remained largely unchanged for many centuries during the Middle Ages, and was reprised and elaborated in the sixteenth century.[39]

In the early modern era, as the Renaissance movement unfolded, the German physician and medical scientist, Theophrastus Bombastus von Hohenheim (commonly known as 'Paracelsus'), 1493–1591, further developed the notion of *melancholia* as a form of madness and insanity, and was the first to introduce distinctions between different forms of the illness, based on more astute behavioural observation. Paracelsus was a contemporary of Luther, and in some ways the two pursued parallel careers.[40]

In the late sixteenth and early seventeenth centuries, a number of English medical researchers and writers began to test new hypotheses about the illness.[41] Robert Burton, the most notable of these, published his monumental compendium, *The Anatomy of Melancholy* in 1621[42], a long and comprehensive study of the illness, drawing on history, science, medicine, philosophy, poetry and theology in order to gain some wider and more encompassing perspective. Burton's *Anatomy*

---

38. Depression is described in the *Ebers Papyrus* (1550 BC). See Sameh M Arab, 'Medicine in Ancient Egypt (Part 3),' *Arab World Books*, accessed August 2013, http://www.arabworldbooks.com/articles8c.htm.
39. Jackson, *Melancholia & Depression*, 29–45.
40. Luther and Paracelsus may seem an odd comparison; however, both were shaped by the same traditions and influenced by the emerging Renaissance spirit of Reformation. See Midelfort, *A History of Madness*, 81–82.
41. Jackson, *Melancholia & Depression*, 104–115.
42. This classic has been in continuous publication since it was written. See Bibliography for details.

is still an important work on *melancholia* and depression, drawing together, as it does, all the western traditions up to that time.

During the seventeenth and eighteenth centuries medical science moved away from the traditional humoral model towards various theories of chemical movement in the body and brain. Mechanical models were proposed, suggesting that the movement of particles and matter through the body was the primary cause of the illness.

The nineteenth century was a time of great cultural awareness of melancholy. There was an explosion of new science. Medical researchers in Britain, Europe and America began to theorise about melancholia as a neurological or neuro-anatomical disease, having its root cause and main effect in the brain itself.[43]

It is interesting and noteworthy that even in the modern era, in which medical neuro-science has radically rejected the traditional hippocratic humoral model for explaining mental illness, elements of this 'old science' remain embedded in some current contemporary psychological methodologies and systems. This shows that, despite the faultiness of Hippocrates' anatomical and bio-chemical understanding, there was a certain phenomenological validity to his theory of the four basic temperaments or personality types, which is still used today.[44]

The Birth and Development of 'Depression'

It was at the opening of the twentieth century that Swiss Psychiatrist, Emil Kraepelin, in successive editions of his *Lehrbuch*,[45] began to translate mental illness case histories into various nosological categories, which were revised many times, with the increasing availability of new data.[46] By the 1920s depression – as a distinct general

---

43. Jackson, *Melancholia & Depression*, 104–40.
44. Jung's theory of personality and its clinical development via the *Myers–Briggs Personality Indicator (MBTI)* and the *David Keirsey Temperament Sorter (KTS)*, still work with the model of the four basic temperaments observed and defined by ancient philosophers and medical theorists, Hippocrates, Plato and Galen. See 'About David Keirsey', Keirsey.com, accessed April 2, 2013, http://www.keirsey.com/drdavidkeirsey.aspx.
45. There were five successive editions of this iconic textbook for psychiatry. The last edition is still in print today: Emil Kraepelin, *Psychiatrie: Ein Lehrbuch Für Studierende und Ärzte*. (New York: Arno Press, 1976).
46. Allan V Horwitz, *Creating Mental Illness* (Chicago: Chicago University Press, 2002), 38–54.

type of mental disorder—had been identified. Through the work of three researchers in the 1930s–40s, Meyer, Gillespie and Henderson, manic depressive disorders then began to be differentiated from other depressive states.[47]

As Jackson explains, various debates and discussions have taken place on the proper categorisation of depressive illness ever since this time, trying to find some consistent and reliable taxonomy that is universally stable. Discussion has focused on dichotomies like 'exogenous and endogenous', 'psychotic and neurotic' and the like. Today, while categorical structures are in place in all advanced health systems and are reviewed regularly, the nosological debates still rage and the taxonomy continues to change. Recently in Australia, for example, Gordon Parker of the *Black Dog Institute* launched a campaign for the reintroduction of a category of depression that has not been current for many years: 'melancholic depression'. This presented different values and criteria on how to organise the many disparate and changing types of depressive illnesses which are manifest in the community.[48]

A main driving force in the shaping of depression's medical identity (especially in the treatment of moderate–severe cases) during the twentieth century has been the development of the *Diagnostic and Statistical Manual of Mental Disorders (DSM)*. This manual, used in most western psychiatric medicine, has been through five major editions; the first published in 1952,[49] and a fifth edition released in May 2013.[50] Earlier editions of the DSM were strongly influenced by

---

47. Jackson, *Melancholia & Depression*, 188–236.
48. See ABC news summary, Rebecca Barrett, 'Push for Melancholia to be Listed as Illness', *ABC News Online*, March 17, 2010, accessed August 2013, http://www.abc.net.au/news/stories/2010/03/17/2848524.htm. Hear an interview about this issue with Gordon Parker on ABC Radio Life Matters program:, Gordon Parker, 'Melancholia as an Illness', audio of interview with Richard Aedy, *Life Matters*, ABC Radio (March 25, 2010), accessed September 2013, http://www.abc.net.au/rn/lifematters/stories/2010/2855014.htm.
49. *Diagnostic and Statistical Manual of Mental Disorders: DSM-III*, 3rd edition, edited by The American Psychiatric Association (Washington: APA, 1980).
50. See the *ME Agenda Patient Community* website's article about the planned new edition of the DSM: 'Press Release: DSM-5 Publication Date Moved to May 2013'" ME Agenda, accessed September 2013, http://meagenda.wordpress.com/2009/12/10/press-release-dsm-5-publication-date-moved-to-may-2013/.

the psychodynamic approach to mental illness, seeing it as a sliding scale of abnormality. They also operated with a causal ontology of illness, and so regarded the individual story of the person as part of the aetiology and, therefore, the total picture of the illness which treating psychiatrists needed to take into account.

DSM and Psychiatric Descriptivism

In 1980, the controversial third edition of the manual (DSM–III) completely abandoned the psychodynamic approach to mental illness, and went with a strictly scientific medical paradigm. It introduced a clear demarcation between normal and abnormal, and took an intentionally 'atheoretical' descriptivist approach, no longer seeking any significant understanding of the patient's personal story, experiences or subjectivity. Neither is there any serious investigation into the aetiology of the illness. Instead it limits the diagnosis of mental illness to the immediate observable behaviours and signs that can be recorded against a defined profile, as determined by statistical consensus. This 'regulatory' model for the diagnosis of mental disorders has been retained and developed in the subsequent editions and revisions of the DSM, including the recently released DSM–V.[51] Despite hopes and expectations that this new edition would represent a step back from the strong regulatory model of diagnosis, it has largely continued along the same path. In the area of depression it has, if anything, become even more categorical and descriptivist, introducing a controversial new category of depressive illness that encompasses grief (for example, over the death of a loved one). While it has long been recognised that prolonged or complicated grief can grow into depression, it is now proposed that grief is itself a major depressive sickness. This is a very unwelcome change in many quarters, and is widely regarded as a further development in the psychiatric establishment's out-of-touch 'pathologisation' of normal human life experiences and responses.

Growing Dissatisfaction with the Current Psychiatric Model

The continued development of this positivist and descriptivist approach has drawn considerable criticism from many quarters,

---

51. *The Diagnostic & Statistical Manual of Mental Disorders: DSM-V*, fifth edition, edited by the American Psychiatric Society (Washington: APA, 2013).

including those who treat and deal with depression sufferers outside the medical establishment and mental health systems.

Jennifer Radden claims that such descriptivist medicine sacrifices too much of the individual journey's integrity. Each person's experience of depression is dimensioned and complex and cannot be reduced to a series of categorical determinations without reducing the person herself.[52]

John Swinton, writing specifically from the perspective of human spirituality, also criticises the psychiatric treatment of mental illness over the course of the twentieth century. He describes medical science, as it works in practice today, as a 'powerful ideology' which ultimately squeezes out human experience and suffering. He observes, 'It draws on empirical research that is designed to develop *universal* methods and treatments that will deal with the symptoms of the *typical* illness within the *average* patient.' There is precious little room left here for any spiritual understanding or awareness to find a foothold.[53]

Likewise, Tim Farrington, a survivor of bipolar depression and the mental health system, speaks about the alienation that was piled on top of the suffering of his severe and long-term illness by the reductionist mentality of psychiatric medicine.[54]

Pharmacotherapy

Besides the use of electro-convulsive therapy (ECT),[55] one of the most controversial aspects of modern psychiatric treatment for depression is the extensive use of antidepressant drugs. A system of diagnosis based on a descriptivist approach inevitably will tend to take a mechanistic and reductionist attitude towards treatment, and the flourishing depression drug industry has been there to provide

---

52. Radden, *The Nature of Melancholy*, 48–9.
53. Swinton, *Spirituality and Mental Health Care*, 49.
54. Tim Farrington, *A Hell of Mercy: A Meditation on Depression and the Dark Night of the Soul* (New York: Harper Collins, 2009), 54.
55. Much could be written here about the history of this therapy and its current use. It has an ongoing role as a treatment for severe depressive illnesses which are resistant to other forms of treatment. For an overview, see Michael Gitlin, 'Pharmacotherapy and Other Somatic Treatments for Depression', in *Handbook of Depression*, second edition, edited by Ian H Gotlib and Constance L Hammen (New York: Guilford Press, 2009), 568–69.

the tools.[56] Much has been written on the explosion of antidepressant drug prescriptions during the 1980s–1990s and the way in which this has fed the culture of drug dependency in western culture. 'Drug cartography', the process used by psychiatrists in navigating the complex landscape of drug effects, has become the key strategy in depression's medical treatment. Despite the faith that is placed in this drug treatment by the psychiatric profession, the actual effectiveness of these drugs for depression has recently been seriously questioned.[57]

Growing Demands for Shrinking Resources

The other manifest problem with the mental health system in Australia (as well as in the UK and the US) is that the incidence of severe depression and other mental illnesses requiring specialist treatment is growing, while mental health services are being withdrawn and scaled down. This puts the mental health services under huge pressure and, in the view of many, has created an *ongoing crisis* of mental health care.

Primary Medical Intervention

Looking at these wider influences and movements in the medical treatment of more severe cases of depression needs to be balanced with the experiences of many who receive good—and even excellent —medical help for cases of mild–moderate depression from their general medical practitioner. The reduction of specialist mental health services has resulted in the need to develop strategies for handling more such cases of depression at the primary health care level. In Australia, preventative strategies and early diagnosis and treatment of such cases by general practitioners have been aided by *beyondblue*.[58]

---

56. Radden, *Moody Minds Distempered*, 84. Radden also refers to drug research in which there are 'drugs searching for disorders' rather than disorders in search of effective drug treatment. See also Edward Shorter, *How Everyone Became Depressed: The Rise and Fall of the Nervous Breakdown* (New York: Oxford University Press, 2013).

57. Jay C Fournier, Robert J DeRubeis, Steven D Hollon, Sona Dimidjian, Jay D Amsterdam, Richard C Shelton and Jan Fawcett, 'Antidepressant Drug Effects and Depression Severity: A Patient-Level Meta-analysis', *The Journal of the American Medical Association* 303, no. 1 (January 6, 2010) 47–53.

58. *beyondblue* initiates projects aimed at equipping and supporting general medical practitioners in the treatment of depression in the community, for

Anecdotal evidence would suggest that most people benefit from this primary health care treatment, and that they receive support and encouragement along with well-supervised drug therapy. However, clinical studies confirming this effectiveness in the general population have not yet been done.

Psychology and Counselling

Diversity and Complexity

The widening of the depression discussion in western culture has also made its mark in the area of psychology and counselling. Since depression's profile has grown in the Australian community in the last decade, the number and variety of available psychological interventions have also increased.[59] The *beyondblue* consumer guide, *A Guide to What works for Depression* (produced through extensive community research), lists no fewer than nineteen different psychological interventions for the treatment of depression, some of which are well established and some of which are relative newcomers to the clinical and counselling worlds.

Along with the widely-used models such as cognitive behavioural therapy (in its various subtypes and forms), psychoanalysis, family therapy, interpersonal psychotherapy and so on, the *Beyond Blue researchers* also list acceptance and commitment therapy (ACT), animal-assisted therapies, art therapy, dance therapy, eye movement desensitisation and reprocessing therapy (EMDR), hypnosis, music therapy, narrative therapy (NT), marital therapy, neurolinguistic programming, problem solving therapy (PST), psychodynamic therapy, reminiscence therapy, and supportive therapy.[60]

Likewise, counselling styles and models have diversified as community awareness and openness have grown. Counsellors too

---

example, 'Re-orientating General Practice Towards Preventative Mental Health Care for Adolescents, Utilising the Practice Nurse: A Pilot Study', *beyondblue*, accessed October 2013, http://www.beyondblue.org.au/resources/research/research-projects/research-projects/re-orientating-general-practice-towards-preventative-mental-health-care-for-adolescents-utilising-the-practice-nurse-a-pilot-study.

59. Gilbert, *Psychotherapy and Counselling for Depression*, xii.
60. Jorm *et al*, *A Guide to What Works for Depression*, 19-28.

use a range of models and approaches, from narrative counselling, cognitive behavioural approaches, Jungian psychoanalysis, and psychodynamic models of various kinds.[61]

It is clear that a number of these psychological and counselling interventions overlap, or at least use similar strategies, and that therapists and counsellors will often mix and match their methodologies according to their own personal style, preferences and experience. As with depression itself, it is increasingly difficult to sort out and categorise these interventions. The sometimes hazy distinction between psychology and counselling means that it is not always immediately clear exactly what kind of therapy or counselling is being offered. The distinction between 'psychologist' and 'counsellor' may also sometimes be hazy, apart from the demarcations that are formally fixed and defined according to training and professional standards.[62]

The Pre–eminence of Cognitive Behavioural Models

For all this variety, however, it is clear that the overwhelmingly favoured psychological interventions in use today are the various forms of cognitive and cognitive-behavioural therapy. Not only in Australia, but also in other western communities, CBT has emerged as the pre-eminent base level model, not just among clinical psychological therapists, but also among counsellors who have also begun to use this approach and its variants very widely.

Cognitive interventions are based on the supposition that the way in which people interpret their experiences determines how they think and feel about them, and how they deal with them in terms of coping behaviours. Depressive people are unduly negative in their interpretation of experience, especially in regard to themselves, their

---

61. 'Explanation of Theoretical Approaches', British Association of Counselling & Psychotherapy, accessed August 2013, http://www.bacp.co.uk/seeking_therapist/theoretical_approaches.php.
62. The professional standards for registered practising psychologists in Australia are set at a high level by the *Australian Health Practitioner Regulation Agency* (AHPRA) and the *Australian Psychological Society* (APS). Counsellors can register with the *Australian Counseling Association* (ACA), an independent NGO, at level 1, after only Diploma level studies. This difference in professional standards and culture creates a formal demarcation between psychological therapy and counselling.

situation, and their futures. This skewed view of life distorts how they process information and interactions with others, and powerful negative patterns (schemas) of thinking and feeling develop. These harden into negative core-beliefs and assumptions which come to underpin all cognition and affect.

CBT seeks to address depressive illness by teaching clients to recognise and critically examine their negative core beliefs in order to reject them as false and irrational. They are then coached in actively choosing more realistic and positive attitudes and directions, using a structured collaborative process, thereby progressively helping them re-orient their thinking and feeling.

Most recent studies show that CBT, when used for depression, is as effective as antidepressant medications in the relief of acute distress, and may be longer lasting. There is also some evidence that CBT may be successfully used to prevent the onset of depression in people at risk who are not currently depressed.

Since Aaron Beck and others first developed cognitive approaches for the treatment of depression in the 1960s, associated variant types of CBT have been developed. Behavioural activation therapy (BT) concentrates not on the cognitive aspect of the depressed person's life, but on the activities in which the person engages. Specifically, it involves doing activities that are rewarding and pleasurable. This helps to reverse inactive habits and lifestyles which tend to characterise depressive illness.[63] Acceptance and commitment therapy (ACT) and mindfulness based cognitive therapy (MBCT) do not work on a depressed person's thoughts or behaviour. Instead, they work directly on peoples' emotions, teaching them to notice and accept their feelings, especially unpleasant ones which they may normally avoid or displace. MBCT is based on the belief that it is unhelpful for depressed persons to avoid emotional suffering, and that such feelings can only be processed by accepting them in order to then freely choose how to respond to them.

Interpersonal Psychotherapy

The other distinct type of psychological therapy which has an established track-record for the treatment of depression is

---

63. Jorm *et al*, *A Guide to What Works for Depression*, 20.

interpersonal psychotherapy (IPT). This type of therapy focuses on a depressed person's key relationships and the patterns, roles, skills, expectations and habits that have been established in them. Together, the client and therapist identify and explore these interpersonal issues rather than what is going on in the client's own mind. Interpersonal psychotherapy often focuses on family relationships with parents, siblings, partners and spouses. It may focus on adjusting to the loss of relationships and issues of grieving, or on the acceptance of change in long-established roles and interactions.

Despite studies from the US, which have proved its effectiveness for depression, IPT is taking longer to develop its profile in Australia, even though it was recently included in Federal Government funded Medicare programs. It is still relatively unfamiliar to Australian psychotherapists and has taken some time to find its place in the psychology teaching programs here.

Narrative Therapy and Counselling: An Inclusive Paradigm

In this brief survey of psychological and counselling interventions for depression, I mention one more therapeutic model: Narrative Therapy. *NT* has steadily been emerging, both in its own right and as an approach used in the context of other helping models. Now an international movement, this form of therapy began here in Adelaide, SA with psychotherapists, Michael White, and David Epston (of New Zealand) in the 1970s. It involves the powerful paradigm of language and narrative in people's self-awareness and self-construction. In recent years several scholars and therapists have begun to explore the use of NT for depression.[64]

The narrative dimension of human life and wellbeing is an increasingly important issue for people in western cultures today because, as Dan Blazer shows, the loss of almost all sense of a *shared story* has left post-modern people deeply disconnected and disoriented. Without a meta-narrative's integrating influence, we quickly lose our language, identity, direction and sense of meaning. Where the Christian-biblical meta-narrative once served to provide

---

64. Damien Ridge, *Recovery from Depression using the Narrative Approach: A Guide for Doctors, Complementary Therapists and Mental Health Professionals* (London: Jessica Kingsley Publishers, 2008). See also Hilary Clark, editor, *Depression and Narrative: Telling the Dark* (New York: State University of New York Press, 2008).

some sense of 'common landscape', people today must somehow construct their own. Blazer suggests that today's dramatically increased incidence of depression is, in part, a natural human response to the increasingly pervasive meaninglessness caused by this 'denarrativisation' in post-modern western culture.

In this environment narrative therapy is rapidly emerging as a key means of help. It is used with depressed persons to help them tell and then retell (reframe) their stories. It is in the telling of this narrative that the client's negative stories, beliefs, problems, issues and values are externalised-expressed in a form that is open to review and reinterpretation by the client, assisted by the therapist and, sometimes, also by others. The aim is to discover the deeper and richer layers of the client's story, thus enabling new possibilities to emerge and deep level changes to take place in the client's self-story. Unlike the typical deficit-corrective approach adopted in most psychological therapies, NT is oriented towards discovery, imagination and creativity.

I include NT in this brief survey not because it has, at this time, developed a particularly high profile as a depression intervention (though it may well do so in future), or has demonstrated its effectiveness via a raft of clinical studies,[65] but because it is inherently inclusive of, and open to, those who find conventional clinical models of therapy unhelpful.

NT's significance in this regard is twofold. Firstly, it appears to be influencing and contributing significantly to other forms of therapy, adding depth and making the therapy process more accessible and 'friendly' to a wide range of people. Narrative as a medium has a certain ability to transcend educational and socio-economic differences, and may indeed be a universal form, open to people of many cultural and ethnic backgrounds. Secondly, NT provides an alternative paradigm for depressive clients who connect and identify more readily with the artistic, literary, creative and imaginative aspects of human life.

---

65. NT is commonly criticised by some sectors of the psychological community because of the lack of empirical evidence that it is effective. Because it does not operate completely by the values of scientific positivism, it does not fit into conventional models for measuring effectiveness. See Jennifer Wallis, Jan Burns and Rose Capdevila, 'What is Narrative Therapy and What is it Not? The Usefulness of Q Methodology to Explore Accounts of White and Epston's (1990) Approach to Narrative Therapy', in *Clinical Psychology & Psychotherapy*, 18/6 (November/December 2011): 486-97.

Though quite structured, NT is less positivist and empiricist, and more qualitative and constructivist in its epistemology. It is therefore more open to the questions of human experience, subjectivity, meaning and spirituality.

The Re-emergence of Spirituality

The decline of mainline Christianity in many western countries has been matched by the advance of medical science, especially psychiatry. These medical developments have coincided with the growth of developmental psychology, and together they have offered promising new possibilities for the treatment of mental illness. As described earlier in this chapter, during the twentieth century religious approaches to depression have continued to fall into disuse, as psychiatric and psychoanalytical approaches (carrying with them Freud's assertion that religious faith is neurotic and pathological) have advanced as a rapidly growing and powerful new orthodoxy. Despite the movement towards clinicalising Christian pastoral care in the 1950s and 1960s, shrinking awareness and resources have meant that the churches have played a dwindling role in mental health care.

However, since the early 1990s there has been a steady growth in awareness and understanding of spirituality and religion in the psychiatric community in western countries. Alongside this movement is the growing wider discussion of spirituality's deep connections with depressive illness in the western world.

The spiritual–religious dimension of human life has not disappeared and been replaced by psychology as a system of meaning, as Freud prophesied, but has persisted and re-emerged as an important dimension of human health and life. Mainline Christian faith and practice, while in many respects marginalised in the milieu of mental health, continues to carry with it traditions and resources that are helpful for depressed persons. More diverse post-modern spiritual understandings of depression are also emerging, influenced by the rapid advance of cultural pluralism in western countries.

a. Post–Modern Spiritualities

The current re-emergence of spirituality in the medical treatment of depression is marked less by mainline Christian faith than by postmodern forms of spiritual consciousness, which are characteristically non-institutional and often highly individualistic. Non-Christian and non-religious types of spirituality have grown and found a place in clinical models of pastoral care. These models of spirituality often do not centre on any shared system of beliefs, but on issues of personalised meaning, relationship, identity and transcendence. When defined more broadly in this way, there is evidence that, although institutionalised religion (chiefly Christianity) has declined somewhat, *spirituality* still plays a key role in the lives of all people and is a vitally important aspect of mental health. These popular 'DIY' types of spirituality often bend and blend mainline religious symbols and language, mixing Christianity with Buddhism and other faith traditions, along with psycho-spiritual understandings.[66]

Australian cultural studies scholar, David Tacey, in his recent book *Gods and Diseases*, claims that, as a culture, Australia is still holding on to secularism and its rejection of the spiritual and supernatural, and that this is the very reason we have one of the highest rates of depression, self-harm and suicide in the western world. His Jungian perspective on spirituality (which, admittedly, falls far short of Christian faith) leads him to suggest that today we need to be far more open to the spiritual dimension of life in order to find a proper state of balance for our souls.[67]

Spirituality and Medical Research

In the last twenty years a consistent pattern has emerged in mental health research indicating that depression sufferers who have some kind of spiritual involvement or religious faith recover more quickly, have longer lasting remissions and respond better to ongoing treatment. These studies have looked at many different facets of spirituality in relation to depressed patients, including prayer, the significance of the conscience and the health-effects of participation in religious community life.[68]

---

66. Mercieca, *The Upside of Down*. Lewis, *Sunbathing in the Rain*. Stephanie Sorrell, *Depression as a Spiritual Journey* (Winchester: O Books, 2009).
67. David Tacey, *Gods and Diseases: Making Sense of our Physical and Mental Wellbeing* (Sydney: Harper Collins, 2011).
68. There are several major studies in this area. I list here four notable examples, two

This research has mostly been done from a scientific and empirical perspective, and has been based on documented outcomes. As such, it is pragmatic in its attitude: it does not offer any judgements about the reality or inherent truth of spiritual and religious beliefs and practices, but has concluded that it benefits the patients by aiding the treatment of mental illness.

The research and writing of American psychiatrist, Harold Koenig, has been seminal in this area, as has been his founding of the *Centre for Spirituality, Theology and Health, Duke University*, promoting clinical research. Koenig's work has been influential internationally, stimulating a whole new growing edge of clinical research in religion, spirituality and mental health, which has produced a profusion of literature.[69]

In the UK, the work of Andrew Sims has followed similar lines over the last decade. Working through the Royal College of Psychiatry, he has done much to nurture the opening-up of the conservative British psychiatric establishment to spirituality and religion, as important and integral aspects of mental health treatment.[70] Sims has produced fascinating research into the ontological interface of mental health and Christian faith and theology, taking up the themes of creation and relationship paradigmatic to this connection. This is a real adventure into the mysterious borderland of psyche and the spiritual.[71]

Listening to Spiritual Experiences of Depression

Possibly the most exciting and insightful recent research into the spirituality of depression sufferers is the 2001 study conducted by

---

major works and two journal articles: Harold G Koenig, *Faith and Mental Health: Religious Resources for Healing* (Philadelphia: Templeton Foundation Press, 2005). Jeff Levin and Harold G Koenig, editgors, *Faith, Medicine, and Science: A Festschrift in Honor of Dr David B Larson* (New York: Routledge, 2005). David R Williams and Michelle J Sternthal, 'Spirituality, Religion and Health: Evidence and Research Directions', *Medical Journal of Australia* 186, no. 10 (21 May 2007 Supplement): S47–S50. Millard J Ardmur and Martin Harrow, 'Conscience and Depressive Disorders', in *The British Journal of Psychiatry*, 120 (March 1972): 259–64.

69. Center for Spirituality, Theology and Health, Duke University, accessed October 2013, http://www.spiritualityandhealth.duke.edu/about/hkoenig/.
70. Andrew Sims, 'Mysterious Ways'.
71. Andrew Sims, *Is Faith a Delusion? Why Religion is Good For Your Health* (New York, Continuum, 2009).

Scottish scholar, John Swinton, 'Living With Meaninglessness'.[72] Unlike those conducting pure medical research into the therapeutic benefits of spirituality and religion for the depressed, Swinton approaches the issues of spirituality and mental health as a theologian and pastoral care-giver, from a positive faith perspective. He is interested in actually *listening to* and *taking seriously* the spiritual experiences of depressed persons, rather than treating them as objectified phenomena. Using the powerful qualitative research methodology known as *hermeneutic phenomenology*, he gets at the lived spiritual experience of people with depression. He identifies seven common themes:

- Meaninglessness and a sense of having no direction or purpose.
- Feeling abandoned by God and others.
- A sense of desperate clinging on to God or others for survival.
- Deep feelings of loneliness and withdrawal–lack of energy and confidence to relate, despite being lonely.
- The feeling of being slowly ground down, having nothing to hope for but more pain and despair.
- A sense of being trapped into living and the desire to die, marked by ambivalence about God and his will to keep you living.
- The view of depression as a crucible, a purifying and refining fire that is ultimately for the individual's growth and benefit.[73]

Swinton's research shows the deep integration of spiritual faith into the person's whole wellbeing. In his conclusion he notes

> Depression is a profoundly spiritual experience. It is a condition that affects a person in their entirety, producing a deep spiritual, existential, physical, psychological and relational crisis that embraces them in all five dimensions. It is a truly holistic form of psychological distress that demands a fully holistic response. Although the participants in this study all had specifically religious forms of spirituality, the spiritual nature of their experiences of loss of meaning, desolation and abandonment are spiritual crises that apply to everyone who encounters the experience of depression.[74]

---

72. Swinton, *Spirituality and Mental Health Care*, 93–135.
73. Swinton, *Spirituality and Mental Health Care*, 112–24.
74. Swinton, *Spirituality and Mental Health Care*, 131.

Mainline Christian Spirituality and Depression

So far in this section we have focussed on non-mainline and non-Christian spirituality, rather than on the biblical Christian traditions. These mainline Christian traditions are, in some cases, also now beginning to re-engage with the spiritual needs of depression sufferers, bringing to the table their theology, spiritual resources and practices which have been developed through ministry to the depressed in past eras. There is a deep tradition of contemplative spirituality in Roman Catholicism which deals with the reality of human darkness and how God may deal with, and walk with us, in depression. The *Dark Night of the Soul* of St John of the Cross, while not dealing exclusively with depression, opens up the possibility that God may be using sadness and suffering to bring the soul closer to himself.[75]

One of the treasures of western spirituality is Ignatius Loyola's prayer against depression: a short twelve-line prayer to Christ, seeking his protection and strength. In many ways this prayer is also a catechetical document, leading the prayerful into a deeper reflection on their own weakness and darkness in the light of Christ's strength.[76]

Possibly the most striking example of contemporary depression spirituality from this contemplative tradition is Henri Nouwen's *The Living Voice of Love*, a series of devotional thoughts written during, and after, his terrible and almost fatal struggle with clinical depression.[77]

Because of Luther's own depressive illness and its influence on his theology, depression has, of course, developed deep roots in Lutheran spirituality.[78] A recent exploration of this is the 2008 book by American Lutheran pastor, Todd Peperkorn: *I Trust When Dark my Road: The Lutheran View of Depression*,[79] together with his blog

---

75. Stephen J Pietsch, 'Depression and the Dark Night of the Soul' (Postgraduate paper, Adelaide College of Divinity, 2011), accessed November 2013, http://www.alc.edu.au/assets/education/about/academic-publications/paper/The-dark-night-of-the-soul.pdf.
76. See Saint Ignatius Loyola, 'Prayer against Depression–by Saint Ignatius of Loyola', *Catholic Online*, accessed August 2013. http://www.catholic.org/prayers/prayer.php?p=616
77. Henri JM Nouwen, *The Inner Voice of Love: A Journey Through Anguish to Freedom* (New York: Image Books, 1996).
78. Pietsch, 'Reflection on Depression in Luther's *Table Talk*, 5–7.
79. Todd Peperkorn, *I Trust When Dark My Road: A Lutheran View of Depression* (St

site.[80] Peperkorn's book, like a lot of contemporary reflection on depression, arose out of his own experience; in his case shaped by the context of parish ministry in a local Lutheran church. He relates and interprets his experiences using biblical and orthodox Christian categories, and draws on the Lutheran theology of justification by grace, showing how depression had eroded his understanding of God's grace and unconditional love for him, and how connecting with this justifying grace is an important ingredient in his ongoing recovery. He draws on the themes of suffering in Lutheran theology, reflecting on Luther's theology of the cross, to underline the objective reality of God's gracious presence with depressed persons, even when they feel utterly abandoned by him.

Representative of the huge range of popular evangelical Protestant spiritual resources on depression is John Lockley's *Practical Workbook for the Depressed Christian*.[81] This particular work is a good exemplar because of its high profile as a spiritual resource among evangelical Christians in Adelaide at the present time. Lockley offers a compassionate and grace-centred approach to depression. However, like so much other evangelical literature of this type, it tends to reduce, over-simplify and trivialise depressive illness. Like many similar authors, he does not really see depression as a spiritual issue, but as a medical issue, an illness which is to be overcome through appropriate treatment, faith and loving Christian support. There is not a great emphasis on what spiritual growth might happen *through* the experience of depressive suffering, or on how personal faith might be deepened or damaged through it. The assumption is that Christians need to focus on recovering from the illness in order to get on with being positive and hopeful again. Like many spiritual 'self-help' resources of this type, it displays little real understanding of the lived experience of depression. The author assumes, for instance, that a depressed person is capable of reading the book and working consistently at overcoming their depression through the exercises given. The problem is that, for most severely depressed persons, such purposeful and focussed activity is clearly impossible.

Louis: LCMS World Relief and Human Care, 2009).
80. See *I Trust When Dark My Road*, http://www.darkmyroad.org/.
81. John Lockley, *A Practical Workbook for the Depressed Christian* (Bletchley: Authentic, 2002).

Pastoral Care Attitudes and Approaches

A Lack of Understanding and Empathy

Rather than immediately jumping into a description of contemporary pastoral care in relation to depression, thereby orienting this discussion to the perspective of the pastoral theologian or caregiver, it is important to look at pastoral care here from the *receiving* end. What do depression sufferers experience and report about the pastoral care they receive from their pastors, carers, church bodies and congregations?

For many depression sufferers the church has not been an understanding and supportive community. What many writers have described[82] is borne out in my own experience of the pastoral care of depressed persons, both as a pastor in parish ministry and as a tertiary lecturer. In my church body, despite the depression-awareness initiatives that have saturated the whole Australian community, there is a low level of awareness about depression, and it seems clear that this is the experience of other churches as well.[83] Sadly, many people who seek help from fellow Christians and church members are met by judgements based on ignorance and the resulting lack of empathy.[84] It

---

82. See the list of unhelpful religious and spiritual things people say to the depressed at 'The Things People Say', *Christian Depression Pages*, accessed August 2013, http://www.christian-depression.org/cdp/sayings.php. See also Lockley, *A Practical Workbook for the Depressed Christian*, 358–379. See also Pietsch, 'Depression and the Soul'.
83. Looking at people's shared experiences and impressions of this on blog sites shows that it is disturbingly common. See 'Christian Culture's Stigmatization of Depression', BaptistPlanet, accessed August 2013, http://baptistplanet.wordpress.com/2009/10/30/christian-cultures-stigmatization-of-depression/. See also the blog comment by the Welsh Emerging Church theologian, Dyfed Wyn Roberts, 'Depression, Stigma and Church', *Dyfed Wyn Roberts*, April 18, 2011, accessed August 2013, http://www.dyfedwynroberts.org.uk/index/depression-stigma-and-church. Finally, see a sociological study involving Presbyterian respondents which shows the same problem: Christopher G Ellison, Wei Zhang, Neal Krause and John Marcum, 'Does Negative Interaction in the Church Increase Psychological Distress? Longitudinal Findings from the Presbyterian Panel Survey', *Sociology of Religion* 70, no. 4 (winter 2009): 409–31.
84. Simpson, *Troubled Minds, Mental Illness and the Church's Mission*, 98–120. The author has done a superb job here of identifying and analysing the major issues. See also Beverly K Yahnke, 'Prescriptions for the Soul: The Taxonomy of Despair', (paper presented at the Mercy Conference St Louis, MO, May 1, 2007), accessed

is clear that pastors and care-givers themselves are often among the offenders here, passing off the suffering of the depressed person as something that can be dealt with via a change of attitude or a lifestyle adjustment.

Quite apart from the common human difficulty of even beginning to understand what depression is without firsthand experience of it, there is the latent (or sometimes overt) expectation in the church that by their very nature as regenerate beings, Christians are, or ought to be, continuously happy and cheerful. When a depressive person is met by such attitudes, it often just confirms the negative beliefs they have already begun to form about themselves, their lack of faith and their spiritual failure.

A Lack of Pastoral and Theological Engagement

As described earlier in this chapter, the rise of medical and psychiatric models for understanding and treating depression in the twentieth century has coincided with the church pulling back, unsure of its credentials for ministering to the mentally ill, in the face of the widespread rejection of spiritual reality by the mental health professions. During the 1950s and 1960s, highly psychologised forms of Christian pastoral care and counselling developed in which the theological and ecclesial model of pastoral care gave way to quasi-clinical and therapeutic constructions.

In the 1980s there was a strong move back toward the theological, ecclesial and biblical emphases of pastoral care and counselling as a result of the paleo-orthodox movement, led by pastoral theologian, Thomas Oden, among others.[85]

The biblical counselling movement also reacted to the predominance of the social sciences in pastoral care and, as with other human struggles, regards the Bible as the source of all understanding of, and treatment for, depression. Whatever shade or type of biblical counselling one consults, there is the same basic schema at work: scripture reshapes and corrects wrong thinking and feeling. This

---

September 2013, http://www.doxology.us/downloads/35_yahnke2.pdf, 4–8.

85. Other protagonists in this movement, particularly those who sought to reattach the church to its biblical and historical traditions of pastoral care, include Carl Braaten, Eugene Peterson, Andrew Purves and Marva Dawn.

approach has continued to be used, particularly by Protestant evangelical Christians.

Despite these movements in the wider scene, and the growth of depression as an illness over the last thirty years, there has been relatively little creative pastoral and theological energy brought to bear on this area. Considering the long tradition of the Christian church's participation in the discussion about and pastoral care of melancholy and depression in past eras, little fresh research or writing has been done. Much of what has been written is, in many ways, simply 'reploughing the fields' of biblical counselling or 'Christian-oriented' medicine and psychiatry of one kind or another.

However, it is important to acknowledge that there have been some helpful contributions. During the 1990s, Donald Capps[86] and Howard Stone[87] (both concentrating on the theological theme of hope) produced helpful books that offer not only pastoral insights from the social sciences, but also some deeper theological reflections that draw the reader into ecclesial and pastoral ministry practice.

More Recent Research and Reflection

In 2004, medical practitioner, Lanny Hunter, and theologian, Victor Hunter, (brothers, co-authors and survivors of clinical depression) published a now widely-appreciated book, dealing with depression as an illness of the whole person, in which the spiritual plays a key role.[88] Emphasising the need to embrace the cross in the midst of depressive suffering, the authors draw on the resources of the Christian tradition, particularly on those who developed their spirituality in the context of depressive suffering.

Until recently the traditional themes of comfort and consolation (*consolatio*) have not been taken up by contemporary Christian pastoral care and counselling. As Leonard M Hummel points out, today the word 'consolation' tends to denote 'a paltry gift in lieu of success–a consolation prize'. Yet this powerful theology-practice from the tradition of the church has rich possibilities for enacting

---

86. Donald Capps, *Agents of Hope: A Pastoral Psychology* (Minneapolis: Fortress: 1995).
87. Stone, *Depression and Hope*.
88. Hunter and Hunter, *What Your Doctor and Your Pastor Want You to Know about Depression*.

God's redemption in the lives of those suffering the spiritual distress of depression. Hummel has reopened this field of pastoral theology and practice, not only from the perspective of depression, but also as a pastoral approach to suffering life generally.[89]

Once again, however, the most significant research on the pastoral care of people with mental health issues (including depression) is that of Scottish scholar, John Swinton.[90] He shows that through the intentional practice of loving friendship, Christian communities can help those with mental illness to find hope, personhood and freedom. His research with depressed persons[91] shows the power of understanding and non-critical acceptance. This openness and friendship must be based on real listening, which entails the willingness to suspend summary evaluation and judgment of others' experiences, even though they may be alien to one's own.

This research also showed the importance of Christian practices, symbols, the liturgy, the sacraments, ritual, language and music as means of spiritual connection for persons who are struggling with the cognitive-affective fog of depression. Swinton also makes special mention of the importance of using lament psalms and hymns in public worship and private devotion.[92]

The writing of Lutheran psychologist and educator, Beverly Yahnke,[93] likewise emphasises the importance of a 'ministry of mercy' characterised by gracious and receptive listening. She also points out the importance of 'keeping vigil' with the depressed, and being present and available. As a diverse and many-layered form of spiritual despair, depression requires pastoral care givers to be patient and humble. Yahnke also bemoans the lack of deeper understanding about depression among pastors, pastoral theologians, and in pastoral theology and counselling text books. As well as quality listening, the

---

89. Hummel, *Clothed in Nothingness*, 7.
90. John Swinton, *Resurrecting the Person: Friendship and the Care of People With Mental Health Problems* (Nashville: Abingdon Press 2000). Swinton's hermeneutic-phenomenological model for researching human spiritual experience allows for much closer listening to the voices of persons with mental illness than conventional empiricist models, and is open to qualitative human data. His research is therefore very useful for pastoral carers.
91. Swinton, *Spirituality and Mental Health Care*, 93-134.
92. Swinton, *Spirituality and Mental Health Care*, 93-134.
93. Yahnke, 'Prescriptions for the Soul'.

pastoral care of the depressed requires the sensitive, discerning and wise application of the Word of God, which may also entail prayer, blessing and other pastoral acts.[94]

Amy Simpson's *Troubled Minds: Mental Illness and the Church's Mission*[95] has drawn much-needed attention to the church's sad failure to give care and understanding to the mentally ill, and has offered important resources and directions for how Christian congregations can offer mercy and compassion.

From a pastoral ministry point of view, the most encouraging sign in this area is the re-emergence of the *Seelsorge* tradition.[96] This tradition of pastoral care carries through the historical threads of Gregory the Great's *cura animarum*, and is the very stuff of Luther's own pastoral theology and practice. It brings together much of the spiritual wisdom about depression of past eras and resonates strongly with the best pastoral research today, emphasising the classical spiritual practices of the church: the pastoral care and counsel of the Christian community and its clergy; loving and faithful Christian friendship; the liturgy, symbol and ritual; the means of grace (the word and sacraments); prayer, and the devotional life.

Conclusion

This brief overview of depression in contemporary life and experience gives us just a glimpse of how pervasive, complex and serious a problem this illness is in our time. Yet it remains peculiarly invisible. Readers of this chapter have sometimes commented, as they come to its end, 'I had no idea'.

But our contemporary struggle with the rise of depressive illness is not unique. It has always been present, ebbing and flowing in response to the tidal changes of culture, economics, religion and philosophy. While modern science has offered new treatments, strategies and remedies, the complex and mysterious 'anatomy of melancholy' (to borrow Burton's famous title) continues to evade us as it 'morphs' its way through history, displaying its 'disagreeing likeness'.

---

94. Yahnke, 'Prescriptions for the Soul'.
95. Amy Simpson, *Troubled Minds, Mental Illness and the Church's Mission*.
96. Pietsch, 'Seelsorge—A Living Tradition'.

When it comes to caring for and helping depression sufferers, we may, therefore, have as much to learn from the wisdom of past eras as we do from modern medicine and psychology. Our world is different from the worlds of Galen, Luther, Burton and even Freud, and yet the thread of continuity between our time and earlier ages is strong, composed as it is, of many strands.

Chapter 4
'Comforting the Melancholy' Meets 'Counselling the Depressed'
A Contemporary Dialogue with Luther

> '...to read Luther is to transform him with the contemporary questions brought to his theology; to read him is to risk the transformation of one's own perception, biases and judgements.'
> Christine Helmer & Bo Holm,
> *Transformations in Luther's Theology.* 2012.

We have now explored Luther's letters to depression sufferers and the sixteenth century context in which they were written. We have also taken some time to explore the multiple faces of depression in our own world. The main point of this book, however, is to bring these two worlds together into creative conversation. What can we learn from Luther? What insights from his pastoral wisdom are still wise today? Are there aspects of his spiritual understanding of melancholy which show up the gaps and blanks in our contemporary constructions of depression?

Addressing these questions entails more than 'filtering' Luther's insights and practices to fit in with today's world view. It also entails hearing *his* critique and listening to the questions *he* raises. This may uncover issues, needs and possibilities which are not currently in view, have been forgotten, or remain unaddressed in the church's pastoral care of depression sufferers.

This encounter between Luther's theology-practice and our own will be worth little unless it is truly mutual. If it is to be more than a balstering of our own pre-existing modern and post-modern assumptions, we must go beyond a 'utilisation' of Luther, undertaken entirely on our own terms. As we noted earlier, any authentic encounter with Luther must be an 'actualisation'[1] of Luther's theology, in which his voice is really heard. Such an actualisation is what has been attempted in the six reflections which follow in this chapter, developing the major consolatory themes found in Luther's letters to the melancholy. As we do so we will visit the key *loci* of Luther's consolation more than once,[2] in order to deepen and enrich our understanding of his insights, from various contemporary perspectives.

Reaching the Heart: Cognitive–Behavioural Insights for Pastoral Care of Persons with Depression

Luther had what psychologists today recognise as a strong *cognitive-behavioural* understanding of the dynamics of depressive illness and employed these insights in his pastoral letters to depression sufferers. Luther's phrase 'depressed thoughts' (*cogitationes tristitiae*) or 'heavy thoughts' (*schwere Gedanken*) is one of his main descriptors of depressive experience. He recognised that the faculty of thought (*cogitatio*) is one of the central presenting issues in depression.

Many of the twenty-one letters in this selection were written between 1530 and 1534. During this time, as we know, Luther was reflecting on the deeper nature and cognitive–behavioural dynamics of depressive melancholy because he was intensively involved in the pastoral care of depressed persons. He says a lot about depressive melancholy in his *Table Talk* which reflects exactly the same cognitive–behavioural understandings and strategies we find in these letters.[3]

We find at the core of Luther's understanding here the two functions, *affectus* and *intellectus*, working in concert to comprise the 'heart'. Balanced and moderated by the conscience, these two dimensions form the 'nerve centre' of the human soul. For Luther, this inner seat of the faculties is where human experience of all kinds is formed. Depressive melancholy is, therefore, a sickness of 'the

---

1. See Stephen Pietsch, 'Exploring Transformation in Luther Studies', in *Lutheran Forum*, 49/1 (Spring 2015): 30-1.
2. The reader will note a cyclical pattern emerge in this chapter as we make the many connections which make up the larger picture,
3. WA TR II, No.1270, 19-20; WA TR II, No.1299, 33; WA TR III, No.3798, 623-624. See also Tony Headley's excellent account of Luther's cognitive–behavioural understanding of depression in 'Martin Luther on Depression'.

heart' in which affect and cognition are both distorted and darkened so that they no longer correspond meaningfully to external reality.[4] This distortion is frequently mediated by the conscience which, under diabolic attack, is burdened with fear and guilt over past misdeeds that have been forgiven and left behind, or by false accusations of new sins. This attack from the devil inflames the individual's guilty fears. When the conscience is attacked in this way, the heart turns inward to self-negativity and despair. The mind devises punishments for itself as it imagines a wrathful God. The emotions conspire to confirm these false perceptions, in a vicious cycle of self-destruction that, unchecked, leads to death.[5]

Luther realises that addressing the false beliefs of the depressive requires strong and practical measures to help break the cycle of despair and self-sabotage. Using the wisdom of his ancient and medieval sources in combination with his grace-centred theology, he advises his addressees to practise intentional changes in their behavioural responses to their moods and feelings, thereby interrupting the repeating pattern of depressive cognition and affect.[6]

He advises his depressive readers to manage their environments in order to avoid circumstances that sabotage them, such as excessive solitude,[7] where there is no influence to counter the inner negative depressive feedback loop of thinking and feeling.

He shows an understanding of the differences between milder and more severe experiences of depression. In less-developed cases, he often moves people towards managing their thinking through

---

4. In his *letter to Queen Maria of Hungary* of 1531 (See Appendix), whose depression was causing her struggles of conscience, Luther wrote: 'Our Lord is not so angry as we may be accustomed to think and feel .'
5. It is quite clear that in Luther's understanding and experience, depressive melancholia was associated with bodily illness which was potentially fatal. Joachim of Anhalt almost died of it in 1534, as did Melanchthon in 1540. Spalatin did die of it in 1545. Besides the possibility of physical degeneration, there were instances of suicidal depression, as we see in the case of the severely depressed Jonas von Stockhausen who was looking to end his life (See Appendix).
6. All through Luther's letters to the melancholy he encourages leisure and sporting activities like hunting, riding, playing chess, seeking out company and conversation.
7. Most notably in our selection, his *letters to Jonas von Stockhausen* (See Appendix: 319–320), *Jerome* and *Matthias Weller* (See Appendix).

diversional activities of various types. In other cases, he realises that a more patient and prayerful walking–beside–the–person is required.[8]

Luther speaks about this cognitive–affective dimension of depressive illness not only from an external observational standpoint, but also from personal experience. He discloses to his readers his own cognitive struggles quite often, using the 'rhetoric of vulnerability' to support his exhortations to his readers to move towards practical actions in fighting the illness.[9]

It is important to see that, for Luther, the cognitive–behavioural understanding of depression is mediated through the over–arching framework of his Christian faith and practice. He uses the biblical dynamic of law and gospel as a powerful 'cognitive–behavioural tool' in helping people move through their guilt, shame and fear, to receiving the forgiveness and freedom of grace. In fact this experiential structure of justification is the central powerhouse in Luther's cognitive–behavioural approach.

Luther sees the devil as a strong and malevolent force behind the depressive cycle of suffering and despair. He characterises the devil as the planter of 'heavy thoughts', tailored to the individual's scruples and fears. For Luther, this is experientially real and self–evident. However, he uses even the devil as a 'device' in his cognitive strategy against melancholy, by unmasking and naming the old enemy's poisoning of the mind. The depressed thoughts may then be 'disowned' by the sufferer, and this in turn disarms the debilitating false judgements which fuel depressive cycles of thinking and feeling.

This is a major connection between Luther's horizon and ours which reveals an affirmative correlation between his sixteenth century

---

8. We see this particularly in the prolonged and chronic cases of depression represented in this selection, Jerome Weller and Joachim of Anhalt. Luther moves from basic coping strategies to a more patient and spiritually supportive approach, as it becomes clear that the despondent moods have become more chronic and protracted.
9. In Luther's *letter to Joachim of Anhalt* of 23 May 1534 (See Appendix) he appeals to the young prince not to waste his youth in gloomy ruminations, citing his own past mistakes: 'I myself, who have spent a good part of my life in sorrow and gloom, now seek and find pleasure wherever I can. Praise God, we now have sufficient understanding [of the Word of God] to be able to rejoice with a good conscience and to use God's gifts with thanksgiving '. Similarly, in his letter to Barbara Lißkirchen of 1531 (See Appendix), Luther empathises respectfully with *his* reader, recalling his own struggles with the same temptation.

constructions of depressive illness and contemporary depression experience. In viewing Luther's use of cognitive and behavioural insights through this lens of the human sciences of psychology and counselling, we can explore what Luther's approach may have to offer today, not only to the practice of cognitive and behavioural therapy and counselling within a contemporary Christian frame of reference, but also for the pastoral care and counsel of depressive persons.

Luther's insights come from a different era to our own and are differently expressed, yet, as Tony Headley observes, they correspond to a surprising extent with cognitive-behavioural therapy for depression today.

> As implied above, one finds a heavy cognitive emphasis in Luther's views of depressionLuther makes a number of very astute observations about the role of cognition in depression . . . This emphasis on cognition and behaviour fits nicely with modern understandings . . . of depression. Like Luther, authors like Aaron Beck emphasize similar cognitive bases for depression.[10]

This understanding was deeply integrated with his theological framework which incorporated sin and forgiveness, faith and trust in God, the word of scripture, prayer and blessing as well as the devil and his evil influences on believers in the world. As we have seen above, his spiritual anthropology reflects a sophisticated psychodynamic understanding of depression. In the letters we see how Luther identifies and addresses the way in which his readers selectively abstract negative impressions and observations, magnifying issues beyond their real significance and catastrophising the future.[11]

There are also several examples of Luther assisting his addressees to move towards the modification of their beliefs and schemata. In the case of Johannes Schlaginhaufen, Joachim of Anhalt and Jerome Weller, Luther played a prolonged pastoral counselling role, and put in sustained efforts to help these friends work towards breaking old cognitive patterns and establishing new ones.

---

10. Headley, 'Martin Luther on Depression'.
11. See Luther's *letter to Barbara Lißkirchen*, 1531 (See Appendix); The *letter to Prince Joachim of Anhalt*, Christmas Day, 1535 (See Appendix). Clearly, in these letters Luther is addressing his readers' false and cognitively distorted beliefs and fears. See Headley, 'Martin Luther on Depression'.

Luther clearly used metacognitive methods too, inviting his readers to step back from their own suppositions and evaluate them more objectively in the light of the external Word of God. In his 1545 letter to Spalatin, there is a long opening *argumentatio* inviting the reader to examine the evidence of the situation and revisit his interpretation of reality:

> The Lord says, 'I do not wish the death of the sinner, but rather that he repent and live'. Do you really think that in your case alone the Lord's hand is shortened? Or has the Lord in your case alone ceased to be merciful?.[12]

CBT and Pastoral Care of the Depressed

It is important to acknowledge the great gift of God which cognitive-behavioural psychology has been in the treatment of mood disorders over the last fifty years. As a *human* science, it works on the *human* level and, as we have seen, it continues to be a highly effective treatment for depression sufferers when it is well-used by any therapist, Christian or not.

There is, however, an important difference to be appreciated between CBT which attempts to incorporate Christian faith and spirituality into its therapeutic program of treatment and CBT which is conducted within the integrated framework of the individual therapist's Christian faith. Many Christian psychologists and counsellors whose faith is integrated with their life and work, do not name themselves as 'Christian therapists' even though their practice is strongly influenced by their faith and spiritual values. They may or may not use cognitive methods drawing on the theological framework and language of their own Christian faith, according to the spiritual orientation and openness of their client.

Today, however, an increasing number of Christian pastoral care-givers and pastors are receiving training in cognitive-behavioural techniques, and there are a number of practitioners offering forms of CBT which they claim are intrinsically 'Christian', and therefore of greater value to Christians than those offered by other therapists. There are diverse understandings of the ways in which CBT can and should interact with Christian faith, and how they should be used

---

12. See Appendix.

by church care-givers and pastors as part of a Christian model of helping.

As we look more closely at Luther's pastoral use of cognitive-behavioural strategies, we are presented with an opportunity to see a theologically integrated approach which offers us not only helpful theological-pastoral insights, but also assists us in evaluating the many models of CBT on offer today which claim to be biblical or Christian.

Grace as a Cognitive–Affective Dynamic

The larger frame of reference within which Luther uses cognitive-behavioural tools is the teaching of justification by grace. It is evident in almost all the twenty-one letters that Luther's consolation is not built around his ability to soothe or calm his readers, but on God's grace which is 'able to comfort us far more than all the distress and unhappiness–under heaven, on earth or in hell–can depress and terrify us'.[13] Luther seeks to bring light into people's experiences of hopelessness and despair with the external spiritual counterpoint of grace, reminding them of their new state of being in Christ. As we will discuss more fully in the course of this chapter, in Luther's use of cognitive behavioural methods this justifying and forgiving grace of Christ is *the* central transformative power at work.

Luther's theological–experiential hermeneutic of law and gospel provides the driving dynamic in the strategies he uses to bring his readers to an experience of this grace. Its impact is partly due to the affirmation and acceptance of the fallen human state. God's law is realistic about sin and suffering. But the Gospel moves on towards an horizon of complete forgiveness and redemption through Christ's death and resurrection, and the individual's personal incorporation into these realities through her own baptism and the life of faith. As shown above, in the 1545 letter to Spalatin, Luther frequently invites his readers (who have become stuck in a consuming consciousness of the law and judgement) to a metacognitive re-evaluation of their own spiritually-skewed and depressed thinking. His goal is to *free* sufferers from the belief system in which they are condemned by God and without hope,[14] to embrace the realisation that they are forgiven

---

13. *Luther's letter to Queen Maria of Hungary,* 1531 (See Appendix).
14. In cognitive terms this strong belief system with its patterns of thinking or

and dearly loved by Christ, whose gracious presence suffers with them and supports them in their depression. In this way Luther uses law and gospel as 'objective poles of reality', enabling his readers to move from the reality of their lives under the law to a new reality of grace and salvation.

Temporal and Eschatological Perspectives

Clearly, Luther's theological horizon of hope reaches beyond the prospect of peace and wellbeing in this earthly life. Unlike today's forms of cognitive and cognitive-behavioural therapy, which are based on positivist human science and see temporal human life as the sum of our existence, Luther's vision of wellbeing and hope is primarily eschatological.

For Luther, hope, joy and peace in this life are the harbingers of the coming kingdom of Christ who conquers sin and suffering, the very things that hold us captive in this world. The joys we receive in this life are based upon the hope and assurance of salvation and eternal life. The temporal melancholy thoughts and sufferings of Queen Maria of Hungary were countered by the new reality of God's eternal kingdom of peace and hope, which is experientially available now, by faith in Christ and his promises. In this letter, Luther prays that God would write this new doctrine on Maria's heart. Further, he prays 'that it will go much deeper, *into* your heart, deeper even than your own life and the things Your Grace holds dear on this earth.'[15]

Faith Based CBT?

Luther's theological use of cognitive dynamics in his pastoral consolation is qualitatively different from much of what is described as 'Christian CBT', 'Faith based CBT' or 'Spiritually Modified CBT' today.[16] Besides the obvious dissimilarity of scientific paradigm and

---

schemata, produces powerfully negative automatic thoughts which arise and dominate the sufferer's thinking and emotions, as we see in the case of the young Prince Joachim of Anhalt. In his case, as in the case of most of Luther's addressees, this self-destructive depressive belief system was aided and abetted by the surrounding church and culture, an oppressive religious system of control based on mortal fear.

15. See Appendix.
16. David Powlison, 'Cure of Souls (and the Modern Psychotherapies)', Christian Counseling & Educational Foundation, accessed January 2011, http://www.ccef.

method, there is a deeper, more fundamental difference of inner structure and orientation. On close examination, many models of 'Christian' CBT are shown to be essentially little more than ordinary CBT (conceptualised within a secular frame of reference), with spiritual imagery and language spliced into the appropriate spaces. These models treat faith as an added component or modification to the established framework. This 'branding' is intended to enhance its marketability to, and therefore, its clinical effectiveness with spiritually active Christian patients. God's grace is not seen as the major transformative power for healing and hope or as a larger frame of meaning.

David Hodge summarises the results of several studies in which forms of 'faith based' CBT have been used with various different targeted sample groups.[17] It is evident in the results from these studies that the 'spiritual aspects' of the therapy are regarded merely as 'plug-in variations' that may or may not make CBT more empirically effective. The clinical figures take into account only the measurable nomothetic data, and leave aside the possibilities of spiritual effects and outcomes. In these forms of 'Christian CBT' it is CBT, and not Christian Faith, that provides the main frame of reference.[18]

---

org/cure-souls-and-modern-psychotherapies. Powlison's excellent 'VITEX-COMPIN' distinction is very helpful in understanding the model Luther uses, in which the Christian Faith has its own integrated resources for the cure of souls, to which he adds psychological insights gleaned from others (a COMPIN approach). Many contemporary practitioners of 'faith based' or 'spiritually modified' CBT, use a VITEX approach, where psychology is the main driving force and active agent and Christian content is at best, a cosmetic add-on.

17. David R Hodge, 'Spiritually Modified Cognitive Therapy: A Review of the Literature', in *Social Work*, 51/2 (April 2006): 157–66.

18. This mismatch also opens up the issue of how the non-Christian therapist relates to the spiritual world of their client, especially since their clinical outlook may be basically agnostic or atheistic. How can they understand and work within the complex and subtle environment of a person's faith-world while themselves remaining outside of it? The difficulty of this question is underlined by an article summarising a panel discussion between four leading cognitive therapists in the UK: Rob Waller, Chris Trepka, Daniel Collerton and James Hawkins, 'Addressing Spirituality in CBT', *The Cognitive Behaviour Therapist* 3, no. 3 (September 2010): 95–106. In the section of the article on working with Christians, it is suggested that a therapist should try to 'hold their client's religious beliefs lightly' themselves, in order to facilitate the therapeutic discussion and treat them as

Luther's use of human cognitive dynamics is fundamentally different from forms of 'Christian' CBT which ultimately centre on *self*-acceptance and *self*-validation through the modification of maladaptive beliefs. As we consider Luther's approach, in which the self gains its significance and validity from the unconditional love of God in Christ, we see that his cognitive orientation is not towards the self but towards the objective external reality of God's actions and words, as unmoving declarations of God's attitude of acceptance and love. At the centre of Luther's practice stands Christ, not the self.

'CBT Using Biblical Principles'

Luther's cognitive strategies of pastoral care are also distinct from what is known today as 'biblically modified CBT' or 'CBT using biblical principles'.[19] This model works on modifying a depression sufferer's negative and self-defeating beliefs and schemata by *conforming* them to 'biblical truth'. In these models there is often an emphasis on helping the individual move to new and God-pleasing *attitudes, actions and practices* which accord with God's revealed truth. This is different from Luther's emphasis on the sufferer being brought into a *new or renewed relationship*, which is first received as pure *gift* on account of Christ's suffering, death and resurrection.

Contemporary models of 'biblically based' CBT often express the goals of treatment in terms of the law's commands rather than the Gospel's free gift: 'The ultimate purpose of counselling is to love God with all the heart, mind and soul.'[20] Luther's 'goals of treatment' turn this statement and its theology completely around. He wants to help his readers *receive* a new reality that *transforms* their lives: that God so loves them that he sent his only son to suffer and die and be raised *for them*.

'functionally true as far as the therapeutic relationship is concerned' (page 98). This unearths further questions of personal integrity and trust in the client-therapist relationship, and shows the lack of understanding of spiritual beliefs and convictions.

19. Ruby Lauderdale-Akhigbe, *Combining Biblical Perspectives and Cognitive Behavioral Therapy in the Treatment of Anxiety, Depression, and Low Self-Esteem* (Pennsylvania: Dorrance Publishing, 2010), 74–92.
20. 'A Combined Treatment Approach: Cognitive-Behavioural Therapy and Spiritual Dimensions', The Centre for Cognitive-Behavioural Therapy, accessed October 2013, http://www.centreforcbtcounselling.co.uk/christian.php.

Grace–centred Models of CBT

In any use of CBT that claims to be Christian in its inner structure and nature as well as its methodology, the biblical teaching of grace is the central powerhouse and transformative cognitive–affective core. If God's objective Gospel of total forgiveness and acceptance is not the alternative solid ground offered to depression sufferers, who are sinking in the quicksand of their own negative thoughts and feelings, then what unique benefit does Christian CBT have to offer apart from a surrounding environment of familiar religious concepts and language?

It is worth noting at this point that there are forms of 'Christian' CBT that genuinely attempt to enact Luther's dynamic of grace as their centre, and which do use cognitive behavioural methods to bring people to a deeper experience of this grace and hope in their lives. Two notable examples are Daniel Kruger's eleven week *Gospel Therapy*[21] cognitive–behavioural study program for depression, and Roger Sonnenberg and David Ludwig's older program, *Living with Purpose*.[22] Despite their weaknesses, these programs do present a biblical doctrine of grace as the conceptual main-frame of their programs, making use of CBT insights and strategies to serve this central dynamic.

CBT in Pastoral Care and Counselling with depression sufferers

Several critical questions emerge at this juncture: Do cognitive–behavioural strategies practised within a Gospel–centred theological framework have a role to play in the work of pastors, chaplains, caregivers and others who minister to depressed persons? In the light of pastoral care's distinctive *theological* purposes and goals, is it desirable and appropriate to utilise cognitive and behavioural *psychological* tools and methods? As we engage with these questions, it is helpful to recognise that Luther did not discover human cognitive–behavioural dynamics. He learned from the long tradition of 'psychology' which his humanist education had opened up to him.

---

21. 'Gospel Therapy: A New Vision of Life Through Christ', Gospel Therapy, accessed February 1, 2013, http://www.gospelgospelGospeltherapy.com. See also Roger Sonnenberg and David J Ludwig, *Living with Purpose–Getting More out of Life* (Cedar Rapids: Family Films Publishing, 1978).
22. Sonnenberg and Ludwig, *Living with Purpose–Getting more out of life*.

Luther learned the technique of using categories and structures from the science of his day, by incorporating them into a *larger theological-pastoral frame of reference*, and adapting them to his own theological and pastoral ends.

Psychologist, Bob Roberts suggests that this is also a sound and sensible way for contemporary Christian pastoral carers to make use of insights from cognitive behavioural psychology. He suggests that we first need to properly understand our own theological tradition, and then, on the background of this knowledge, select or 'cherry pick' the insights and methods that are useful and able to be profitably incorporated into our theological frame of reference.[23]

A number of the pastoral strategies which Luther uses in his letters to depression sufferers are in harmony with today's cognitive-behavioural methods, and are valid and effective at the level of pastoral practice:

- Helping depressed persons to think about their thinking, using scriptural teaching, especially the doctrine of grace.
- Developing strategies and plans for redirecting negative thoughts through activating alternative behaviours.
- Working on developing positive schemata through spiritual practices.
- Transpersonalising depressive thoughts and impulses through recognising their spiritual significance as diabolic attack which needs to be actively rejected.

Jones and Butman, however, in their thoughtful theological critique of CBT, give a well measured warning. Besides the naturalistic–positivist tendency to reject spiritual experience, cognitive–behavioural models of therapy raise several other theological issues and questions, for example, self–deception and evil, the spiritual nature of emotion, and the nature of being fully and truly human.[24] Any taking over of material from CBT on the part of the pastoral carer must take account not only of the immediate, but also the deeper theological

---

23. Robert C Roberts, 'Faith and therapy', audio and transcript of interview with David Rutledge, *Encounter*, ABC Radio National (February 24, 2008), accessed September 2013, http://www.abc.net.au/radionational/programs/encounter/faith-and-therapy/3297546.
24. Stanton L Jones and Richard E Butman, *Modern Psychotherapies: A Comprehensive Christian Appraisal* (Downer's Grove: Intervarsity, 1991), 223.

dimensions inherent in it. It is therefore important for pastoral carers to be theologically critical and discriminating in what strategies they take on board, and how they use them.[25]

Assailed by the Enemy: Interpreting Luther's Demonology of Depression

The devil's attack on Christian believers in the form of depressive 'heavy thoughts' is a major theme present in twelve of the twenty-one letters we have examined. Given Luther's emphasis on depressive melancholy as the devil's attack in his pastoral reflections in the *Table Talk*,[26] it would have been reasonable to expect this theme to be more strongly represented in this correspondence. On examining the letters more closely, however, an explanation emerges. While in the *Table Talk* Luther is sharing his thoughts freely in the casual context of after-dinner conversation, in these letters he is doing something different; he is responding to the pastoral needs of his readers in a considered and responsible manner, befitting the role of *consolator*. Casual conversation is one thing; formal pastoral consolation is a different genre, requiring a different rhetorical *dispositio*.

Luther knew full-well that drawing undue attention to the devil's attacks in the case of some of his depressed addressees could spark an anxiety reaction, making their situation worse. In the case of his seven letters to the nervous and highly-suggestible Prince Joachim of Anhalt, for example, Luther barely gives the devil a single significant mention.[27] This shows us something important for understanding

---

25. As Paul Vitz points out, Christianity and science do not just represent different parallel paradigms but may in some areas be understood as 'competing worldviews', in which case the Christian pastoral carer needs to look very carefully indeed at what assumptions and values come packaged into the methods and techniques he borrows from psychology. See Paul C Vitz, *Psychology as Religion, The Cult of Self-Worship* (Grand Rapids: Eerdmans, 1977), 33–42.
26. Pietsch, 'Reflection on Depression in Luther's *Table Talk*' 20–25.
27. He makes reference to the devil only once in his consolatory letters to Prince Joachim, in a letter written on Christmas Day 1535, some 18 months after the prince's severe depressive breakdown in 1534. Here Luther uses the devil as a comic exemplar to make his point: 'Who can terrify us except the devil? But greater than the devil is He that is in us, weak though our faith may be. Even if the devil were holy and sinless, we acknowledge that we are sinners. And even if the devil were so strong that he did not require Christ's help and strength, we

his demonology discourse in these letters: that he is using it with discerning judgement, as something which is not helpful and appropriate for every situation.

Luther has a subtle and psychologically sophisticated understanding of how Satan works through melancholy moods and depression, picking on our existing vulnerabilities or fears:

> I myself know well from experience how the devil, when he finds an opportunity, gladly climbs over the fence—especially where it is lowest; and where it is wet already, there it pours. Out of one struggle, as from a single spark, he happily creates a fire or a flood.[28]

Luther nowhere actually suggests that depressive illness is aetiologically caused by the devil or demonic spirits, or that it is, in itself, a form of demonic oppression or possession *per se*. His image of the devil in the above quotation, 'climbing over the fence where it is lowest' shows his understanding that, as with other life-circumstances, the devil uses the opportunities he finds in a person's depressed moods to aggravate their sadness and suffering.[29] In order to do this, he gains access to human thoughts and feelings in order to plant his poison there.[30]

Luther depicts the devil in 'vivid colour' as a real personal being, and moreover, as a cruel attacker, who hates all Christians because he hates Christ and persecutes believers for their whole lives. So, if we are to withstand these assaults, we must learn how to deal with this pest.[31] His chief mode of attack with those in the grip of melancholy is to produce spiritual confusion, distorting their spiritual perception and feeling, creating a troubled conscience and parading their sins and weaknesses before them. He knows how to exploit the peculiar weaknesses of those who are spiritually depleted by depression.

---

need the dear Saviour. We must be weak, and are willing to be, in order that Christ's strength may dwell in us ' (See Appendix).
28. *Letter to Queen Maria of Hungary*, 1531 (See Appendix).
29. Pietsch, 'Depression and the Soul', 5.
30. In all twelve letters where Luther deals with the devil's role in depressive illness Luther attributes his readers' dark and negative thoughts to the devil's interference. See particularly his *letters to Queen Maria of Hungary* (See Appendix) and *Matthias Weller* (See Appendix).
31. *Letter to Jerome Weller*, August 15 1530 (See Appendix).

He accuses the sufferer falsely, raking up past and long-forgiven misdeeds.[32] Satan snatches from our memories all comfort, tearing the sufferer's thoughts away from Christ and pushing her in the direction of thinking about herself. He leads the sufferer to look to herself instead of others, blocking the channels through which God may wish to bring help and comfort, and ultimately take over God's role as saviour and Lord.[33]

Using a depressed person's negative thinking and damaged conscience, the devil portrays Christ falsely: as an angry and accusing judge waiting to condemn, or as a disinterested and distant tyrant who has simply turned his back. Lying in wait until his victims are alone and vulnerable to attack, the devil turns solitude into torture instead of rest. He chips away at his victims constantly, hoping to break down their faith. He seeks to lead the depression sufferer further into isolation, sadness and despair, and ultimately to death.[34]

At some points, particularly where the sufferer is physically or spiritually vulnerable, Luther advises his readers not to enter into disputation with the devil, but rather to laugh at and scorn him, showing utter contempt and derision.[35] At other times, where he thinks his addressee is strong enough to do so, Luther advises to engage the devil in disputation, by declaring his faith in Christ, his status as a forgiven child of God and his trust in God's promises. He sometimes provides his reader with a short 'speech' for this very purpose.[36]

As Heiko Oberman points out more than once,[37] we misunderstand and underestimate Luther if we characterise his awareness of the devil merely as some grotesque superstitious hangover of his late medieval upbringing, or as a neurotic paranoid obsession that flared

---

32. *Letter to George Spalatin,* August 21 1544 (See Appendix).
33. *Letter to Barbara Lißkirchen,* 1531 (See Appendix).
34. *Letter to Matthias Weller,* October 7 1534 (See Appendix).
35. Stolt, *Laßt uns Fröhlich Springen,* 99.
36. 'Accordingly, if the devil should say, "Do not drink", you should reply to him, "On this very account, because you forbid it, I shall drink, and what is more, I shall drink a generous amount". From the *letter to Jerome Weller* of July 1530 (See Appendix).
37. Oberman, Heiko A. 'Luther Against the Devil', in *The Christian Century* 107/1 (1990): 75–79, accessed July 2010, http://www.religion-online.org/showarticle.asp?title=750.

in response to opposition or difficulty. Luther rather saw Satan as a 'false and pathetic figure who cannot accept or inhabit reality, or even properly exist within it. Instead he haunts the edges of human life, hoping to despoil and destroy'.[38]

Luther 'cuts the devil down to size' by describing his influence and the means of his defeat in theological and experiential terms. Luther sought to oust the devil from his medieval status as a figure of terror and show him for what he is: a carping pest, whose daily chipping away at the Christian's faith and life is part of the tiresome *Anfechtung* all Christians must learn to deal with. Luther's view of the devil, particularly as exemplified in his letters to the depressed, is therefore not one that fosters fear. Rather it engenders resistance among the faithful[39] and puts in their hands the weapons of faith and hope in Christ. Luther encourages his readers to recognise the devil as their attacker and accuser and deal with him according to Christ's authority over him.[40] The devil is, therefore, a vital and integral part of Luther's *theological world view*. His awareness and experience of the evil one flows not primarily from the lurid demonology of sixteenth century Germany but from the biblical images and narratives, as theological commentaries on the experience of the Christian living in this world. Oberman comments:

> There is no way to grasp the milieu of experience and faith unless one has an acute sense of this view of Christian existence between God and the Devil: without a recognition of Satan's power, belief in Christ is reduced to an idea about Christ–and Luther's faith becomes a confused delusion in keeping with the tenor of his time.[41]

---

38. Pietsch, 'Reflection on Depression in Luther's *Table Talk*', 24.
39. James 4:7: 'Resist the devil and he will flee from you'.
40. Nigel Goring Wright, *A Theology of the Dark Side: Putting the Power of Evil in Its Place* (Eugene: Wipf & Stock, 2002), thinks that the devil should be played down much more lest he gain too much influence over Christians by having a higher than necessary profile. This point rests on the assumption that if the devil is left alone he will not stir up as much trouble on his own. Luther's view of the devil is based on the New Testament's warning (1 Peter 5:8) that the devil actively seeks to harm Christians. To Jerome Weller he writes that the devil 'hates and persecutes every single brother of Christ'. Therefore to name, renounce and rebuke him is the best way to 'play him down' and put him in his place.
41. Oberman, *Luther: Man between God and the Devil*, 2.

Far from failing to escape the medieval fog of superstition surrounding the devil, Luther gained a clear *practical theological* perspective on the devil and his work, and it was this that enabled him to *make use of* the evil one for his own theological and pastoral purposes. Perhaps more than any other theologian before or after him, Luther cleared the fog of fear by unmasking the devil as the evil, deceptive, but ultimately hollow, adversary that he is. Oberman observes that 'the manger and the altar confront the devil with the unattainable. Both the demonic intangible adversary of God and the Son of God are present in this world, but only Christ the Son is corporeally present. Anyone who goes further, making the devil into a living being, is superstitious'.[42]

Besides his advice to scorn and revile the enemy loudly, sometimes using quite filthy language, Luther employs the rhetorical method of *scripting* or writing short dramatic dialogues or speeches in which the confrontation between the sufferer and Satan is 're-storied' to reflect the victory of Christ and faith: 'Therefore, if the devil says, "Do not drink", you should reply: "On account of that, because you forbid it, I will drink, and what is more, I will have a generous amount".[43]

In these little dramatic fragments, Luther makes use of the burlesque *Narrenspiel* of the *Carnival*. The devil, for all his elaborate subterfuge, is duped and routed by the believer simply asserting his good conscience and trust in God, and is always left at the end of the 'sketch' looking like an imbecile.[44] In this way Luther changes the medieval 'story' of fear and superstition by speaking the new narrative of faith and freedom, and moreover, by placing it on the lips of vulnerable melancholy souls who find themselves spiritually attacked. Luther's 're-framing' or 're-narrating' of the devil reduces his power and recasts him as a minor rather than a major character in the Christian life. We see in these letters, therefore, how he deviated radically from the medieval consciousness of the diabolical, strengthening the resistance of Christians by putting the gifts of God in their hands: the Word and promises of Christ which produce faith and hope.

---

42. Oberman, *Luther: Man between God and the Devil*, 156.
43. *Letter to Jerome Weller*, July 1530 (See Appendix) This reflects the same habit we find in the *Table Talk*, where Luther uses even more embellished scripts, stories and anecdotes of the same kind.
44. Pietsch, 'Reflection on Depression in Luther's *Table Talk*', 21–3.

There is, however, a carefully tuned paradox in Luther's use of the devil in these letters. While he treats Satan as an empty fool, he also takes seriously the damage he can still do as a spiritual and psychological attacker who, in his desperate rage, hounds vulnerable souls to despair and death through his accusations and lies. As Luther says to Jerome Weller, because the devil hates and persecutes every Christian to the end of the world, we must not grow tired of watching and fighting against him.[45]

The devil's Existence

Clearly some sections of the western Christian church no longer believe in the existence of the devil as a personal evil being, although the debate has been recently reignited by the re-emergence of *exorcism, deliverance ministries* and the renewed emphasis in many quarters of the church on *spiritual warfare.*

The devil cannot simply be written out of spiritual reality today because he is deemed offensive to our enlightened reason or irrelevant. Carl Braaten observes, 'Theology always moves forward in the creative tension between tradition and innovation; we are free to interpret the tradition, but not to arbitrarily whack away what we don't like, and modernity is in itself no criterion of truth or reliability'.[46] Besides the devil's existence being strongly attested in scripture and the church's tradition, and recognised by many (perhaps a majority) of Christians globally, there is the recent widespread re-emergence of the occult, demonic oppression and even demonic possession, which adds experiential weight to the church's historic teaching. The claims stands: 'In fashion or out, what is believed and experienced as spiritual reality by so many Christians will not be denied.'[47]

Those who have objected to belief in the devil's existence because he is a figure of fear and superstition who has sometimes been used to improperly exert spiritual control over others, need to take account of Luther's demonological discourse in these letters. Luther *empowers his readers* with the freedom of faith. Likewise, those who object to the existence of the devil for fear of it leading to a false *Manichean*

---

45. *Letter to Jerome Weller*, August 15 1530 (See Appendix).
46. Carl E Braaten, 'Powers in Conflict: Christ and the Devil', in *Sin, Death, and the Devil*, edited by Carl E Braaten and Robert W Jenson (Grand Rapids: Eerdmans, 2000), 96.
47. Pietsch, 'Reflection on Depression in Luther's *Table Talk*', 28. See also Wright, *A Theology of the Dark Side*, 30.

theology (in which good and evil battle for control of the cosmos), should read Luther's advice to Jerome Weller: 'this devil is conquered by mocking and despising him.'[48]

The best theological 'defence' of the devil's existence is perhaps offered, once again, by Oberman. Writing in 1982, in the wake of twentieth century theological modernism, he maintains that we should listen to Luther and not turn away in embarrassment from recognising the existence of the evil one. If we deny the devil's existence, we turn away from the reality of evil and, ultimately, from the reality of Christ.

> Where the gospel is preached and bears fruit, the devil is there to get in the way—that is his nature, today more than ever! Fear of the devil does not fit in with our modern era, for belief in the devil has been exorcised by attractive ideologies. But in the process our grasp of the unity of man has been lost: living with the real Christ in one's faith means being a whole person as opposed to an intellect that subscribes to a mere idea of Christ.[49]

It is here that Luther's view stands in direct conflict with the predominent scientific view of depression in our contemporary world. Medical science and psychiatry, with their strong empirical positivist framework, do not allow for the existence of the devil or demonic spirits. When psychiatrists are confronted with the suggestion that persons suffering with depression may be under 'spiritual attack' from the devil, they are understandably sceptical. Given the naturalistic framework in which they operate, it cannot be expected that many medical scientists—even those sympathetic to Christian faith or some other form of religious spirituality—would be open to the biblical view of the devil and his work in and among humanity. It may reasonably be assumed that this is why so little has been written on this issue in recent times.

---

48. *Letter to Jerome Weller*, July 1530 (See Appendix).
49. Heiko A Oberman, *Luther: Man between God and the Devil*, translated by Eileen Walliser-Schwarzbart (New York: Yale University Press, 2006), 156. See also Pietsch, 'Depression and the Soul', 5.

Depressive Psychosis and Diabolic Experiences

Although the devil has disappeared from the discussions of the mental health treatment community, he has *not* disappeared from the experience and language of severely depressed persons. Quite apart from the possibility of theological interpretations of depression as the devil's attack, there is still present among depression sufferers today a dimension of 'diabolic experience' that Luther himself knew only too well: immediate awareness of the devil through seeing, hearing and 'feeling' him.[50]

Among the symptoms regularly noted in cases of severely and psychotically depressed patients is the perception of direct contact with the devil. Sometimes, psychotically depressed people hallucinate that they *are the devil* or *are possessed by the devil* or are *being oppressed by the devil*. The study which is still often quoted (though it is now 40 years old) on the nature of depressive–psychotic delusions is the 1967 series of interviews conducted by Aaron T Beck with 280 psychotically depressed individuals, in which fourteen per cent of the patients reported some kind of encounter or relationship with the devil.[51] These patients were persons who had been diagnosed as psychotic and had shown that they were delusional in other areas as well.[52]

Though less common now, perhaps because of the gradual loss of religious awareness in western culture over the last fifty years, diabolic and demonic delusions are still experienced today by psychotically depressed persons.[53] In my own pastoral experience over the last

---

50. William H Meller and Robert H Albers, 'Depression', in *Ministry with Persons with Mental Illness and Their Families*, edited by Robert H Albers, William H Meller and Steven C Thurber (Minneapolis: Fortress, 2012), 14–5.
51. Aaron T Beck and Brad A Alford. *Depression: Causes and Treatments*, second edition (Philadelphia: University of Philadelphia Press, 2009), 37.
52. More than one psychiatrist has been bold enough to say that Luther was suffering with psychotic delusions, too. There was a tradition of 'Luther psycho-history' in the twentieth century. It was the Danish Psychiatrist, Paul J Reiter, who first proposed that Luther's encounters with the devil were symptoms of a psychotic illness in his *Martin Luthers Umwelt, Charakter und Psychose, Sowie Die Bedeutung Dieser Faktoren Für Seine Entwicklung und Lehre* (Copenhagen: Leven & Munksgaard, 1937). This hypothesis was later used by other scholars, including Erik H Erikson in his highly popular *Young Man Luther: A Study in Psychoanalysis and History* (London: Faber & Faber, 1958).
53. Anthony P Morrison, 'The Interpretation of Intrusions in Psychosis: An

twenty years in parish ministry, I have encountered people in care with psychotic mental illness, some of them severely depressed, who had come to be convinced that the devil was interfering with their lives.

But are all such experiences *delusional*? Here we find ourselves walking in that characteristically ambiguous borderland between spirituality and mental illness which leads into the territory of speculative theological metapsychology. However, taking an open-minded theological standpoint, we need to ask: *Are* some of these people in fact experiencing the devil's attack and interference *through* or *in the context of* their mental illness? Or must these experiences and perceptions all be seen as unreal; simply part of the range of delusions and hallucinations they experience *because of* their illness, like the 'black cat sitting at the end of their bed'?

While it is difficult to find any literature dealing with this specific issue, John Peteet's approach to integrating the biological and spiritual aspects of depressive illness offers an opening: '[B]oth mood states and spiritual experience have distinct but overlapping brain correlates, as discussed above. It is therefore misleading to assume that biological, psychological or spiritual dimensions of the self are immiscible.'[54] Could this 'overlap' that Peteet refers to be the very territory where the devil does his secret and destructive work?

It is telling that, while one does not find much about this issue in the writing of the psychiatric community today, it certainly does emerge in the literature in which the *actual experiences of persons with mental illness* are *listened to* and reported. A Scottish woman who took part in a narrative research project on recovery from mental illness made an interesting comment: 'Psychiatrists never give any credence to the fact that there may be other realities which the brain tunes into when it's affected by psychosis.'[55] Are some experiences of the devil indeed

---

Integrative Cognitive Approach to Hallucinations and Delusions', in *Behavioural and Cognitive Psychotherapy* 29/3 (July 2001): 257–276. See also 'How To Get Rid of Severe Depression', depression-guide.com, accessed May 4, 2012, http://www.depression-guide.com/severe-depression.htm.

54. John R Peteet, *Depression and the Soul: A Guide to Spiritually Integrated Treatment* (New York: Routledge, 2010), 193.
55. 'Fighting the Devil', Scottish Recovery Network, accessed July 10, 2012, http://www.scottishrecovery.net/Stories-from-the-narrative-research-project/fighting-the-devil.html.

more than false perceptions arising from psychic pathology? Clearly, many people with experience of depressive illness would answer 'yes'.

Psychotherapy and the Diabolic

How are experiences of the devil or demons dealt with in the context of psychological therapy? Treatment models for depression that seek to integrate various types of psychotherapy with Christian theology are increasingly popular among Christians. Do these models of therapy see the devil or the demonic as significant or important for understanding and treating depression? Or do they see them as outmoded and irrelevant? Do Luther's insights in this area have anything to offer contemporary Christian psychologists? We reflect on these questions by comparing Luther's insights with two recent and respected works on theologically integrated psychotherapy.

McMinn and Campbell's *Integrative Psychotherapy*[56] is widely considered a new benchmark in the integration of theological and psychological approaches to pastoral counselling. It covers Christian counselling of depression, integrating various psychotherapeutic models and methods. It also takes into account Luther's theology of sin and grace as central theological dynamics for Christian counselling. However, the devil plays no role in this model's theological or psychological design. It seems clear that the authors have simply written him out of the picture. This is especially disappointing since this resource, which claims to offer a comprehensive integrated approach, offers nothing to the Christian counsellor or therapist who encounters persons whose faith experience has brought them into contact with the demonic.

The second work consulted was Siang-Yang Tan's comprehensive study, *Counseling and Psychotherapy: A Christian Perspective*. Tan identifies the reality of demonisation and the need for *spiritual warfare* in the face of such demonic attack. He gives criteria and guidelines for the diagnosis and treatment of these serious problems, which clearly equate to what is more generally described as *demonic oppression*. He suggests that this type of demonisation requires

---

56. Mark R McMinn and Clark D Campbell, *Integrative Psychotherapy: Toward a Comprehensive Christian Approach* (Downers Grove: IVP Academic, 2007).

spiritual warfare, incorporating discernment of spirits, deliverance ministry and prayer.[57]

While Tan's analysis, drawing on the Pentecostal tradition of demonology, takes the experience of spiritual attack seriously, the author proposes a rather unsophisticated one-dimensional picture of this issue, 'demonisation'. We find nothing of Luther's biblical insight that the devil works against all believers all the time to undermine their faith, attacking people at their point of vulnerability, striking at the heart-the seat of cognition and affect-at which point the Christian needs to resist him by turning to God's word and power. There seems to be little understanding of the devil's continual harassment through the big and small everyday struggles of life; the struggles which take on larger dimensions for those battling depression. Luther's perspective is that demonic interference is not an extraordinary occurrence, but part of living as a Christian which brings into clear view the need to live by word and sacrament, faith and prayer.

Narrative Reframing

It is here that Luther offers a significant contribution. He used the rhetorical narrative device of *scripting* short scenes for his readers, in which they, as the speakers, would rebuke and humiliate the devil, 'turning the tables' on him as he sought to attack and terrify them. In these short 'dramas' the devil is a passive character who appears only long enough to be 'ticked off' and sent packing. What Luther is doing in these passages of his letters is enabling his addressee to *externalise* depressive thoughts and feelings. This happens as the sufferer re-stories the experience of depression, moving out of the role of victim and taking the initiative in changing the narrative direction of the situation.

It is certainly clear that Luther was not reducing the devil to mere figure or metaphor, as some depression writers do today in their narrative treatments; he knew and experienced Satan as all too real, and his rhetorical counter-attacks are meant to be effective as real weapons against this malicious enemy.

In the same way that some therapists today use psychodrama as a means to empower persons who see themselves as passive victims,

---

57. Siang-Yang Tan, *Counseling and Psychotherapy: A Christian Perspective* (Grand Rapids: Baker Academic, 2011), 332-33.

Luther's scripts express and seek to elicit a response of defiant resistance and opposition to the devil, using sarcasm, irony and sometimes the power of offensive language.

Both Galvin[58] and another therapist, Har Man-kwong,[59] describe how their clients have used demonological language to re-name and re-story their situations by externalising and naming the problem. Interestingly, Galvin describes his work with a Lutheran counselling client who adopted the same biblical image that Luther uses to describe the depressive thoughts with which the devil attacks believers: the 'flaming darts' of the evil one (Ephesians 6:16).[60]

A brief case history illustrates this well. Phil was a recovering alcoholic in his late thirties, who was also struggling with severe depression associated with his broken marriage. A keen reader of theology, he had discovered Luther's commentaries on Genesis, through which he, too, began to reframe his addiction and his depressive moods as the devil's attack on his faith and conscience. In certain situations he began to speak about the devil 'having a go' at him, as he related experiences from his past and present life. He took particular strength from the humorous aspects of Luther's devil discourse, which seemed to disarm the spiritual attack he was experiencing. This helped to break the tension and negativity of the depressive moods that descended on him daily, particularly as evening fell.

Another striking example of the the devil being used in the external reframing of depression is in a narrative poem written by the same Christian Scottish woman mentioned above, and recorded as part of the same narrative research project in mental health recovery:

> Then, towering above me, who but Lucifer fell. His face was expressionless and cold as ice as well. I sensed that he was

---

58. Ray Galvin, 'Narrative Therapy in Pastoral Ministry: A Postmodern Approach to Christian Counselling', Just solutions, accessed April 2011, http://justsolutions.eu/Resources/NarrTherGalvin.pdf, 167–68.
59. Har Man-kwong, 'Overcoming Craving: The Use of Narrative Practices in Breaking Drug Habits', in *International Journal of Narrative Therapy & Community Work*, 1 (2004): 17–24, accessed April 20, 2012, http://www.dulwichcentre.com.au/overcoming-craving.html.
60. Galvin, 'Narrative Therapy in Pastoral Ministry', 167. Luther uses this image very graphically in his letter to Jonas von Stockhausen of November 27 1532 (See Appendix).

waiting with a question yet unsaid. A new strength slowly gathered in my tormented head. I raise myself up slightly, and in not a little fright, I announced my faith in Jesus and declared him to be right, he cast his cloak upon me and said, 'your servant Ma'am'. I think that I now know that I was there put to a test, and by the grace of God alone allowed to come out blest.[61]

Despite the fact that post-modern societies have largely rejected the devil's existence, he still plays a strong rhetorical role in contemporary depression literature, particularly in depression autobiography and poetry in which people are narrating and processing their own experiences.[62] Despite the fact that these writers may not see the devil as real in a completely *literal* sense, they clearly are drawing on the biblical images in their use of demonological rhetoric, expressing something that is deeply real for them *symbolically*.[63] It seems that some personal depression stories are just too dark to be told without the devil playing a role.

Cognitive Transpersonalising

An associated aspect of Luther's *narrative* methodology is his *cognitive* technique of transpersonalising depressive feelings using the devil as a 'target'. Bruce Parmenter's fascinating study on this[64] shows how Luther used this method to help a chronically depressed colleague, Johann Schlaginhaufen (also a recipient of one of the twenty-one letters in our selection), whom Luther nicknamed '*Herr Turbicide*'.[65] Luther displaces the source of the depression and fear from the sufferer to the devil, in this way establishing the crucial psychological distance between 'I' and 'Not I'. This moves the inner

---

61. 'Fighting the Devil' (Scottish Recovery Network).
62. Solomon's *The Noonday Demon* and Merritt's *The Devil Within* are cases in point.
63. The word 'symbolically' is not used here in the popular modern sense of 'token', but in the deeper sense, as something powerful and real which gives access to dimensions of that which is symbolised itself. See Alexis Deodato S Itao, 'Paul Ricoeur's Hermeneutics of Symbols: A Critical Dialectic of Suspicion and Faith', *Krittike* 4, no. 2 (December 2010): 1–17.
64. Bruce R Pamenter '"Devil Talk": A Case History of Martin Luther's Pastoral Counselling with "Herr Turbicide" Compared to a Moder Case of Depression', in *American Journal of Pastoral Counselling*, 7/1 (2003): 67–72.
65. Haile, *Luther: A Biography*, 187–92.

self-destructive vortex of negative cognition and affect to a different arena, in which they can be effectively opposed and rejected. There are numerous examples of this transpersonalising among the letters in our selection.[66] As we have noted variously above, Luther coaches many of his addressees in transpersonalising their depressive thoughts and feelings by recognising them as the devil's malign interference rather than their own valid perceptions.

Parmenter describes his study of Luther's cognitive method as 'a journey back to the future'. He proposes that it can and should be used in certain pastoral counselling situations today. In his article he gives the case history of a forty-five-year-old woman who was a long-term depression-patient, and describes a turning point in her treatment as she was able to move her negative inner discourse from 'I' to 'Not I'.

Recognising and Responding to Spiritual Attack

In Luther's theological-pastoral practice in these twenty-one letters, he recognises and uses the devil as a 'device', a kind of spring-board from which to launch his readers onto Christ's grace and mercy. Luther speaks about the devil only in order to witness to Christ's victory over him, especially in the hearts and consciences of his depressive readers. The point to be harvested from Luther's practice here is that, in the pastoral care of depression sufferers, the devil's attacks and accusations should not be allowed to stand unchallenged by the word of Christ's forgiveness and grace and his promises to protect and keep those who belong to him.

In most cases today we do not need to do this as elaborately and in such 'theatrical' terms as Luther did for his sixteenth century readers, who felt their lives greatly impinged upon by demonic supernatural beings. His concern was to reduce a medieval monster to its true size and to teach people the power of Christ's name and word so that they might learn how to repel the devil's lies themselves.

Our task today is also to help people respond in faith to spiritual attack. But our context is appreciably different to Luther's. Today, in a world where science constructs and explains reality, and where the individual largely develops personal meaning *internally*, people need

---

66. The *Letter to Elsa von Canitz* of August 22 1527 (See Appendix); *Letter to Barbara Lißkirchen* of 1531 (See Appendix); *Letter to Mrs Jonas von Stockhausen* of November 27 1532 (See Appendix).

Seehelp chiefly to *recognise* and name spiritual attack in order to then unmask its deception.[67] Persons struggling with depressive illness in particular need to be alerted to how their thoughts and perceptions are being manipulated, how their consciences are being distorted, and how their faith in God's word is being 'white-anted' *from outside*. Speaking the authoritative word of Christ's forgiveness and mercy in opposition to the lies of the devil[68] strengthens and gives hope. Supporting people in prayer against the evil one is also part of this task.

On the other hand, we find in these letters that where Luther judges that tackling this issue head-on will not be helpful because of the particular spiritual sensitivity and vulnerability of his reader, he refrains from demonological rhetoric altogether.

In pastoral care and counsel today, too, carers need to be responsive and responsible in their use of demonological language with depressed persons.[69] Caution and care should be exercised here because depressed persons who are spiritually vulnerable or who have an oversensitive conscience, may fixate on negative images of the devil and his power in their lives. An even more conservative approach should be taken by pastoral carers with persons who are psychotically depressed and prone to delusions and false perceptions, and may therefore be highly suggestible. There is significant danger here because, as we observed above, psychotic delusions frequently tend to negatively distort religious images, themes and beliefs, including the demonic.

Luther's Devil Today?

True, Luther's world was very different from ours. Today reality is no longer perceived to be teeming with supernatural beings and forces who are self-evidently present and making themselves felt in the fabric of everyday life. For most post-modern westerners, the cosmos is instead scientifically apprehended. Today it seems almost possible for people to live in the world yet never become personally aware of

---

67. John W Kleinig, *Grace Upon Grace: Spirituality for Today* (St Louis: CPH, 2008), 236–39.
68. 'The only way to drive away the devil is by believing in Christ and saying "I am baptised, I am a Christian".' (WA TR VI, No.6830, 217:26–27).
69. Wright, *Theology of the Dark Side*, 115–30.

a spiritual or supernatural realm. In such a context it is not feasible or even possible for us to adopt Luther's whole sixteenth century world view, with its strong awareness of spirits, devils and demons. However, Luther's *theological view of the devil* is not just a relic of this past era, but reflects a present reality. Biblical teaching about it is therefore of continuing importance, both in its own right as an integral part of the historic Christian tradition, and as an intrinsically functional element of Christ-centred pastoral care.

As Oberman intimates, the recognition of the devil's presence in the world as a malevolent and purposeful will and his impingement on our lives is important. It is a needed antidote to post-enlightenment human naivety about evil as that which lies, destroys, kills and separates us from God and his gifts.[70] It is therefore in the recognising, naming and renouncing of this enemy and his lies that the power of his deceptions is broken, and the believer begins to hear and trust the true life-giving Word of God. That word, first spoken into the newly-opened ears of Christians at their baptism,[71] where they renounce the devil and confess faith in the Triune God, is the word of forgiveness and life which puts into action the 'genuine demythologising' of the devil, and establishes Christ's kingdom and gracious rule. In this way the devil's schemes backfire on him and he ends up serving God's loving purposes.[72]

Nigel Goring Wright's point—that the devil should not be given *too much* credit or 'air time'—must be acknowledged as a wise one. Luther's way of down-playing the devil's influence in the lives of his depressed readers was to scorn and ridicule him. While this may also have its place today, the crucial thing is that depression sufferers receive the help they need from the Word of God, in order to recognise and reject the devil's attacks on their hearts, minds and consciences.

---

70. This is the crucial point about the devil as he is depicted in the New Testament, notably by Jesus himself (Jn 8:44); that he cannot be reduced to an irrational and impersonal force of evil, but is defined in his individuality by his purposeful enmity and hatred of God and humanity. See Wright, *Theology of the Dark Side*, 41 & 67 ff.
71. Many baptismal rites (including that of the LCA) incorporate this 'opening of the ears and mouth' as a ritual action, recalling Jesus' healing of the deaf and mute man in Mark 7:31-37.
72. Kleinig, *Grace Upon Grace*, 233.

In this way, they can experience God's healing and comforting grace and mercy for their individual needs.

All Things in Christ: Justification By Grace As Comfort For the Depressed

As many have observed, pastoral concerns about the comfort of souls were what first gave rise to Luther's Reformation theology of justification by grace.[73] What has, in subsequent eras, become a strongly constructed and defended Christian doctrine began as Luther's pastoral response to the spiritual suffering he saw all around him: terrors of conscience and fears, not only of death, but of the horrors that lay beyond for the sinner. It is no surprise then, to find that this same teaching is what drives all Luther's consolatory writings. Martin Treu observes that all Luther's comfort of the suffering can be described as the 'specific pastoral aspect of his teaching on justification.'[74]

Yet even for those who had heard and embraced the Reformation preaching of the Gospel, the ingrained habits of spiritual guilt over sin and hyper-scrupulosity ran deep, and the residual fear of God's wrath lingered. For the depression sufferers of Luther's era, this guilt-ridden religious fear of judgment and damnation was a common and understandable point of vulnerability, providing a ready focus for people's anxious depressive fixations. There are several examples of this among these twenty-one letters.[75] Luther's comfort for depressive melancholics struggling with such fears was to reassure them of God's mercy and forgiveness in Christ, and his promise that they are, despite all perceptions to the contrary, justified, loved and cared for by God in this life and forever. On Christmas Day 1535, he wrote to the neurotically scrupulous Prince Joachim, 'What can distress us–

---

73. Hummel, *Clothed in Nothingness*, 23. See also John Thomas McNeill, *A History of the Cure of Souls* (New York: Harper, 1951), 163.
74. Martin Treu, 'Die Bedeutung der Consolatio für Luthers Seelsorge bis 1525', in *Lutherjahrbuch*, 53 (1986): 7–25.
75. *Letter to Prince Joachim of Anhalt*, Christmas Day 1535 (See Appendix), *Letter to Barbara Lißkirchen* of 1531 (See Appendix); *Letter to Queen Maria of Hungary* of 1531 (See Appendix).

other, perhaps than our sins and bad conscience? Yet Christ has taken these from us, even while we sin daily.'[76]

For Luther, the means by which the soul receives God's justifying and comforting grace is the *conscience*, as the 'mirror' of the heart's true state. The self's needs, hopes and fears are written here, where the present reality and ultimate destiny of the soul before God are sensed and felt. If the conscience is clouded by guilt and fear (real or imagined), then nothing else in life can give joy and hope. When the conscience is right before God in Christ, the whole person is truly free and at peace, even if suffering severely in some other way. If the conscience is at peace then nothing else can truly make us despair.[77]

In Luther's theology, the conscience is much more than a moral compass. It is the spiritual-psychological-physical nerve centre of the whole person, the arbiter of intellect and affect and the interpreter of all the faculties. In depression, the conscience-and with it, all these other faculties-turns in against the self in a storm of self-destruction driven by shame, fear and despair.

Luther's Christian consolation, centred in God's justifying forgiveness in Christ, is summed up in his letter to Maria of Hungary:

> Therefore Your Grace ought to thank God that you have a good conscience before him in Christ, because that far outweighs every temporal bodily suffering we may have. . . For God's grace is able to comfort us far more than all the distress and unhappiness under heaven.[78]

Luther's teaching of justification by grace spoke powerfully to spiritually depressed people in the sixteenth century, when the church, through its system of penance, ruled people with the fear of God's judgement.

As we encounter Luther's consolation today, however, our job is to test it in our our own contemporary context. Does the good news of justification by grace work in the same way today in the post-modern west—a context in which society, the power of the Christian church, morality and spirituality are so changed? Are contemporary consciences still attuned to moral and religious guilt in the same way?

---

76. *Letter to Prince Joachim of Anhalt*, Christmas Day 1535 (See Appendix).
77. *Letter to Queen Maria of Hungary*, 1531 (See Appendix).
78. *Letter to Queen Maria of Hungary*, 1531 (See Appendix).

Is such guilt a pathological effect of depression? How is the conscience affected by depression today? Are these issues felt, expressed and dealt with today via different constructs and language?

Medical Constructions of Depressive Guilt

Despite the differences in our contemporary context, over-blown guilt is still as much a part of depressive illness today as it was in Luther's era. Psychiatric profiling of depressive illness has placed guilt well up on its list of common symptoms. Recent psycho-neurological research has identified the links between depression and the part of the brain that processes feelings of guilt and shame, which is unusually active in many depressive patients.[79]

Because depression is an illness that distorts the thinking processes, it works with the raw negative cognitive-affective material already present and available in the sufferer's mind and memory. Most people have actions or episodes in their past about which they feel guilty. When depression interacts with these, it sometimes results in distorted guilt which takes over more and more of a person's thinking and feeling.[80]

This guilt may be associated with past failures in relationships, trauma, or abuse. It may flow from an awareness of past sins against God and others. Peteet points out that negative forms of spirituality or religiosity can compound depressive guilt, as when, for example, a person is told that their depression signals a lack of faith or punishment for some particular misdeed.

As in some of the cases of depression Luther dealt with, in some severe cases today too, guilt can become a psychotic delusion in which the sufferer feels himself responsible for wrongs or problems for which he cannot possibly be considered culpable, or feels guilty for not measuring up to impossibly high standards.[81]

---

79. Jorge Moll, Ricardo de Oliveira-Souza, Roland Zahn and Jordan Grafman, 'The Cognitive Neuroscience of Moral Emotions', in *The Neuroscience of Morality: Emotion, Brain Disorders, and Development*, edited by Walter Sinnott-Armstrong, Volume 3 of *Moral Psychology* (Cambridge, MA: MIT Press, 2008), 1–17. See the excellent summary from Rick Nauert, 'Brain Scans Show Depression's Link to Guilt', PsychCentral, accessed March 19, 2013, http://psychcentral.com/news/2008/08/26/brain-scans-show-depressions-link-to-guilt/2826.html.
80. Peteet, *Depression and the Soul*, 74.
81. H Gordon, 'Guilt: Why is it Such a Burden?' *Bishop John Robinson Fellowship*

The exaggerated guilt often experienced in depression is widely seen by psychiatrists as a distortive cognitive effect of the illness which goes away by itself when the depression is effectively treated, without attempts to resolve or reconcile the past actions or events that are believed to have caused the guilty feelings. There is therefore a strong supposition among psychiatrists that depression-related guilt is really an effect of the illness itself, and that attempts to deal with it through confession or counselling are beside the point.[82]

However, despite depression-related guilt often being associated with the medical pathology of the illness, these guilt feelings are sometimes also related to real relationships, events and misdeeds, and have a real basis in experiential reality. As Swinton points out, this means that the guilt experienced by depressive persons also needs to be taken seriously and respected, not merely diagnosed or treated as pathological. While a depressive person's guilt may well be distorted by their illness, it cannot be reduced merely to that, any more than the person herself can be reduced to her illness.

The medical literature on this issue of guilt and forgiveness in depression shows that, despite voices calling for greater spiritual awareness, the empiricist-positivist mindset of medical science is still dismissive of the spiritual realities involved.[83] Until a more open and inclusive theoretical model for integrating medical science with theology and spirituality can be developed, these difficulties seem insoluble.[84]

Clinical Models of Forgiveness?

Comparing the theology of forgiveness and justification in Luther's letters with therapeutic understandings of guilt and forgiveness in psychiatric practice once again highlights their fundamentally different orientation.

Newsletter 9 (February/March 2000): 4–6. The author identifies that depressive people often feel not only guilt over real misdeeds or moral failures on their part (transgression guilt), but also over forms of guilt that are unreasonable and more indicative of personal shame (perfection guilt and rejection guilt). See also Swinton, *Spirituality and Mental Health Care*, 162.

82. Peteet, *Depression and the Soul*, 58.
83. Swinton, *Spirituality and Mental Health Care*, 162.
84. Peteet, *Depression and the Soul*, 193.

As one would expect, almost all the research and writing on the area of guilt and forgiveness in the medical science community concentrates on its lateral human dimension: forgiving others' misdeeds and being forgiven by other people for one's own.[85] There is undoubtedly a 'spiritual' dimension in this, which is of great significance, particularly for the healing of persons through relationship. Our spiritual life does after all include our standing in relation with one another. However, for Luther (and for many contemporary Christian theologians) this misses the core of the issue, which is how humans stand *before* God, not just temporally but also eschatologically. It is our guilt before God and our reception of forgiveness through Jesus Christ by faith (our justification) that are of ultimate importance for healing and the restoration of hope.

While many Christian psychiatrists may be quite comfortable with such a theological understanding of forgiveness, it still pushes well beyond the boundaries of spirituality that can be formally accepted in the field of medical science research. While Koenig,[86] Peteet[87] and others in the psychiatric field are able to acknowledge spirituality on the human experiential level (which remains well within empirical limits), it is a different matter to reach beyond the scientific empiricist paradigm to discuss justification as an objective spiritual reality.[88]

For Luther, forgiveness is not a psychological or emotional effect, or a form of 'positive religious coping'.[89] Its benefits include–but also

---

85. Peteet, *Depression and the Soul*, 56–7. See also Loren Toussaint and Jon R Webb, 'Theoretical and Empirical Connections Between Forgiveness, Mental Health, and Well-Being', in *Handbook of Forgiveness*, edited by Everett L Worthington (New York: Routledge, 2005), 349–62. See also 'Forgiveness: Letting Go of Grudges and Bitterness', Mayo Clinic, accessed July 10, 2012, http://www.mayoclinic.com/health/forgiveness/MH00131.
86. Harold G Koenig, Michael E McCullough and David B Larson, *Handbook of Religion and Health* (New York: Oxford University Press, 2001), 118–35.
87. Peteet, *Depression and the Soul*, 29–63.
88. There are underlying layers to this discussion. While John Peteet's integrated perspective on medical science and spirituality does genuinely reach out a hand beyond naturalistic medical empiricism, the discussion is still ultimately determined by what can be known and shown on the empirical level, i.e. the self, humanity, human effects, human society, etc. The discussion is therefore locked into a '*von unten*' scientific frame of reference.
89. Koenig, McCullough and Larson, *Handbook of Religion and Health*, 129–31.

reach beyond–immediate wellbeing, because it is a spiritual reality that profoundly alters the individual's being and identity forever, by altering his relation to the triune God.

It may be for this reason that medical writers who deal with forgiveness are seldom able to let forgiveness itself stand alone as an active agent. Forgiveness seems always to be seen as *instrumental*; a step towards what will *really* help: building positive virtues, strong confidence, and so on.[90] It is used as a means for the patient's return to full and productive functioning. Its place in medical thinking about depression depends on its measurable therapeutic effect.[91]

For Luther, forgiveness is itself not just a means of recovery to full health, but resurrection from death to life. It is a gift which, in being received, not only increases our wellbeing but transforms our *whole-being*. It has power to heal and, moreover, to *save* body and soul.[92]

Guilt and Forgiveness in Psychotherapy

If justification is, as Luther said, the article on which the church stands or falls,[93] then its encounter with contemporary psychology here is a particularly crucial juncture. If psychology is left to play the leading role here, as it was in the 1960s when Carl Rogers' 'client centred therapy' became the preferred model for Christian pastoral counselling, the issues of sin, guilt and forgiveness are inevitably reduced to fit within the rationalist empirical boundaries of human science. Justification of sinners by grace is replaced by self-acceptance in one form or another.[94] As Erickson puts it, this amounts

---

90. Peteet, *Depression and the Soul*, 90–1.
91. Swinton, *Spirituality and Mental Health Care*, 84–5, speaks about the flawed assumption inherent in most medical scientific discourses on spirituality and faith: that God can only be *functionally* present, and that it is actually the *belief itself* that is significant in the context of the patient's mental health. Swinton makes the point that reality includes not only the empirical, but also the super-empirical which cannot be measured and quantified by conventional closed empirical methods of inquiry.
92. From Luther's point of view, today's medical approach to guilt and forgiveness is nothing but 'the law dressed up as Gospel—in other words, a means by which people ultimately seek to save and heal themselves by self-improvement.
93. Luther expressed this thought in different words in various places, most notably in his comments on Psalm 130:6 in his *Commentary on the Psalms* of 1532–1533: '*quia isto articulo stante stat Ecclesia, ruente ruit Ecclesia*' (WA XL iii, 352:3).
94. Tillich attempted this, translating justification into the modern therapeutic

to 'justification by self-esteem'[95] and ultimately to an inversion of Jesus' parable of the Pharisee and the tax collector, in which self-esteem and not God's grace wins the day.[96] Sin is characterised as the outcome of psychological damage, and guilt is displaced, discounted or denied. Once established as a 'victim', one may be absolved of guilt and responsibility. Justification becomes a process of human psychological self-reconciliation, in which God's approval is an added confirmation of what is really important: that one forgives, values and loves oneself.[97]

In Luther's theology, justification by grace is proclaimed as a word from *outside* this naturalistic framework. It does what no human helping is able to do: forgive sins. Robert Coles relates a fascinating story of how psychoanalyst, Anna Freud, once came to see this very point herself in the course of treating a patient, commenting:

> I thought to myself that this poor lady doesn't need us at all. No, she's had her fill of 'us', even if she doesn't know it... What she needs, I thought, is forgiveness. She needs to make peace with her soul, not talk about her mind. There must be a God somewhere to help her, to hear her, to heal her.[98]

At this point let us turn the tables and consider the opposite arrangement, in which *theology plays the leading role* in this encounter. If we change the order, bringing contemporary psychology together with Luther's justification theology within his larger *theological* frame

---

concept, 'acceptability'. See C FitzSimons Allison, 'Pastoral Care in the Light of Justification by Faith Alone', in *By Faith Alone: Essays on Justification in Honor of Gerhard O Forde*, edited by Joseph A Burgess and Marc Kolden (Grand Rapids: Eerdmans, 2004), 309.

95. Richard C Erickson, 'The Psychology of Self-Esteem: Promise or Peril?' in *Pastoral Psychology*, 35/3 (Spring 1987): 163-71.
96. Allison, 'Pastoral Care in the Light of Justification by Faith Alone', 310-11.
97. In 1972, Psychiatrist Karl Menninger wrote his famous work, *Whatever Became of Sin?* (Stroud: Hawthorn Books, 1973), a now old, but still very insightful, critique of psychology as a conceptual framework for issues of sin and morality. See also Beverly Yahnke, 'Christian Psychology and Spiritual Care: Approaches to Ministerial Health', (paper presented at the Midwest Ministerial Health Conference, October 1, 1998), 8-10, accessed November 2012, http://www.mtio.com/articles/aissar43.htm.
98. Robert Coles, *Harvard Diary: Reflections on the Sacred and the Secular* (New York: Crossroad, 1988), 180.

of reference, their meeting is far more fruitful. This arrangement allows us to incorporate insights and methods from psychology in a way that enhances our understanding of Luther, and helps us to harvest his theological wisdom at a practical level for the comfort and care of depressed persons. Alexis Trader demonstrates this model of integration comprehensively in his close study of the spiritual care of the fathers of the early church, drawing on insights from Aaron Beck's cognitive therapy.[99] He shows that when psychological insights are used selectively and strategically, they become valuable bridges between our theological tradition and contemporary practice. In the case of Luther's counsels for depression, there are at least two such valuable bridging possibilities from modern psychotherapy which emerge.

Justification and Metacognition

As we noted earlier, Luther enacted his teaching of justification by grace in his pastoral letters through his *metacognitive* use of God's gracious justification of the sinner, apart from good works, and most importantly of all, apart from the guilty feelings, perceptions and thoughts of his depressed readers. He uses the external *forensic* word of justification, which is true and valid whatever the individual experiences, as a solid 'mooring post' of spiritual reality, in order to help his readers challenge their own thinking. He wrote to George Spalatin, a man depressed and tortured with guilt after a humiliating error of pastoral judgement: 'Do you really think that in your case alone the Lord's hand is shortened?'[100] Or has the Lord in your case alone ceased to be merciful?'[101]

What Luther is doing is what Siang-Yang Tan describes in his suggestions for using CT with Christians today:[102] helping his friend critique his own perceptions and beliefs by holding them up next to the light of an external objective reality. However, while Luther's metacognitive method depends on this very objectivity and externality of what *God* says and has promised *extra nos*, its

---

99. Alexis Trader, *Ancient Christian Wisdom and Aaron Beck's Cognitive Therapy: A Meetings of Minds* (New York: Peter Lang, 2011).
100. Isa 59:1.
101. *Letter to George Spalatin,* August 21 1544 (See Appendix).
102. Tan, *Counseling and Psychotherapy,* 274–76.

point is that this external objective justification become an internal, subjective cognitive–affective experience for the addressee, if it is to bring comfort.

Building Justification Narratives

The second bridging connection we find between Luther's justification theology and modern psychology and counselling is the use of *narrative* recasting. As we will explore more fully later in this chapter, in some of his letters Luther draws his readers into the unfolding of the eschatological *Heilsgeschichte* of the biblical narrative. As he challenges and recasts the story of George Spalatin's terrible fall from grace (to use the example mentioned above), he draws Spalatin into the story of Israel, fusing time and narrative together so that the reader has the sense of the biblical story playing out in the present, with a cast of characters drawn from various moments in history.[103]

As contemporary psychology is recognising, narrative methods have great potential for helping depressed persons. Ray Galvin's story of Franz, to which we referred earlier, illustrates the point. Franz (who happened to have a Lutheran background) had an underlying grasp of the Christian teaching on sin, grace and justification which enabled him to re-author his story of sin and condemnation via the Christ-story, so that he could *appropriate and experience* justification.[104]

This Christian use of narrative therapy opens up pathways through which depressive people can learn to re-author their stories of sin, guilt and condemnation, by fusing them with Christ's story of death and resurrection, in order to build 'justification narratives'. Or, to express it in more accurate theological terms, as we are transformed into Christ's image it is actually the Spirit who re-authors the stories of our lives, by providing us with the experiential wisdom[105] to see ourselves in terms of God's judgement and promise, as those made right with him.[106] Lois Malcolm and Janet Ramsey explore this in

---

103. Robert Kolb observes the same fusing of time and narrative in Luther's other works, particularly his sermons. See Robert Kolb, *Luther and the Stories of God: Biblical Narratives as a Foundation for Christian Living* (Grand Rapids: Baker Academic, 2012), 29–33.
104. Galvin, 'Narrative Therapy and Pastoral Ministry', 165–67.
105. Oswald Bayer, *Martin Luther's Theology: A Contemporary Interpretation*, translated by Thomas H Trapp (Grand Rapids: Eerdmans, 2003), 21.
106. Janet L Ramsey and Lois E Malcolm, 'On Forgiveness and Healing: Narrative Therapy and the Gospel Story', in *Word & World*, 30/1 (Winter 2010): 31.

some depth, offering insights on how narrative therapy focussing on forgiveness and healing can use the Gospel stories. Through justification, God provides us with a radically different future–an alternative story in which this Triune God is the protagonist whose own plotline becomes ours.

Justification in Contemporary Theology and Pastoral Care

How Luther's consolation of justification gels with the human sciences is, however, only one of the issues to be worked through. There is the question of whether contemporary theology still affirms the Reformation's teaching of justification by grace as a means of comfort. Do depressed people still frame their deep struggles and fears in terms of guilt and terror before God's wrath? Does Luther's sixteenth century understanding of the melancholy 'terrified conscience' coincide with the experience of depressed persons today?

The teaching of justification by grace through faith has historically stirred up controversy and debate, just as it did in Luther's day and is doing now. It has a history of upsetting the homeostasis.[107] Theology's work of reviewing and restating the church's teaching in new generations has gone on for centuries and continues today. Because of its central place in the teaching and life of Christians, the doctrine of justification will always be part of this ferment. We cannot take time and space in this study to do much more than acknowledge these movements, and note the importance of the current conversations.[108]

The question remains, however, of how justification by faith is received and understood among contemporary Christians and in society generally. Paul Tillich wrote in 1950 that the teaching of

---

107. Allison, 'Pastoral Care in the Light of Justification by Faith Alone', 305–14.
108. Besides the debate between John Piper and NT Wright on the interpretation of St Paul's writing on justification, there has also been lively discussion about the 'Finnish school of Luther research', which draws out the dimension of 'Christ present in faith' in Luther's teaching, and explores faith in Christ as *theosis*. In 1999 the doctrine of justification became the topic of controversy, once again, when the *Joint declaration on Justification* was signed by the Roman Catholic Church and Lutheran Church bodies around the world (including the Lutheran Church of Australia). This has variously been both enthusiastically welcomed and vehemently condemned. Besides all this, over the last thirty years theologians have proposed various modern and post-modern interpretations of Luther's doctrine, seeking to explicate the truth of justification by faith for the church's changing post-enlightenment context.

justification by faith is 'so strange to the modern man that there is scarcely any way of making it intelligible to him'.[109] He considered that even then, before secularism had reached the peak of its influence in western culture, the biblical teachings of sin, law, grace and justification had already slipped, almost irretrievably. The outworking of this has continued. For one thing, we see how many Christians today have lost their view of the eschatological horizon. They no longer think of *eternal hope* but of 'my best life now' as the key to their destiny and meaning.[110] Psychology's humanistic influence on some schools of pastoral theology has reshaped justification as *self-realisation*. Erickson suggests that today religion's legitimate function—its 'doctrine of justification'—is considered to be affirming the value and worth of persons by enhancing their self-esteem, quality of life and human dignity.[111]

Luther's teaching of justification by faith comes as a jagged and jarring word that upsets this human spiritual edifice. It is not just unintelligible, but offensive.[112] It deconstructs human spirituality and self-confidence; it points to the shattering diagnosis of the law which brands all human sufficiency as filthy rags, before declaring the gift of Christ's death for our sins and his resurrection for our complete justification.

Theodor Dieter insightfully observes that much popular Christian spirituality today shows no understanding of Luther's teaching: that in justifying us freely by grace, God has effected our complete and radical deliverance from the comprehensive, overwhelming and impossible demands of the law, and so has brought us out of one realm and into another. This does not accord with today's belief in the sufficiency and autonomy of persons, and so justification by faith is understood by many as 'recasting the law's demands for the purpose of a more tolerable life'.[113]

Yet, despite its incompatibility with contemporary culture, the biblical teaching of justification remains, and 'stubbornly continues

---

109. Allison. 'Pastoral Care in the Light of Justification by Faith Alone', 307.
110. Allison. 'Pastoral Care in the Light of Justification by Faith Alone', 306.
111. Erickson, 'The Psychology of Self-Esteem', 163-71.
112. Allison, 'Pastoral Care in the Light of Justification by Faith Alone', 305.
113. Theodor Dieter, 'Why Does Luther's Doctrine of Justification Matter Today?' in *The Global Luther, A Theologian for Modern Times*, edited by Christine Helmer (Minneapolis: Fortress, 2009), 195.

to occupy its seat' in the church and the world. Mark Mattes observes that human beings are still spiritually homesick and hungry for the deep legitimation and '*righ*teousness' that can only be *given* by him who created them for *him*self. Why else do they spend their lives seeking, working and striving to *justify* their lives by other means? While human beings remain so, the question of one's ultimate justification can never be irrelevant: 'In this regard, the problem is not an absence of anxious consciences . . . but rather that people fail to discern and critique the idols by which they justify themselves'.[114]

Tillich, who early on recognised the growing incongruity of Luther's justification teaching in modernist culture, noted that it nevertheless remains the irreducible substance of Christian faith, and that efforts to 'modernise' it by substituting different concepts, constructions or language that may speak to new generations, fail to convey its truth.[115] It corresponds to and aligns the human soul with another great 'irreducible', the first commandment, which shows us that we may find our identity, purpose, destiny and justification in no other god.

This leads us to recognise that the deep human sickness of sin and guilt is still there, under the surface, even if it is unnamed and unacknowledged.[116] Mattes points out that people's unawareness that they are experiencing the effects of the law does not mean that they are unaffected by them. True, it no longer expresses itself today predominantly in theological terms, as guilt produced by sin against God and others. It has instead found expression in the explosion of psychological and mental health syndromes and disorders we have experienced in the west over the last half century, the most widespread and common of which is depression.[117]

---

114. Mark C Mattes, *The Role of Justification in Contemporary Theology* (Grand Rapids: Eerdmans 2004), 182.
115. Paul Tillich, *The Shaking of the Foundations* (New York: Scribner's, 1950), 153.
116. Allison, 'Pastoral Care in the Light of Justification by Faith Alone', 314.
117. This analysis is shared by many psychological therapists and expressed from many different perspectives. Dorothy Rowe speaks about the deep relationship between depression and the human search for rightness and correctness. See Dorothy Rowe, 'Depression's Punitive Conscience', *the guardian*, November 12, 2009, accessed October 2013, http://www.theguardian.com/commentisfree/2009/nov/12/robert-enke-depression-suicide.Jungian psychotherapists, Nancy Carter Pennington and Lawrence H Staples, *The Guilt Cure* (Carmel: Fisher King Press, 2011), propose that unaddressed guilt, which

As noted in Swinton's research, one of the unexpected spiritual effects of depression is that it may allow the sufferer to see spiritual reality with a new and shocking simplicity and clarity.[118] In pastoral conversation with such a person on one occasion, in which we were talking about prayer, she began to reflect on her illness's spiritual aspects, and commented, 'I am grateful for one thing. Depression has taught me how powerless I actually am and how totally dependent I am on God'. A successful professional who had experienced depression as a debilitating sickness with physical as well as psychological effects, she had been stripped of all her personal power, independence and competency. Her means of self-justification–her achievements and skills, assumptions of personal autonomy and spiritual self-sufficiency–had been melted away and she became aware, as never before, of her need of God's grace.

Depression's 'Punitive Conscience'

While psychiatric science identifies the symptom of *pathological guilt* simply as an effect of depression, other scientists view it more existentially. Echoing Luther's much earlier insights, British psychotherapist, Dorothy Rowe, describes depression's gravest danger as its 'punitive conscience'.[119] As in Luther's day, depressed persons today are often fixated on their guilt and may interpret their suffering as punishment for their sins or misdeeds, if not from an angry God then from a malevolent fate. Today the stricken conscience has not, as some commentators claim, disappeared or been superseded, but has been *internalised and privatised*. In a culture where the self is constructed *in, by and for the individual* rather than *in, with and for the community*, the conscience is hidden in the private interior world of the sufferer and not expressed or externalised in the process of confession, as it may have been in earlier and less secularised eras.

In today's secular environment, this punitive conscience is a dangerous and destructive force in the life of a depression sufferer. It is oriented inwards and 'stands before itself' instead of 'before God'. It may no longer dread and secretly hate this righteous God, but

---

no longer has any means of resolution or expiation through spiritual means, lies behind many mental health issues today.
118. Swinton, *Spirituality and Mental Health Care*, 122–23
119. Rowe, 'Depression's Punitive Conscience'.

dreads and secretly hates itself. In depression the punitive conscience becomes its own relentless and wrathful deity, condemning and damning itself through self-loathing, anxiety, self-sabotage and the negative misappropriation of all circumstances and encounters. It may finally reject itself utterly. This private hell of the depressed conscience, where the sufferer has become judge and jury, may also lead it to take on the role of executioner, who enacts this ultimate self-rejection in suicide. It is not hard to see how depression has sometimes been understood as a form of destructive self-idolatry in which the self assumes God's place, meeting out wrath, condemnation and death.

Justification as Comfort for the Depressed

Though alien to some contemporary western sensibilities, Luther's justification teaching has an experiential dynamic which makes it very practical in addressing depression at a personal spiritual level in pastoral care. As we observed earlier, it is comprised of a dialectic which spans and unifies the *inner-subjective* and *outer-objective* aspects of human experience; the two dimensions which are frequently dualised so that they remain in sterile conflict.[120]

On the one hand, it places to the fore God's 'alien righteousness', 'imputed' or given from without. This enables depressive persons to fix onto the external anchor of God's declared attitude of grace and forgiveness, and his gift of his own righteousness which makes sinners right before him. For depressed persons, who are so frequently locked into their own spiralling self-negativity and guilt, this shifts the focus of attention to the counterpoint of God's promises and assurance of unconditional acceptance in Christ.

On the other hand, the teaching of justification by grace, though depending completely on God's external objective work of justification in Christ, is deeply experiential, touching the depressed person's inner

---

120. This is frequently the experience of depression sufferers with current models of medical treatment. Their *profound inner experience* of depression is all but ignored, and their treatment is based heavily on the external and objective elements of their illness. See Swinton, *Spirituality and Mental Health Care*, 49–54.

cognitive and affective faculties. It unfolds into a comprehensive life–reality.[121]

This is Luther's 'theology of the heart' in action; the *verbum externum* is received as experience in the believer's inmost core. Using the words of scripture and scriptural images, Luther anchors his consolations in the unchanging reality of God's objective external promises, but there can be no belief without also 'feeling it in the heart'.[122] Knowing about one's salvation as an outward reality is only one half of it. This is why Luther uses such powerfully affective and tender language in his comfort of the depressed, taking advantage of images and metaphors to bring home the power and beauty of God's grace.

Learning the 'Language of the Heart'

This dialectic joins the outer reality of God's grace with the inner reality of a person's feelings and thoughts, breaking the bondage of despair. This is Luther's unique gift for our practice of pastoral care of depressed persons today. The task that comes with it is the same kind of *close attention* and care which Luther exercised in choosing the right way to express and convey God's mercy and grace to his diverse addressees. As we observed earlier, we too need to find the right rhetorical *dispositio*, the right approach that will enable us to speak the heart–language of those suffering with depression today. It will not be the language of power 'from above' that was appropriate to Luther's era, but the 'from alongside' language of vulnerability. This pastoral heart–language must go much farther than the 'head–language' spoken by the medical profession, in which the illness is reduced to its biological materiality and the *person* (as a soul) is largely ignored. It must reflect the external truth of God's radical justifying grace in a way that reaches both *intellectus* and *affectus*. This will of course be attuned differently for different contexts and persons, and require sensitivity, discernment and deep listening.

---

121. Richard C Eyer, *Pastoral Care Under the Cross: God in the Midst of Suffering* (St Louis: CPH, 1994), 134–35.
122. Stolt, 'Joy, Love and Trust', 6–7.

Confession and Absolution

The church's historic means for pastorally enacting and delivering the comfort of justification is the practice of confession and absolution. While Luther's letters obviously could not enact the formal process of confession and absolution, I would suggest that in many places they at least proclaim Christ's absolution, using the consolatory rhetorical *dispositio* appropriate to such pastoral letters, sharpened suitably for each reader.[123]

This raises the possibility of confession and absolution with depression sufferers today. There may sometimes be legitimate concerns with depressed persons about inadvertently drawing undue attention to their sins if they already have an over-scrupulous conscience. Care and judgement must be exercised in this regard. However, in confession and absolution there is also the opportunity to draw even greater attention to the forgiveness of God, which is directly announced to the person by name. The very externality and objectivity of confession and absolution may sometimes create one more objective spiritual anchor-point for the depressed person whose symptoms include guilt, shame and self-loathing. The words spoken by the confessor come from Christ himself, and carry a divine authority that directly challenges the depressive's inner accusing voices.

In the context of private confession, there is the opportunity for the carer to shape the words of absolution according to the needs of the individual. There is also the opportunity to pray for the person, and have pastoral conversation and counsel before and/or after the rite itself.

---

123. Many examples could be cited, but I quote here only two notable extracts. In his 1531 letter to Queen Maria of Hungary he writes, 'And if he is our gracious God, whose pledge we have, namely his son, given through baptism, the sacrament [of the Lord's Supper] and the Gospel, we should certainly not doubt, but rather rely completely on his grace, which covers everything' (See Appendix). Similarly, on Christmas Day, 1535 Luther comforts Prince Joachim on Anhalt: 'What can distress us-other, perhaps, than our sins and bad conscience? Yet Christ has taken these from us, even while we sin daily' (See Appendix).

In His Good Time: Suffering, Patience and the Cross

One of the key ingredients in Luther's consolation of the melancholy is his compassion for their pain and his understanding of this pain's spiritual dimensions and meanings. Because Luther's writing on this issue in the twenty one letters is so deeply rooted in his wider theology regarding suffering, it is important at this point to briefly sketch this background theology, in order to properly understand his approach to suffering in the letters themselves.

The view of suffering Luther expresses in these letters is the mature fruit of life-experience and long theological-pastoral reflection.[124] Unlike the philosophers and theologians of later modernity, he was not interested in *explaining* suffering or justifying God as good and loving in light of his will to allow or send suffering. Luther was not greatly attracted to rationalistic systems which satisfy human logic. He was interested rather in describing how the soul 'suffers divine things'.[125] In doing so, he was fully aware that, from the perspective of human reason, his theology had 'ragged edges'. He did not engage in speculation about why such suffering occurred, or seek to silence the voice of the sufferer by rationalising (and thus invalidating) their pain, but tried to speak honestly on the basis of scripture and the comforts offered there.[126]

---

124. Luther's theology of suffering followed a pathway of development, changing in form and orientation depending on his audience at the time. Early in his career, he began to develop it in his first lectures on the Psalms, the *Dictata super psalterium,*1513-1516 (WA III and WA IV, 1-414). It is expressed in the *Heidelberg Disputation* of 1518 (WA I, 353-374), where he developed his *theology of the cross*. We find it expressed in consolatory form in his *Fourteen Consolations* of 1520 (WA VI, 104-134), and again in the form of a disputation in the *Bondage of the Will* of 1525 (WA VIII, 600-787). Also very important is his *Sermon on Cross and Suffering* of 1530 (WA XXXII, 29-38), which expresses his theology of suffering in a simpler and more pastoral way. For a recent summary, see Ronald K Rittgers, *The Reformation of Suffering: Pastoral Theology and Lay Piety in Late Medieval and Early Modern Germany* (New York: Oxford University Press, 2012), 110-24.
125. *Luther's Marginal Notes on Tauler's Sermons*, 1516, WA IX, 97:12-14. Human beings are essentially passive (receptive) in spiritual things. Their reason and logic therefore do not play a key role in God's working.
126. 'When such trials of "why?" come, be careful that you do not answer and let these attacks take over. Rather close your eyes, slay reason and take refuge in the word of God. Do not let that "why?" come into your heart. The Devil is too

Luther's view was that while human beings obviously bring much suffering on themselves and one another, and suffer the attacks of the devil, it is ultimately God who, in his strange wisdom, allows suffering and even sends it.[127] The experience of suffering in life, including the experience of depression, often leaves people with a dark and disturbing sense of the *Deus absconditus*: God hidden. The soul finds itself left in the dark, confused and wondering why. We do not, and cannot, understand this hidden and mysterious work of God. He is acting in and through history, in our personal circumstances and in the whole of creation, in secret and veiled ways which to us may at times seem strange, dark and even disturbingly cruel. *Deus absconditus* is not available to us or our reason; this is why Luther offers no 'theodicy' to satisfy the bewilderment of those who experience suffering. To do so is in fact not only false, but dangerous.[128] As he wrote to the anxious and depressed Barbara Lißkirchen, we are not invited to delve into God's hidden counsels, but to know him as he has revealed himself to us (*Deus revelatus*)[129] in his Son, Jesus Christ and his work of salvation. Here we see disclosed God's full and ultimate will to reconcile, redeem and restore all things, including those things which here and now lie shrouded in darkness and pain.

Luther uses two different terms to describe God's hidden and revealed works: *opus alienum* (God's alien work) and *opus proprium* (God's proper work). God uses his alien work (sufferings, trials and afflictions) to accomplish his proper work (life and salvation). Suffering drives us to cry out to God, who comforts us with his promises that he will end our suffering.[130]

---

    strong, you will not be able to master it.' *Luther's Lectures on Isaiah*, 1527–1530 (WA XXXI ii, 361:20-23).

127. See Luther's *Sermon on cross and suffering*, 1530 (WA XXXII, 29-38).
128. Leonard Hummel comments, 'In the throes of various tempests we may seek safe harbour in aiming for an understanding of our suffering, but if we do so we will crash into the wrath of God hidden beneath the surface of that suffering.' See Hummel, *Clothed in Nothingness*, 29.
129. Martin Luther, *The Bondage of the Will*. WA XVIII, 684-688. Translated by E Gordon Rupp and Phillip S Watson. 'Luther: On the Bondage of the Will', in *Luther and Erasmus: Free Will and Salvation*, edited by E Gordon Rupp and Phillip S Watson (Philadelphia: Westminster Press, 1969), 200-8.
130. Luther first uses these two terms to explain God's hidden and revealed works quite early, in his *Dictata super psalterium* 1513-1515 (WA III, 246:19 & WA IV, 87:24) then subsequently in various places, to explain the Christian's

With this theological background in mind, we now turn our attention to how we find this theology expressed in the twenty-one letters. All of these letters were written after 1525, and so represent Luther's latter development as a theologian. This shows through, I suggest, not only in the theological shape of his spiritual counsel, but also in his pastoral insight and compassion as he seeks to comfort and uplift his depressed readers.[131]

Here in these letters, as in his other writings, Luther maintained a position to which many today take offence: that God not only allows but also sends suffering to the lives of people in order to bring about their ultimate blessing and redemption. In fact, according to Luther, *tentatio* (trial and affliction) is the *key* experiential ingredient of faith and its growth, and the touchstone of true theology.[132] In his letter to Prince Joachim on June 9, 1534, he writes:

> But God acts rightly in wishing Your Grace to be accustomed to suffering at this time. Therefore, Your Grace, you should be glad that God has taken you to school this once, and will teach you how to suffer a good hiding.[133] He wishes the rod to remain rod, not to make an executioner's sword of it, so that Your Grace may go on suffering the rod.[134]

He sees the young prince's suffering not only as an inevitable part of life, but as part of his spiritual formation and preparation (a point he also makes in his letters to Jerome Weller,[135] Elsa von Canitz[136] and Queen Maria of Hungary[137]).

God does not send suffering for its own sake, but as part of his larger will to bless, heal and save us, the 'working' of which is hidden from and incomprehensible to us while we suffer,[138] and may even

---

experience of suffering.
131. Mennecke-Haustein, *Luthers Trostbriefe*, 13 (footnote 15).
132. *Luther's Preface to the Wittenberg Edition of Luther's German Writings,*1539. WA 50, 660:1–16).
133. Here Luther uses a colloquial German expression: 'a good shilling's worth', meaning 'a good hiding'.
134. See Appendix.
135. See Appendix
136. See Appendix.
137. See Appendix.
138. Luther's understanding of this hidden working of God does not imply some

remain so for our entire earthly life. God's gifts and mercies often come to us *sub contrario* (in the form of the opposite), in what feels to us like his wrath, or perhaps, even more disturbingly, his cold disinterest.

Tentatio teaches us how to truly appreciate God's *word*, God's *time*, God's *wisdom* and God's *mercy*. In his letter of June 23, 1534 to Prince Joachim, Luther again explains how God worked for the blessing and salvation of Israel as they waited at the banks of the Red Sea, with Pharaoh's army swooping down on them. This entailed their willingness to trust God, and patiently endure despair and the immediate threat of death for a little while so that, at just the right moment, God would answer their cries and destroy Pharaoh in one stroke, thus securing Israel's freedom and safety. Humanly, we cannot see or begin to imagine God's hidden work in our lives, but with eyes of faith we see God's love and mercy at work in our trials and agonies, just as we see it at work in Christ crucified. Faith enables us to trust in Christ that what we suffer here and now, horrible as it might be, somehow hides within it the mercy and love of God.

In the midst of depressive suffering, particularly in situations where the illness is protracted, Luther encourages his readers to be prayerful, patient and trusting, thereby leaving the questions and confusion of suffering to God's loving wisdom, even in seemingly hopeless situations. Prayer needs to take on a receptive rather than a demanding attitude, confident that in ways beyond human reckoning, God is answering our cries for help. Once again, to Prince Joachim on June 23, 1534, whose severe bout of depression was dragging on, he writes that

> we truly do not know how we should pray, but he as a true Father, knows and sees how we should pray, and he acts according to this knowledge, and not according to how we pray... Therefore, Your Grace, I hold that our Lord is striving even now and indeed has it in mind to improve Your Grace's

---

kind of static 'plan' which is being inexorably unfolded through history and individual human lives. Rather, God, in his will to ultimately bless, save, and redeem, acts and responds dynamically in history and in individual lives. See Eyer, *Pastoral Care Under The Cross*, 47.

situation, and that he will help you even more powerfully, for this is what we are now asking.[139]

Luther emphasises more than once that our suffering, though unbearable *to us*, is small compared to the suffering Jesus Christ endured *for us* in order to bring us salvation and hope. To Maria of Hungary in 1531 he writes,

> but [he] tests us to see if we honour him and have courage to suffer, while he himself, though blameless, has willingly taken on himself incomprehensible suffering for our sin, and so all this is from the all-gracious heart of his father, our dear God.[140]

This puts our human agonies into perspective and shows their true meaning. They are not evidence of God's wrath or lack of care for us or his powerlessness to help. Christ suffered for us more than we can ever suffer, in order to redeem our suffering. Here and throughout these twenty-one letters to the depressed we find strong cadences of Luther's *theology of the cross*. It does not appear in its familiar *disputational* or *polemical* forms, but is expressed here in the form of *consolatory rhetoric*, highlighting the pastoral comfort of the cross: that God is most truly known by the believer through the cross of suffering, embraced and held within Christ's far greater and meritorious suffering for our sake.[141]

This is a mystery of which human reason, caught in the consuming uncertainty of earthly existence and its inevitable pain, can make no satisfying rational sense. It requires not understanding, but faith. Luther offers no theory to help align God's will with *our* understanding and sense of love and justice, since this is not within the ken of any

---

139. See Appendix.
140. See Appendix.
141. As Hans Joachim Iwand shows, this pastoral aspect of Luther's *theologia crucis* is not to be seen as a secondary or derived emphasis, but is organic to Luther's own understanding and is present in his earliest expositions, notably in his 1517 *Commentary on the Seven Penitential Psalms* (WA I, 158–220). See Hans Joachim Iwand, 'Lecture on the Theology of the Cross', [paper presented at the Beinroder Konvent in Herbst 1959), trans Aaron Moldenhauer, 2004, accessed September 2013, http://gnesiolutheran.com/lecture-on-the-theology-of-the-cross/.

human being. This is the frontier at which human reason reaches its limits.[142]

This theology did not flow out of inexperience or indifference to human suffering on Luther's part. He knew the suffering of depressive melancholy only too well, with all its horrors. He knew what it is to wonder how God can turn to good such terrible pain and agony as severe depression. He was fully aware that in such darkness, depression sufferers may find themselves confronted by a God who seems to have become their mortal enemy; who appears even to break his own word.[143]

It is in situations of severe spiritual suffering like depression, in which the believer is tempted to despair, that receiving comfort and consolation through other Christians becomes crucial.[144] God uses others to speak his words of grace and assurance to those who can no longer appropriate it themselves because they are utterly sunk in the mire of despondency. Luther himself commented that as a young monk he may have died of his deep melancholy without the comfort of his mentor, Johann von Staupitz.[145] He sees his work of comforting depression sufferers as his chance to render, as a fellow-Christian, the same service of comfort to others. The church is one body of Christ and so 'one brother is compelled to bear the burden of the other'.[146] In Luther's view, this mutual comfort among believers is not an optional ministry for those in the church who may 'feel called' or 'have gifts' in pastoral care. It is the vocation and duty (*Trostamt*) of *all* Christians, part of Christ's new command to love. It is *God's means* of care and comfort, through which *he* speaks and acts.[147] Christians never suffer

---

142. *The Bondage of the Will* (WA XVIII, 671–676). Luther points out the ultimate foolishness and futility of human reason for apprehending the eternal work of God.
143. See Luther's *Lectures on Genesis*, especially Gen 22, where he deals with God's testing of Abraham (WA XLIII, 200–270). In Luther's understanding of 'God hidden', the divine will to save and bless is hidden from the experience and understanding of the sufferer.
144. *Letter to Matthias Weller*, October 7 1534; *Letter to Jerome Weller*, August 15 1530; *Letter to Jonas von Stockhausen*, November 17 1532 (See Appendix).
145. The *Table Talk,* from November 1530 (WA TR I, No.122, 47–49) and February1533 (WA TR I, No.461, 199–201).
146. *Letter to Jerome Weller* of August 15 1530 (See Appendix).
147. This mutual consolation and conversation of the brethren flows from Luther's

alone; God gives us one another as comforters, prayer-partners and helpers.[148]

Depression and Meaning

What do the contemporary health-sciences make of Luther's view? Unlike Luther, contemporary medical science and psychology, following standard empirical scientific lines, generally regard suffering itself as intrinsically neutral and meaningless.[149] They admit that some exceptional people may turn their suffering to advantage and make it meaningful by their attitude, using their experiences to, in some way, nurture their personal growth. However, the benefit in this case is due to *their* decisions and actions, not to the suffering itself. Suffering's immediate causes may show its nature; it may be due to human error or evil. Alternately, it may come from natural and accidental causes. However, even if the immediate 'what' and 'why' of it is known, suffering itself leads to no *new or deeper insight, maturity or meaning*. It is an inherently meaningless experience with no benefit or purpose.

Viewed from this perspective, depression is therefore a particularly pernicious form of suffering. Since its causes are often mysterious and its progress is so destructive, it is experienced as agonisingly meaningless and ultimately nihilistic.[150] It was Victor Frankl who noted that it is when pain is empty and meaningless that suffering becomes intolerable, especially for post-enlightenment humans, for

---

monastic formation, the *officium consolandi*—the duty to comfort others as one has been comforted according to 2 Cor1:3-6. See Mennecke-Haustein, *Luthers Trostbriefe*, 20-2.

148. Luther's thoughts in these letters to the depressed draw considerably on the theology in his *Fourteen Consolations of 1519*, where he describes the mystery of the church as the Body of Christ: 'Therefore when I suffer, I suffer not alone, but Christ and all Christians suffer with me . . . Even so others bear my burden and their strength becomes my own. The church's faith supports my fearfulness . . . the prayer of others pleads for me . . . Who would not then rejoice in his pains? For it is not he that bears his sins and pains; or if he does bear them he does not bear them alone, but is assisted by so many holy sons of God, even by Christ himself' (WA VI, 131:15-29).
149. Yahnke, 'Christian Psychology and Spiritual Care', 10.
150. Examples from depression-autobiography abound. Perhaps most expressive of the agonising meaninglessness of depression is the famous masterpiece: William Styron, *Darkness Visible: A Memoir of Madness* (New York: Random House, 1990).

whom purpose and progress towards the future are so important.[151] This sense of existential meaninglessness is often thought to be depression's deepest dimension of suffering, and is widely regarded as its distinctive marker in our post-modern era.[152]

Like medical science, psychology holds the alleviation of human suffering as its most sacred and cherished goal, and in the last twenty years has devoted vast amounts of energy to research and development in order to provide more effective treatments to relieve the increasingly widespread suffering of depression.[153] A glimpse at the research literature shows the huge commitment of resources being made in this area, especially through initiatives like *beyondblue* and the *Black Dog Foundation*.[154]

Luther located the meaning of depressive illness in God's hidden purposes, and held out hope to sufferers on the basis of divine promises of help and relief. For him, depression calls the Christian into the exercise of faith and hope, and deeper still into the *tentatio* by which faith and hope are strengthened and confirmed as the believer is conformed to Christ. Contemporary psychology on the other hand, locates meaning in the *human* quest to improve the quality of life, by learning how to better avoid and remedy suffering of all kinds, including the psychological suffering of depression. This quest is intensified by the underlying assumption that suffering is especially intolerable because life in this world is 'all there is' and that there is no eschatological horizon beyond it.

Positive Psychology and Depressive Suffering

Not all contemporary psychology, however, takes such a dim view of depressive suffering. The *positive psychology* school, moving away

---

151. It is noticeable how frequently and easily suffering comes to be identified as, in itself, 'evil' in this positivist world view: suffering is seen as the worst thing that can happen to one and must be avoided at all costs. See Scott M Peck, *The Road Less Traveled: A New Psychology of Love, Traditional Values and Spiritual Growth* (New York: Touchstone, 1978).
152. John Swinton's research into spirituality and depression identifies this deep sense of hopelessness and meaninglessness as central to depression as a spiritual experience. See Swinton, *Spirituality and Mental Health Care*, 95–6.
153. The scholarly work that periodically publishes and summarises this astounding body of research is Gotlib and Hammen, *Handbook of Depression*.
154. See *beyondblue*'s comprehensive online resources. The *Black Dog Institute* website is similarly impressive.

from the deficit-solution paradigm that has shaped most traditional forms of psychotherapy, adopts a more accepting and attentive stance towards suffering, as a potentially *productive* force for change and growth. Seligman views depressive and other psychological illness as suffering to be endured and learned from for the sake of 'the flourishing life'.[155]

Positive psychology sees suffering as an aspect of human life that can be managed but not eliminated. It serves the function of helping human beings to build stronger character by developing positive habits, values and virtues. James Davies develops this approach by proposing that suffering is a natural and essential part of the human journey of personal growth that provides moments of reflection and redirection. Depression is one such experience; an urgent call to stop and review what is happening in life and discern a new way forward.[156] It is not a sickness to be anaesthetised, but a healthy call to change-an encounter to be engaged relationally for the sake of growth towards wholeness.[157]

These positive psychological views of suffering as 'productive' are closer to Luther's understanding inasmuch as they allow the experience of suffering room in the human life. However, they still see suffering as a means to greater subjective wellbeing, to be *used* for human ends and judged by human criteria. The acceptance of suffering is based on its production of meaning through self-improvement and growth.

'Christian Psychology' and Depressive Suffering

It is interesting to discover that a body of current Christian psychological opinion supports Luther's view that God's will

---

155. Martin EP Seligman, *Flourish: A Visionary New Understanding of Happiness and Well-being* (New York: Free Press, 2011), 78–96. Seligman has contributed greatly to new movements in education in which resiliency and the ability to overcome negative experience and emotions are taught in schools. He relates his part in setting up a new wellbeing initiative at Geelong Grammar School (Victoria) in 2005, which many Australian scholars have now imitated.
156. James Davies, *The Importance of Suffering: The Value and Meaning of Emotional Discontent* (Hove: Routledge, 2012), 2, 100–05, 139–43.
157. Positive psychological approaches to depressive illness have been influenced by emerging *evolutionary* theories about depression as part of the dynamics of human survival. See Randolph M Nesse, 'Is Depression an Adaptation?', in *Archives of General Psychiatry*, 57/1 (January 2000): 14–20.

encompasses suffering as a means to ultimately bless and redeem the believer. In addition to this wider general picture, the two recent comprehensive works on Christian psychotherapy which we used earlier as exemplars also support this view.[158]

Unlike Luther, however, contemporary Christian psychological writers tend to place their emphasis on God passively *allowing* rather than actively *sending* suffering as a means for his people to grow in faith.[159] The point of difference is that whereas Luther draws attention to the fact that God is intentionally working *through* the depressive suffering of his addressees, contemporary writers' views are framed more as responses to the searching theodic questions which are commonly asked today: Why is this happening to me? Why is God allowing me to go through such pain?

This reflects the distance between Luther's world and ours, and shows how different our post-modern image of God is to his. Our assumption today tends to be that God is good, loving and powerful *on our terms* rather than his. As we will see later in this reflection, this is no small cultural difference that has come with the passing of time, requiring some adjustment of language. It indicates a profound theological shift, which requires deeper consideration.

However, some psychological models are more compatible with Luther's theology. As in previous reflections, Ray Galvin's writing on the use of *narrative discourse* with Christian depressive clients suggests fresh possibilities for learning from Luther's views on suffering, and fruitfully adapting his approaches to the contemporary context.[160]

Luther knew how narrative has the ability to help the counsellor avoid the propositional 'deadlocks' that arise in rationally oriented models in order to create room for growth and movement. From the pastoral *argumentatio* in his letter to Prince Joachim of June 23 1534,[161] we see how Luther is coaching the prince on how to 're-author' *his* suffering story within the wider framework of God's gracious purposes instead of the narrow framework of his individual depressive isolation.

---

158. McMinn and Campbell, *Integrative Psychotherapy*, 48–51, 311. See also Tan, *Counseling and Psychotherapy*, 331–33.
159. Tan, *Counselling and Psychotherapy*, 330–32.
160. Galvin, 'Narrative Therapy in Pastoral Ministry', 144–64.
161. See Appendix.

Intentional narrative strategies utilising biblical narratives in the re-authoring of clients' depressive stories offers a rich range of possibilities. Biblical suffering narratives and the characters that drive them carry what NT Wright calls the 'authority of story' which invites us to discover our own journey within the unfolding truth of the divine drama.[162]

Utopian Expectations and Depression

Obviously, Luther's *theological* views on suffering and God's work through it are not widely accepted in a predominantly secular western culture like Australia. Nevertheless a comparison of Luther's pre-enlightenment social and cultural paradigm with ours is revealing. The society in which he lived was far more accepting of suffering than ours. Depressive melancholy was common and on the increase in early Renaissance Germany, as were the plague, poverty, political turmoil, civil unrest and religious uncertainty.[163] Odo Marquard observes that in such contexts, where suffering is severe and inevitable, people tend to accept it and get on with the struggle of living. It is to some degree thus normalised so that theodic questions about how God could allow such suffering tend not to arise.[164]

Post-enlightenment western societies have taken on very different thinking and expectations in this regard. The individual has become the 'prime unit', leading to an emphasis on personal happiness and self-fulfilment as an achievable goal.[165] Achieving and keeping this *happiness* has become life's prime concern, to the point of its attaining the status of a 'right'.[166]

---

162. Nicholas Thomas Wright, 'How Can the Bible Be Authoritative?', in *Vox Evangelica* 21 (1991): 7-32, accessed October 2013, http://www.biblicalstudies.org.uk/pdf/vox/vol21/bible_wright.pdf.
163. Andrew Pettegree, 'Time and Space: Living in Sixteenth-century Europe'" In *Europe in the Sixteenth Century* (Oxford: Blackwell, 2002), 1-11, accessed March 22, 2013, http://www.blackwellpublishing.com/content/BPL_Images/Content_store/Sample_chapter/978063_207016/pettegree.pdf.
164. Odo Marquard, 'Unburdenings: Theodicy Motives in Modern Philosophy', in *In Defense of the Accidental: Philosophical Studies*, translated by Robert M Wallace (New York: Oxford University Press, 1991), 8-28.
165. John Swinton, *Raging with Compassion: Pastoral Responses to the Problem of Evil* (Grand Rapids: Eerdmans, 2007), 38.
166. The United States Declaration of Independence of 1776, drafted in the midst of enlightenment idealism about human dignity and human rights, maintains

Swinton points out that one of the influences which has contributed greatly to this thinking is the astounding success of medical science over the last century. Medicine has found effective treatments for so many of the world's serious illnesses, and alleviated so much physical suffering that an expectation has been created that suffering should no longer be part-at least not a significant or long-lasting part-of our experience.[167] This expectation is one of the social factors that has driven the boom in the prescription of antidepressant and other psychotropic drugs since they became more widely available in the years following the second world war. Faith in the power of antidepressant medication as a means of life-stability and wellbeing still persists.[168]

In societies which harbour such utopian expectations of pain-free living, suffering is seen as the first and foremost threat to happiness and is considered intolerable. When suffering is prolonged, particularly in situations where another party is thought 'responsible' for it, people frequently feel a sense of outrage and injustice. Deprived of the level of wellbeing to which they feel entitled, they consider that they are being robbed of life itself. Reality of course is that they are surrounded by others who are also suffering, and who are, like them, missing out on 'a happy life'.[169]

Whatever objections may be raised to Luther's theological views of suffering by contemporary secular culture, the *realism* of his sixteenth century vision of life is certainly still compelling today, and provides a telling critique of the utopian dream. He had no illusions about the inbuilt tragedy of fallen human existence and he knew that the painful suffering of depression is a common experience of the inner darkness shared by all humanity. His view finds agreement among more than

---

that all people have certain inalienable rights: life, liberty and the pursuit of happiness. As the US's cultural influence in the West has grown over the last century, so has this fundamental expectation of a happy life.
167. Swinton, *Raging with Compassion*, 38.
168. David Healy, *The Antidepressant Era* (Cambridge: Harvard University Press, 1997).
169. Nancy Colier, 'The Myth of Happiness and Why it Makes Us Un-Happy', *Psychology Today*, September 18, 2012, accessed February 10, 2013, http://www.psychologytoday.com/blog/inviting-monkey-tea/201209/the-myth-happiness-and-why-it-makes-us-un-happy.

one contemporary social-cultural commentator. Eric G Wilson[170] and Darian Leader[171] point out the falseness and unsustainability of the West's dream of happiness, and the craziness of thinking that life will not, at some point, disappoint or depress us as we experience loss, pain or difficulty.

Wilson in particular questions the assumption that depression and melancholy should be viewed as abnormal forms of suffering at all. Throughout history they seem rather to have been part of the mainstream of human experience.[172]

Contemporary Pastoral Theology and Depressive Suffering

As Luther's pastoral consolations for the suffering are considered in the light of contemporary theology, the obvious emergent issue is the question of suffering and God's will. For depression sufferers who frequently experience spiritual struggles, this is a crucial issue. How are we to understand the reality of our suffering, especially depressive suffering with its sense of meaninglessness and despair, within the framework of Christian teaching about God's love? This theological question is unavoidable at this point of the reflection because Luther's pastoral comfort in the twenty-one letters depends on and reflects a particular theological view of this question which is highly controversial both at the 'theoretical' and practical levels.

Luther's teaching about suffering in the Christian life, as summarised briefly above, is as theologically challenging and contentious today as it was in his own lifetime. As we address ourselves to it, it is therefore necessary to understand it clearly for what it is before we see how it stands in today's theological discussion. An important beginning point is that, despite claims that Luther's view of suffering amounts to a theodicy,[173] it is not, at least not in any modern sense.[174]

---

170. Eric G Wilson, *Against Happiness: In Praise of Melancholy* (New York: Sarah Crichton Books, 2008).
171. Leader, *The New Black*.
172. Wilson, *Against Happiness*, 38–57.
173. David Ray Griffin, *God Power, and Evil: A Process Theodicy* (Louisville: Westminster John Knox, 2004), 101–15. See also Thomas Adams, 'Luther's Two Theodicies'. *Without Authority*, January 20 2007, accessed May 20, 2012, http://woauthority.blogspot.com.au/2007/01/luthers-two-theodicies.html.
174. Some theologians have used the word theodicy in a 'pre-modern' sense to describe the acceptance of suffering in view of God's love, as, for instance, in

More precisely, theodicy was the intellectual enterprise first launched by Leibniz in the nineteenth century.[175] It postdates Luther and is conducted along a different 'set of tracks' altogether. Luther's theology is not offering a rationalist or functional system that harmonises and explains conflicting factors, but is deeply experiential and pastoral in its concerns, especially as it is applied to the lives of people suffering spiritual trials such as depressive melancholy. It is *Seelsorge* and is inclusive of the whole person–intellect together with the conscience and the affects. Lastly and most importantly, it must be noted that Luther was not trying to justify or defend God against charges that he is unloving or unjust. Any such project is beyond human reason, a 'theology of glory'.[176]

'Deus Domesticus'?

Luther's view of the role of suffering in the life of the Christian could be said to be the complete opposite of a theodicy. He believes that God uses suffering and even evil to accomplish his good purposes in the world.

This is quite offensive to the ears of many modern and postmodern Christians. A God who sends suffering? A God whose will it is that I go through cancer or grief or depression? For my *good*? To propose this is heresy for many contemporary theologians.[177] Today, it is said, we must present to the world the God of love, and leave behind the dark wrathful deity of Luther's world. We must show that this God is as enlightened as we are if he is to be acceptable to us and to future generations. It could be said that Luther's *Deus absconditus* and *Deus revelatus* are today supplanted by a *Deus domesticus*–our 'household God', tamed, domesticated and 'correct' in every way.

Repudiating this false spirituality, Kenneth Leech reflects on why only the 'God who is God' is of help to the depressed:

---

    the book of Job or in Rm 8.
175. Gottfried Wilhelm Leibniz, *Theodicy* (Chicago: Open Court, 1998).
176. Robert Kolb and Charles P Arand, *The Genius of Luther's Theology: A Wittenberg Way of Thinking for the Contemporary Church* (Grand Rapids: Baker Academic, 2008), 121.
177. John Swinton, while finding some aspects of Luther's theology of suffering appealing is, like many contemporary theologians, finally unable to accept his position on God's use of suffering for good. He in fact finds any such suggestion offensive. See Swinton, *Raging with Compassion*, 20-1.

> One of the central features in the understanding of God in the Jewish and Christian Traditions is insistence that God cannot be known directly. Only the idols can be known directly. They can be looked at, objectified, brought under our control. They are the tame gods, gods of the status quo, the gods who know their place . . .[T]he true and living God is known only in the consuming fire of the burning bush, the thick darkness of Sinai, the thick darkness of Calvary. Only by entering into this darkness can we come to know God and ourselves, . . . only by staying with the darkness does it become aglow with divine glory.[178]

Contemporary theologian, Hans Schwarz likewise characterises this post-modern God-image as a 'shamanistic' view of God.[179] In such a religious system, we human beings install 'God' in our self-constructed cosmos to serve our wishes in response to our works of service. In this theology God is brought down to 'human scale' in order to correspond with *our* notions of what is just and right. God's actions must conform to *our* ideas of goodness or love.

Schwarz points out that one of Luther's prime discoveries was that if God is indeed God and not a human construct, then he cannot be domesticated or tamed or bargained with in order to secure one's needs.[180] The God who is God is not our household idol. He is separate and free and he has no 'need of' us. He is almighty and sovereign and beyond our human and inherently sinful and self-interested expectations of him.

This places a different light on questions such as: 'Why has God allowed this to happen?' and 'Why is there suffering in the world?' so widely asked today. What right do we have to demand that God justify himself to *us*? What does he owe us? Schwarz comments:

> If we think through the matter, we are so caught up in our existential deficiency and inferiority to God, that we cannot expect anything from God but his rejection. As Augustine

---

178. Kenneth Leech, *We Preach Christ Crucified* (London: Darton, Longman and Todd, 1994), 83.
179. Hans Schwarz, 'Martin Luther's Central Insights for Today', public lecture delivered at Australian Lutheran College, Adelaide, May 2012, 1-2.
180. In Luther's day the medieval system of penance was just such an elaborate system, set up to broker an accommodation between God and humanity.

stated it bluntly: 'We have all deserved eternal death'. This means that we can neither offer anything to God or expect anything in return.[181]

Yet God has revealed his love for us in his Son, Jesus Christ, out of his own undeserved grace, an act of freedom and self-giving on his part. But he is never wholly to be known or understood, and never to be taken for granted.[182] When *we* think we have 'leg-roped' him, we find the noose empty; he is *absconditus*.[183] This is exemplified by the particular spiritual *Anfechtung* of depression which, like Luther and his readers, many contemporary believers have experienced as utter spiritual darkness and abandonment. In the lonely misery of this illness, as we reach for God, our ready supply of security, we may even find that he appears to have become our enemy.[184]

Luther's theology is, at this point, confrontingly honest and realistic.[185] Writing about his own depressive *Anfechtung* he says that 'the soul is stripped of its own garments, of its shoes, of all of its possessions, and of all of its imaginations, and is taken away by the word . . . into the wilderness'.[186] He shows that the horrors which may befall a human soul are even greater than we can imagine. And yet, as Parker Palmer observes from his own experience of depression, this

---

181. Schwarz, *Martin Luther's Central Insights for Today*, 5.
182. Jane E Strohl, 'For God Leads Down to Hell and Brings Back: Theodicy and the Word of Comfort in Luther's Theology' (Luther Lecture 2008, Pacific Lutheran Theological Seminary, October 29, 2008), accessed September 2013, http://www.plts.edu/docs/strohl_luther_lecture_2008.pdf.
183. 'God is, as the tradition (especially Martin Luther) put it, hidden (*absconditus*). The Latin has a more active flavour to it than the English, as when someone absconds with the "goods" and leaves behind only an absence, a nothingness.' Gerhard O Forde, *Theology is for Proclamation* (Augsburg: Fortress, 1990), 16.
184. Hunter and Hunter, *What your Doctor and your Pastor Want you to know about Depression*, 83.
185. John Douglas Hall points out that this experiential honesty and realism is one of the vital features of Luther's theology of suffering and the cross, and offers an indispensable-if sometimes quite disturbing-critique of today's culture of spiritualised humanistic optimism. See John Douglas Hall, 'Theology of the Cross: A Usable Past', Evangelical Lutheran Church of America, *accessed June 18, 2012*, http://www.elca.org/~/media/Files/Growing%20in%20Faith/Vocation/Word%20and%20Service%20Ministry/TheTheologyoftheCross_pdf.ashx.
186. *Operationes in Psalmos*, 1519-1521. WA V, 176:18-20.

is a 'dangerous but potentially life-giving place',[187] where we may over time come to see that even though (or perhaps precisely because) our 'religious coping' has been destroyed, God is closer, more merciful and more powerful to save than we could ever have imagined. He is in fact gracious and powerful enough to encompass our deepest depression within his vision of creation reconciled and restored.

Depression and the Cross

Luther asserts that a true theologian (a real Christian) is one who 'comprehends the visible and manifest things of God through suffering and the cross'.[188] Accordingly, he offers no theodic comforts and consolations to his depressed readers, but tries to help them to receive and apprehend their suffering *through the cross*. There, where God is humiliated and apparently defeated, he reveals his unlimited and unmerited grace for sinners, poured out by Christ through his passion and death, through which he encompasses and redeems the suffering of the world and every individual in it. Moreover, Christians are called to *share in* the cross. The life of faith is marked by the experience of suffering.[189] When we feel ourselves attacked or forsaken by the fearful hidden God, as depression sufferers often do, we are being *conformed to* Christ; that is, we share in Christ's suffering so that he is revealed to us and in us.[190]

The cross embodies a paradox which characterises our own experience of life and faith: in the cross God is simultaneously hidden and revealed. His divine love is displayed there, but disguised under suffering and wrath, so that only with eyes of faith and trust can we see and know it. It is only here that we may *truly experience Christ*,

---

187. Parker J Palmer, 'All the Way Down: Depression and the Spiritual Journey', in *Weavings: A Journal of Christian Spiritual Life*, 13/5 (September–October 1998): 6, accessed October 2013, http://www.wmeades.com/id220.htm.
188. *The Heidelberg Disputation of 1518*, Thesis 20. (WA I, 362:2–3).
189. In Luther's *Sermons on John*, 1538, where he comments on chapters 14–15, Jesus is preparing his disciples for the suffering they will endure because of him. Luther speaks about the Christian's experience of suffering: 'Anyone who is deeply rooted and well-grounded will often imagine that he has neither God nor Christ. He will feel nothing but death, the devil and sin passing over him like a violent storm and a dark cloud' (WA XLV, 598:32–35).
190. *Sermon on Cross and Suffering*, 1530 (WA XXXII, 29–38).

where God's hidden (alien) work is revealed as his proper work, and made visible in the realm of suffering human beings.

God's self-revelation on the cross shows him, on the one hand, scandalously at one with our sin and weakness. On the other hand, however, it shows us miraculously at one with his holiness and love, as we are conformed to his cruciform image by our suffering.[191] Ironically, it is our very feebleness that enables us to know and receive God's help, as we begin to realise and acknowledge our utter weakness and need. It is only when we are weak that we can truly be strong.

For depression sufferers, this insight often comes as deep comfort and relief, since they are incapable of anything but weakness and need, and feel utterly spiritually bankrupt.[192] Here is a God who is nevertheless prepared to meet them right where they are. Through the cross, their suffering becomes a sign that Christ has bound himself to them.[193]

Depressed believers sometimes say they feel 'unable to believe', as if 'God has just disappeared' and left a blank space in their lives.[194] Others sense God only through the lens of a distorted depressive conscience, as an angry judge. Such people are friends of the cross, where Jesus was made utterly helpless, abandoned, judged, condemned and left for dead, with and for them.[195]

The true comfort of this theology is not that 'God shares our pain' (that 'misery loves company', as Forde put it),[196] but, as Luther wrote to the depressed Queen Maria of Hungary in 1531, that our suffering

---

191. 'Through the suffering of Christ, the suffering of all his saints has become utterly holy, for it has been touched with Christ's suffering.' Martin Luther, *Sermon on Cross and suffering*, 1530 (WA XXXII, 38).
192. In my pastoral experience this is especially true where people have been involved in church communities where they have been expected to 'put out' in terms of outward displays of faith and acts of service. When their depression strips them of their capacity to do these things, they see this as a reflection of the state of their faith, which reveals the spiritual problem that they understand faith primarily as doing instead of receiving.
193. William Hordern, *Experience and Faith, The Significance of Luther for Understanding Today's Experiential Religion* (Minneapolis: Augsburg, 1983), 94–6.
194. Swinton, *Spirituality and Mental Health Care*, 114–16.
195. Hunter and Hunter, *What Your Doctor and Your Pastor Want You to Know about Depression*, 83, 88–89.
196. Forde, *On Being a Theologian of The Cross*, viii.

is held within the embrace of Christ's.[197] Our depressive experiences of being alone and condemned, forsaken and lost do not place us beyond God's love but at its very heart. Suffering, affliction and the cross then become 'the most precious treasury of all'.[198]

This pastoral theology of the cross is to be distinguished from what Dorothee Soelle identified as 'Christian masochism', a distorted view of the Christian's faithfulness and patience in suffering which sees suffering itself as spiritually virtuous.[199] Beverly Yahnke describes a chilling example of this distortion in an account of one pastor's misapplication of Luther's theology of the cross in the case of a depressed woman. He counselled that depression was her cross to bear obediently and humbly, and discouraged her from seeking medical or psychological treatment to relieve her misery.[200] Such a view of suffering often springs from a type of theodicy which explains human suffering as God breaking down our pride or demonstrating our powerlessness presupposing a God who only becomes great by making us small, or who somehow takes pleasure in our affliction for its own sake.[201] In Luther's view of human suffering in the light of the cross, the opposite is the case: God himself (In Christ) is the one who is broken down, for and with humanity.

Depression and Theologies of Glory

Standing in stark contrast to Luther's approach are contemporary interpretations of suffering which are essentially what Luther called 'theologies of glory'. The theologian of glory does not receive the suffering of the cross, but seeks to transcend and overcome it, usually by rational means. Such theologies look at the cross and see not the pivotal event in which all our destinies are tied up, but a single stage in the linear process of salvation, to be moved past, preferably as quickly as possible.

In relation to the cross of depression, theologies of glory increasingly take their cue from western culture's ideal of happiness and fulfilment. They seek 'solutions based on method' rather than

---

197. See Appendix.
198. *Explanation of the Ninety Five Theses*, 1518.Thesis 55 ('WA 1, 613:25).
199. Dorothee Soelle, *Suffering* (Philadelphia: Fortress: 1975), 9–32.
200. Yahnke, *Christian Psychology and Spiritual Care*, 1–3.
201. Soelle, *Suffering*, 19.

'hope based on grace'. Formulae and principles are proposed, often accompanied by manuals and guides. These offer strategies for 'victorious depression-free living'. Scripture is enlisted in the form of disjointed sound bites which bypass the cross's interpretive centrality and place up-front the language of triumphalism.

As Parker Palmer[202] identifies, most hollow of all in such theology is the characteristic call to greater 'surrender' and dedication to the Lord, as if this may be presupposed as the underlying problem and solution of depressive illness in general. When those whose depression has drained them of willpower and energy see that this 'fulfilled, empowered Christian life' is beyond them, they frequently give up and turn away from faith, or begin an even darker journey towards despair.[203] In seeking to move past depression by means of false religious optimism, theologies of glory actually stifle the soul by denying its pain and silencing its voice.[204]

Depressive Suffering Transformed

Richard Eyer picks up the intent of Luther's consolation in his letters to the depressed in his judgement that pastoral care consists not in removing others' suffering, but in helping the sufferer receive and interpret their suffering in the light of the cross.[205] Through faith, human suffering is changed by the reality of the cross. Just as God transformed Christ's passion and dying into victory over sin and death, so our crosses are transformed in Christ. Under the cross, the suffering of depression may too be transformed, not into 'happiness' or 'pain-free-ness' but into *hope*, which looks forward to both a temporal and eternal future, knowing that the cross in one's life is not a sign that God has forsaken, but that he is truly and graciously present. In the presence of hope, depression may persist, but its stranglehold on the soul is broken and its power to 'steal the future' is taken away.[206] As Luther writes to Joachim, God is teaching the sufferer through this

---

202. Palmer, 'All the Way Down', 2.
203. Alexander J Davidson, *Through a Foreign Land: Coping with Depression* (Adelaide: Lutheran Publishing House, 1984), 17-8.
204. Hunter and Hunter, *What Your Doctor and Your Pastor Want You to Know About Depression*, 85-7.
205. Eyer, *Pastoral Care Under the Cross*, 28-9.
206. Davidson, *Through a Foreign Land*, 84-6. See also Stone, *Depression and Hope*, 52-3.

experience in the crucible of depressive suffering, to turn to him and the hope and strength only he can give, instead of turning to human sources of happiness and security which, even at their best, are always ultimately only temporary and passing.

Prayer

As in Luther's practice, so in contemporary situations of pastoral care with the depressed, prayer is the constant companion of pastoral comfort. Luther models the persistent and patient life of prayer that he exhorts his readers to practise. He knows from experience how hard it is for those in the grip of melancholy to pray, so he gives his strong leadership and example by pledging his prayers on their behalf, praying with and for them in the text of his letters, and teaching about the nature of prayer in the life of the suffering Christian.[207]

The struggle to pray is also a common theme among depressed believers today, along with other kinds of spiritual resistance. This may be associated with anger towards God, feeling abandoned by God, a distorted and terrified conscience, loss of faith or simple exhaustion and the inability to focus.

Intercessory prayer and, when appropriate, prayer *with* the person keep open the spiritual dialogue which the depression sufferer may be unable to sustain themselves.

Cruciform Listening

In Luther's situation of geographic isolation from those he was consoling, he was forced most of the time to 'listen' via the reports of others before pastorally responding by letter. The most notable exception[208] was his relationship with Prince Joachim of Anhalt, whom he visited repeatedly during the latter's depressive crisis in

---

207. Luther's practice of prayer as a consistent and frequent feature of pastoral care is indicated particularly in his ministry to Prince Joachim of Anhalt during 1534. See his letters of June 9 (See Appendix) and June 12 (See Appendix) in which it is clear that Luther is using the *Our Father* as a form of intensive intercessory prayer. See also his letters of June 23 (See and June 26 (See Appendix) in which he teaches the prince about the receptive posture of prayer and the practice of patience and perseverance in prayer.
208. As noted earlier, Luther also spent considerable time and attention on helping his friends, Jerome Weller and Johann Schlaginhaufen, particularly while they were lodgers in his house.

1534. It is apparent from some of Luther's letters that, despite other urgent projects and work pressures, he put in considerable time, travelling to Dessau (at Joachim's request) to make himself personally available to the depressed prince, to listen and attend to the prince's situation. Luther's engagement is shown not only by the genuinely compassionate and caring language he used in his letters, but also by the skilful and incisive counsel he gave to Joachim, whose situation he knew intimately and had considered deeply.

It is almost a truism to say that such listening is a key element of care-giving to depressed persons today, and yet its importance is still far from fully appreciated by pastoral care-givers, especially as it is understood in the light of Luther's theology of the cross. Swinton's research shows that deeply engaged listening is mysteriously powerful. In several interview extracts it emerged that when someone offers their full attention and understanding to a depressed person, this is experienced as powerfully healing.[209]

Such listening is more than empathetic; it is cruciform; it 'suffers' the other. It enters into the other's distress, bearing and coping with it, just as Christ enters into our suffering and we enter into his. Listening to a depression sufferer requires a level of emotional and spiritual maturity which enables understanding and acceptance of the other's profound negativity and pain, and the willingness to endure them. To use Luther's taxonomy again, it involves the *affectus* and the *intellectus*–the very *heart* of the carer. It is difficult, costly and taxing and *calls the listener to cruciform suffering* of the sufferer. Just as the person in the grip of their despair is suffering divine things, so the listener suffers these things through that person.

The Silence of the Cross

Luther sometimes surprises his reader not by what he says but by his ability to leave things unsaid. Likewise John Swinton reflects that today there are also moments in which it may be important for the pastoral carer not to speak, but to keep silence and wait.

He points out that the silence of Jesus at various moments during his passion and crucifixion is as meaningful and loaded as his

---

209. Swinton, *Spirituality and Mental Health Care*, 126–28. See also Meller and Albers, 'Depression', 27–9.

speaking, and calls us to listen, as we recognise both the authentic human suffering of the cross and the divine mystery of love enacted there. Likewise, Swinton proposes, 'In solidarity and awkward presence with the sufferer we must learn the practice of listening to silences. Reflection on the cross of Christ moves us to become sensitive to the subtle nuances of the experience of pain, desolation, brokenness and suffering'.[210]

Care-giving to those in deep depression, who frequently go into extended periods of silence, may at times call for just such patient and discerning silence on the part of the carer. Such silence is not merely waiting, but *accommodating silence* which recognises the mystery that God is present and at work. It expresses our willingness to *share* the sufferer's situation rather than *comfort ourselves* through ineffective attempts to overcome or resolve the pain.[211] Henri Nouwen notes, 'The friend who can be silent with us in a moment of despair or confusion . . . who can tolerate not knowing, not curing, not healing and face with us the reality of our powerlessness, that is a friend who cares'.[212]

The Word of the Cross?

While Luther's theology of suffering holds its own in the contemporary world, there remains the question of *how we may pastorally embody it* in a culture that is so out of tune with its claims. Against the backdrop of our culture of human positivity today, Luther's stark realism cannot help but appear negative and unhelpful. In light of this, would we today choose to counsel people by saying: 'God is giving you this cross of depressive suffering to strengthen you', as Luther did with Joachim of Anhalt?[213] Given the importance of compassionate listening and respectful silence, how appropriate is it to offer this kind of comfort?

John Swinton points out that many contemporary people find little comfort and help in such counsel because, even if they are people of faith, they may simply not be able to see a 'good' beyond the terrible

---

210. Swinton, *Raging With Compassion*, 101.
211. Eyer, *Pastoral Care Under The Cross*, 74.
212. Henri Nouwen, *Out of Solitude: Three Meditations on the Christian Life* (Notre Dame: Ave Maria Press, 1974), 34.
213. The Letter of June 9 1534 (See Appendix).

pain of their immediate personal situation.[214] Typically, we know that clinically depressed people tend to fit into this category. Locked into the vortex of their own inner negativity, their ability to see any possibilities beyond it is impaired. To them, a God who is capable of causing such awful suffering may well be highly offensive.[215] In this case, Luther's counsel may not readily be heard as comfort and encouragement, but as a rational explanation–another 'theodicy' which does not help.[216]

Richard Eyer's perspective on how Luther's theology can find legitimate expression today affirms this point.[217] He believes that it is presumptuous for any pastoral carer to claim knowledge of God's will for another person, and suggests that the task of interpreting suffering belongs to the sufferer rather than the carer. Unlike Luther's sixteenth century pastoral relationships, today the pastoral carer's relationship with the sufferer is marked by a greater equality of power, education and social standing. Unlike Luther's, our culture also emphasises personal autonomy and self-determination.[218] Today it is perhaps therefore no longer culturally appropriate or helpful to make judgements or declarations about others' lives as Luther did, even if they are sincere and true. Eyer suggests that the pastoral carer's role here is rather to support sufferers as they wrestle with God in the midst of their crises, believing that the crisis holds potential

---

214. Swinton, *Raging With Compassion*, 10.
215. Luther insists that this being 'offended' is part of becoming a theologian and learning through testing experiences of God and his word: 'I myself was offended more than once, and brought to the depth and abyss of despair so that I wished that I had never been created a man' (*Bondage of the Will*, 1525, WA XVIII, 719:9-11).
216. John Douglas Hall identifies the importance of properly applying Luther's theology of the cross in today's context in a pastorally sensitive and faithful manner. This may at times mean remaining silent rather than offering counsel, as Luther would have done in his context. See John Douglas Hall, *The Cross in Our Context: Jesus and the Suffering World* (Minneapolis: Augsburg-Fortress, 2003), 42-6.
217. Eyer, *Pastoral Care Under The Cross*, 46-7.
218. Luther's personal profile, credibility and power enabled him to speak into the lives of others with unprecedented pastoral authority. However, in the post-modern era the individual is empowered to interpret their own experience and act with personal autonomy. This is becoming increasingly the case in the area of mental health, notably with depression. See Mercieca, *The Upside of Down*, 82-3.

for the deepening of their faith; that there is greater value in sufferers themselves coming to a point of recognising and naming the cross in their lives.[219]

On the other hand, Matt Rogers relates how hearing that God was at work for his good through his depression (though it was not clear how) was highly significant. Even though it was of little apparent help to him while he was searching for an *explanation* for his suffering, it nevertheless prepared him to see its reality as he began to recover. In hindsight, he saw how those words had enabled him, despite his confusion, to endure the illness and its trials. It was truth that he had needed to hear, but which could only be fully understood and appreciated at a later point.[220] While offering theories or speculations about God's *precise purposes* for someone's depressive illness is simply foolish and disrespectful, there is the theological question of the pastoral carer's calling to proclaim God's loving purpose to a depression sufferer in the midst of their darkness, even if it does not have an immediate and felt comforting effect.

People certainly require different expressions of care depending on where they are at the time, and, as one pastor has noted, 'timing is almost everything'. Discerning the moment in which it will be helpful to offer spiritual counsel is only possible after patient listening. The most faithful Christians will go through phases in their depression of not wanting to hear any God-talk at all. They may be confused, angry or simply too exhausted. Sometimes, however, people need to either express or hear someone else reaffirm that although we don't know how or why, God *is* working for good in their situation. At times, depressed persons under pastoral care will return to 'check' this point in order to find reassurance. What is particularly humbling is that sometimes these people may be, by all human measures, marginally Christian, and yet they display a simplicity and depth of trust in God's grace which alludes more 'churched' Christians.[221]

---

219. Eyer, *Pastoral Care Under the Cross*, 46–7.
220. Matt Rogers, *Losing God: Clinging to Faith Through Doubt and Depression* (Downers Grove: IVP, 2008), 95–147.
221. This observation arises not only from my own extensive pastoral experience with depression sufferers but from discussion with other pastors and chaplains who have worked with the depressed and mentally ill.

Counter-intuitive Comfort

Luther's theology of suffering and its implications for the pastoral care of depressed persons, continues to be controversial, even offensive. It rejects contemporary spirituality's reduction of God to a 'tame deity'. It does not lead into the sterile speculation of theodicy, but to the very epicentre of God's self-disclosure in the weakness and suffering of the cross. Christ's passion and death gather in the suffering and sickness of all, and in a special way embrace the lonely God-forsakenness and despair experienced by depressed persons.

Luther's theology, with its grittily realistic stance towards suffering and its understanding of God as graciously present at the lowest point of human wretchedness, is a crucial focus for all ministry to depression sufferers.

Kenneth Leech reflects:

> In facing our spiritual dis-ease [depression] in its various forms and degrees of severity, we must indisputably encounter it. It is a tragic loss to treat suffering as if something has simply gone awry. Spiritual maturity is not the accumulation of skills and techniques. It is not being transfigured into having problem-free lives. It comes in attending to and encountering the dis-ease and darkness of our own humanity. It comes as a result of being opened up and confronted by realities which disturb and transform us: the reality of the word of God, challenging, piercing, shaking us; the reality of the encounter with ourselves, with God and with the depths in other people, through silence and darkness. Common to these encounters is the element of struggle, of conflict. We are formed through struggle.[222]

The Comforting Word: Luther's Use of Scripture as Consolation for the Depressed

Luther's consolation consistently draws its content from scripture, making extensive use of biblical quotations, allusions and references. Even where Luther is comforting his readers using his own words, they

---

222. Kenneth Leech, *Spirituality and Pastoral Care* (London: Sheldon Press, 1986), 31.

frequently resound with the cadences of scripture. Close examination of his sentences often reveals that they are conflations of two or more biblical quotes, arranged to speak to the situation of the reader. A wide range of biblical material is covered across the twenty-one letters in the selection: the Gospels and Epistles, Old Testament narratives, the prophets, and most assiduously, the Psalms.[223] Especially in letters to his young male addressees, he makes use of the Old Testament wisdom literature, chiefly Proverbs and Ecclesiastes.[224]

This saturation of biblical material reflects Luther's understanding of pastoral care as lived theology, in which scripture is not only the authoritative source, but also the *vivia vox* speaking to the hearer in the present. Wherever Christians give care and counsel to one another, the words of scripture are unavoidably involved, since they alone can be relied upon as God's own counsel.[225] For Luther, scripture was a door into spiritual reality, filled with living characters and events, inside which our time is 'collapsed' into the biblical narrative so that, to the reader of scripture, Pharaoh, Israel, Moses, Paul and Peter are present 'in the here and now'. Luther regarded reading and receiving scripture as a profound personal encounter with the performative word of the living God, which started externally but moved inward to the heart and conscience, affecting and transforming the whole person. A Christian's best response to distress and suffering is therefore to 'give oneself to scripture in order to feel the power of its comfort'.[226] This importance of being directly and personally addressed by scripture is illustrated by Luther's letter to Johann Agricola about his wife Elizabeth, who was suffering with depressive melancholy. He exhorts Agricola, 'So do not give up impressing upon her that when the Word

---

223. Across the selection of letters, Luther refers to and quotes from Ps 13, 34, 50, 51, 55, 57, 77, 118 and 147.
224. In Luther's letters to Prince Joachim and Jerome Weller, he takes on the role of mentor or teacher in his consolations, using the Old Testament's wisdom literature as a source of life-training. Part of the struggle of these serious young men with depression was the need to mature in their understanding and expectations of happiness and suffering within the larger picture of the Christian life.
225. In his *Misuse of the Mass*, 1521, Luther makes the bold claim, 'To try to give consolation without the Word of God is the work of the devil himself' (WA 8, 491:14-15).
226. *Sermon on Cross and Suffering*, 1530 (WA XXXII, 34:29-31).

of God is taught, whether you are present or not, it has something to say to her'.[227]

Inherent in Luther's use of biblical texts is his distinction of law and gospel. There are several situations in which Luther clearly recognises the need to speak a word of gentle rebuke, challenging an attitude or behaviour that is sinful and contributing to the reader's problems. Christian *consolation*, as practised in Luther's day is not to be confused with today's tendency to treat the sufferer of depression simply as a victim of an evil fate. While Luther certainly did not equate depressive illness itself with sin, he knew that victims of the illness were sinners, and indeed had their own particular sinful idolatries. Using Proverbs 25:27 and Ecclesiasticus 3:21 and 27, Luther points out to Barbara Lißkirchen that by prying into God's secret counsels concerning predestination and election, she was ignoring (and transgressing) the first commandment by seeking to usurp God's sovereignty. In so doing, she only made her despair and anxiety worse by seeking answers that she could never find. However, this application of scripture as law is always completed by means of a word of grace. As always, for Luther the heart of all comfort and help in this life's sufferings is the message of justification and forgiveness in Christ. He goes on to reassure Barbara Lißkirchen of her salvation through faith in Christ and, using a startling allusion to John 20:27, writes to her the beautiful blessing: 'May our dear Lord Jesus Christ show you his hands and his side[228] and greet you with a friendly heart, and may you see and hear only him until you find your joy in him. Amen'.[229]

Luther incorporated scripture into the rhetorical arrangement of his letters at various points and in different ways. He often used scriptural quotations in constructing his consolatory *argumentatio*, carefully creating interpretive bridges between scripture and the life experience of the reader. He frequently brings scripture into 'metacognitive' encounter with the beliefs or suppositions of the sufferer, challenging their negative and ungracious view of themselves

---

227. See Appendix.
228. Cf Jn 20:27.
229. *Letter to Barbara Lißkirchen*, April 30 1531 (Appendix).

and/or their situation. Typically, scripture is referenced or quoted towards the end of the *exhortatio*, in some cases as part of it.[230]

As noted earlier, we find here again that Luther sometimes uses scripture in his consolations in ways that correspond strongly with contemporary narrative therapy and counselling methods. He suggests to his readers alternative narrative readings of their situation. To the depressed and suicidal Jonas von Stockhausen, Luther wrote about Jonah and Elijah and even Jesus himself, who were all weary and sick of life in this world, but who knew it was God's will that they endure, and so fought against their desire to die. In offering this alternative narrative frame for von Stockhausen's battle with suicidal thoughts, Luther lifted up and sanctified his terrible struggle, and showed him a new way forward.

As observed in chapter 3, Luther sometimes (usually towards the end of a letter) assembles a 'bouquet' of biblical texts which complement and amplify one another. At first glance, it may seem as if he is simply 'piling up evidence' for the point he is making, but on closer study it becomes clear that he has brought together a number of texts that, as a composite, lead into deeper and richer spiritual insights, as the reader rereads and meditates on the letter over time.[231] These 'bouquets' reveal a lot about Luther's pastoral theology, particularly his emphasis on Christ as the true comforter of the suffering.[232]

Scripture and Contemporary Pastoral Theology

However, before we look into how Luther's methods of biblical consolation may be appplied today, we need to discuss whether his use of scripture is still theologically and pastorally appropriate. This task potentially opens up a huge range of questions. It is not feasible to grapple here with all facets of the complex contemporary

---

230. *Letter to Jonas von Stockhausen,* November 27 1532 (See Appendix)
231. A feature of consolatory letters in this period is that they were read and reread not just by the individual but in family and community groups where the biblical references and quotations could be studied.
232. For example, in his *Letter to Matthias Weller,* October 7 1534 (See Appendix). Luther weaves six short biblical quotes (1 Thess 5:14; Isa 40:8–9; Deut 28:47; Mt 6:25; 1 Pet 5:7 and Ps 55:22) into a 'bouquet' of biblical comfort. Each verse carries its own 'fragrance' to be appreciated, but together these verses form a clear and powerful call to receive God's freely-offered comfort.

debate about the Bible's authority, historicity or authenticity. For the purposes of the discussion, therefore, let us assume an acceptance of the Bible's authority as the divine word of God, since Luther's views and practice can only be meaningfully considered on that basis.

This issue aside, there are other questions to be addressed which *are* germane to the fundamentally *pastoral focus* of our inquiry: Does Luther's approach to the application of scripture require any theological modification? Can his direct application of the text to life still be accepted in today's highly sophisticated context? On the other hand, we also need to ask: Are there aspects of Luther's practice which bring to light needs or weaknesses in today's pastoral care practice? Does Luther indeed have something to teach us today about the pastoral use of scripture with depressed persons?

Scripture as Comfort Today?

As we have discovered, for Luther pastoral consolation of the suffering arises directly out of scripture as the written Word of God. However, for some pastoral theologians today such an immediate connection between the ancient word of scripture and the complexity of contemporary life seems impossible. Steven Pattison contends: 'At best there are some parts of the Bible which may be deemed to relate tangentially to contemporary problems.'[233] Pattison goes on to assert that the Bible's cultural, cosmological and scientific framework is totally outmoded and anachronistic in today's world, and judges that anybody who would seek to take it seriously as a means of pastoral care must be a fundamentalist or biblicist.[234]

Scripture does not, of course, directly or explicitly address all human struggles and concerns in every age. From Luther's sixteenth century perspective, scripture did not explicitly deal with the plague, the papacy, the Turk or civil unrest, and yet Luther and his contemporaries found it to be an accurate mirror of their human struggles, and heard it speaking directly to their sufferings. As God's Word, which speaks into time and history, scripture has shown its

---

233. Stephen Pattison, *A Critique of Pastoral Care*, third edition (London: SCM, 2000), 107–14.
234. Pattison, *A Critique of Pastoral Care*, 113.

ongoing power to touch the underlying sin and suffering of humanity, whatever its persistent or changeling outward manifestations over time may be. To dismiss this is to dismiss most of the church's tradition of pastoral theology, from Gregory the Great to Eugene Peterson.

In the specific area of contemporary pastoral care and counsel for the depressed, there are numerous examples of depression sufferers finding comfort and hope in scripture. One glowing example is Teresa Smith's autobiographical work on her journey with the psalms of lament through long term depression, in which she shares how these ancient prayers from another time, culture and context enabled her to find *her* voice and hear *God's* voice in the midst of severe mental suffering.[235] In light of contemporary Christians continuing to experience scripture's ability to console and strengthen in this way, the claims of Pattison and others seem rather pale.

Text and Context

Pattison claims that from the standpoint of contemporary biblical hermeneutics, it is simply nonsensical to place the ancient texts of scripture into the context of people's pastoral struggles and problems today, since this wrenches the text out of its original context in an arbitrary and simplistic fashion. Pattison's point has some merit: the glib, trite or uncritical pastoral application of biblical texts with no concern for their inner layers of context and meaning lacks both pastoral and biblical integrity.

However, within a theology which receives Scripture as the living Word of God addressed to the *Anfechtung* of all humanity, Pattison's point, while well-taken, cannot be as seen as absolute. As NT Wright observes, if there is one thing that is found plentifully in Scripture it is recognisably authentic human experience:[236] feelings, thoughts, hopes and fears, many of which resonate deeply with humans in any era. As for Luther, so today this deeply human literature is the very means through which God mysteriously forges his connections with human hearts.

---

235. Teresa S Smith, *Through The Darkest Valley: The Lament Psalms and One Woman's Life-long Struggle Against Depression* (Eugene: Resource Publications, 2009).
236. Wright, 'How Can the Bible Be Authoritative?' 2-4.

Leonard Hummel, following the pastoral care of seven contemporary persons suffering with a range of different life-struggles, including depression, shows how each of these believers was addressed by Scripture in their individual situation. Some found narrative connections for their own lives; others found themes and images leading back to the doctrinal teaching they received as children. Others, still, were led by Scripture back to the liturgy where God's comfort was enacted to them sacramentally. For all of these persons, Scripture was a source of pastoral comfort and healing.[237]

Scripture and Cognitive Psychology

While secularly oriented psychotherapy for depression has no place for the biblical text, among Christian psychotherapists and counsellors Scripture is widely used, although to varying degrees and in significantly different ways. As we briefly explore this point of critical encounter, let's consider today's main types of Christian therapy and counselling, and compare their use of Scripture with Luther's.

As we will see, Luther is surprisingly relevant for today. The methods he employs in applying Scripture in his pastoral letters are also helpful for our context, and indeed some of them correspond positively with contemporary psychotherapy and counselling for depression. Moreover, the theological implicit critique he offers on the way in which Scripture is used by some of today's therapists and counsellors is very telling.

Most significant in this regard are Luther's use of cognitive and behavioural strategies. As we noted in an earlier, some contemporary forms of CT and CBT which label themselves 'Christian' integrate Christian faith and practice in only the most perfunctory manner, while other Christian practitioners of cognitive therapy set out to use Scripture with far greater depth and integrity.

However, more is needed here than a deep commitment to the authority of the Bible. The proper use of Scripture requires *theological and hermeneutical discernment*. Luther's basic distinction of law and gospel in Scripture offers a crucially important 'guiding light' at this point. Some of the current Christian psychological literature

---

237. Hummel, *Clothed in Nothingness*, 49–71.

which advocates the use of Scripture in cognitive and behavioural therapies is less than clear in its theological hermeneutics. Typically it uses Scripture to set goals or standards for personal change and growth, but ignores the fact that Scripture's central teaching is God's gracious forgiveness towards fallen humanity, through his Son. In this case the client is receiving the message of the law as an impetus for change rather than the transformative news of God's unconditional forgiveness and love in Christ.[238]

From a contemporary Lutheran standpoint, this is an inadequate and unhelpful use of the Bible, in which its message is reduced to 'positive human content' and offers nothing more than good advice on how to make constructive changes in one's thinking.

Besides missing the Gospel-core of Scripture, this approach also potentially puts depressed persons under the greater pressure of renewed spiritual commands, which-when received by a severely depressed and spiritually weakened conscience-quickly turn to accusations and judgements.[239]

The biblical *kerygma* of God's grace, on the other hand, is a spiritually regenerative force; the beginnings of a new life through the death and resurrection of Christ.

McMinn & Campbell and Siang-Yang Tan offer strong grace-centred cognitive approaches to the use of Scripture in CT and CBT. They illustrate how thought restructuring and behavioural change may make use of scriptural reframing, decentring and metacognitive methods, in which law and gospel are well-distinguished so that each has its proper voice and performs its proper function.[240]

An exciting development has been the use of traditional forms of Christian meditation and contemplation on Scripture within cognitive

---

238. For example, John CG Sturdy, 'Christian Cognitive Therapy', *John's Christianity Page*, June 10 2007, accessed January 2013, http://www.cb1.com/~john/Religion/CCT.html.
239. In pastoral counselling with many depressed persons, I have frequently noted how their 'personal hermeneutical filter' is fatally skewed towards the law. Even when God's grace is expressed to them, they feed back what they have heard in terms of the law, talking about 'where they have failed' and 'what they now have to do'. In this way they load the burden of the illness back onto their own shoulders.
240. Tan, *Counseling and Psychotherapy*, 274-75. McMinn and Campbell, *Integrative Psychotherapy*, 288-90.

models of therapy for depression. Initially cognitive therapists began to explore this area by experimenting with Zen Buddhist forms of meditation such as mindfulness and acceptance. However, Christians have now also explored forms of biblical meditation and mindfulness using Scripture.[241] Howard Stone, for example, details his use of the ancient contemplative Christian discipline, *lectio divina* (sacred reading of Scripture), within a cognitive therapy framework. Such meditative approaches slow down the depression sufferer's thinking and facilitate, through slow reading and rereading of the scriptural text, a gradual refocussing on the external voice of the word and what it is saying to them.[242]

Narrative Therapy with Scripture

Luther's narrative use of biblical texts in his letters corresponds to a surprising degree with the methods and strategies of contemporary narrative therapy and counselling. While NT, as it was first developed by White and Epston in the 1970s, was resistant to any idea of a universal or shared meta-narrative (like the biblical story),[243] Christians have since adapted NT very successfully, using the scriptural meta-narrative as a *primary resource* in helping people re-author their own stories.

McMinn and Campbell, in their *Integrative Psychotherapy* model, show how narrative techniques can be incorporated into the treatment of Christians with depression. While taking on board the basic point that we, as individuals, construct our own stories, the authors propose that truth is not only constructed but also *revealed*, and that the biblical meta-narrative has a rightful and important role to play in narrative therapy and counselling with Christians.

---

241. Tan, *Counseling and Psychotherapy*, 276. To some extent this kind of *repeated reading* was also what Luther's addressees did with his consolatory letters, as they returned again and again to find comfort from his words in difficult times. This is possibly one reason Luther included so many scriptural quotations and allusions in his letters.
242. Stone, *Depression and Hope*, 121–22.
243. An excellent article examining this aspect of narrative therapy is: Cameron Lee, 'Agency and Purpose in Narrative Therapy: Questioning the Postmodern Rejection of Metanarrative', in *Journal of Psychology and Theology*, 32 (2004): 221–31.

> Throughout the Old Testament we see God telling the people of Israel to build altars, practice rituals and establish ceremonies to help them tell their story . . . [I]n the New Testament the story is expanded . . . And ever since, through the history of Christianity, believers have gathered to tell the old, old story through worship and fellowship. It is a grand story, a meta-narrative, but it is also a highly personal story that gives each individual Christian a renewed perspective on the past, present and future.[244]

In much the same way as a modern narrative therapist may do, Luther seeks to collaborate with his readers in the *co-construction* of their personal stories.[245] He helps them to link past, present and future by using the threads of the biblical story of sin and grace, as expressed through 'sub-stories' such as God's rescue of Israel at the Red Sea, or his merciful care of Elijah as he struggles with the will to die. In doing so, Luther once more models the key interpretive dynamic of law and gospel with insight, compassion and imagination.

The Biblical and Nouthetic Counselling Models

Like Luther, the contemporary *biblical counselling* movement and its close cousin, *nouthetic counselling* have sought to be faithful to Scripture as the authoritative Word of God, and open to its power to speak directly to human hearts and lives. However, as in the case of some types of CT and CBT, the biblical and nouthetic models operate with a theology of Scripture which is distinctly different to Luther's; an approach which is *correctional and rehabilitative* rather than *transformational and regenerative*.

The biblical and nouthetic counselling models, in their various forms, understand depressive illness in basically the same way–as a spiritual 'misalignment' of the human heart and mind resulting from sin. The depressed person is one who has moved outside of godly biblical patterns of thinking, feeling and behaving, resulting in illness and misery. What is needed, therefore, is primarily a program of correctional therapy and rehabilitation to help the person repent of their wrong habits, and move back into right thinking and feeling in conformity with God's Word.

---

244. McMinn and Campbell, *Integrative Psychotherapy*, 305-6.
245. McMinn and Campbell, *Integrative Psychotherapy*, 305.

Here once again, Luther's approach to Scripture offers an incisive critique. His christocentric hermeneutics and associated distinction of law and gospel enable Scripture to be heard as more than the correction (*nouthesia*) of the law. To be sure, Luther recognises the role that sin sometimes plays in depressive illness, and does not shrink from giving the appropriate rebuke and correction when he thinks it necessary. However, this word of law is not in itself the healing agent; it only prepares the way for the proclamation of the Gospel—the grace, forgiveness and freedom of God in Christ. Scripture holds at its centre Christ and his death and resurrection for humanity's forgiveness and healing, and speaks its word of law and gospel in order to perform this in the heart of the believer. This transforming word does much more than reform or rehabilitate; it resurrects and regenerates.

The Pastoral–Hermeneutical Challenge

Luther's pastoral application of scriptural texts to the life-situations of his depressive readers was the work not only of a gifted *Seelsorger*, but also an adept biblical theologian. As a monk, then a theologian, Luther had prayed, meditated, studied and lectured on the Bible for decades. He knew Scripture intimately. This biblical scholarship together with his deep *experiential knowledge* of Scripture enabled him to pastorally apply biblical texts with great insight, integrity and skill, especially to those whose melancholic struggles he himself shared. His use of Scripture in the twenty-one letters is subtle, affective, deeply considered and hermeneutically pertinent. He divides and proclaims law and gospel with a surgeon's skill, in order to bring hope and healing.

This recognition gives cause for reflection on how thoroughly pastoral carers are equipped today in the area of biblical theology: 'It shows the real challenge for pastoral carers in using Scripture in pastoral care and counsel today–that we do not know it well enough and so lack skill in its pastoral application. We may know the situation of the person we are helping, and we may know what the scriptures say, but lack the kind of deep biblical–pastoral formation needed to bring the two together in a faithful and creative encounter'.[246]

---

246. Pietsch, 'Reflection on Depression in Luther's *Table Talk*', 39.

Ian Dickson's 2003 study on the use of the Bible in pastoral practice shows that clergy and pastoral carers generally have little depth of knowledge and experience in applying Scripture pastorally, sticking to the widely used 'fashionable runs' rather than exploring the deeper diversity of Scripture in any hermeneutically or pastorally imaginative way.[247]

Examining Luther's use of biblical texts in the pastoral consolation of depression sufferers, which flows from his *scholarly and experiential* knowledge of Scripture, exposes a general weakness in pastoral care today. In so doing, it challenges us to a new and deeper engagement with Scripture, not just as a 'resource' external to our own lives, to be 'administered' to others, but as a word that has addressed us and found interpretive grounding in our life and practice.

Scripture and Power Dynamics

Luther's society was radically different to ours and the framework of his rhetorical *disposition*—or more precisely, his use of Scripture within it—raises questions for our contemporary practice in relation to the appropriate use of power in pastoral care relationships.

In church communities, especially Lutheran ones, Scripture carries great authority. How this authority interacts with the power-dynamics at work in pastoral care relationships is an oft-forgotten but crucial issue. Among Christians who hold the Bible up as the source and norm of all teaching and life in the church, to quote Scripture is to exercise power and to deploy its ultimate authority as God's definitive word. This can be a great help where, within the law-gospel dynamic, the message of God's grace is conveyed to the hearer. The great risk, however, is that a depressive person whose natural hermeneutical filter is geared negatively, will hear Scripture being quoted as demand, compulsion or judgement, even though the words shared by the carer are offered with the opposite intention.

Depressed persons have sometimes experienced the application of Scripture to their situation as a denial of their feelings or an attempt

---

247. JN Ian Dickinson, 'The Use of the Bible in Pastoral Practice', Cardiff University, Cardiff School of History, Archaeology and Religion, December 2003, accessed April 14, 2013, http://www.cardiff.ac.uk/share/research/projectreports/previousprojects/biblepastoralpractice/the-use-of-the-bible-in-pastoral-practice.html.

to silence their expression of pain. In conversation about this book, a friend described to me how he, as an depressive eighteen-year-old, had sought help from his pastor. The pastor listened for a few moments before quoting Psalm 27:1. It was made clear to him that this Word of God was the authoritative answer to his depressive struggles and that, in view of this answer, no further voicing of those struggles was appropriate. Scripture was used to silence and deny the sufferer's complaint. This wonderful verse of Scripture could have been spoken with such comfort, had it been shared by a carer who had entered compassionately into a pastoral encounter and prepared the way for it to speak to the sufferer by first listening and understanding.

This highlights the importance of the carer using the power of Scripture's authority with insight, patience and skill, having listened properly to the situation of the other, and understanding their particular needs and fears before God, so that they know–as far as possible–how a word of Scripture will be heard and received. The carer who speaks the Word of God to a person suffering with depression needs to do so within the context of a relationship of mutual understanding, empathy and trust.

The Word of God in Public Worship

It is clear that the public dimension of the Christian life is assumed in Luther's letters, and that he sees his pastoral advice as an extension of the ministry of the word already being received through the Divine Service of the Christian community.

Moreover, it is important to address this point because of the recognition of contemporary researchers that public worship, with its proclamation of the Gospel, comfort and nurture of the sacraments and the mutual care of the Christian community (created and permeated by word and sacrament), are key elements in the pastoral care of the depressed. Lanny and Victor Hunter affirm that Scripture's central agency in public worship is integral to the spiritual work that addresses depression. They observe that it is in the context of the church's worship that the Word of God moves from its written form to its bodily and material forms, first in the sacrament and then in the sacramental community, so that the isolation and self-slavery of the depressive person present in the worshipping assembly begins to be broken down:

> The Bible always connects the individual person to the community. When one weeps, all weep. When one rejoices all rejoice. When one suffers, all suffer. When one celebrates all celebrate. Pastoral care and spiritual direction take seriously the role of the community in relation to the individual person.[248]

Swinton probes this spiritual dynamic of the church's public liturgy more deeply, examining extracts from narratives written by Christians struggling with depression, penetrating to the reality of doubt and despair experienced by many such Christians. He notes that the dimensions of the word of God that are enacted in liturgical worship through symbol, art, music and ritual became 'sensory handles' that enable the participation of severely depressed persons in worship, when their cognitive ability to 'believe' has fled.[249]

Meditation and Visualisation

As we hve noted already, some of the most striking instances of Luther's pastoral use of biblical texts in these twenty-one letters are those in which he draws his readers into *visualising* the biblical narrative, while placing themselves directly into it.[250] Luther here shows how he himself interacts with Scripture by entering the world of the text, imaginatively super-imposing it over the present moment and its circumstances as a means of interpreting personal experience in the light of God's word and promise.

The way in which Luther uses this meditative visualisation as a pastoral tool for helping his depressed readers is, in some ways, analogous to the practice of visualising scenes from the Gospels developed by Ignatius Loyola. It seems likely that Luther and Ignatius were tapping into the same spiritual tradition here.[251] They recognised that with people who are in some way troubled

---

248. Hunter and Hunter, *What Your Doctor and Your Pastor Want You to Know About Depression*, 94.
249. Swinton, *Spirituality and Mental Health Care*, 129–30.
250. The *Letter to Prince Joachim of Anhalt*, June 23 1534 (See Appendix) and the *Letter to George Spalatin*, June 23 1534 (See Appendix).
251. Both Ignatius and Luther were influenced by the *lectio divina* tradition which, typically in the phase of *contemplation*, uses the imaginative visualisation of scriptural narrative as a way to help the reader of Scripture move more deeply into the text.

or depressed, the cognitive and reasoning faculties may be compromised or dysfunctional, but that the imagination and senses are often heightened, and may offer the best opportunity to reach the individual's inner spiritual world.[252]

While Luther's visualising of the biblical text is essentially rhetorical and not developed into a *meditative technique* like that of Ignatius, it does open up the question of how such imaginative visualisation might be intentionally used as a way of bringing God's Word to depressed persons.

It is necessary at this point to make two related and important distinctions. First, Luther's practice of visualising the biblical text is theological and pastoral in its orientation and not, in the contemporary psychological sense, therapeutic or curative. Luther's primary objective is not to help the sufferer benefit from imagining the text through the calming effect of the images themselves, as a positive 'self-help' alternative to negative depressive catastrophising. Luther's understanding of visualising the scriptural narrative is that by stepping into the text in faith, believing in Christ's gracious presence through his word, the reader receives Christ's benefits.[253] It is an encounter with Christ, the living word, through Scripture. The point of this is not to achieve a favourably altered state or to manage one's moods (as in psychological visualisation techniques), but to be encountered by Christ's gracious presence.[254]

Second, while Luther's purpose in leading others into imaginative visualisations of the scriptural narrative was undoubtedly that this should help them, his focus was not simply on 'fixing' the suffering of

---

252. This can be observed commonly with depressive persons' strong tendency to catastrophise the future. Without strong thinking and reasoning faculties to moderate their thoughts, they interpret sensory input in a highly imaginative but negative way, visualising the worst outcomes possible. However, such an active imagination may sometimes be open to other influences and possibilities too. See an explanation of this from David Purves, 'Creative Imagination and its Role in Stress, Anxiety and Depression', YouTube video, 5:34, posted by 'TheMoodControl', October 24 2011, accessed December 10 2012, http://www.youtube.com/watch?v=eSPyhCyysmg.
253. John W Kleinig, 'Meditation', John W Kleinig Resources, accessed April 12 2013, http://www.johnkleinig.com/files/7113/2730/7599/Meditation.pdf.
254. See Luther's pamphlet, *A Brief Instruction on What to Look for and Expect in the Gospels*, 1521 (WA XI, 13–14).

depression, but on transforming the person's suffering through God's comfort, in particular his gifts of faith and hope.

Unlike much of the popular spiritual literature on this topic available today, Luther's approach to visualising scriptural narratives is not all about 'overcoming depression' by spiritual means, but about receiving God's consolation and help according to his wise will. With these two important qualifications in view, it is appropriate to consider whether the church, in its pastoral care and counsel of depressive persons, may indeed take up such intentional approaches in its ministry of the word. In this post-modern age, in which many are drawn by the 'accommodating space' afforded by the narrative paradigm, here is an opening for the depressed—those whose 'story has gone missing'—to find their place in the biblical salvation story of Jesus Christ, through the ministry of grace-centred and biblically resourced counselling.

Of Good Cheer: Luther's Practical Theology of Joy

This theme is the single most significant emphasis in the twenty-one letters examined in this book. It stands at the very heart of Luther's comfort of the depressed. Luther's theology of joy, the development of which may be traced from his early writings through to his mature work,[255] is brought to bear in these *Trostbriefe* in a compelling and powerful way. In the process of analysing the letters, it becomes clear that the potency of this joy-theology for comforting the depressed is that it functions as the exact 'countervailing force' to depression's sadness and despair.[256] Depressive sadness is sustained by the individual's ongoing negative self-orbit in a growing cycle of self-defeat. Luther shows how God's gift of joy is able to break into and transform this destructive pattern and bring emotional relief and comfort, as God himself is revealed as the source and centre of life in place of the powerless and despairing self.

---

255. Stolt, *Laßt uns Fröhlich Springen*, 93–8.
256. Adam Potkay, *The Story of Joy: From the Bible to Late Romanticism* (Cambridge: Cambridge University Press, 2007), 73.

As Stolt,[257] drawing on Günther Metzger's seminal work[258] on this aspect of Luther's theology observes, it is clear that *Fröhlichkeit* (*laetitia*) is the 'foundational emotion' (*Grundgefühl*) of the Christian's life. In Luther's culture, this joy was both felt and expressed far more intensely than today. When Luther wrote '*Laßt uns fröhlich springen*', this was not just figurative but descriptive of how people of his time (adults as well as children) actually expressed joy and gladness: by leaping and jumping, dancing and clapping hands.[259] Generally speaking, Luther's *Gefühlswelt* was far more lively than ours. The difficulty, insecurity and pain of sixteenth century life created the conditions not only for dread and sorrow, but also for exuberant rejoicing in God's goodness, and enthusiastic celebration of life's good and pleasurable gifts when they were there to be had. In this way, Luther too experienced joy all the more deeply in times of severe *Anfechtung* and suffering.

The Christian's joy arises from the personal experience of God's grace, which shows that God himself is good, comforting and 'joy-rich' (*gut, tröstlich und freudenreich*)[260] and loves sinners, not an angry judge who inspires fear and terror (*Furcht und Angst*).[261] For Luther, God is the source and giver of the believer's joy. When Christians experience joy, it is the product of God's saving and self-giving actions. God's comforts bring *Fröhlichkeit* and *Freude*. Joy is an important fruit of the Spirit in the Christian's life because it witnesses to the Spirit's work in the believer's heart and shows that, even in pain and adversity, faith and its fruit are still present. God therefore wants his people to be joyful, both inwardly and outwardly; inwardly for their own sake and outwardly for the sake of others.[262]

---

257. Stolt, *Laßt uns Fröhlich Springen*, 93–4.
258. Günther Metzger, *Gelebter Glaube, Die Formierung Reformatorischen Denkens in Luthers erster Psalmvorlesung, dargestellt am Begriff des Affekts* (Götingen: Vandenhoek & Ruprecht, 1964).
259. Stolt, *Laßt uns Fröhlich Springen*, 95–7.
260. From Luther's 1531 German translation of Psalm 54:8 (WA Bi III, 56:21–23).
261. See Stolt, *Laßt uns Fröhlich Springen*, 55–6.
262. In the first of Luther's consolatory letters to the depressed Joachim of Anhalt in May 1534, he writes: 'So be joyful, both inwardly, in Christ himself and otwardly in his gifts and good things. This is what he wants. This is why he is with us. This is why he provides his gifts—that we may use and enjoy them, and that we may praise, love and thank him forever and ever.' (See Appendix).

The foremost source of joy is, of course, the Gospel itself; God's grace and favour for sinners through his Son, which gives a free conscience and the assurance of eternal life (sometimes called the *internal* or *inward* comfort). In the light of this loving mercy, *all* good gifts and pleasures may be received and used with thanks and 'enjoyed' with a good conscience. Music, laughter, good company, food, drink, sport, and so on (the so-called *external* or *outward* comforts) are gifts of joy from a God who first gave his own Son.[263]

Just as sobriety and self-denial had been the signs of piety in the old faith, so during the Reformation the outward joyful expression of faith, and the proper enjoyment of life's pleasures, were increasingly seen as the index of the Spirit's liberating and renewing activity in the Christian's life.[264]

Conversely, a lack of joy was a sign that something was not right spiritually in a person's life. This is an important emphasis in Luther's comfort of the depressed, some of whom were still oppressed by the fears and scruples associated with their former highly penitential spirituality. In this old model of the spiritual life, enjoyment was suspect and represented the danger of sin, as in the case of Joachim of Anhalt.

In Luthers letters to the depressed, as elsewhere in his writings, there are numerous examples of Luther aligning joy with a good conscience and the restoration of God's favour and friendship through the forgiveness of sins.[265]

But joy is more than this. In these letters, as in the table talk from around the same period, Luther uses this joy as a *weapon* to be strategically deployed against the dreaded *tristitia* and the devil, who uses sadness and despondency to attack the Christian's faith.[266] For example, in the second of his three letters to the severely depressed Jerome Weller, from the Coburg in 1530, Luther advises mocking and laughing at the devil, joking and playing games, going out and enjoying

---

263. See also the *Letter to Jerome Weller*, July 1530 (See Appendix).
264. Potkay, *The Story of Joy*, 73.
265. *Letter to Queen Maria of Hungary*, 1531 (See Appendix). See also the *Letter to Joachim of Anhalt*, Christmas Day 1535 (See Appendix).
266. See also Stolt, *Laßt uns fröhich springen*, 99.

a drink as ways to *practise* his Christian joy, so as to confound and humiliate the enemy, who would rather he was miserable and alone.[267]

One of the hallmarks of Luther's strategy of joy is his habit of encouraging and sometimes *commanding* his addressees to 'be comforted', or to 'be joyful'.[268] Such imperatives may sound strange to our ears since, in our culture, joy is understood as a product of our own internal emotional lives which comes or goes as it pleases, in response to things which are largely outside our immediate control. For Luther, however, joy is above all an *extra nos* supernatural gift of the Holy Spirit, and is freely given and available to the believer. Indeed God wants to make us joyful at all times and expects us to be, even–indeed especially–in the midst of suffering and sadness. When Luther commands his readers to 'be joyful' he is really telling them to make use of what is already freely available and accessible to them by grace through faith. We therefore are free to *act* in faith on God's promise and *be* joyful, even if this may initially mean defying our inner feelings of joylessness. As Potkay puts it, Luther sees joy as both a 'subjective attitude' and a 'set of outward practices'.[269] His use of the imperative, '*Sei fröhlich*', assumes that at the level of decision and behaviour, the will rather than the feelings may sometimes need to lead the way towards the deeper experience of *Freude* and *Fröhlichkeit*. Joy may therefore be most present in the life of the suffering Christian, and suffering may indeed intensify it.

As we have noted at various points, Luther draws on the long tradition of coaching his depressed readers in joyful and enjoyable activities, using a number of different channels. He adopts the use of light–hearted humour and wit with Joachim of Anhalt, joking about their mutual friends and Luther's publishers.[270] Luther also dispatched Francis Burkhart to Dessau[271] to continue engaging the prince in the practice of simply having fun and enjoying himself in good company, through games, conversation and laughter.

---

267. See the *Letter to Jerome Weller*, July 1530 (See Appendix).
268. The *Letters to Joachim of Anhalt*, May 23 1534, June 9 1534 and June 23 1534 See also the *Letter to Mathias Weller*, October 7 1534 (See Appendix).
269. Potkay, *The Story of Joy*, 73-6.
270. *Letter to Joachim of Anhalt*, June 12 1534 (See Appendix).
271. *Letter to Joachim of Anhalt*, June 12 1534.

Along with the enjoyment of food, beer and wine to stimulate enjoyment and gladden the heart, music is prescribed as a powerful comfort. Though this topic is addressed directly in only two of the twenty-one letters, it is nevertheless of special significance among Luther's strategies of joy against depression and sadness. In his letter of October 1534 to Matthias Weller[272] (the musician brother of Jerome) who was suffering a severe bout of depressive melancholy, and in his letter of June in the same year to Joachim of Anhalt,[273] Luther speaks of the anti-depressant power of music. He refers, in both letters, to 2 Kings 3:14-15 where Elisha calls for a musician to inspire him so that he is able to prophesy, and to Psalm 57:7-8 where David calls for the harp and lyre with which to make melody in praise and thanks to God.

Luther writes to Matthias Weller, 'If the devil returns and plants worries and sad thoughts in your mind, resist him manfully and say, "Get out, devil! I must now play and sing unto my Lord Christ".'[274] Luther also suggests the repertoire for Weller's spiritual 'music therapy': the *Te Deum* and the *Benedictus*, canticles of praise-the medicine of joy for the depressed and despondent heart.

Two key points emerge here: firstly, that the gift of music itself has power to lift up the despondent heart. Secondly, and more significantly, it is a means of praising God by which, as Luther writes to Joachim, 'all the saints *made themselves joyful* with psalms and stringed instruments'. Luther reflects here, almost certainly from his own experience, how music used to glorify God is a powerhouse of joy that reaches and uplifts the heart (the intellect and affects) so that, as he wrote to Matthias Weller, 'sad thoughts go away'.[275]

What emerges in these letters is Luther's conviction that joy is not only felt at the intellectual and affective levels, but is also deeply connected with the physical senses and appetites; indeed, receiving and using God's many and diverse gifts of joy is the means by which

---

272. *Letter to Matthias Weller*, October 7 1534 (See Appendix).
273. *Letter to Joachim of Anhalt*, June 26 1534 (See Appendix).
274. See Appendix.
275. While it can only be mentioned in passing here, this aspect of Luther's strategy against depression is very important and, given the profound role of music in Luther's theology, really deserves its own thematic treatment. It opens up many exciting horizons for the use of Christian music to minister to persons with depression today.

the whole person (intellect and affects, body and senses) participates in God's gracious and generous provision. While actively engaging in such joy, through means which integrate the whole person in this manner, the pattern of depressive and self-undermining thoughts and feelings is disrupted, and an alternative possibility for thinking, feeling and acting is introduced.

Joy and Happiness

The Positive Psychology movement uses the concept of *joy* (along with other emotions and qualities of life) in its construction of *happiness* as *subjective well-being (SWB)*.[276] This new psychology has gone away from focussing on mental illness and sought to work proactively towards helping people build positive, healthy, joyful and happy lives. Positive psychology (with its associated disciplines) is a growing and complex research arena. There is no doubt that this new direction has been a refreshing influence in all kinds of fields, including Christian education, pastoral care and counselling.[277]

As we reflect on the nature of joy, and how it may be brought into the experience of depression sufferers today, it is important to evaluate the understanding of joy within the structure of positive psychology. Is there any convergence here with Luther's theology of joy, on which Christian pastoral carers might draw in supporting and helping depression sufferers?

The designation 'joy' comes up in positive psychology literature in association with other more or less synonymous terms. It is often associated with words such as pleasure, fulfilment and satisfaction, in describing the affective elements of *subjective well being* (SWB) as the framework used for analysing and measuring all-round personal happiness with life. Seligman identifies that positive emotions and feelings such as joy are strongly associated with better health, longer

---

276. See Martin EP Seligman, *Authentic Happiness, Using the New Positive Psychology to Realize Your Potential for Lasting Fulfillment* (New York: Atria Books, 2003) and more recently, Seligman, *Flourish*.
277. Paul C Vitz, 'Psychology in Recovery', *First Things*, March 2005, accessed September 2013, http://www.firstthings.com/article/2007/01/psychology-in-recovery-41. See also Christopher Kaczor, 'Positive Psychology and Pastoral Practice', *Homiletic & Pastoral Review*, April 29 2012, accessed October 2013, http://www.hprweb.com/2012/04/positive-psychology-and-pastoral-practice/.

life, stronger relationships and professional success. Closely aligned with this key-insight into the effect of good emotions, positive psychologists propose that religious faith and practice improve SWB, and they are becoming increasingly interested in spirituality and 'transcendence' as key elements of human health.[278]

There is some common ground with Luther's theological understanding of joy here. Like Gerson and Constantinus (the 'psychologists' on whose work Luther drew in his consolation of the depressed), Seligman and others have identified the key importance of positive emotions such as joy, delight, satisfaction, and so on in human wellbeing and the crucial role they play in spirituality and faith as elements of human happiness. This affirmation is especially welcome in the church today, which, in some places, is still battling with the joyless and opresive legacy of extreme pietism.

However, comparing this *subjective wellbeing* model of joy with Luther's spiritual understanding highlights a fundamental difference between them. The concepts of joy, happiness, satisfaction, fulfilment, and so on in positive psychology are constructed within a consciously humanist scientific framework. Within that therapeutic framework they are undoubtedly valuable and valid, and have proved helpful in enabling many people to improve their lives.

On the other hand, Luther's view of joy is consciously theological and spiritual; in his world there was no 'secular' option. He saw joy not as something generated by natural human efforts, but as a supernatural gift and fruit of the Holy Spirit. Joy is the delighted recognition that God is for us and with us now and forever in Christ, and is therefore ours even in the midst of unhappiness, dissatisfaction, illness and misfortune of all kinds—in circumstances in which subjective wellbeing has been badly damaged or even shattered. This spiritual joy is not produced through the positive nurture of strengths or virtues, but is grasped by faith.

While the new openness in positive psychology to religion and spirituality is to be appreciated, we must recognise that it still operates within a humanist scientific framework, not a theological one. The true goal of Christian pastoral care is not to produce happier and more satisfied persons, but to help people discover the joy, hope and comfort of Christ through his word and gifts.

---

278. *Vitz*, 'Psychology in Recovery'.

Despite this basic difference, however, Luther's encouragement to his depressed readers—to enjoy the good gifts of life and cultivate good relationships—is certainly not in disagreement with many of the strategies used by positive psychology to build and strengthen the resilience and coping resources of depressed persons.

Activating Pleasure and Joy

Luther's behavioural strategies against depressive illness, in which he seeks to stimulate joy and positive affect through light-hearted company, games and other activities, owe, as we have seen, much to the medieval psychology of Jean Gerson and Constantinus Africanus. This same tradition is also mirrored in some of the models used today in cognitive-behavioural psychology, in particular *Behavioural Therapy* (BT), also called *Behavioural Activation* (BA).

In BT/BA, patients are, after careful individual assessment, scheduled to take part in pleasurable, enjoyable and satisfying activities, where they are coached and encouraged by the therapist. As we see in Luther's consolation of Joachim of Anhalt, activational strategies make use of externally introduced activity and input as a means to interrupt the negative pattern that has been established by a depressive person's own inner thoughts and attitudes. This external 'kick-starting' strategy also counters the negative behavioural patterns of self-isolation, avoidance, withdrawal and inactivity that make depression worse and prolong its hold.[279]

Unlike CBT, BT/BA does not work directly on changing a person's beliefs and attitudes as a means to improving their mood and affect, but begins in the second phase of the cognitive-behavioural cycle, tapping into the possibilities offered by activity that is rewarding, satisfying or pleasurable. A number of studies indicate that BT/BA works as well as CBT, and may even work better than CBT in cases of severe depression.[280]

---

279. Jorm *et al*, *A Guide to What Works for Depression*, 20. See also the current standard work on Behavioural Activation for depression: Christopher R Martell, Sona Dimidjian and Ruth Herman-Dunn, *Behavioral Activation for Depression: A Clinician's Guide* (New York: Guildford Press, 2010).
280. Pim Cuijpers, Annemieke van Straten and Lisanne Warmerdam, 'Behavioral Activation Treatments of Depression: A Meta-analysis', in *Clinical Psychology Review*, 27/3 (2007): 318-26. See also D Ekers, David Richards and Simon

Because BT/BA is based on relatively uncomplicated psychological theory and does not carry with it as heavy a loading of scientific ideology, it also commends itself as a model of therapy well-suited to use in Christian contexts, in combination with theological language and practices not unlike the theology of joy in Luther's letters to the depressed. Maria Armento's 2011 thesis on this topic[281] comprehensively investigates the opportunities that BT/BA presents for Christian counsellors and psychologists.

Humour

The use of wit and humour in helping people suffering depression was part of the established wisdom that Luther inherited from earlier masters of consolation. He drew on the *homo facetus* tradition[282]—the witty and entertaining conversationalist who had the gift of humour, and could break a person's negative mood and get him to relax and laugh, as we can see in his letters to Joachim of Anhalt. Humour was part of his 'weaponry of joy': one of God's gifts for the enjoyment of life.

It has long been known in the field of medical science that laughing has a relaxing physiological effect on the human body that is similar to that of exercise. It reduces stress hormones, relieves muscle tension and releases endorphins into the brain, which is why laughter is a pleasant and joyful experience.[283]

What does psychological research say about laughter's effects on depression sufferers? *beyondblue* assess the distinct model of treatment known as *Humour Therapy* quite unfavourably, citing the lack of strong evidence that it helps people with depression.[284] Other researchers are more positive about the general benefits of humour

---

Gilbody, 'A Meta-analysis of Randomized Trials of Behavioural Treatment of Depression', in *Psychological Medicine*, 38/5 (May 2008): 611–624.

281. Maria Elizabeth Anne Armento, 'Behavioural Activation of Religious Behaviours: Treating Depressed College Students with a Randomised control Trial' (Ph.D. dissertation, University of Tennessee, Knoxville, 2011), accessed January 5 2013. http://trace.tennessee.edu/utk_graddiss/1052.
282. Dicke, 'Homo facetus: vom Mittelalter eines humanistischen Ideals', 299–332.
283. Melinda Smith and Jeanne Segal, 'Laughter is the Best Medicine, The Health Benefits of Humor and Laughter', *Helpguide.org*, last updated May 2013, accessed August 2012, http://www.helpguide.org/life/humor_laughter_health.htm.
284. Jorm *et al*, *A Guide to What Works for Depression*, 40.

simply as part of natural traffic and dialogue between persons; something to be recognised and used in the context of helping relationships for the joy and comfort that it brings. There is a growing body of serious psychological literature which suggests that there are benefits for depression sufferers in humour.[285]

Cognitive Therapist, Nando Pelusi advances the view that humour can assist in the breaking down of depressive thoughts and feelings by promoting more *flexible* attitudes, and broadening the tolerance and perspective of depressive individuals. A feature of many depressive people is that their thinking tends to be kept within tight and rigid categories. Laughter triggers a psychological change of 'vantage point' for the depression sufferer, from being the unhappy *victim* or *enemy* of circumstance, to seeing and accepting oneself as a small *part of* the wider circumstance.[286] There is freedom especially in being able to laugh at oneself, not derisively but with an appreciation of the ironic and the ridiculous which is to be found in human experience. We see this beautifully modelled by Luther in his series of letters to the serious and forlorn Prince Joachim in 1534. He jokes about his publishers, talking about them as if they are pets who 'must be fed' regularly, before turning the humour around onto himself, describing how his publishers had finally gotten the better of him after all, having him 'saddled up with bit and bridle' like a horse.[287]

Depression and Music Therapy

Contemporary research into music therapy continues to rediscover the powerful joy-dynamic of music and music-making for people suffering with depression. Several smaller studies have shown that

---

285. Anna Bokarius, Khanh Ha, Russell Poland, Vladimir Bokarius, Mark H Rapaport and Waguih William IsHak, 'Attitude Toward Humor in Patients Experiencing Depressive Symptoms', in *Innovations in Clinical Neuroscience* 8/9 (September 2011): 20–3. See also So Hee Kim, Yean Hee Kim, Hwa Jung Kim, Soon Haeng Lee and Si On Yu, 'The Effect of Laughter Therapy on Depression, Anxiety, and Stress in Patients with Breast Cancer Undergoing Radiotherapy', in *Journal of Korean Oncology Nursing*, 9/2 (August 2009): 155–62.
286. Nando Pelusi, 'How to Cultivate Humor: If You're Suffering Depression, Humor Can Change Your State of Mind', *Psychology Today*, last reviewed March 25 2013, accessed August 2013, http://www.psychologytoday.com/articles/200405/how-cultivate-humor.
287. *Letters to Joachim of Anhalt* (See Appendix).

music therapy for depression is an effective adjunct treatment to other interventions, and that it enhances the benefits of other forms of psychotherapy.[288] Larger studies still need to be done to confirm and further explore these findings.

In the Christian pastoral care of depression-sufferers, the spiritual dynamic of music which Luther knew so well comes into view, suggesting possible deeper dimensions to be explored in music therapy in Christian contexts: receptive techniques involving the use of music as an aid for reflection and prayer, as well as more active involvement in music–*making*. The playing of music and singing of praise which happen communally in the public liturgy direct us again to the opportunities for consolation and healing that are offered in the church's worship, where music becomes the core medium for prayer, praise and the Word of God.

These 'Grey and Latter Days'

In 1967, when Martin Franzmann coined this phrase in his famous hymn O God, O Lord of heaven and earth,[289] he sensed already then the movement in western culture which has led to what Dan Blazer calls a new *age of melancholy*. Blazer[290] describes the human situation of our 'greyed-out' post-modern era in terms that, I suggest, are neatly captured in one word: joylessness.

In contrast to the pre-modern world, where the extremes of joy and sorrow stood in bold contrast to one another in everyday life, today we live a much more homogeneous and emotionally equalised existence. In the wealthy West, technology and social management keep (or *appear* to keep) chaos, death and war at bay most of the time. We have more security, safety and predictability in life than ever before. But much less joy.

---

288. 'Music Therapy 'Helps Treat' Depression', NHS Choices, accessed April 2013, http://www.nhs.uk/news/2011/08August/Pages/music-therapy-for-depression.aspx. This randomised controlled trial confirms the other studies done recently.
289. *Lutheran Book of Worship* (Minneapolis: Augsburg Publishing House, 1985), No. 396.
290. Blazer, *The Age of Melancholy*, 148–59.

The Shrinkage of Language and Experience

Birgit Stolt observes the shrinkage of the expression of joy in the German language during modernity and post-modernity. In Luther's world, joy was felt and expressed with a great intensity. Leaping, dancing and singing for joy were common spontaneous expressions of emotion.[291] Today, apart from the sporting arena where we are watching our team score goals, and the unself-conscious joyful responses of little children, such actions are considered rather 'over-the-top'. Likewise, our English vocabulary of joy has paled in its intensity. The words 'joy' or 'joyful' do not appear in everyday English usage much anymore except as a sarcastic put-down sometimes used in youth culture to describe whatever is 'geeky' or outmoded.[292] One must go to poets and theologians to hear it spoken in earnest; those living in the corners of our culture where language and meaning has not yet been completely 'greyed out'.

The Loss of Contrast

In our post-modern industrialised communities, we are faced by spiralling complexity together with unlimited but uninformed choice. We are expected to realise our potential in a world of expanding possibilities that no human being can keep up with.[293] We are saturated with information yet the very volume of it all prevents us from really acting on or responding to it.

Consequently, people are frequently paralysed by boredom and purposelessness. In all sectors of life, definition and differentiation are blurred and greyed. Moral and ethical issues are caught up in complexity that seems insoluble; there are always 'shades of grey' and 'grey areas'. One view must be as valuable as another. There are many ways forward; so many that *my* way is impossible to find.[294]

Joy requires and creates contrast. It needs a spectrum of real human experience which entails the acceptance of *extremes*—

---

291. Stolt, *Laßt uns Fröhlich Springen*, 300–6.
292. The words 'joyous' and 'joyful' are sometimes used as synonyms for 'lame' or 'stupid'. This shows the cynical and joyless edge to western youth culture. The very idea that something could be joyful-that it could really touch or change the individual's inner life-is scorned.
293. Greenfeld, *Mind, Modernity, Madness*, 4–6.
294. Solomon, *The Noonday Demon*, 407–8.

those things we hate in the twenty-first century and do our best to ameliorate. We work hard to protect people from extremes. We shield our children from danger, difficulty and disappointment of all kinds. But where contingency, tension and resistance are removed, how do people learn to adapt or become world-aware and resilient? Where the reality of life's difficulty and pain is masked and minimised, how do they recognise beauty, goodness or love when they encounter them? Unless they know suffering, how can they know joy? Joy can only be experienced where the bright and sombre colours of life have not been blended to nondescript grey.

Joylessness and the Loss of Hope

Where joy and sorrow are greyed out, so will hope be. Blazer's sociological analysis of western culture today shows how this grey joyless context has led to a dangerous loss of hope,[295] creating the conditions for our new age of melancholy, in which depressive illness becomes the widespread response to the disorientation and despair of life. He quotes Andrew Delbanco, whose description of the issues within a narrative framework over a decade ago is still insightful:

> Human beings need to organise the inchoate sensations amid which we pass our days–pain, desire, pleasure, fear–into a story. When that story leads somewhere and thereby helps us navigate through life to its inevitable terminus in death, it gives us hope. We must imagine some end if we are to keep at bay the ... suspicion that one may be adrift in an absurd world. The name for that suspicion–for the absence or diminution of hope–is melancholy ... the dark twin of hope.[296]

The current epidemic of depression is, in this sense, no less spiritual than the *melancholia* of the sixteenth century. The loss of meaning and joy, and ultimately of hope, creates a void that cannot be filled, a crisis of being in which the soul cries out for comfort and rescue.

---

295. Blazer, *The Age of Melancholy*, 151–52.
296. Andrew Delbanco, *The Real American Dream: A Meditation on Hope* (Massachusetts: Harvard University Press, 1999), 1–2.

Joy as Emotion and Practice

For Luther, joy is both a *subjective experience* and a *spiritual practice*. Sometimes it is led by the feelings and emotions which overflow into actions and practices such as praise, prayer, service, and so on. At other times it needs to be *led by* actions and practices, giving rise, in turn, to the affective and emotional experience of joy. This theology describes the surprise and delight of joy which visits the soul in response to the good and beautiful, but also helps the believer to seek the comfort of joy when his thoughts and emotions are depressed, through the external means of God's word and gifts.

Post–Modern Subjectivity

Many post-modern Christians have benefited from the influence of the positive psychology movement and its emphasis on *subjective wellbeing*, in which positive emotions and moods are seen to be linked to internal attitudes and values. We have seen this growing emphasis on *experiencing* the joy of faith celebrated in the Pentecostal and evangelical streams of the western church, and more widely too. In our 'greyed-out' new 'age of melancholy' this subjective-experiential dimension of joy is vital for Christian faith, and for helping depressed people find comfort, hope and relief in believing.

However, even when it takes account of external factors and influences, this construct of joy easily comes to depend on the inidividual's own ability to generate good affect. In this case joy risks becoming *primarily* a subjective experience, something that arises within the heart, 'bubbling up and over' as a spontaneous response from within. Certainly, this 'delight' aspect of joy is found in the Bible and in Luther's theology, and who would ever wish to deny or denigrate it?

Yet if it becomes the *mainstay* of spiritual joy, then joyful Christian living becomes little more than a spiritual form of *subjective wellbeing*; it depends on the individual's emotions and moods, and comes and goes with them. This overly 'internal' view of joy, therefore, often leaves people suffering depression in their own feelings, which move inevitably back towards despondency and negativity.[297] Luther's

---

297. Hunter and Hunter, *What Your Doctor and Your Pastor Want You to Know about Depression*, 85–6.

insight—that joyful and joy-expressing practices can also lead to joyful emotions—is a vital countervailing emphasis, and provides an invaluable activational spiritual strategy for helping depressed persons experience joy.

'Received Joy'

Luther's understanding of joy is not primarily *subjective* in the contemporary psychological sense, but *receptive*. It is part of the Christian's *vita passiva*—the life received from God through his word and gifts, not the life we build for ourselves through our careful cultivation of *subjective wellbeing*. Christian joy is therefore primarily the Holy's Spirit's *gift*, received by faith. While we certainly participate in it, we cannot create or 'realise' it for ourselves and it does not ultimately depend on what is happening in our own emotions, moods or situation in life. If, in our despondency and depression, we act on God's promises and engage in joyful behaviour of some kind, this too is faith receiving and using God's gift. Joy is therefore available to us in the midst of unhappiness and misfortune, even in deep depression. It is perhaps most readily recognised and received in the midst of such suffering, in the shadow of the cross. Suffering and pain do not necessarily diminish life's richness and joy, but may indeed deepen it. We may, at times, need to let go of our attempts at self-constructed wellbeing in order to experience joy because our human ideals get in the way of God's *real* gifts.

Rhetoric of Joy

Luther's theology of joy is still vibrant today, charged as it is with the Gospel's timeless good news of God's grace and mercy in Christ. However, as we have noted in earlier reflections, the rhetoric Luther sometimes used in his letters, while appropriate to his era and to his unique position, needs to be modified for the contemporary pastoral care context. His frequent authoritative imperatives to his readers in the twenty-one letters, 'Be joyful' or 'Be of good comfort', may not always be appropriate or helpful in today's pastoral care situation, in which the carer and the sufferer are on a much more equal footing in terms of education and power.

The rhetorical *dispositio* of imperatives in contemporary language tends to be not just authoritative, but *authoritarian*, and is tied up with giving orders, imposing one's own wishes and controlling the behaviour of others.[298]

To be sure, the underlying point is valid and very valuable. In our culture, where emotions and feelings are usually seen as entirely internal, individual and subjective experiences, people often need to learn the insight that the experience of joy may frequently be found by taking a joyful outward attitude, and getting involved in joyful and enjoyable activity.

However, with the pastoral care of depression sufferers today, this kind of encouragement and coaching needs to be done much more carefully, adopting a respectful, collaborative rhetorical *dispositio*,[299] and only if and when trust and respect has been established in the helping relationship. Gilbert points out at length how important it is to establish this rapport through intentional empathy, non-judgement and tolerance. The use of language and speech-forms which support and build such collaboration between helper and sufferer, is a key strategic factor in the pastoral care of depressed persons.[300]

Joy and the Liturgy

These considerations lead back, once again, to the vital importance in Christian pastoral care of helping people with depression come to worship. The whole movement of the liturgy is really a divine process for the transaction of joy. Through confession and absolution, the ministry of the word and prayer, and the Eucharist, the worshipper is transferred from his sterile self-orbit to a new orbit around Jesus Christ and the forgiveness, healing and life he gives through word

---

298. In Australia's highly egalitarian culture, the only relationships in which direct imperatives are used in contemporary language (apart from rude or abusive situations) are those in which there is an overt imbalance of power in favour of the speaker, for example, a parent speaking urgently to a young child for their own safety, military orders given to subordinate ranks, etc. This is different to Luther's day, where he could write to equals and superiors (even kings and princes) using the direct imperative as a means of emphasis and positive direction in the context of consolation.
299. It is important to note at this point, that Luther does not *always* use highly power-laden rhetorical forms in his consolations. He can, on occasions, speak from a position of vulnerability, sharing with the reader his own experience as a depression sufferer.
300. Gilbert, *Psychotherapy and Counselling for Depression*, 148–64.

and sacrament. Worship is, in this sense, all about joy as the true *Grundgefühl* of the Christian life. Whether it is solemn and high in its tone, or lively and expressive, the core 'joyful exchange' is the same: Christ takes what is ours and gives all that is his, including his joy!

Lanny and Victor Hunter point out that the liturgy's ritual is an extremely important structural feature of worship for depression sufferers, and an indispensable tool in pastoral care.

> The use of ritual not only provides alternative ways for expressing certain realities, but also may provide the only way to express them. This is especially true of sacramental expressions in which the framework of worship is a critical part of pastoral care from a Christian perspective... All things human—judgement, challenge, forgiveness, grace, sin, shame, suffering, healing, guilt, reverence, love, uncertainty, fear, hope and purpose—belong to the language and symbols and reality of both worship and pastoral care.[301]

Joy and Christian Community

The liturgy, pastoral care, mutual encouragement and service all find their integrative context in Christian community. Luther's *activational* approach to evoking joy in his readers assumes that God's gift of joy comes to us through the en*joy*ment of other persons, events and activities that cheer the spirit and provide consolation. This insight, which is fundamental in Luther's theology and practice of joy, highlights the importance of Christian fellowship and friendship in the pastoral care of depressed persons. It also shows the much-overlooked importance of intentionally incorporating depressed persons into small group activity, volunteer acts of service to others and team-activities which support and strengthen their sense of community.

Sadly, however, it is the case in many Australian church contexts that depressed persons do not find this kind of Christian care and support. Despite the community education initiatives like *beyondblue* and other agencies in Australia and other western nations, depression is poorly understood in many local congregations. Depressed church

---

301. Hunter and Hunter, *What Your Doctor and Your Pastor Want You to Know about Depression*, 94. See also Swinton, *Spirituality and Mental Health Care*, 128-30.

members frequently fall through the 'pastoral care cracks' in local community churches. They often pick up that, even though the clergy and members are well-intentioned, there is little real understanding of their situation and are tempted to withdraw, feeling vulnerable and unsafe.[302] Because depression is a widespread and common problem in the church community as well as in the wider population, this ignorance and lack of empathy can only be regarded as a serious deficit in the spiritual care of local churches.

---

302. Hunter and Hunter *What Your Doctor and Your Pator Wany You to Know about Depression*, 125–26. My pastoral experience in Australia would accord strongly with Swinton's observations. I frequently encountered the reality that church members were unable to empathise with and accept those with depression. See also the series of video diary entries published by Cordelia Ophelia, 'CordeliaOphelia', YouTube Channel, accessed September 2013, http://www.youtube.com/user/CordeliaOphelia.

Chapter 5
Of Good Comfort
A Summary—Interpretation

> 'Always forwards towards Luther...'
> Bishop Anders Nygren, LWF Assembly, 1947.

Three Types of Critical Encounter

As the contemporary horizon of depressive illness has been brought into reflective dialogue with Luther's pastoral consolation of depression sufferers of his era, *three different types of critical encounter* between these two 'worlds' have emerged:

a. *Points of modification*, where it becomes clear that Luther's understanding and practice needs to be either disclaimed or modified for the contemporary context because of social, cultural or scientific differences between his era and ours.
b. *Points of synergy*, where Luther's understanding and practice coincides with today's, and may be brought together with contemporary approaches in productive partnership and dialogue, to enhance current theology and practice.
c. *Points of transformation*, where Luther's theology and pastoral care critique contemporary understanding and practice by revealing or recovering valuable theological and pastoral insights and possibilities which challenge and have potential to transform current theology and practice.

In this threefold outcome, aspects of Luther's theology and practice which are no longer valid and appropriate, or which need to be modified, have first been identified and differentiated, thus helping to clarify the remaining material. Then the points where Luther's perspective coincides with and enhances current practices have been noted. Finally, the areas in which Luther's theology and practice speak critically and creatively into our current context are identified, highlighting the points of encounter on which his understandings may spark a rethinking of current assumptions and approaches.

It now remains to reflect briefly on each of these three areas of encounter which have emerged, in order to more fully appreciate their meanings for pastoral theology and practice in ministry to persons with depression.

Points of Modification

Luther's Authoritative Rhetoric and Today's Context

Luther's rhetorical *dispositio* sometimes creates problems when placed in the contemporary context. In post-modern societies, authoritative institutions and individuals do not have credibility for a majority of people, even when they are beneficent and caring. This is especially true when it comes to speaking in a definitive or declarative manner to people about issues in their personal lives.

Some of the rhetorical language Luther uses in his letters reflects the strong spiritual authority of the church over people's lives in the Reformation era.

Moreover, as a doctor of the church, and as a world-famous figure, Luther's unique status allowed him to speak from a rhetorical *dispositio* of considerable *personal* power and credibility. Luther's own direct experience of depressive illness gave him a certain confidence of conviction about what would help other sufferers. His theological-pastoral judgements and insights are often, therefore, presented as factual judgements, in the form of direct speech. Likewise, his counsel comes in the rhetorical form of *exhortatio* and imperative–a common and acceptable form of speech for Luther to use in his society, but which sounds very strong to our ears today.

Obviously this socially constructed rhetoric is not appropriate to helping relationships today, especially in an equality-conscious culture like Australia. All psychological practice and counselling today works with a far more collaborative approach to relationships and a much greater equalisation of power. Today pastors and pastoral counsellors need to deploy language very carefully and respectfully, in ways which reflect, suggest, encourage and empower the client.

Of course, all professional therapy and counselling relationships still have power dynamics. One of the major areas of accountability in counselling and therapy is appropriate use of power, particularly the way it is subtly used in the form of language. Abuse and coercion are to be avoided at all costs. It is clear, therefore, that we cannot speak to counselling clients or to those under our pastoral care as Luther often did, within the power-structure of his relationships–with bold declaratives, exhortatory imperatives and commands.

While it is generally expected that today's pastoral carer, counsellor or therapist may at some appropriate point offer input or even advice, it is not acceptable today to tell the client what they should do. In a pastoral encounter it may also be expected that the carer proclaim God's Word to the client; here too the forms of speech and rhetorical impact of the carer's proclamation need to be carefully chosen, taking into account the type and degree of trust and mutuality that has been established. Today's cultural context requires a different rhetorical *dispositio*, reflecting a different relationship between counsellor and client from Luther's day.

This is also increasingly the case among depression sufferers who today frequently reserve the right to interpret their own life-situations rather than simply hand over this right to medical, psychiatric or other professionals. People are less and less willing to 'be told' about their own lives or their own health by powerful professionals. In contemporary western culture the acceptance of others' power to judge one's state of being is increasingly seen as one of the things that shames and humiliates persons with depression, and adds to the stigma of perceived incompetence, unreliability and inferiority. This can be seen in the wider discussion regarding mental health, in which people are exploring multiple pathways of healing and wellbeing, trusting their own awareness and intuition above others' diagnostic and therapeutic determinations.

Luther's Medical Understanding of Depressive Illness

As noted at various points in the previous chapters, an obvious area in which Luther's perspective on depressive illness must be disclaimed is his medical understanding. The hippocratic humoral paradigm of *melancholia* in Luther's era was the accepted scientific and medical orthodoxy which informed the treatments offered by physicians. Like others, Luther read the medical literature on *melancholia* that had become popular and available through the influence of Renaissance humanism.

It is important to note, however, that while Luther subscribed to what later turned out to be a thoroughly misguided medical theory of depressive illness, his own pastoral engagement with depression sufferers did not in any way rest upon it. He was, as we have seen, far more interested in the spiritual and theological aspects of depression, and sought to offer his consolation and advice on *that* basis.

Twentieth and twenty-first century medical science has progressed to far deeper insight and understanding of depressive and other mental illness as brain-based. Greater knowledge is now being gained of mental illness through neurological and neuro-psychological research.

It seems however, that medical scientists and pastoral carers who work collaboratively with them might draw further important insights from the way in which history has unfolded here. When we note the pace of recent medical progress, and how primitive and ill-conceived the humoral model of depression accepted in Luther's era seems to us today, we might wonder how and why Hippocrates' ancient understanding was able to hold its own as the accepted scientific orthodoxy for so long. It was fundamentally an *observational* model and while it remained unchallenged by new forms of medical inquiry, functioned as a reasonably consistent and credible explanation.[1]

This demonstrates the reality that now more than ever, in this age of rapid scientific progress, medical and neurological scientists ought to be modest in their claims to understand the human person and know with certainty the mysterious complexities of the body and mind that have baffled researchers for centuries. What is known as 'scientifically certain' today may soon be shown to be inadequate or even mistaken.

---

1. In fact, *some* of the treatments prescribed under the humoral model-based as they were on observational data-remain valid today. Now as then, depression sufferers are advised to ensure good exercise, sleep, balanced nutrition and social engagement as active measures in their recovery.

Our understanding of the nature and meanings of depressive illness continues to grow. Like Luther, who accepted the challenge of embracing and integrating the new knowledge that was rapidly emerging in Renaissance Germany, we too need to be prepared to grow beyond where we are. As we have seen, the work of medical researchers such as Andrew Sims and John Peteet tends to indicate that neuro-scientific and theological understandings of mental illness are slowly moving closer to one another and beginning to seriously explore their common ground. In such an environment, medical professionals and religious pastoral carers need to remain open to the changing horizon and the possibilities which it may unfold.

Points of Synergy

Rhetoric of Vulnerability

We noted earlier that Luther's authoritative rhetoric is sometimes unhelpful in the contemporary context. However, rhetoric is capable of taking many shapes, and may be *disposed* (arranged) in a number of ways in relation to its hearers and readers. In our use of pastoral rhetoric today we need to make sure that the *dispositio* we take up is appropriate to our hearers and the relationship we have with them, and is not being received as manipulative, condescending or oppressive.

It is interesting to note that Luther does not *always* use highly power-laden rhetorical forms. He can, on occasions, take up a *dispositio* of vulnerability, sharing with the reader his own experience as a depression sufferer. At these moments he does not appear as the authoritative doctor, but as the fellow sufferer, using the very distance between these two dispositions as a rhetorical means to come closer to his reader. It is here, where Luther openly admits to his own human vulnerability, that his words are most winning, comforting and helpful to those who read them today.[2]

---

2. I have often found in seminars and public presentations that when shown Luther's frank disclosures of his own depressive struggle, audiences are frequently not only surprised, but deeply impacted. One pastor commented to me, 'So if Luther could feel so depressed maybe it does not mean the depressed people in my church have got it all wrong.'

An important clue to this use of rhetorical language in contemporary Australian society is the way in which *beyond blue* ambassadors and other depression survivors speak and write in the public domain. As fellow-sufferers, they speak 'from below' and 'from alongside', using what might be termed a 'rhetoric of vulnerability'.[3] Their rhetoric employs a different *dispositio*. It is often in the form of shared personal narrative that offers points of connection via which the hearer or reader may begin to reflect on, interpret, and reframe their own experience. It also has a destigmatising effect on depression and those who suffer it, revealing the falseness of common assumptions about depression sufferers and their quality as persons. It is highly affective and 'authoritative' simply because it is offered from a rhetorical *dispositio* appropriate to contemporary western culture.[4]

Cognitive–Behavioural Strategies

As explored throughout the previous chapter, the greatest point of synergy between Luther's pastoral consolations in these letters and pastoral counselling of depressed persons today is the use of cognitive and behavioural methodologies. As we have seen, by drawing on the 'psychology' of his day, Luther employed what psychologists today clearly recognise as CBT strategies, including metacognitive approaches to belief modification, cognitive transpersonalising, and behavioural activation.

However, for those giving pastoral care to the depressed today, the highly significant thing to note in Luther's use of these tools is the way in which he harnesses them to serve God's external word of justifying grace. He uses metacognitive methods to re-ground his readers in the reality of God's love. He uses cognitive transpersonalising as a means of spiritual direction in the context of the devil's assault on the conscience in depression. He also makes use of behavioural activation

---

3. See *beyondblue* ambassador, Kyle Vander Kuyp's account of his depression, 'Kyle Vander Kuyp', *beyondblue*, accessed October 2013, http://www.beyondblue.org.au/connect-with-others/ambassadors/ambassador-profile/kyle-vander-kuyp.
4. Another notable example is Australian Poet, Les Murray, in his many poems, interviews and most recently, in his depression memoir, Murray, *Killing the Black Dog*. See Les Murray talking about his depression: Murray, 'Les Murray on Killing the Black Dog (p 1).'

in order to move his addressees from habitual negative rumination to engagement in the God-given joy of Christian life and faith.

Just as Eastern Orthodox pastoral theologians today are exploring the cognitive-behavioural 'psychology' of the church's ancient Fathers as a resource for their engagement with current psychological models in pastoral care,[5] so Luther's letters too need to be more deeply explored and analysed, in order to probe the internal structures and dynamics of his fusion of theology and cognitive behavioural psychology.

The Narrative Paradigm

As we have seen, there is a strong positive correlation between Luther's consolatory practices and contemporary forms of narrative counselling and therapy. We noted the way in which Luther makes use of narrative strategies, collaborating with his reader in order to help *re-author* and *re-frame*. He makes special use of the biblical metanarrative as a resource for his readers to 'resituate' and 'reorient' their story of melancholy and depression, by helping them find themselves *within* the biblical narrative of hope and redemption. His unique way of 'collapsing time' so that his addressee is 'placed into' the biblical narrative, with its spiritual dynamics, drama and emotion, is a very striking feature.

The growth and development of narrative counselling and therapy as a highly adaptable and available means of helping depression sufferers has created many openings for Christian pastoral carers and counsellors to explore its possibilities. Here again, there is an important and potentially fruitful opportunity to mine Luther's letters to depressed persons to investigate more closely how he has shaped and crafted his narrative practices theologically, particularly how he has done so in relation to the biblical metanarrative.

---

5. Trader, *Ancient Christian Wisdom and Aaron Beck's Cognitive Therapy*. Archimandrite Hierotheos Vlachos, *Orthodox Psychotherapy: the Science of the Fathers*, translated by Ester E Cunningham Williams (Levadia: Birth of Theotokos Monastery, 2005).
See also Sandra Lee Dixon, John Doody and Kim Paffenroth, editors, *Augustine and Psychology* (Lanham: Lexington Book, 2012).

Music and Pastoral Care

Luther's recognition of the powerful joy-dynamic of music for depression sufferers is well borne out by contemporary research into music therapy for depression. Christian music therapists continue to rediscover the possibilities of music for treating depression, and the importance of music as both an expressive and effective healing agent in the context of worship as well as therapeutic consultations.

Luther's particular emphases in the use of music also seem to resonate strongly with today's experience. While there is no doubt that listening to music is beneficial, Luther advises his readers to be actively involved in *music-making*. However, Luther's key insight is the spiritual joy-dynamic of joining music to praise of God. This lifts music up off the human plain so that it becomes a means by which the heart is brought into the heavenly realm. Music used in this way is the divine 'medicine of joy' for depressed Christians.

Once again, this area opens a new horizon of research into the deeper aspects of Luther's understanding of music and its spiritual effects, and how these might be used in pastoral care and by Christian music therapists.

Points of Transformation

Theology as the Proper Frame of Reference

As noted already in relation to cognitive behavioural psychology, Luther very intentionally shaped his pastoral consolations in these twenty-one letters with his biblical Reformation theology as the main frame of reference, while drawing from various other historic and contemporary sources to supplement and assist him. As we have seen, he boldly adapted the current epistolary forms, rhetorical methods, medical insights and psychological wisdom of his era to serve within his wider theological framework of pastoral care. He drew on Renaissance humanism, with its rich reprising of classical and medieval knowledge, but always in order to serve his driving pastoral desire to speak and enact the Gospel of Christ to the suffering.

This approach has much to commend it to the church today. Even though the church's pastoral care is no longer the captive of the human sciences, as it was in the latter half of the twentieth century, there is still much confusion among pastoral carers about the integration of psychology, psychotherapy and Christian pastoral care. The dominance of clinical and psychological interventions for depression in our culture still tends to create pressure for Christian pastoral carers to give up their spiritual means and practices, and bow to the authority of science, as the only significant frame of reference for addressing mental illness.

However, as Luther shows, the church needs to carefully maintain its own legitimate language and categories for understanding and addressing depressive illness as a *spiritual reality*. Pastoral carers, while drawing on psychological and medical insights, have their own unique theological frame of reference in which to operate, in order to minister to the depressed with the spiritual means entrusted to them.

While psychology and medical science offer us important insights and strategies, especially in areas such as cognitive-behavioural dynamics, we need to continually evaluate and re-assess how we use these insights, and how we relate them to our own over-arching theological and spiritual framework. Our questions need to be: 'What philosophical values and assumptions come packaged into this material?' and 'How may we appropriate it *theologically*, and express it in sound pastoral practice?'.

In the face of the dominance of clinical interventions for depression today, maintaining a theological frame of reference requires an ongoing commitment on the part of pastoral carers; a continuing engagement with the living tradition of the church's *Seelsorge*, in which they engage in theological and biblical reflection.

Depression and the Devil

As we receive and interpret Luther today, it may be tempting to simply throw away elements which obviously do not fit with our culture's modern and post-modern world view. Luther's view of evil and the evil one is a shocking challenge to the post-modern naiveté of many contemporary theologians, however, it is not readily deconstructed. In fact, those aspects of it which seem the most ill-fitting today may, on closer examination, prove to be the most important of all.

While Luther's demonology is a controversial and confronting issue which some Luther scholars today would rather discard as part of an outdated medieval world view, no such 'simple disposal' is possible. The reality of the devil's work is part of the fundamental architecture of Luther's theology and also, therefore, part of the deep structure of his pastoral consolation.

Moreover, the devil's existence and activity is part of the biblical faith and tradition that continues to be important in the public teaching and faith experience of the church today. It is frequently also part of the spiritual experience and discourse of depression sufferers today, as it was in Luther's day.

Unlike some contemporary teachings about the role of demonisation and spiritual oppression in depressive illness, Luther sees the devil's temptation and attack as 'par for the course' in the lives of *all* believers; depressed persons happen to have their particular vulnerabilities, which the devil exploits in order to undermine their faith.

Nevertheless, the pastoral application of this theology with depressed persons is not to be lightly or casually undertaken. It requires the pastoral carer or counsellor to develop a shared world of meaning with the client. It may, as we have seen, be greatly aided by insights and approaches from contemporary psychology, such as narrative reframing and cognitive transpersonalising, as modes of pastoral dialogue and conversation through which the devil's attacks and temptations are placed in the light of Christ's liberating redemption, forgiveness and hope.

Depression, Justification and the Conscience

It is often claimed that the significance of justification by grace has waned in our era because people no longer feel guilty and fear God's punishment. Yet it is evident from the number of psychological and mental health issues associated with internalised and unresolved guilt and shame, that the deep sickness of sin and its toxic bi-products still wound the sensitive human heart and conscience. With some depressed persons, the conscience is distorted and damaged so severely that it turns inward and becomes its own despairing and angry judge, meting out condemnation and wrath against itself.

Luther's insight that pastoral care for the depressed centres around the healing of the sick conscience, through the proclamation of justification by grace and the forgiveness of sins, is a truly transformational one. It brings the external and objective message of forgiveness and hope into contact with the depressive person's inner despair, unfolding into a comprehensively renewing life reality. Just as this life-changing Gospel is the core of Christian faith, so it is the heart of Christian pastoral care. No psychologist or psychiatrist has access to this healing and recreating power. The pastoral carer's unique task is to appropriately proclaim this Gospel using the heart-language of the sufferer, to reach not only the intellect but also the emotions, will and, mostly crucially, the conscience.

Depressive Suffering and the Cross

Luther's theology of suffering offers a valuable, if sometimes disturbing, critique of the spiritualised human optimism offered so widely by Christian churches today. He claims that God is revealed to us and in us not through wellbeing and success, but through the cross of bitter suffering. The scandle of Luther's teaching is that when depression sufferers feel abandoned or even attacked by this God, as they often do, they experience his hand conforming them to the image of his Son. In the cross of depression, with its emotional and spiritual agony and powerlessness, Christ is at one with us and we with him. Through the cross of Christ, suffering becomes a sign that Christ has bound himself to us in order to transform and ultimately redeem our suffering.

It is not too much to say that for those giving sustained pastoral care and counsel to the depressed, some seasoned experiential knowledge of the cross of suffering is essential. Such spiritual maturity is needed if the carer is to understand and bear with the negativity and pain they will encounter in the sufferer. Giving pastoral care in this context requires patient 'cruciform' listening, and the forbearance to understand and respect long periods of silence as well as the expression of strong emotions. However, most challenging of all, it requires wisdom to know when and how to name the work of God in the sufferer's life. Sensitivity, patience and wisdom are required to help the carer discern how and when to speak the word of the cross and the word of resurrection and hope.

Joy as Gift and Practice

The theology and practice of joy found in Luther's letters is arguably the most significant point of transformation to emerge in this study. It stands out so strongly because it is a distinct alternative to the contemporary positive psychological quest for happiness and wellbeing. Springing from the Gospel of justification by grace, joy is based on the objective external Word of God, but crucially, is also a subjective affective experience of that grace. While in contemporary western culture joy is generally seen as an internal spontaneous emotional experience, in Luther's biblical understanding it is an *extra nos* gift promised by God, to be freely received in faith. For Luther, joy is 'in the Lord'; it is a gift of the Spirit and is therefore not ultimately dependent on life-circumstances or conditions. It may even be most intensely experienced in the midst of deep suffering and despondency, as Luther expresses in his commentary on the Magnificat:

> But where there is this experience, namely, that He is a God who looks into the depths and helps only the poor, despised, afflicted, miserable, forsaken and those who are nothing, there a hearty love for him is born, so that the heart overflows with gladness and goes leaping and dancing for the pleasure it has found in God.[6]

This joy may well up, even from the depressed heart, as a response to God's grace and goodness, or it may need to be 'worked at' through participating in joyful activities such as eating, drinking, making music and enjoying good company. It is on this point that a potentially transformative strategy emerges. Luther's theological use of behavioural activation strategies to stimulate his readers' enjoyment of the outward and material joys of life commends itself as an intentional approach for the pastoral care and counsel of depressed persons. Luther's focus on outward enjoyment could be extended to include other kinds of community participation, including Christian fellowship activities and acts of service. Behavioural Activation (BA) is a therapy with a proven track record in the treatment of depression today. It is readily adaptable to a theological frame of reference, since it is relatively simple and uncomplicated by difficult psychological presuppositions. Further investigation and research into the pastoral adaptation of this psychological intervention is a fertile field for future research.

---

6. WA VII, 538–604. Translation by Birgit Stolt in *Joy, Love and Trust*. 11.

The Use of Scripture

The use of Scripture in Christian pastoral care and counselling continues to be disputed territory. On one hand, it is rejected by liberal and secular pastoral carers who have abandoned any notion of 'Scripture'. On the other hand, it is used in a rigid and prescriptive manner by the conservative biblical counselling movement. Luther models superbly how to avoid the problems of both these extremes by a) using his deep knowledge and experience of Scripture skilfully and discerningly, according to the issues of context involved, and b) applying Scripture as law and gospel so that those in need may be led ultimately to forgiveness, peace and hope through faith in Christ.

Recent research shows that the use of the Bible in pastoral care is generally rather shallow, reflecting a low level of both biblical knowledge and *experiential biblical wisdom* among pastoral carers. On this score, we have a lot to learn from Luther. His deep and comprehensive understanding of Scripture, particularly of its human–divine narrative dimension, gave him an understanding of the human heart and conscience, as well as insight into how to apply the biblical counsel to them. He looks into the 'streets and alley–ways' of both the Old and New Testaments and sees human beings who are, spiritually if not culturally, like himself, and like us. He sees God's law and judgement on human sin, and he sees Christ's mercy and grace. As has been shown in previous chapters, he is able, like an expert physician, to apply the right scriptural medicine for the healing of the soul.

This kind of deep biblical knowledge, experience and skill requires a more thorough and ongoing engagement with Scripture on the part of pastoral carers than is currently the norm. It entails more than pastors or pastoral carers merely undertaking more academic biblical study in their training–though that too is important. It requires the *lived experience of Scripture* through spiritual and pastoral formation.

Luther also shows in these letters how to use basic psychological strategies as an aid in applying Scripture with depressed persons. He often uses Scripture as a major part of his metacognitive strategy for testing and challenging depressed persons' false beliefs and thinking. He makes use of biblical narratives to help his readers reframe and reconsider their own depression stories. Both these psychological strategies have the potential to be further developed for use within a theological framework.

Another area that warrants further research and investigation is Luther's use of meditative visualisation of scriptural narratives with depressed readers. This type of imaginative narrative engagement with Scripture is already well developed in the Ignatian spiritual tradition, however, Luther's approach, following the interpretive pattern of law and gospel, has its own distinct gifts to offer.

Pastoral 'Risk–taking'

This final point of transformation is perhaps somewhat controversial. As one examines and reflects on these twenty-one letters, it becomes more and more evident that Luther was a theological and pastoral risk-taker. In his desire to move towards and meet his readers where they are, he often goes out to the edge of his theological boundaries, especially in his pastoral use of rhetoric. He understood that pastoral practice, especially with those who are *in extremis*, requires the carer to respond flexibly and sometimes daringly in order to meet an extreme situation. Pastoral care is about doing theology in a *particular space*, with *a particular person*, not producing a correct balanced theological response that will stand up under all theological scrutiny. One has the impression when reading these letters that Luther is far more concerned about reaching his readers with his message of comfort than about satisfying theological correctness, at least in the *systematic* sense. He realises the need to do his theology faithfully 'in the moment' in order to meet people where they are and establish spiritual contact with them.

However, Luther was not a *reckless* risk-taker. He did not see himself as a prophet in receipt of direct revelations from the Spirit, who therefore trusted in the authority of his own religious impulses. His pastoral risk-taking was possible because he had a highly stable biblical centre of gravity. Luther was securely based in his theology and in Scripture. Reading these letters, one has the sense that Luther knows exactly how far he can 'lean out of the boat without tipping it over'.

In today's cultural climate, in which all kinds of theological and pastoral correctness and procedure seem to dictate how pastoral and human care may occur, Luther's kind of pastoral risk-taking is even more important.[7] Reality, especially spiritual reality, seldom runs along the artificial tracks that are built for it. Pastors and carers for the depressed therefore need to know how and when and where to push beyond these lines in order to reach, support and comfort those in need, while at the same time remaining firmly rooted in their theology and pastoral integrity. They need to learn and gain experience in 'how to lean out of the boat' in order to reach those they serve. This need to take responsible pastoral risks is the reason that pastors and pastoral carers must be well-formed biblically and theologically, as well as appropriately informed by the human sciences.

Conclusion

These twenty-one letters offer ongoing wisdom and inspiration to Christian pastoral carers today for their ministry to the depressed, and open up new horizons for future exploration As Anders Nygren said in 1947, so today, we find ourselves saying not 'backwards to Luther', but 'forwards to Luther'.

As we observed at various points in this study, Luther lived 500 years ago, and in a very different society to ours. Yet in this research journey we have been able to confirm that his pastoral insights and practices still speak to us powerfully today, in some cases in a very immediate and direct manner, and in other cases with the help of interpretation and adjustment for today's changed context.

All the key elements of Luther's consolation identified in the chapters above contribute to this. However, by way of final reflection, these many aspects can be boiled down to two essential and related features.

Firstly, in these letters Luther was able to communicate an honest understanding, acceptance and affirmation of his readers' human experience of the pain and despair of depressive illness. It quickly becomes evident to the reader that Luther knows and empathises with the experiential reality of depression.

---

7. Today guidelines, rules and procedures have run wild in all kinds of human and pastoral care. This is counter-productive. People frequently do not fit into these devised structures, and carers are not free to make informed judgements in the moment.

Secondly, this platform of receptive understanding allows Luther to address the word and grace of God to his readers in experiential and practical terms, which can be received and used at the immediate level of daily life.

These two features are as effectual today as they were in Luther's world, and are the reason that his letters to depressed persons are still able speak so pertinently and powerfully to so many contemporary readers.

Appendix: Luther's Letters of Consolation to the Depressed: Translations

1. Elisabeth (Mrs Johann) Agricola

WA BR IV, No.1112, 210–211.[1]

June 10 1527

To the honourable and virtuous Mrs. Elizabeth Agricola, wife of the schoolmaster in Eisleben, my dear friend: grace and peace.

My dear Elsa:
I intended to write to you earlier, but Mr. Matthes[2] left before I got around to it. I am assuming that by this time your master is back home again and that, God willing, you are feeling better.

You must not be so fearful and anxious. Remember that Christ is near and that he carries your troubles, for he has not abandoned you, as your flesh and blood would have you think. Just call out to him honestly, from the heart and you can be certain that he hears you, for you know that it is his way to help, strengthen, and comfort all who ask him. So be of good comfort, and remember that he has suffered far more for you than you can ever suffer for his sake or for your own. We also mean to pray; in fact we are already praying earnestly that in his Son, Christ, God will accept these prayers and strengthen you in this weakness of body and soul.

With this, I commit you to God. Amen.

Greetings to your schoolmaster and your whole family from all of us.

Whitmonday, 1527.

Martin Luther.

---

1. Translation by Stephen Pietsch (June 2015).
2. Luther refers to the postal courier.

2. Johann Agricola

WA BR IV, No.1111, 210.[3]

Early July 1527

To his brother in the Lord, Johann Agricola, at Eisleben, a teacher of Christian young people.

Grace and peace.

If you are able to help at all in the matter Stephanus[4] will explain to you, please do so. Until now we have, with varying success, been deceived. Nevertheless it seems to me that this person has not deceived us or our efforts, when we actually talk it over. She is wretched and needs loving attention, for which you have willing helpers.[5]

It seems to us like a solution, if it will help, for your Elsa to have a change, and breathe the air to which she is accustomed,[6] and rest here with us for a few days. As soon as you make a decision about this, we are glad to support your charming wife, that excellent and honest lass, in whatever way will be helpful for her.

Goodbye. My Kate is vomiting and nauseous, and is once more sick (with a 'good sickness' I hope), with a dizzy head (caused by what, I do not know).[7] She heartily wishes your Elsa well.

My little John is cheerful and strong, and is a ravenous and thirsty little chap, thanks be to God.

Martin Luther

---

3. Translation by Fraser Pearce (November 2010).
4. Postal couriers who carried and delivered letters often also were entrusted with verbal messages from the sender.
5. The nature of this matter is unclear. Who was trying to deceive Luther? Clearly, Luther decided not to commit the details of the matter to paper, either for the sake of confidentiality or to save time. Some of Luther's statements seem to point to the possibility that the woman he refers to in this first section of the letter is Elizabeth Agricola; however, the fact that Luther takes up the matter of Elizabeth Agricola's situation quite openly in the next paragraph suggests that this first section of the letter deals with an entirely different issue. Added to this, it is very unlikely that Luther would have had any access to Elizabeth Agricola in the days prior to his writing this letter in order to make the judgments he does here.
6. Elizabeth Agricola was a native of Wittenberg.
7. The 'good sickness' Luther mentions almost certainly indicates that Katie was pregnant.

3. Johann Agricola

WA BR IV, No.1119, 215–220.[1]

Early July 1527

To John Agricola, servant of Christ in Eisleben, my friend in the Lord: grace and peace.

My dear Agricola:
I have enthusiatically and gladly welcomed your Elsa here. Her sickness is, as you see, more to do with the soul than the body. I am comforting her as well as I know how, and as much as I can. You could have done the same, except that in situations like this a woman believes anybody else in preference to her own husband, for she thinks that everything her husband says is motivated by love rather than good judgment.

In summary, her illness is not a matter for the apothecaries (as they refer to them), nor should it be treated with the poultices of Hippocrates, but requires the efficacious plasters of Scripture and the Word of God. For what has the conscience got to do with Hippocrates? Therefore I would dissuade you from using bodily medicine and recommend instead the power of God's Word. However, it is the way of our wives to think that the Word is not relevent to them but only to us, their husbands, who are their defenders and guardians. So do not give up impressing upon her that when the Word of God is taught, whether you are present or not, it has something to say to her. I have to fight this same battle all the time with my own Katie. Our wives must watch out in case, when they do need to make use of the Word, they find, to their sorrow, that it is too difficult.

Otherwise everything is well. Farewell in the Lord.

Martin Luther.

---

1. Translation by Stephen Pietsch (June 2015).

4. Joachim of Anhalt

WA BR VII, No.2113, 65–67.[2]

May 23 1534

Grace and peace in Christ.

Enlightened Prince, gracious Lord,

Master Nicolaus Hausmann informed me that Your Grace had been a little unwell, but that you were, thanks be to God, once again on the mend.

I have often noticed that almost all the members of Your Grace's family have reserved, quiet and serious natures,[3] and this has led me to think that Your Grace's illness may well be caused by melancholy and depression. I really wish, therefore, to encourage Your Grace, who are a young man, always to be joyful, to participate in riding and hunting, and to seek out the company of others who may be able to enjoy these things with Your Grace in a godly and honorable way. For loneliness and melancholy are poisonous and deadly to everybody, especially to a young man. This is why God has commanded us to be joyful in his presence; he does not want an offering of sadness. This is frequently recorded by Moses[4]; also in Ecclesiastes 12: 'Enjoy yourself, young man, while you are young and let your heart make you glad.'[5] No one realises how much harm it does a young person to avoid enjoyment and fall into being lonely and depressed.

Your Grace has Master Nicholas Hausmann and many others there with you. Be joyful with them; for gladness and good cheer, when honourable and decent, are the best medicine for a young person—in fact for everybody. I myself, who have spent the better part of my life in sadness and negativity, now look for and find enjoyment wherever I can. Praise God, we now have enough understanding to be able to enjoy God's gifts in good conscience and with thanksgiving, for he created them for this very purpose and is delighted when we do this.

---

2. Translation by Stephen Pietsch (June 2015).
3. Luther is referring to Prince William of Anhalt, who became a begging friar in 1473 and of Prince Joachim's two paternal aunts, who became abbesses.
4. That is, in the books of Moses, the Pentateuch.
5. Actually Eccl 11:9.

If I am mistaken and have done Your Grace an injustice, I hope that Your Grace will be generous enough to excuse me. However, I truly think that Your Grace is reluctant to enjoy anything, as if this were sinful. This has often been my problem, and sometimes still is. To be sure, enjoying sin is of the devil, but participation in proper and honorable pleasures with good and God-fearing people—even if the talk and joking might sometimes go too far—is God-pleasing.

So, be joyful, both inwardly in Christ himself and outwardly in his gifts and good things. This is what he wants. This is why he is with us. This is why he provides his gifts—that we may use and enjoy them, and that we may praise, love, and thank him forever and ever.

Age and other concerns will show how futile this present depression and melancholy is. Christ cares about us and will not abandon us.

To his keeping I commit Your Grace forever. Amen.

Your Grace's willing [servant],

Martin Luther, Doctor.

Pentecost Eve, I 534.

5. Joachim of Anhalt

WA BR VII, No.2116, 70.[6]

June 9 1534

Grace and peace! Gracious prince and Lord!

Along with this letter I send back everything which travelled with me,[7] and thank you for it all most profusely.

On the way back, I diligently and almost without ceasing thought of you, Your Grace, and prayed the *Our Father* several times as well.

Phillip M has since pointed out to me that Your Grace has not been especially unwell until just recently, to which I said 'Then it's no wonder that His Grace has so easily become anxious; he is unaccustomed to it'.

---

6. Translation by Stephen Pietsch (October 2010).
7. Luther had been visiting the court at Dessau to attend and minister to Prince Joachim in his depressive illness. The prince provided Luther with horse-drawn transport and an armed guard for his journey back to Wittenberg after his visit to Dessau.

But God acts rightly in wishing Your Grace to get used to suffering at this time. So, Your Grace, you should be glad that God has taken you to school this once, and will teach you how to suffer a good hiding.[8] He wishes the rod to remain a rod, not to make an executioner's sword of it, so that Your Grace may go on suffering the rod.

Come, Your Grace, my Lord and prince, be cheerful and remember that other brothers are suffering too, as St Peter says, and perhaps even more than you are.[9] For Christ says 'Because I live, you also will live'.[10]

When I have fed my printers a little, I will come again and bring the Pomer[11] with me, as he has promised me today.

And with this, I cheerfully commend you to God.
Tuesday after Corpus Christi (9 June), 1534.

6. Joachim of Anhalt

WA BR VII, No.2119, 73–74.[12]

June 12 1534

To the most enlightened and highborn prince and Lord, Lord Joachim, Prince of Anhalt, Prince of Ascania,[13] Lord of Bernberg, my gracious Lord. Grace and peace in Christ!

Gracious Prince and Lord,

Johann Beichling has brought me an excellent report that Your Grace is in good spirits, and that you are again finding pleasure in eating.[14] For as I have certainly said, and prayed all along and continue to do at all times now, (like my good Lord, the Provost)[15] 'O God, let my prince be healthy and happy'. And I hope that he will do it.

---

8. Here Luther uses a colloquial German expression: 'a good shilling's worth' meaning 'a good hiding'.
9. 1 Pt 5;9
10. Jn 14;19
11. Luther's nickname for Bugenhagen.
12. Translation by Stephen Pietsch and Brian Van Wageningen (June 2010).
13. "Ascania" is the older dynastic name for the house of Anhalt.
14. People acting as couriers of written mail from one place to another routinely delivered verbal messages as well.
15. Luther is referring to Joachim's older brother, Prince Georg, who was at that time provost (dean) of the Cathedral in Magdeburg.

When I have fed my publisher bosses a little bit so that I may have some peace from them, I will (God willing) bring with me the 'Pomer',[16] the 'Pomersche'[17] and 'Hamester'[18] so that my gracious wife may see how the 'Pomer' and the 'Pomersche' are looking so 'happily married'.

So to God be commended. Amen! And may Your Grace be joyful indeed. My *Our Father* and I myself are with Your Grace.

Now, Your Grace needs to be a bit careful of Master Francis[19] when it comes to the game of chess. For he thinks he can play very well, and I would give a beautiful bunch of roses to be able to play as well as he allows himself to think he can.

He knows how to place his knight, and how to move his rook and how to position his pawns, but the queen is his master in the game, and perhaps elsewhere too! That he understands the best! Amen.

June 12, 1534

Your Grace's willing [servant]

Martin Luther

7. Joachim of Anhalt

WA BR VII, No.2120, 75.[20]

June 13 1534

My gracious beloved prince and Lord, Prince Joachim of Anhalt.

---

16. 'Pomer' is Luther's nickname for Johannes Bugenhagen (a native of Pomerania).
17. The feminine form of 'Pomer', a nickname Luther transferred to Joachim's sister-in-law, Margarethe, the wife of Prince Johann (who also came from Pomerania). Mennecke-Haustein (*Luthers Trostbrief*, 249–250) speculates that Luther's statement about Bugenhagen and Margarethe being "happily married" can only be a joke about the obvious good will and friendliness that existed between the two Pomeranians. However, the circumstances referred to in this paragraph are far from clear and the exact nature of this 'in-joke' is unknown.
18. The identity of 'Hamester' (Hamster) is unknown. The best guess scholars have offered is that it is the pet name of Margarethe's seven-year-old daughter.
19. Francis Burkhardt, a close friend of, and frequent visitor to, Joachim during this bout of depressive illness.
20. Translation by Stephen Pietsch (June 2009).

To Your Grace's hands, in haste.

Grace and peace in Christ! Gracious prince and lord!

Dr Augustinus[21] was in such a hurry that I am was hardly able to write anything.

Christ our Saviour will help Your Grace, should the moment come. Then his promises will not fail you.

I wish, as soon as I have fed my publishers a little, to do as Your Grace has written, and as I have promised.

With this, I commend you to God. Amen.

Your Grace's willing servant

Martin Luther.

8. Joachim of Anhalt

WA BR VII, No.2121, 76–77.[22]

June 23 1534

For the attention of my gracious prince and Lord etc., quickly written, composed as a supplication from a poor comforter and 'paraclete', until God provides something better.[23] Amen.

Grace and peace, which is true joy and comfort in Christ.

Gracious Prince and Lord, it must surely be of no small benefit that Your Grace is not yet rid of this fever and spiritual attack, since we had thought that you must be rid of it – that our prayer had been heard and accepted by God, true as he is to His promise, on which basis which we trust and pray.

But I think he is rather doing with Your Grace what he did with the children of Israel in Egypt (not to mention what he did with others and is even now doing with me), namely glorifying himself in the burning bush before Moses (Exodus 3), saying that he had heard the Israelites' cry and wanted to rescue them, so that Moses and Israel might have been under the impression that God would do it first thing tomorrow.

---

21. Dr Augustinus Schurf, Luther's physician.
22. Translation by Stephen Pietsch (November 2009).
23. Luther is referring to his hope of visiting the court at Dessau again in order to once again comfort and attend to the prince.

But as God begins to help, the situation gets worse than before. Israel were tormented to the extent that they even regretted that they had ever prayed and believed. They began to despair of God's salvation altogether.

On top of that Pharaoh suffered many plagues, but even that did not help. Israel had to continue to be tormented and imprisoned until the time came when the promised redemption they had wished for arrived in all its glory, and their enemies were drowned in the Red Sea.

For St Paul says in Ephesians 3, if our prayer is acceptable, God will do far more than we could ever think or wish.

When God takes hold of things, it seems to us that he is trying to make things even worse. On this point we can learn from what the apostle says in Romans 8: we truly do not know how we should pray, but he as a true Father, knows and sees how we should pray, and he acts according to this knowledge, and not according to how we pray.

In the same way, therefore, a father has also to act against his child by not giving him what he asks for, but rather what the father knows he should ask for. Though the child cries about it, no harm is done. His request is no less acceptable to the father if the father does not respond on this occasion or in the way the child wishes or asks.

In the same way, a doctor often must not act how, when and where his patient wishes, and yet he loves the patient and truly wants to help him. By his leaving aside the patient's longing and asking, nothing bad happens, and it is therefore, as a result, none the worse for the patient.

Therefore, Your Grace, I hold that our Lord is striving even now, and indeed has it in mind to improve Your Grace's situation, and that he will help you even more powerfully, for this is what we are now asking. I have no doubt that our requests are well-pleasing to God. This kind of prayer is what the Lord commands—and it is in fact his own work in us, and so must please him. And he will, I hope, do more for you than heal your fever, for Your Grace is an exceptional person.

Therefore let Your Grace be comforted. Christ is ours—yes, in every way ours, just as we long for him. And even if he makes himself an obstacle to reason, no matter.

God willing, I will soon be with Your Grace, once those who are plaguing me have eaten a little,[24] to stay with you for a week, and if I can manage longer, I will.

Christ, our Lord is himself with Your Grace; that is certain. To His grace and protection I commit you.

St John's Eve

9. Joachim of Anhalt

WA BR VII, No.2122, 78–79.[25]

June 26 1534

Grace and peace of mind, and also comfort and strength of body, from Christ Jesus, our dear Lord and comforting Saviour.

Gracious Prince and Lord:

While Master Francis[26] is again returning to Your Grace to entertain you, did not want to see him go without a word from me, even if I had nothing to write except 'Good morning' or 'Good evening.' I have every hope of Your Grace's condition improving, although improvement could be slow.

I am always faithfully praying my meager *Our Father* on Your Grace's behalf. As I do so, I recall that when I was ill it sometimes took a longer time and sometimes a shorter time before I received help, and that I received more than I prayed for.

Now, of course, I am speaking here about spiritual consolation, for earthly comfort is worth little unless it arouses spiritual consolation. Elisha, for instance, was roused by his minstrel,[27] and David himself says in Psalm 57 that his harp was his pride and joy: 'Awake, my glory; awake, psaltery and harp.'[28] And all the saints cheered themselves with

---

24. Here Luther is referring to his publishers who were pestering him to complete material due for publication. His joke is that, like Pharaoh, whom he mentions in this letter, he too must suffer plagues.
25. Translation by Stephen Pietsch (June 2015).
26. Francis Burkhardt was a teacher of Greek in Wittenberg, who was made rector of the university in 1532. An intimate friend of Prince Joachim, he was later attracted to politics and in 1536 became vice-chancellor of Electoral Saxony.
27. Cf 2 Kgs 3:15.
28. Ps 57:8.

psalms and stringed instruments. This is why I am glad that Master Francis is returning to Your Grace, for he is an upright and decent man, who will be able to cheer Your Grace's heart with good and Christian conversation, singing, and other things.

I tender to Your Grace my best good wishes and pray that Master Francis' services will help in the restoration of health and the defeat of the attacker. Amen. Unless I die or am laid low before I can do so, I too mean to visit Your Grace (this is certain) as soon as I can free myself from the collar, bridle, saddle, and spurs of the printers.[29]

With that, I commit Your Grace to God. Amen.

Friday after Saint John's Day, 1534.

10. Joachim of Anhalt

WA BR VII, No.2279, 335–336.[30]

December 25 1535

May our dear Lord Christ comfort Your Grace with his incarnation. He became incarnate to comfort and show his good will to all people, as the beloved angels today sing, 'Glory to God in the highest, and on earth peace, good will toward men.'[31]

I trust that Your Grace will have no doubt or despondency concerning the Faith or the Gospel, since Your Grace has now been well instructed in that which is the truth, as opposed to the lies of the devil and the pope. If we stand firm in the Faith and teaching, what does it matter even if hell and all its demons descend on us? What can distress us—apart from, perhaps, our sins and a bad conscience? Even so, Christ has removed these from us, even while we sin daily. Who can frighten us except the devil? But greater than the devil is He that is in us,[32] weak though our faith may be. Even if the devil were holy

---

29. Luther was occupied with seeing the first edition of his translation of the complete Bible through the press; it appeared in this same year. Luther finally visited the prince with several friends from July 15 to July 19, and again from July 24 to July 28.
30. Translation by Stephen Pietsch (June 2015).
31. Lk 2:14.
32. Cf 1 Jn 4:14.

and sinless, we admit that we are sinners. And even if the devil were so strong that he did not require Christ's help and strength, we need the dear Saviour. Weak we must be, and are willing to be, in order that Christ's strength may dwell in us; as Saint Paul says, 'Christ's strength is made perfect in weakness.'[33]

Your Grace has certainly betrayed or crucified the dear Lord. But even if Your Grace had, Christ nevertheless remains gracious. He prayed even for those who crucified him. Therefore, be of good comfort. In Christ's strength resist the evil spirit, who can do no more than trouble, frighten, or kill.

The dear Lord Jesus Christ, our friend and our consolation, be with Your Grace and not leave Your Grace comfortless.

11. Elizabeth von Canitz

WA BR IV, No.1133, 236-237.[34]

August 22 1527

To the honourable and virtuous Miss Elsa von Canitz, currently in Eicha, my dear friend in Christ: grace and peace in Christ Jesus.

Honoured, virtuous Miss Elsa:

I have written to your dear aunt, Hanna von Plausig, and asked her to send you to me for a time. It is my intention to use you as a teacher for young girls and through your undertaking this work, set others an example. You would have accommodation and meals in my home, so you would be in no danger and have nothing to worry about. So, I now ask you not to decline [my request].

I hear too that the evil enemy is attacking you with depressive thoughts. O my dear young woman, do not let him frighten you, for whoever suffers the devil here will not have to suffer him later. It is a good sign. Christ suffered all this too, and so did many holy prophets and apostles, as the Psalms amply show. In view of this, therefore, be of good comfort, and willingly endure this, your Father's rod. He will relieve you of it in his own time. If you come, I shall talk to you further about this.

---

33. 2 Cor 12:9.
34. Translation by Stephen Pietsch (May 2015).

Herewith I commit you to God's keeping. Amen.

Thursday after St Agapitus' Day, 1527.

12. Queen Maria of Hungary

WA BR VI, No.1866, 194–197.[35]

1531

Grace and peace from God, in Christ, our Lord and Saviour.

Enlightened and highborn Queen

I have heard from N[36] how distressed Your Grace has been, and I can only think that such distress does not come from a single cause, and as is often the case, misfortunes do not come alone.

I myself know well from experience how the devil, when he finds an opportunity, gladly climbs over the fence—especially where it is lowest; and where it is wet already, there it pours. Out of one struggle, as from a single spark, he happily creates a fire or a flood.

Therefore this is my humble request and warning, Your Grace: resist as far as possible your own thoughts, which actually are *not* your own, but most certainly those which the devil has stirred up.

Our Lord is not so angry as we may be accustomed to think and feel, but tests us to see if we honour him and have courage to suffer, while he himself, though blameless, has willingly taken on himself incomprehensible suffering for our sin, and so all this is from the all-gracious heart of his Father, our dear God.

If we think about it, this suffering which his beloved son has taken all on himself, for our sake, is so great that we should see our own suffering as insignificant by comparison. So compared to the gall and vinegar which he suffered, our present suffering could only be considered fine wine and malvaiser.[37]

And if he is our gracious God, whose pledge we have, namely his son, given through baptism, the sacrament and the Gospel, we should

---

35. Translation by Stephen Pietsch (June 2011).
36. Luther uses only the initial 'N' here to refer to the person who has passed on news of the queen's illness. The person's identity is unknown.
37. A high quality wine imported from Southern Europe.

certainly not doubt, but rather rely completely on his grace, which covers everything. This is also God's will.

What does it matter then if body and life, father and mother, brothers, kingdom, crown, honour, wealth and anything else one could mention pass away? For if God's grace remains ours, then God is our father and his son is our brother, and heaven and his creation are our inheritance, and all the angels and saints are our brothers, cousins and sisters. So if we lose everything, we have after all, lost less than a halfpenny's worth and even if we had no kingdom, heaven or earth, we still have God himself and eternal life!

Therefore I now ask God the Father himself that he, through his dear Holy Spirit, would write on Your Grace's heart what is so richly found in Scripture, and keep you thinking about this. Moreover, I pray that it will go much deeper, *into* your heart, deeper even than your own life and the things Your Grace holds dear on this earth.

I write this because I most certainly hope that Your Grace will have no further heavy burden or battle with the devil, either concerning sins or the conscience or matters from the past which do not concern the conscience.

Therefore Your Grace ought to thank God that you have a good conscience before him in Christ, because that far outweighs every temporal bodily suffering we may have. Ah, we will never do or suffer for ourselves—much less for God—as much as he has done and suffered for us.

So know, Your Grace, that to our Lord God, the highest service and pleasure and the best sacrifice is that we should fight against such depressive and melancholy thoughts, and allow them no room. For God's grace is able to comfort us far more than all the distress and unhappiness under heaven, on earth or in hell can depress and terrify us.

As he says in Psalm 147, 'God takes pleasure in the one who fears him and trusts in his goodness'. And also in Psalm 51, 'the sacrifice of God is a downcast spirit and an empty heart'. And as Psalm 50 commands, one should not keep struggles and misfortunes in the heart but cast them away, fleeing to God and calling on him. The text then also says 'Call upon me in your need and I will help you, and you will thank me'. It does not say 'Look at your needs' but rather 'Turn to me and cry to me and you will never be in need again'.

For God is above all troubles, and if it is God's will that his grace should comfort us, then no misfortune can depress us, as Paul says in Philippians 3, 'The peace and comfort you have in God will overcome all things'.[38]

With this, I commend you to God . . . closing greetings etc.

Your Grace's servant

Martin Luther

13. Barbara Lißkirchen

WA BR VI, No.1811, 86–88.[39]

April 30 1531

Grace and peace in Christ.

Virtuous and Dear Lady:

Your dear brother Jerome Weller has informed me that you are deeply troubled with spiritual attack[40] concerning eternal election. I am very sorry to hear this. May Christ our Lord save you. Amen.

Now, I know all about this sickness. I myself was brought to the very edge of eternal death by it. As well as praying for you, I would like to counsel and comfort you, though it is difficult to discuss such issues in writing. Nevertheless, if God will grant me the grace, I will not let this go, but do what I can. I will show you how God helped me out of this and by what methods I now daily protect myself against it.

First of all, you must resolutely fix in your heart the point that thoughts like yours are certainly the whisperings and fiery darts[41] of the wicked devil. Scripture says in Proverbs 7, 'He who searches out the lofty things of majesty will be cast down.'[42] Now, such thoughts as yours are pointless, searching into the majesty of God and his

---

38. Phil 3:21
39. Translation by Stephen Pietsch (June 2015).
40. Luther uses the word *Anfechtung* here, indicating already that he sees this woman's struggle as a supernatural spiritual assault. This point is taken up directly, in his first *argumentatio*, where he describes her thoughts as the fiery darts of the devil (Eph 6).
41. Eph s 6:16.
42. Cf Prov 25:27.

high providence. Jesus ben Sirach says in the third chapter: 'Do not search out things that are beyond your strength. The things that God has commanded, think rather about them.'[43] There is no benefit in your gawping at things about which you have not been commanded. David also lamented in Psalm 131 that it was bad for him to look into things that were too high for him.[44] That is why these thoughts of yours certainly do not come from God, but from the devil, who plagues us with them, making God out to be the enemy so that we despair. God has strictly forbidden this in the First Commandment. He wants us to love, trust, and praise him in whom we live.

Second, when such thoughts assault you, you should learn to question yourself like this: 'Please, in which Commandment does it say that I should think about and deal with this?.' When it is clear that there is no such commandment, learn to say: 'Get away with you, tiresome devil! You are trying to get me worried about myself. But God says everywhere that I should let him care for me. He says, 'I am your God.'[45] That is, 'I care for you; depend upon me, wait for me, and let me take care of you.' This is what St Peter taught: 'Cast all your worries upon him, for he cares for you.'[46] And David taught, 'Give your burden to the Lord, and he will sustain you.'[47]

Third, if, despite this, these thoughts continue (for the devil does not like giving up), you too must refuse to give up. You must always turn your heart away from them and say: 'Don't you hear, devil? I will have nothing to do with such thoughts. In fact God has forbidden me to. So hop it! I must now think of God's commandments, and in doing so, I will let him take care of me. If you are so smart, go up to heaven and dispute with God himself; he can answer you quite well enough.' This is the way you must always reject these thoughts and turn your heart to God's commandments.

Fourth, of all God's commands the highest is this, that we hold up before our eyes the image of his dear Son, our Lord Jesus Christ. Every day he will be our clear mirror in which we can see how much

---

43. Eccl 3:21, 22.
44. Cf Ps 131:1.
45. Cf Ex 20:2.
46. Cf 1 Pt 5:7.
47. Ps 55:23.

God loves us and how well, in his endless goodness, he has cared for us by giving his dear Son for us.

In this way, this way, I say, can one learn the true art of dealing with predestination. This way, it will be clear that you believe in Christ. And If you believe, then you are called. And if you are called, then you are most certainly predestinated. Do not let this mirror and throne of grace be torn away from the eyes of your heart. If such thoughts still come and bite like fiery serpents, pay no attention to these 'serpent-thoughts'. Turn away from them and look at the bronze serpent, that is, Christ given for us. Then, God willing, you will feel better.

But, as I have said, it is a struggle to get rid of such thoughts. If they enter your mind, throw them out again, just as you would immediately spit out some filthy muck that fell into your mouth. God has helped me to do this in my own situation. It is his critical command that we keep before us the image of his Son, in whom he has revealed himself to be our God (as the first commandment teaches) who helps and cares for us. So God will not allow us to help or take care of ourselves, which would be to deny him, and to deny the first commandment, and Christ as well.

That miserable devil, who is God's enemy and Christ's, tries to use these thoughts (which are against to the first commandment) to tear us away from Christ and God and make us think about ourselves and our own worries. If we do this, we take upon ourselves God's job, which is to care for us and be our God. In paradise the devil wanted to make Adam equal with God so that he would be his own god and care for himself, robbing God of his divine work of caring for him. The result was Adam's tragic fall.

That is enough advice for now. I have also written to your brother Jerome Weller[48] so that he too warns and encourages you diligently, so you learn to ignore these thoughts. Let the devil, from whom they come, search them out. He knows very well what has happened to him before in this situation: he fell from heaven into the abyss of hell. In summary: We should bother ourselves with things God has not told to worry about. It is the devil, and not God, who pushes that idea.

---

48. This letter is not extant.

May our dear Lord Jesus Christ show you his hands and his side[49] and greet you with a friendly heart, and may you see and hear only him until you find your joy in him. Amen.

The last day of April, 1531.

Martin Luther.

14. John Schlaginhaufen

WA BR VI, No.4353, 561.[50]

December 12 1533

To the venerable man in Christ, Mr. John Schlaginhaufen, pastor in Köthen, faithful minister of the Word, my brother.

Grace and peace in Christ. My dear Pastor:

I thank you for the gift of the medlars.[51] How well this land produces such fruit. I like them better than the Italian ones—when they are just a little bit greener, but they must still be ripe.

I regret to hear that you are still sometimes depressed. Christ is as near to you as you are to yourself, and he will not devour you, because he shed his blood for you. Dear friend, honor this good, faithful Man. And believe that he favours and loves you more than Dr. Luther or any other Christian. What you expect from us, expect even more from him. For what we do, we do at his bidding, but what he who bids us does, he does naturally from his own goodness.

With this I commit you and yours to God's care. Amen.

In a hurry,

The vigil of Saint Luke, 1533.

Martin Luther.

---

49. Cf Jn 20:27.
50. Translation by Stephen Pietsch (May 2015).
51. A large persimmon-like fruit, native to Germany. They are inedible when green and need to be ripened until brown and almost rotten.

15. George Spalatin

WA BR X, No.4021, 638–640.[52]

August 21 1544

To Doctor George Spalatin,

A man highly respected in Christ, Superintendent of the churches in Misnia,
Most faithful pastor to the people of Altenburg,
and one most dear to his own Lord.

Grace and peace in the Lord, and the consolation of the Holy Spirit, Amen.

I deeply sympathise with you, my dearest Spalatin, and I pray to the Lord that he may strengthen and cheer you. As I enquire what kind of malady you are suffering from, I am told that some think you are plagued by a depressed spirit because of the unfortunate case of the pastor who has married the step-mother of his deceased wife.

If this is so, I beg you, through Christ our Lord—and with all the prayers I can possibly pray—not to get above yourself by dwelling on your own thoughts and feelings, but rather listen to your brother in Christ who is speaking to you. Otherwise your melancholy will destroy you—that melancholy which Paul[53] says 'works death', just as I myself have experienced, and as Master Phillip did too, at Weimar in 1540. As a result of the issue of the Landgrave, depression had all but killed him, but Christ brought him back to life through my words to him.

Let us suppose that you have been guilty, having sinned in this particular case—or that you have committed more and even greater sins than Manasseh, whose offences could not be eradicated from the generations that followed him, right down to the time of Jerusalem's destruction. But in fact your sin is easily remedied and truly only of a temporal nature. So I say again, let us suppose that you are actually to blame. Surely you will not let depression destroy you so that by killing yourself you commit an even greater sin?

---

52. Translation by Elmore Leske (August, 2013). Edited and revised by Stephen Pietsch (August, 2013).
53. 2 Cor 7:10.

It is quite enough that you have sinned. Now let go of it. Don't let your despondency lead to an even greater offence. The Lord says 'I do not wish the death of the sinner, but rather that he repent and live'.[54] Do you really think that in your case alone the Lord's hand is shortened?[55] Or has the Lord in your case alone ceased to be merciful?[56]

Are you the only man whose sin is such that there is no longer a high priest who is able to sympathise with our weaknesses?[57] Surely you do not believe that it is so remarkably new for a person living in the flesh and surrounded by the fiery darts of so many devils to at some point be wounded or even laid low?

You seem to me to be a man who is not experienced in wrestling against sin, conscience and the law—or perhaps Satan has snatched away from your sight and memory all those verses of Scripture by which you were prepared for battle by the work[58] and benefits of Christ. Yes, he has done the same with all your outstanding sermons about grace by which you taught the church, and encouraged and confronted it with great confidence and a joyful spirit. Or it must be that until now, you have been only a trifling sinner, aware of having committed only the tiniest peccadillos.

Therefore I beg you, join us truly great and hard-boiled sinners so that you do not diminish Christ for us, who is not a saviour for imaginary or trivial sins but rather for real sins—not only small ones but great ones—yes even the worst, in fact for all sins committed by all people.

In this way Staupitz used to comfort me in my melancholic periods, saying 'You wish to be a 'painted sinner' and to have a 'painted Christ' as your saviour. You must get used to the fact that Christ is a real saviour and that you are a real sinner. God does not play games or indulge in make-believe. It was no joke that he sent us his Son and gave him up for us. But it seems that Satan has snatched these and similar truths from your memory so that you cannot now recall them, even for your own sake.

---

54. Ez 33:11.
55. Isa 59:1.
56. Ps 77:10.
57. Heb 4:15.
58. Here the Latin word *officio* (office) is more loosely translated 'work' for the sake of English sense. The phrase refers to Christ's office as redeemer and saviour, and the benefits which flow from it to the believer.

Open your ears and listen to your brother, as I sing to you—your brother who stands outside of your depressions and is strong. Yes, he stands there so that you who are weak and harassed by Satan, may rest on him and be cheered and strengthened so that you can stick it to the devil and sing 'I was struck down and overthrown so that I might fall, but the Lord supported me'.[59] Imagine that I am St Peter who stretches out his hand and says to you 'In the name of Jesus Christ, rise and walk'.[60]

In this way, my dear Spalatin, listen and believe everything which Christ is saying to you through me, for I am not mistaken (of this I am certain) and I am not speaking Satan's lies. Rather Christ is speaking through me and is commanding you to trust this brother of yours, with whom you share the one faith. He himself absolves you from this sin of yours, and all sins. In this way let me be a partaker of your sins so that I may help you carry them. Likewise make sure you are a partaker along with us in our consolation which is sure and true, which the Lord himself has commanded, so that we may give orders even to you, in order that you will accept them.[61] For while we hate to see you being tortured by depression, Christ hates it even more.

Do not reject the one giving this command and providing consolation—the one who both hates and condemns your depressions as the vexations of Satan. Do not submit to the devil by allowing him to fashion some different Christ for you than the real one. Your depression is the work of the devil which Christ wishes to destroy,[62] if you will let him. You have taken quite enough of a beating. You have grieved quite enough and been sufficiently repentant, in fact excessively so —more than enough.

You can see my dear Spalatin that I am dealing with you and speaking to you from a true heart. I shall consider it the greatest favour that you return to me by accepting my consolation, that is the forgiveness of the Lord himself, his absolution and restoration to life. By accepting this you will appreciate—later on at least—that you have even offered the most pleasing sacrifice to the Lord himself, as

---

59. Ps 118:13.
60. Acts 3:6.
61. Cf 2 Cor 1:1–7.
62. 1 Jn 3:8.

it is written, 'The Lord is well pleased with those who fear him and hope in his mercy'.⁶³

Therefore bid the depressions of the devil farewell, for he has caused us no small distress over you, and has indeed sought to ruin our happiness as well. If he could he would swallow us all in one gulp. May Christ rather rebuke him—and he will!

May he strengthen and preserve you through his Holy Spirit. Amen.

Comfort your wife with these and even better words. There has been no time to write another letter to her.

At Zeitz, August 21, 1544.

16. Mrs Jonas von Stockhausen

WA BR VI, No.1975, 388–389.⁶⁴

November 27 1532

To the honoured and virtuous Mrs N von Stockhausen, wife of the captain of the guard in Nordhausen, my kind and good friend: grace and peace in Christ.

Honoured and virtuous Lady!

I have written a quick note of consolation to your dear lord. Now, the devil hates both of you because you love his enemy, Christ. For this you must suffer, as he himself says: 'Because I have chosen you, therefore the world and its prince hate you. But be comforted; the suffering of God's saints is precious to him.'⁶⁵

Because I am in such a hurry, I can write little. Take great care not to leave your husband alone for a single moment, and leave nothing lying around which he might use to harm himself. Solitude is utter poison for him. That is why the devil urges him to it. It won't hurt to read or tell him stories, news, or other trivia, even if some of it is nonsense, gossip or tall stories about Turks, Tartars,⁶⁶ and the like—

---

63. Ps 147:11.
64. Translation by Stephen Pietsch (June 2-15).
65. A conflation (with variations) of Jn 15:19; 16:33, and Ps 16:15.
66. Popular light reading at that time included the Chronicles of Marco Polo's travels to the orient, which reported strange and exotic information about the

whatever may get him laughing and joking. Then quickly repeat some comforting sayings from Scripture. Whatever you do, do not leave him alone to be still, so that he sinks into his own thoughts. It does not matter if he gets irritable with this. Act as though it upsets you and tell him off about it, but let it happen anyway.

This quick note will have to do. Christ, who is the cause this heartache for you, will help you, just as he has done lately. Just hang onto him. You are the apple of his eye; whoever messes with you messes him.[67] Amen.

Doctor Martin Luther

17. Jonas von Stockhausen

WA BR VI, No. 974, 386–388.[68]

November 17 1532

To the august and brave Jonas von Stockhausen, captain in Nordhausen, my kind lord and good friend: grace and peace in Christ.

August, brave and dear Lord and Friend!

I am informed by good friends that the evil enemy is attacking you savegely, making you feel sick of living so that you long for death.[69] My dear friend, it really is high time that you stop trusting and following your own thoughts and listen to others who are free of this afflcition. Now, bind your ears tightly to my mouth and let my words go straight to your heart.[70] This is how God will strengthen and comfort you—by means of *our* words.

      Turks, Tarters and other peoples.
67. The sense of this last phrase is somewhat obscure because it is an allusion to Zech 2:8: 'For thus says the Lord of hosts . . . regarding the nations that plundered you: Truly the one who touches you, the apple of my eye, see now I am going to raise my hand against them'.
68. Translation by Stephen Pietsch (June 2015).
69. This is perhaps a freer translation of the German, which has particular words and phrases (*Überdruß des Lebens* or *Lebensüberdruß*) for this experience which do not easily translate into English.
70. This literally says 'bind your ears to *our* mouth etc. since Luther wishes to indicate to von Stockhausen that he is joining his own voice with those of the reader's other friends and advisors, who are giving him the same counsel.

First of all, you know that you should and must be obedient to God and avoid utterly disobedience to his will. Since you certainly must understand that it is God who gives you life and does not now desire your death, your thoughts should give way to this divine will and be obedient to it. Have no doubt that such thoughts, which are in conflict with God's will, were forcibly implanted into your mind by the devil. This is why you must stand resolutely and either ride them them out or, with equal force, rip them out.

For our Lord Christ, life was also miserable and bitter, yet he did not wish to die unless it was his Father's will. He fled from death and held onto life as long as he could, saying 'My time is not yet come'.[71] In just the same way, Elijah, Jonah, and other prophets called and cried out for death in their agony and exasperation, and even cursed the day they were born.[72] Still, even though they were sick of living, they had to fight against it and carry on in this life until their hour had come. You must surely obey and imitate such examples as words and warnings from the Holy Spirit, because you must spit out these thoughts that are driving you and throw them far away.

And if it is hard to do this, just think that you are held tight and bound by chains and that you must force your way out of their strangle hold with toil, struggle and sweat. For the arrows of the devil cannot be pulled out lightly or easily when they are so deeply stuck into your flesh. They must be torn out forcibly. So you have to take heart, resolutely defy yourself and say indignantly: 'No, my good man. No matter how unwilling you are to live, you should and must live! This is what God wants, and this is what I want too. Get lost, you thoughts of the devil! To hell with dying and death! You wont get anywhere with me', etc. Grit your teeth against your thoughts, and by God's will, be more stubborn, hard-headed, and strong-willed than the most unyielding peasant or bad-tempered old woman—indeed, be harder than an anvil or bar of iron. If you fight and struggle against yourself like this, God will certainly help you. But if you do not resist and fight back, but instead give your thoughts free reign to torture you, the fight will soon be lost.

    However, for the sake of clear modern English, I have made these pronouns singular.
71. Jn 7:6.
72. Cf 1 Kgs 19:4; Jonah 4:3; Jer 20:14.

However, the best advice of all is this: Do not struggle against your thoughts at all, but ignore them and act as if you do not feel them. Continue thinking about and remembering other things, and say: 'Alright, devil, leave me alone. I have no time for your thoughts. I must eat, drink, ride, travel, or do this or that.' Or say: 'I have to be joyful now. Come back tomorrow', etc. Get busy with whatever you can find to do – whether it's sport or something else—so that you free yourself from these thoughts, treat them with contempt and get rid of them. If necessary, use fowl and discourteous language, like this: 'Dear devil, if you can't do better than that, then lick my arse. I have no time for you now.' Regarding this read the examples of the nagging nit-picker,[73] the hissing of geese,[74] and the like in Gerson's *De cogitationibus blasphemiae*![75] This is the best advice. Something else that should and will help you are our prayers, especially those of pious Christians.

With that, I commit you to our beloved Lord, the only Saviour and the true conqueror, Jesus Christ. May he guard his victory and triumph over the devil in your heart. May he bring us all joy through the help he gives you and the miracle he does in you. For this we confidently hope and pray, just as he has commanded and promised us. Amen.

In Wittenberg, Wednesday following St Catherine's Day.

Martin Luther, Doctor.

---

73. The 'leuseknicker' Luther refers to here is the 'nitpicker' (one who 'strains at gnats' cf Matt 23:24) whose carping and nagging over trivial issues should be ignored.
74. Luther explains this reference more fully where he refers to the same image in his letter to Jerome Weller of June 19, 1530 (the next letter translated in this appendix). The picture here is of someone dealing with the menacing hisses of geese by simply walking past and ignoring them, thereby 'calling their bluff'.
75. Jean Gerson (1363-1429) was a french mystic and theologian who wrote consolatory tracts on melancholy and depression. It seems there is, however, actually no tract by Gerson with the title *De cogitationibus blasphamiae* (at least none that is still in existence today). Luther amost certainly means to refer to Gerson's *Contra fœdem tentationem blasphemiæ*.

18. Jerome Weller

WA BR V, No.1593, 373–375.[76]

June 19 1530

Grace and peace in Christ.

I received both letters from you, my dear Jerome. Naturally I was very pleased by both (especially the most recent one), in which you write to me concerning my son John[77]—that you are his teacher, and that he is your settled and diligent student.

If indeed I should be able, I will most freely please you in return; Christ will make up where I am deficient!

Master Vitus told me that you are sometimes troubled by a spirit of sadness. This is a trial that greatly damages one's youth, as Scripture says: 'An unhappy spirit dries out the bones.'[78] Everywhere Scripture forbids this sadness, as in Ecclesiastes 11:3:[79] 'Rejoice, young man, in your youth and let your heart be glad in the days of your youth'[80]; and, a little while later, 'Take sadness from your heart and affliction from your flesh.'[81] Also in Ecclesiasticus 30:5[82] it says, 'Do not give sadness to your soul, and do not afflict yourself with your thoughts.' Cheerfulness of heart is the life of a person; it is an unfailing treasury of health, and the exaltation of a man is his longevity. Therefore have pity on your soul, pleasing God, and drive sadness far from you. Sadness has killed many, and there is no profit in it. Thus also Paul says to the Corinthians that 'worldly sorrow works death.'[83]

Therefore, before all things, it is to be firmly established that these evil and sad thoughts of yours are not from God but from the devil. That's because God is not a God of sadness but a God of consolation

---

76. Latin text translated by Fraser Pearce (November 2010). Two sections in German translated by Stephen Pietsch (February 2011). Edited and revised by Stephen Pietsch (June, 2015).
77. This is a little confusing. It was definitely Luther's son, John (Hans) who had recently started his schooling with Weller, yet the Latin seems to indicate that Luther is referring to Weller's son.
78. Prov 17:22.
79. Actually verse 9.
80. Eccl 11:9
81. Eccl 11:10
82. Actually verse 23.
83. 2 Cor 7:10

and joy, just as Christ himself says, 'God is not a God of the dead but of the living'.[84]

What, indeed, is it to live other than to be joyful in the Lord? Therefore, now accustom yourself to thoughts of this kind, so that presently you may repel the sad thoughts, saying 'The Lord did not send you'. This line of thinking is not from him who called you. The fight is hard in the beginning, but with practice it will become easier. For it is not only you who is bearing these thoughts, but all the saints. They fought, and they conquered.

Also, in *The Aeneid*, Virgil says, 'Do not yield yourself to troubles, but rather go more boldly'.[85]

The most important thing in this fight is not to attend to, scrutinise, or follow the appearances of these thoughts, but, just as when a goose hisses at you, to scorn them and pass them by. The one who learns this will conquer and the one who does not learn this will *be* conquered, for to give attention to these things and dispute with them until such time as they should spontaneously stop or yield, is to provoke and strengthen them.

Let the people of Israel be an example to you. They conquered their serpents not by looking at them or struggling, but by turning their eyes in another direction, that is, to the bronze serpent.[86] This is the true and certain victory in this fight. So, my dear Jerome, see to it that you don't allow these sad thoughts to hang around in your heart.

A certain wise man responded to a person who had been tested by the same sad thoughts, who was saying 'How far I have fallen into evil thoughts!' The wise man said 'So then, let yourself fall *out* of them'. So he taught, using this excellent saying.

And another man said to a person complaining of the same things, 'You can't take precautions against birds flying over your head; but you can take precautions against them building nests in your hair'. So you'll do rightly if you instead sport with others or engage in other enjoyable activities, and will not burden your conscience from such diversion. For this pointless, empty sorrow does not please God. Now

---

84. Mk 12:27.
85. Virgil, *The Aeneid*. Book VI, Chapter 4, *romansonline*, translated by Theodore C Williams, accessed September 2013, http://www.romansonline.com/Src_Frame.asp?DocID=Vrg_ae06_04.
86. Nb 21

the sorrow over sins is at once brief and joyful because of the promise of grace and the forgiveness of sins, but worldly sorrow is truly of the devil[87] and without promise—it is just a mess of worries and useless and impossible thoughts about God.

I could go on, but when you receive this, greet the brother to whom I began to write—the postman was in a hurry to get going. I shall write another letter to him, and to Oinotomos[88] and to others. I commend to you your student.

May the Spirit of Christ console and cheer your heart. Amen.

19. Jerome Weller

WA BR V, No.1670, 518–520.[89]

July 1530

Grace and peace in Christ.

My dear Jerome:

You should believe that this trial you are going through is from the devil, who troubles you like this because you believe in Christ. You see how smug and happy he permits the worst enemies of the Gospel to be. Just think of Eck,[90] Zwingli,[91] and others. It is unavoidable for all of us Christians that the devil is our opponent and enemy; as St Peter says, 'Your enemy, the devil, roams around.'[92]

Admirable Jerome, you should rejoice in this trial of the devil because it is a sure sign that God favours and has mercy on you. You say that the trial is heavier than you can bear, and that you fear that it will break and smash you down, driving you to despair and blasphemy. I know this trick of the devil. If he cannot break a person with his first salvo, he tries by persistence to wear him out and weaken him until he falls and admits defeat. Whenever this temptation comes

---

87. 2 Cor 7:10.
88. Latinised version of 'Schneidewein', the name of one of Luther's friends in Wittenberg.
89. Translation by Stephen Pietsch (June 2015).
90. John Eck (1486–1543), a leading Catholic opponent of Luther.
91. The swiss reformer, Huldreich Zwingli (1484–1531), had been opposed to Luther over the interpretation of Holy Communion.
92. 1 Pt 5:8.

to you, avoid getting into an argument with the devil and do not allow yourself to dwell on those deadly thoughts, because doing that is nothing short of giving in to the devil and letting him get his way. Try with all your might to treat those thoughts, which are engendered by the devil, with contempt. In this sort of trial and struggle, contempt is the best and easiest method of winning out over the devil. Laugh at your opponent scornfully and ask who it is with whom you are speaking. Make sure you avoid solitude, for the devil watches and lies in wait for you most of all when you are alone. This devil is conquered by mocking and deriding him, not by resisting and arguing with him. So, Jerome, joke and play some games with my wife and others. In this way you will drive out your diabolical thoughts and find courage.

This trial is more necessary to you than food and drink. Let me remind you what happened to me when I was about your age. When I first entered the monastery I was depressed and miserable, and could not shake off my dependency. Because of it I confessed to Dr Staupitz (a man I remember with joy)[93] and received advice from him. I opened up to him about the horrible and revolting thoughts I had. He said: 'Don't you know, Martin, that this trial is beneficial and necessary for you? God is not putting you through this for no reason. You will see how he means to use you as his servant to accomplish great things.' And so it turned out. I was made a great doctor (I can appropriately say this about myself) though at the time when I suffered this trial I never would have believed that was possible. I have no doubt that this will happen with you too. You will become a great man. Take courage and be sure that such words, especially those which come from the mouths of learned and important men, do not lack a certain prophetic significance.

I remember that a man I once consoled concerning the loss of his son said to me, 'Just you wait and see, Martin, you will become a great man.' I have often thought about those words, because, as I have already said, such sayings can be somewhat prophetic. So take good courage, and cast these dreaded thoughts out of your mind. Whenever the devil annoys you with such thoughts, immediately look for some male company—drink more, joke and play, or take part in some other

---

93. Luther frequently referred fondly to the help he received in the monastery from the Augustinian vicar-general, John von Staupitz, who was Luther's confessor and mentor.

kind of fun. Sometimes it is necessary to drink a little more, play, joke, or even commit some sin, defying the devil so that you give him no chance to make us feel guilty over trivia. We will be overwhelmed if we get over-anxious about falling into some sin or other.

So, if the devil says, 'Do not drink' you should reply: 'On account of that, because you forbid it, I *will* drink, and what is more, I will have a goodly amount.' In this way, one should always do the opposite of what Satan demands. Why do you think I drink wine undiluted, talk speak my mind, feed my face as I do, if it is not to annoy and bother the devil who made it his job to annoy and bother me? If only I could commit some token sin simply for the sake of humiliating the devil, so that he might at last grasp that I own no sin and am conscious of no sin. When the devil attacks and plagues us, we must completely put the whole decalogue to one side. When the devil throws our sins at us and claims that we merit only death and hell, we should tell him: 'I admit that I deserve death and hell. So what? Does this mean that I will be condemned to eternal damnation? Absolutely not, because I know who who suffered and made satisfaction for me. His name is Jesus Christ, the Son of God. Where he is, there will I also be.'

Yours,

Martin Luther

20. Jerome Weller

WA BR V, No.1684, 546–547.[94]

August 15 1530

Grace and peace in Christ.

My dear Jerome

Although I have forgotten whatever it was I wrote to you in my previous letter concerning a depressed spirit—and it may now happen that I write the very same things again, in my desire to stress continually the same core truths—nevertheless, since the trials of us all ought to be shared by all (just as I suffer for you, so you in turn suffer for me), I most certainly wish to revisit the very same subject.

---

94. Translation by Elmore Leske (November 2010).

As there is one in the same enemy who hates and persecutes every single brother of Christ, so we, too, are one and the same body in which each individual suffers for all the other individuals. And this happens solely because we worship Christ. So it comes about that in this way the one brother is compelled to bear the burden of the other.

Therefore you must see to it that you learn how to reappraise this situation. For you have not yet properly learned about the nature of that spirit which is the enemy of spiritual joy. And be sure that you are not alone in bearing this burden, nor are you the only one to be so attacked. We are all bearing this with you, and we are all suffering in you. God who commands 'You shall not kill' certainly declares by this command that he does not want these depressed, death-bearing thoughts, but thoughts that are full of life and joyfulness. This is how even the Psalmist expresses it, saying: 'There is life in keeping with his will.'[95] Ezekiel too: 'I do not wish the death of the sinner, but rather that he turn from his way and live.'[96]

So since it is clear that God is displeased with this kind of depression, we have the strong consolation that, even if we cannot completely escape that demon, we nevertheless can bear it with more maturity, strengthened by those words of God.

I know that it is not in our power to eliminate these thoughts just whenever we wish. But I know, on the other hand, that they will not win the battle, because He says: 'He shall never suffer the righteous to be moved etc.'[97], provided we learn to cast our care onto His very own self.

But the Lord Jesus, our strong wrestler and invincible victor will be with you. Amen.

From the Wilderness, August 15, 1530. I commend to you your pupil, my son.

Would that some day I shall be able to give thanks!

---

95. Ps 19:11.
96. Ezek 18:23.
97. Ps 55:22.

21. Matthias Weller

WA BR VII, No.2139, 104–106.[98]

October 7 1534

Grace and peace in Christ.

Honoured, kind and dear Friend:

Your dear brother has informed me that you are deeply distressed and suffering with depression. He will no doubt tell you all I have said to him.

Dear Matthias, do not follow your own thoughts, but listen to what other people say to you. For God has commanded men to comfort their neighbours, and it is his will that the distressed should take such comfort as from God's himself. This is why our Lord says through St Paul, 'Comfort the fainthearted,'[99] and through Isaiah: 'Comfort, comfort my people. Speak comfortably.'[100] And in a different place our Lord says that it is not his will that man should be despondent, but instead serve the Lord with gladness,[101] and not offer him the sacrifice of sorrow. Moses and the prophets preached all of this, copiously and often. Our Lord also commanded us not to be worried,[102] but to cast our worries onto him, for he cares about us,[103] as St Peter taught from Ps. 55.[104]

So then, because to God wants everyone to comfort his brother, and wants such comfort be received with a believing heart, leave behind your own thoughts. Realise that through them, it is the wicked devil who is tormenting you, and that they are not really your thoughts but his, who cannot bear to see us joyful.

So listen to what we say to you in God's name: that you ought to rejoice in Christ, your gracious Lord and Redeemer. Let him bear your loads, for he certainly cares about you, even though things have not yet improved as you would like. Still, he lives. Expect the best from him. In his eyes, this is the greatest sacrifice; as the Scriptures

---

98. Translation by Stephen Pietsch (June 2015).
99. 1 Thess 5:14.
100. Isa 40:8, 9.
101. Cf Deut 28:47.
102. Cf Matt 6:25.
103. Cf 1 Pt 5:7.
104. Cf Ps 55:22.

say, no sacrifice is more pleasing and acceptable than a yoyful heart that rejoices in the Lord.

Therefore, when you are depressed, and it is all threatening to take over, say: 'Up you get! I must play a hymn to the Lord on my regal[105] (it could be the *Te Deum laudamus* or the *Benedictus*), for the Scriptures teach me that it pleases the Lord to hear a joyful hymn played on stringed instruments.' Then begin playing the keys and singing along, as David and Elisha[106] did, until your depressed thoughts go away. If the devil returns and places worries and sad thoughts in your mind, fight back with renewed courage and say, 'Get out, devil! I must now play and sing to my Lord, Christ.'

You must learn to resist him like this, and not put up with him placing thoughts in your mind. If you allow one thought to enter, and you listen to it, the devil will force ten more thoughts into your mind until he finally overpowers you. So, the best thing you can do is to whack the devil on the snout first. Be like the fellow who, whenever his wife began to nag and gnaw at him, pulled his flute out from under his belt and played soothingly until she got tired of it and left him in peace. So you too should turn to your regal or get some good companions together and sing with them until you manage to put the devil off.

If you really believe that those thoughts come from the devil, then you have already won. But, because your faith is still fragile, listen to us, who by God's grace, know it, and lean on our staff until you learn to walk by yourself. And when good people comfort you, dear Matthias, try to believe that God is speaking to you through them. Pay attention to them and don't doubt that it is most certainly God's word coming to you, in line with God's command, through men, for your comfort.

May the same Lord who has bidden me, and whom I must obey, give all these things to you in your heart and enable you to believe and confess them. Amen.

Martin Luther, Doctor.

Wednesday after St Francis' Day, 1534.

---

105. A portable organ, which in the sixteenth century consisted of a case enclosing reed pipes, with keys on one side and bellows on the other.
106. Cf 2 Kgs 3:14–15.

Select Bibliography

Africanus, Constantinus. *De melancholia libri duo*. Europeana, original copy owned by Bodleian Libraries, Oxford University. http://www.europeana.eu/portal/record/92093/5B63F3F89D5D8FE6D1F9066ECE3A986D81A97BA5.html.

Ardmur, Millard J, and Martin Harrow. 'Conscience and Depressive Disorders.' *The British Journal of Psychiatry* 120 (March 1972): 259–64.

Arikha, Noga. *Passions and Tempers: A History of the Humours*. New York: Harper Collins, 2007.

Ball, Philip. *The Devil's Doctor: Paracelsus and the World of Renaissance Magic and Science*. London: Arrow Books, 2007.

Bandmann, Günter. *Melancholie und Musik: Ikonographische Studien*. Opladen: Westdeutscher Verlag, 1960.

Beck, Aaron T, and Brad A Alford. *Depression: Causes and Treatments*. 2nd edition. Philadelphia: University of Philadelphia Press, 2009.

Berrios, GE 'Melancholia and Depression During the 19th Century: A Conceptual History.' *The British Journal of Psychiatry* 153 (September 1988): 298–304.

beyondblue. Accessed August 2013. http://www.beyondblue.org.au.

beyondblue. 'Ambassadors.' Accessed October 2013. http://www.beyondblue.org.au/connect-with-others/ambassadors.

beyondblue. 'Kyle Vander Kuyp.' Accessed October 2013. http://www.beyondblue.org.au/connect-with-others/ambassadors/ambassador-profile/kyle-vander-kuyp.

beyondblue. 'Re-orientating General Practice Towards Preventative Mental Health Care for Adolescents, Utilising the Practice Nurse: A Pilot Study.' Accessed October 2013. http://www.beyondblue.

org.au/resources/research/research-projects/research-projects/re-orientating-general-practice-towards-preventative-mental-health-care-for-adolescents-utilising-the-practice-nurse-a-pilot-study.

beyondblue. 'Types of depression.' Accessed October 2013. http://www.beyondblue.org.au/the-facts/depression/types-of-depression.

Biebel, David, and Harold G Koenig. *New Light on Depression: Help, Hope, and Answers For The Depressed and those Who Love Them*. Grand Rapids: Zondervan, 2004.

Black Dog Institute. Accessed August, 2013. http://www.blackdoginstitute.org.au/.

Black Dog Institute. 'Facts and Figures about Mental Health and Mood Disorders.' Accessed October 2013. http://www.blackdoginstitute.org.au/docs/Factsandfiguresaboutmentalhealthandmooddisorders.pdf.

Black Dog Institute. 'What It's Like.' Accessed October 2013. http://www.blackdoginstitute.org.au/public/depression/whatitslike.cfm.

Blazer, Dan G. *The Age of Melancholy: 'Major Depression' and its Social Origins*. New York: Routledge, 2005.

Braaten, Carl E. 'Powers in Conflict: Christ and the Devil.' In *Sin, Death, and the Devil*. Edited by Carl E Braaten and Robert W Jenson, 94–107. Grand Rapids: Eerdmans, 2000.

Brampton, Sally. *Shoot The Damn Dog: A Memoir of Depression*. London: Bloomsbury Publishing, 2008.

Brecht, Martin. *Martin Luther: His Road to Reformation 1483–1521*. Minneapolis: Fortress, 1985.

Brecht, Martin. *Martin Luther: Shaping and Defining the Reformation 1521–1532*. Minneapolis: Fortress, 1990.

Brecht, Martin. *Martin Luther: The Preservation of the Church, 1532–1546*. Minneapolis: Fortress, 1999.

Burton, Robert. *The Anatomy of Melancholy*. First published 1621. 1932 ed., edited by Holbrook Jackson. New York: New York Review Books, 2001.

Christian Depression Pages. 'The Things People Say.' Accessed August 2013. http://www.christian-depression.org/cdp/sayings.php.

Clark, Hilary, ed. *Depression and Narrative: Telling the Dark*. New York: State University of New York Press, 2008.

Davies, James. *The Importance of Suffering: The Value and Meaning of Emotional Discontent*. Hove: Routledge, 2012.

Dicke, Gerd. 'Homo Facetus: vom Mittelalter eines Humanistischen Ideals.' In *Humanismus in der Deutschen Literatur des Mittelalters und der Frühen Neuzeit : XVIII. Anglo-German Colloquium, Hofgeismar 2003*. Edited by Nicola McLelland, Stefanie Schmitt and Hans-Jochen Schiewer, 299-332. Tübingen: Niemeyer, 2008.

Dickinson, J N Ian. 'The Use of the Bible in Pastoral Practice.' Cardiff University, Cardiff School of History, Archaeology and Religion, December 2003. Accessed April 14, 2013. http://www.cardiff.ac.uk/share/research/projectreports/previousprojects/biblepastoralpractice/the-use-of-the-bible-in-pastoral-practice.html.

Dieter, Theodor. 'Why Does Luther's Doctrine of Justification Matter Today?' In *The Global Luther: A Theologian for Modern Times*. Edited by Christine Helmer, 189-209. Minneapolis: Fortress, 2009.

Dober, Hans Martin. *Seelsorge bei Luther, Schleiermacher und nach Freud*. Leipzig: Evangelische Verlagsanstalt, 2008.

Doolittle, Benjamin R, and Michael Farrell. 'The Association Between Spirituality and Depression in an Urban Clinic', in *The Primary Care Companion to the Journal of Clinical Psychiatry* 6/3 (May 2004): 114-18.

Dreβ, Walter. 'Gerson und Luther', in *Zeitschrift für Kirchengeschichte* 52/1 (1933): 122-61.

Dudley, Michael. 'Melancholy or Depression. Sacred or Secular?' in *The International Journal for the Psychology of Religion*, 2/2 (1992): 87-99.

Ebeling, Gerhard. *Luthers Seelsorge: Theologie in der Vielfalt der Lebenssituationen an seinen Briefen Dargestellt*. Tübingen: JCB Mohr (Paul Siebeck), 1997.

Ellis, Pete M, and Don AR Smith. 'Treating Depression: the *beyondblue* Guidelines for Treating Depression in Primary Care.' in *The Medical Journal of Australia* 176/10 (20 May 2002): S77-S83. Accessed October 2013. http://www.mja.com.au/public/issues/176_10_200502/ell10082_fm.html.

Eyer, Richard C. *Pastoral Care Under the Cross: God in the Midst of Suffering*. St Louis: CPH, 1994.

Eyers, Kerrie, and Gordon Parker. *Tackling Depression at Work: A Practical Guide for Employees and Managers*. Sydney: Allen & Unwin, 2010.

Farrington, Tim. *A Hell of Mercy: A Meditation on Depression and the Dark Night of the Soul*. New York: Harper Collins, 2009.

Folk-Williams, John. 'Depression and Imagination.' *Storied Mind*. Accessed December 10, 2012. http://www.storiedmind.com/fighting-depression/depression-and-imagination/.

Fournier, Jay C, Robert J DeRubeis, Steven D Hollon, Sona Dimidjian, Jay D Amsterdam, Richard C Shelton, and Jan Fawcett. 'Antidepressant Drug Effects and Depression Severity: A Patient-Level Meta-analysis.' *The Journal of the American Medical Association* 303, no. 1 (January 6, 2010): 47–53.

Gerson, Jean. "Contra fœdem tentationem blasphemiæ." In *Opera omnia: novo ordine digesta et in quinque tomos distribute*. Vol. 3., reprinted ed., edited by Louis Ellies Du Pin, 243–246. Hildesheim: Georg Olms Verlag, 1987.

Gerson, Jean. 'Contra nimis strictam et scrupulosam conscientiam.' In *Opera omnia: novo ordine digesta et in quinque tomos distribute*. Volume 3, reprinted edition, edited by Louis Ellies Du Pin, 241–43. Hildesheim: Georg Olms Verlag, 1987.

Gilbert, Paul Raymond. *Psychotherapy and Counselling for Depression*. 3rd edition. London: Sage Publications, 2007.

Gospel Therapy.'Gospel Therapy, A New Vision of Life Through Christ.' Accessed February 1, 2013. http://www.Gospeltherapy.com/.

Gowland, Angus. 'The Problem of Early Modern Melancholy', in *Past & Present* 191/1 (May 2006): 77–120.

Gowland, Angus. *The Worlds of Renaissance Melancholy: Robert Burton in Context*. Cambridge: Cambridge University Press, 2006.

Greenfeld, Liah. *Mind, Modernity, Madness: The Impact of Culture on Human Experience*. New York: Harvard University Press, 2013.

Gritsch, Eric W. *Martin–God's Court Jester, Luther in Retrospect*. Philadelphia: Fortress, 1983.

Haile, HG. *Luther, A Biography*. London: Sheldon, 1980.

Hall, Douglas John. 'The Theology of the Cross: A Usable Past.' Evangelical Lutheran Church of America. Accessed June 18, 2012. http://www.elca.org/~/media/Files/Growing%20in%20Faith/Vocation/

Word%20and%20Service%20Ministry/TheTheologyoftheCross_pdf. ashx

Hall, John Douglas. *The Cross in Our Context: Jesus and the Suffering World*. Minneapolis: Augsburg-Fortress, 2003.

Hassoun, Jacques. *Cruelty of Depression: On Melancholy*. Cambridge MA: Perseus Publishing, 1997.

Headley, Tony. 'Martin Luther on Depression.' *Light and Life Magazine* (July-August 1999). Accessed October 2013. http://morethancoping.wordpress.com/2011/03/07/martin-luther-on-depression-2/.

Healy, David. *The Antidepressant Era*. Cambridge: Harvard University Press, 1997.

Hollon, Steven D, and Sona Dimidjian. 'Cognitive and Behavioral Treatment of Depression'. in *Handbook of Depression*. second edition, edited by Ian H Gotlib and Constance L Hammen, 586-603. London: Guildford Press, 2009.

Hordern, William. *Experience and Faith: The Significance of Luther for Understanding Today's Experiential Religion*. Minneapolis: Augsburg, 1983.

Horwitz, Allan V. *Creating Mental Illness*. Chicago: Chicago University Press, 2002.

Hummel, Leonard M. *Clothed in Nothingness: Consolation for Suffering*. Minneapolis: Fortress, 2003.

Hunter, R Lanny, and Victor L Hunter. *What Your Doctor and Your Pastor Want You to Know about Depression*. St Louis: Chalice Press, 2004.

I Trust When Dark My Road. Accessed August 2013. http://www.darkmyroad.org/.

Jackson, Stanley W. *Melancholia and Depression: From Hippocratic Times to Modern Times*. Newhaven: Yale University Press, 1990.

Jorm, Anthony, Nick Allen, Amy Morgan, Siobhan Ryan, and Rosemary Purcell. *A Guide to What Works for Depression*. second edition. Melbourne: *beyondblue*, 2009.

Jorm, Anthony F, Helen Christensen, and Kathleen M Griffiths. 'The Impact of *beyondblue*: the National Depression Initiative in the Australian Public's Recognition of Depression and Beliefs About Treatments', in *Australian and New Zealand Journal of Psychiatry*, 39/4 (April 2005): 248-54.

Karp, David A. *Speaking of Sadness: Depression, Disconnection, and the Meanings of Illness*. New York: Oxford University Press, 1997.

Kleinman, Arthur, and Byron Good, editors. *Culture and Depression: Studies in the Anthropology and Cross-cultural Psychiatry of Affect and Disorder*. Berkley: University of California Press, 1985.

Klibansky, Raymond, Erwin Panofsky, and Fritz Saxl. *Saturn and Melancholy: Studies in the History of Natural Philosophy, Religion and Art*. New York: Basic Books, 1964.

Knight, Gavin, and Joanna Knight. *Disturbed by Mind and Spirit: Mental Health and Healing in Parish Ministry*. London: Mowbray, 2009.

Koenig, Harold G. *Faith and Mental Health: Religious Resources for Healing*. Philadelphia: Templeton Foundation Press, 2005.

Koenig, Harold G. 'Religion, Spirituality and Psychiatry: A New Era in Mental Health.' *Revista de Psiquiatria Clínica* 34, sup. 1 (2007): 5-7. Accessed August 2013. http://www.hcnet.usp.br/ipq/revista/vol34/s1/5.html.

Kramer, Peter D. *Against Depression*. New York: Penguin Books, 2005.

Krause, Gerhard. 'Luthers Stellung zum Selbstmord: Ein Kapitel seine Lehre und Praxis der Seelsorge', in *Luther* 36 (1965): 51-71.

Leech, Kenneth. *Spirituality and Pastoral Care*. London: Sheldon Press, 1986.

Levack, Brian P. *The Devil Within: Possession and Exorcism in the Christian West*. New York: Yale University Press, 2013.

Lockley, Paul. *Counselling For Depression*. London: Free Association Books, 2005.

Luther, Martin. *The Bondage of the Will*. WA XVIII. 684-88. Translated by E Gordon Rupp and Phillip S Watson. 'Luther: On the Bondage of the Will', in *Luther and Erasmus: Free Will and Salvation*. Edited by E Gordon Rupp and Phillip S Watson, 101-34. Philadelphia: Westminster Press, 1969.

Luther, Martin. *Luther: Letters of Spiritual Counsel*. Edited by Theodore G Tappert. Volume 18 of *The Library of Christian Classics*. Lousiville, Ky: Westminster John Knox Press, 1955.

Luther, Martin. *Kritische Gesamtausgabe Werke (Weimarer Ausgabe)*. Kritische Gesamtausgabe 1 (1883). 120 volumes. Weimar: Böhlhaus, 1921.

Luther, Martin. *Luther's Works*. American Edition. Volumes 1-55. Edited by Jaroslav Pelikan and Helmut T Lehman. St Louis: Concordia Publishing House & Philadelphia: Muhlenburg Press, 1960-1975.

Melanchthon, Philipp. *De melancholia hypochondriaca positiones inaugurales*. Basileae : Typis Iohan. Iacobi Genathii, 1629. Originally published 1529. E-rara, original copy owned by Universitätsbibliothek Basel. Accessed October 2013. http://dx.doi.org/10.3931/e-rara-17563.

Meller, William H, and Robert H Albers. 'Depression.' In *Ministry with Persons with Mental Illness and Their Families*. Edited by Robert H Albers, William H Meller and Steven C Thurber, 11-32. Minneapolis: Fortress, 2012.

Mennecke-Haustein, Ute. *Luthers Trostbriefe*. 56 Band von *Quellen und Forschungen zur Reformationsgeschichte*. Göttingen: Gütersloher Verlagshaus, 1989.

Menninger, Karl. *Whatever Became of Sin?* Stroud: Hawthorn Books, 1973.

Metzger, Günther. *Gelebter Glaube, Die Formierung Reformatorischen Denkens in Luthers erster Psalmvorlesung, Dargestellt am Begriff des Affekts*. Göttingen: Vandenhoek & Ruprecht, 1964.

Midelfort, HC Erik. *A History of Madness in Sixteenth-Century Germany*. Stanford: Stanford University Press, 2000.

Midelfort, HC Erik. 'Madness and the Problems of Psychological History in the Sixteenth Century', in *The Sixteenth Century Journal* 12/1 (Spring 1981): 5-12. Accessed September 2013. http://www.jstor.org/stable/3003698.

Mindframe. 'Brief Snapshot of Mental Illness in Australia.' Accessed August 2013. http://www.mindframe-media.info/for-media/reporting-mental-illness/facts-and-stats#Snapshot.

Murray, Les. *Killing the Black Dog: A Memoir of Depression*. New York: Farrar, Strauss & Giroux, 2011.

Nouwen, Henri. *Out of Solitude: Three Meditations on the Christian Life*. Notre Dame: Ave Maria Press, 1974.

Nouwen, Henri. *The Inner Voice of Love: A Journey Through Anguish To Freedom*. New York: Image Books, 1996.

Oberman, Heiko A. 'Luther Against the Devil.' *The Christian Century* 107, no. 1 (1990): 75-9. Accessed July 2010. http://www.religion-online.org/showarticle.asp?title=750.

Padfield, David. 'Sin, Guilt and Depression.' *Padfield.com*. Accessed August 2013. http://www.padfield.com/2000/guilt.html.

Palmer, Parker J. 'All The Way Down: Depression and the Spiritual Journey.' *Weavings: A Journal of Christian Spiritual Life* 13, no. 5 (September–October 1998). Accessed October 2013. http://www.wmeades.com/id220.htm.

Parmenter, Bruce R. '"Devil Talk": A Case History of Martin Luther's Pastoral Counseling with "Herr Turbicide", Compared to a "Modern" Case of Depression', in *American Journal of Pastoral Counseling*, 7.1 (2003): 67–72.

Parker, Gordon. 'Melancholia as an Illness.' Audio of interview with Richard Aedy, *Life Matters*. ABC Radio, March 25, 2010. Accessed September 2013. http://www.abc.net.au/rn/lifematters/stories/2010/2855014.htm.

Parker, Gordon, Gemma Gladstone, and Kuan Tsee Chee. 'Depression in the Planet's Largest Ethnic Group: The Chinese.' *The American Journal of Psychiatry* 158, no. 6 (June 2001): 857–64. Accessed September 2013. http://ajp.psychiatryonline.org/data/Journals/AJP/3725/857.pdf.

Peperkorn, Todd A. *I Trust When Dark My Road: A Lutheran View of Depression*. St Louis: LCMS World Relief, 2009.

Peteet, John R. *Depression and the Soul: A Guide to Spiritually Integrated Treatment*. New York: Routledge, 2010.

Pettegree, Andrew. 'Time and Space: Living in Sixteenth-century Europe.' In *Europe in the Sixteenth Century*, 1–11. Oxford: Blackwell, 2002. Accessed March 22, 2013. http://www.blackwellpublishing.com/content/BPL_Images/Content_store/Sample_chapter/9780631207016/pettegree.pdf.

Pietsch, Stephen J. 'A Contemporary Pastoral Reflection on Martin Luther's Understanding of and Approach to Depressive Illness in his *Table Talk*.' Masters thesis, Adelaide College of Divinity, 2011. Accessed November 2013. http://www.alc.edu.au/assets/education/about/academic-publications/paper/Reflection-on-depression-in-Luthers-Table-Talk.pdf.

Pietsch, Stephen J. 'Exploring Transformation in Luther Studies', in *Lutheran Forum*, 49/1 (Spring 2015) 30–31.

Pietsch, Stephen J. 'Depression and the Dark Night of the Soul.' Postgraduate Research paper, Adelaide College of Divinity, 2011.

Accessed November 2013. http://www.alc.edu.au/assets/education/about/academic-publications/paper/The-dark-night-of-the-soul.pdf.

Pietsch, Stephen J. 'Depression and the Soul: a Cook's Tour.' Paper presented for the opening lecture of Australian Lutheran College, Adelaide, Australia, February 8, 2010. Accessed July 2012. http://www.alc.edu.au/assets/education/about/academic-publications/opening-lecture/2010-depression-and-the-soul.pdf.

Pietsch, Stephen J. 'Luther Comforts a Depressed Pastor: Luther's Letter of Consolation to George Spalatin–Analysis and Reflection.', in *Lutheran Theological Journal*, 35/3 (December 2011): 144–48.

Pietsch, Stephen J. 'Seelsorge–A Living Tradition in Pastoral Theology Practice.', in *Lutheran Theological Journal* 43/1 (May 2009): 49–62.

Powlison, David. 'Cure of Souls (and the Modern Psychotherapies).' Christian Counseling & Educational Foundation. Accessed January 2011. http://www.ccef.org/cure-souls-and-modern-psychotherapies.

Radden, Jennifer. *Moody Minds Distempered: Essays on Melancholy and Depression*. New York: Oxford University Press, 2009.

Radden, Jennifer, ed. *The Nature of Melancholy: From Aristotle to Kristeva*. New York: Oxford University Press, 2000.

Rittgers, Ronald K. *The Reformation of Suffering: Pastoral Theology and Lay Piety in Late Medieval and Early Modern Germany*. New York: Oxford University Press, 2012.

Roper, Lyndal. 'Martin Luther's Body: The "Stout Doctor" and His Biographers', in *The American Historical Review*, 115/2 (April 2010): 351–84.

Roper, Lyndal. "To His Most Learned and Dearest Friend": Reading Luther's Letters.' *German History* 28, no 3 (September 2010): 283–295.

Rössing-Hager, Monika. *Syntax und Textkomposition in Luthers Briefprosa*. Wien: Böhlhaus, 1972.

Rowe, Dorothy. 'Depression's Punitive Conscience.' *theguardian*, November 12, 2009. Accessed October 2013. http://www.theguardian.com/commentisfree/2009/nov/12/robert-enke-depression-suicide.

Rowe, Dorothy. 'The Real Causes of Depression.' *Dorothy Rowe*, April 2, 2011. Accessed July 2011. http://www.dorothyrowe.com.au/articles/item/192-the-real-causes-of-depression-february-2007.

Sane Australia. 'Depression.' Accessed October 2013. http://www.sane.org/information/factsheets-podcasts/178-depression.

Schilling, Johannes. 'Gegen Lebensüberdruß und Todessehnsucht, Zwei Trostbriefe Martin Luthers.' *Luther, Zeitschrift der Luther-Gesellschaft* 81 (2010): 2–6.

Schleiner, Winifred. *Melancholy, Genius, and Utopia in the Renaissance.* Volume 10 of *Wolfenbütteler Abhandlungen zur Renaissanceforschung*. Wiesbaden: Harrassowitz Verlag, 1991.

Scottish Recovery Network. 'Fighting the Devil.' Accessed July 10, 2012. http://www.scottishrecovery.net/Stories-from-the-narrative-research-project/fighting-the-devil.html.

Sims, Andrew. *Is Faith a Delusion? Why Religion is Good For Your Health*. New York, Continuum, 2009.

Smith, Teresa S. *Through the Darkest Valley: The Lament Psalms and One Woman's Lifelong Battle Against Depression*. Eugene: Wipf & Stock, 2009.

Solomon, Andrew. *The Noonday Demon: An Atlas of Depression*. New York: Scribner, 2001.

Starobinski, Jean. *History of the Treatment of Melancholy From the Earliest Times to 1900*. Basel: Geigy, 1962.

Stolt, Birgit. 'Joy, Love and Trust-Basic Ingredients in Luther's Theology of the Faith of the Heart.' Luther Colloquy Lectures, October 31, 2001, Institute for Luther Studies at Lutheran Theological Seminary, Gettysburg. Accessed July 6, 2011. http://www.holytrinitynewrochelle.org/yourti84373.html.

Stolt, Birgit. *Laßt uns Fröhlich Springen, Gefühlswelt und Gefühlsnavigierung in Luthers Reformationsarbeit*. Berlin: Weidler, 2012.

Stolt, Birgit. 'Martin Luther on God as Father', in *Lutheran Quarterly*, 8/4 (1994): 385–95.

Stolt, Birgit. 'Luther's Faith of "the Heart": Experience, Emotion, and Reason.' In *The Global Luther: A Theologian for Modern Times*. Edited by Christine Helmer, 131–50. Minneapolis: Fortress, 2009.

Stolt, Birgit. *Martin Luthers Rhetorik des Herzens*. Tubingen: Mohr Siebeck, 2000.

Stone, Howard W. *Depression and Hope: New Insights for Pastoral Counseling*. Minneapolis: Augsburg Fortress, 1998.

Strohl, Jane E. 'For God Leads Down to Hell and Brings Back: Theodicy and the Word of Comfort in Luther's Theology.' Luther Lecture 2008, Pacific Lutheran Theological Seminary, October 29, 2008. Accessed September 2013. http://www.plts.edu/docs/strohl_luther_lecture_2008.pdf.

Styron, William. *Darkness Visible: A Memoir of Madness*. New York: Random House, 1990.

Swinton, John. *Raging with Compassion: Pastoral Responses to the Problem of Evil*. Grand Rapids: Eerdmans, 2007.

Swinton, John. *Spirituality and Mental Health Care: Rediscovering a 'Forgotten' Dimension*. London: Jessica Kingsley, 2001.

Swinton, John, and Harriet Mowat. *Practical Theology and Qualitative Research*. London: SCM, 2006.

Trader, Alexis. *Ancient Christian Wisdom and Aaron Beck's Cognitive Therapy: A Meeting of Minds*. New York: Peter Lang, 2011.

Treu, Martin. 'Die Bedeutung der Consolatio für Luthers Seelsorge bis 1525.' *Lutherjahrbuch* 53 (1986): 7–25.

Vitz, Paul C. *Psychology as Religion: The Cult of Self-Worship*. Grand Rapids: Eerdmans, 1977.

Vitz, Paul C. 'Psychology in Recovery.' *First Things*, March 2005. Accessed September 2013. http://www.firstthings.com/article/2007/01/psychology-in-recovery-41.

Wilson, Eric G. *Against Happiness, In Praise of Melancholy*. New York: Sarah Crichton Books, 2008.

Yahnke, Beverly K. 'Prescriptions for the Soul: The Taxonomy of Despair.' Paper presented at the Mercy Conference, St. Louis, MO, May 1, 2007. Accessed September 2013. http://www.doxology.us/downloads/35_yahnke2.pdf.

Yahnke, Beverly K, 'Christian Psychology and Spiritual Care: Approaches to Ministerial Health.' Paper presented at the Midwest Ministerial Health Conference, October 1, 1998. Accessed November 2012. http://www.mtio.com/articles/aissar43.htm.

Index

A

Absolution, 20, 180, 237, 275.
Acceptance, 40, 41, 62, 109, 113, 120, 122, 123, 134, 143, 146, 147, 171, 178, 189, 193, 202, 210, 214, 233, 241, 253.
Adam, 38, 74, 193, 221, 271.
Altenburg, 77, 78, 273.
Anfechtung, xv, xvi, 7, 8, 21, 30, 72, 83, 88, 97, 152, 196, 211, 222, 269.
Anhalt, vi, xvi, xxiii, 7, 12, 21, 22, 24, 27, 39, 40, 41, 42, 45, 46, 49, 61, 75, 76, 80, 139, 140, 141, 143, 149, 165, 166, 180, 201, 203, 219, 222, 223, 224, 225, 228, 229, 230, 258, 259, 260, 261, 263, 262, 264, 265.
Argumentationes, 55, 56.
Aristotle, xx, 107, 114, 297.
Augsburg, 30, 40, 78, 87, 89, 96.
Augustine, 195, 245.
Avicenna, 107.

B

Bayer, Oswald, xviii, 173.
Beck, Aaron, 122, 141, 156, 172, 245.
Benedictus, 98, 225, 287.
Bible, the, 9, 31, 35, 38, 54, 133, 191, 210, 211, 212, 213, 216, 217, 219, 221, 234, 251, 265, 291.
Blazer, Dan, xix, xx, 110, 123, 124, 231, 233, 290.
Bohemia, 64, 66, 68.
Buddhist, 213.
Burkhardt, Francis, xxiii, 51, 52, 58, 59, 77, 261, 224 264.
Burton, Robert, 101, 107, 114, 115, 136, 290, 292.
Butman, Richard, 148.

C

Calvary, 195.
Capps, Donald, 133.
Carnival, 51, 153.
Catholicism, 45, 129.
Christ, x, xi, 4, 7, 17, 19, 20, 21, 22, 27, 35, 36, 46, 47, 49, 53, 57, 58, 59, 60, 61, 62, 64, 67,

69, 72, 73, 74, 76, 79, 80, 85, 86, 90, 92, 93, 94, 95, 99, 129, 143, 144, 146, 149, 150, 151, 152, 153, 154, 155, 162, 163, 164, 165, 169, 173, 174, 178, 179, 180, 181, 183, 184, 186, 187, 195, 196, 197, 198, 201, 202, 205, 207, 208, 212, 215, 219, 220, 224, 226, 227, 235, 236, 247, 248, 250, 254, 259, 261, 262, 263, 264, 265, 266, 267, 268, 270, 271, 272, 273, 276, 277, 278, 279, 280, 281, 283, 285.
Christology, 53, 80, 215.
Cicero, 11.
Coburg, 16, 87, 88, 89, 91, 92, 95, 223.
Cognitive and diversional strategies, 18
Cognitive-affective, 31, 67, 71, 91, 134, 138, 140, 147, 167, 173, 179,
Cognitive-behavioural, 18, 120, 121, 140, 141, 142, 143, 146, 147, 228, 244, 245, 246, 247.
Cognitive functions, 97.
Cognitive interventions, 122, 214.
Coles, Robert, 171.
Comfort, xii, xiv, xx, xxi, 14, 15, 16, 18, 19, 20, 21, 22, 23, 29, 34, 35, 36, 39, 40, 41, 43, 44, 47, 48, 53, 55, 57, 59, 61, 62, 64, 65, 69, 70, 71, 72, 79, 81, 83, 94, 95, 97, 99, 142, 150, 164, 171, 172, 177f, 179, 182, 185, 186, 192, 195, 196, 197, 198, 200, 203, 205f, 207, 209f, 213, 217, 220, 221, 222, 224, 227, 229, 233, 238f, 251, 252, 254, 261, 263, 264, 267, 268, 273, 275, 276, 285, 286, 296, 298.
Comforter, 5, 12, 20, 21, 49, 53, 57, 58, 85, 187, 209, 262.
Comforting, 15, 21, 30, 137f, 165, 166, 186, 205, 206, 222, 257, 264.
Commandment, 73, 74, 94, 176, 208, 270, 271.
Community, x, xiii, 12, 15, 16, 78, 82, 102, 109, 110, 111, 116, 117, 120, 121, 124, 125, 127, 131, 135, 155, 157, 160, 169, 177, 209, 218, 219, 237, 238, 250.
Confession, 74, 168, 177, 179, 180, 237.
Consolation, x, xi, xiii, xiv, xix, xx, 9, 15, 16, 17, 18, 19, 22, 24, 27, 34, 36, 42, 44, 48, 49, 53, 54, 55, 56, 58, 61, 62, 66, 68, 69, 74, 78, 80, 81, 85, 86, 88, 90, 91, 94, 96, 97, 99, 100, 133, 142, 143, 148, 165, 166, 173, 178, 180, 185, 186, 192, 196, 199, 206, 207, 209, 216, 220, 226, 227, 228, 230, 235, 236, 238, 241, 243, 245, 247, 252, 254, 263, 265, 272, 274, 275, 279, 284, 292, 296.
Counsel, xii, xiii, xx, xxi, 10, 12, 16, 29, 34, 37, 45, 48, 52, 53, 55, 61, 65, 68, 69, 73, 74, 76, 82, 84, 87, 89, 92, 97, 134,

140, 162, 171, 180, 182, 201, 202, 203, 204, 206, 207, 210, 215, 220, 239, 248, 249, 250, 268,
Counselling, xii, 61, 62, 71, 119f, 122f, 131, 132, 133, 134, 140, 144, 145, 146f, 157, 159, 160, 167, 170, 172, 182, 208, 211, 212, 213, 214f, 220, 225, 239, 240, 243, 244, 250, 291.
Cross, the, 55, 60, 92, 129, 132, 178, 180f, 184, 185, 195, 196f, 202f, 234, 248f.

D

Delbanco, Andrew, 233.
Depressed, passim.
Depression, ix, x, xi, xiii, xiv, xv, xvi, xvii, xviii, xix, xx, xxi, 5, 7, 8, 14, 20, 35, 39, 43, 44, 47, 60, 61, 64, 67, 69, 70, 71, 75, 76, 78, 79, 86, 87, 89, 90, 92, 93, 95, 97, 98, 100f, 107f, 111, 113f, 119f, 127f, 136f, 148f, 155f, 176f, 186f, 190f, 196f, 198f, 229f, 238f, 246f, 257, 258, 272, 274, 284, 285.
Depressive, ix, x, xi, xii, xiii, xiv, xvi, xvii, xix, xx, xxi, 3, 4, 5f, 15, 18, 19, 24, 27f, 34, 35, 36, 37, 39, 40, 41, 42, 43, 49, 52, 53, 57, 59, 61, 62, 63, 65, 67, 68, 69, 75, 78, 81, 84, 87, 89, 91, 92, 98, 100f, 108, 109, 112, 115, 116, 121, 124, 126, 129, 131, 134, 138, 139, 140, 143, 147, 148, 155f, 161, 164, 166f, 173, 178, 180, 183, 185, 187, 188, 189f, 192f, 199f, 207, 214, 217, 224, 227, 229, 232, 238, 241f, 248f, 265, 267.
Despair, xi, 3, 4, 8, 20, 21, 55, 69, 83, 91, 92, 128, 132, 138, 139, 140, 143, 151, 153, 166, 179, 184, 186, 193, 200, 202, 203, 204, 206, 208, 219, 221, 233, 247, 248, 253, 263, 270, 282, 299.
Dessau, 40, 41, 42, 44, 46, 47, 49, 50, 51, 52, 53, 57, 58, 59, 61, 202, 224, 259, 262

E

Eck, 282.
Eicha, 63, 266.
Electro-convulsive therapy (ECT), 118.
Elizabeth,
Emperor Charles V, 64, 87.
Experiences, xvii, xviii, 104, 105, 112, 116, 117, 118, 121, 127f, 155, 157, 159, 160, 171, 186, 198, 204, 235.
Diabolic, 155
of life, 2,
of deep fear, 7
of hopelessness, 143
Luther's depressive illness, 30, 101

F

Fall, of humanity, 38, 143, 192, 213, 271.
Freud, Anna, 171.
Freud, Sigmuend, 108, 125, 136.

G

Galvin, Ray, 160, 173, 190.
Georg, Prince, 21, 22, 39, 40, 43.
Gerson, Jean, 17, 18, 19, 68, 84, 89, 90, 98, 100, 226, 228, 279, 290, 292.
Gift, 249.
God, passim.
Grace, ix, 17, 21, 23, 29, 30, 44, 46, 48, 49, 53, 56, 57, 59, 62, 66, 67, 68, 69, 73, 79, 80, 89, 129, 134, 138, 139, 142, 143, 144, 147, 157, 160, 161, 162, 163, 164, 165, 166, 179, 171, 172, 173, 174, 176, 178, 179, 182, 184, 185, 195, 196, 199, 205, 207, 212, 214, 215, 216, 220, 221, 222, 223, 234, 236, 243, 247, 249, 250, 253, 254, 255, 256, 257, 258, 260, 261, 262, 263, 265, 267, 268, 270, 271, 272, 275, 276, 279, 281, 283, 285, 286.
Gracious, 4, 22, 52, 53, 56, 57, 59, 64, 69, 81, 129, 133, 143, 163, 171, 179, 184, 190, 196, 200, 205, 208, 212, 219, 220, 225, 257, 258, 259, 260, 261, 263, 265, 266, 285.
Gregory, the Great, 135, 211.
Guide/guidelines, xx, 9, 112, 119, 120, 121, 122, 158, 199, 227, 228, 229, 252, 290, 291, 292, 295,
Guilty, 35, 93, 139, 167, 168, 172, 248, 273, 284,

H

Habsburg, 64, 65, 66, 68.
Happiness, 89, 107, 142, 165, 188, 191, 192, 199, 200, 206, 225, 226, 234, 249, 267, 275, 298.
Hausmann, 40, 43, 60, 88, 258.
Healthy, 47, 102, 108, 110, 112, 189, 226, 260.
Health, ix, x, xv, 7, 8, 35, 42, 43, 47, 52, 54, 56, 59, 101, 107, 108, 109, 110, 111, 115, 117, 119, 120, 122, 124, 125, 126, 127, 128, 131, 133, 155, 160, 167, 168, 169, 170, 176, 178, 186, 187, 188, 197, 201, 204, 218, 225, 226, 228, 236, 240, 247, 259, 264, 279, 289, 293, 297, 298.
Hippocrates, xx, 37, 107, 114, 115, 242, 257.
Homo Facetus, 50, 59, 229, 291.
Honesty, 32, 79, 196.
Hope, xii, 2, 7, 19, 22, 30, 55, 59, 62, 65, 74, 82, 91, 92, 95, 107, 109, 112, 116, 129, 129, 132, 133, 142, 143, 144, 146, 151, 153, 162, 165, 168, 174, 183, 184, 187, 199, 200, 210, 211, 213, 215, 220, 227, 232, 233, 236, 244, 247, 248, 250, 258, 259, 261, 262, 263, 267, 274, 278, 298.
Hummel, 16, 134, 165, 182, 212, 293.
Humour, 5, 44, 47, 50, 51, 58, 62, 224, 229, 230, 289.

Hunter, Lanny, 133, 196, 198, 200, 218, 219, 235, 237, 293.
Hunter, Victor, 132, 195, 198, 200, 218, 219, 235, 237, 293.

I
Ignatius, 129, 220.

J
Jackson, Stanley, xx, 114, 115, 116, 293.
Jesus, 57, 73, 74, 80, 83, 93, 95, 160, 163, 168, 170, 181, 184, 195, 196, 197, 202, 203, 207, 208, 220, 235, 263, 265, 269, 271, 274, 278, 283, 284, 292.
Joachim of Anhalt, xvi, xxiii, 7, 12, 21, 27, 39, 40, 41, 42, 43, 44, 45, 46, 48, 49, 51, 52, 53, 55, 55, 57, 58, 59, 61, 62, 183, 184, 192, 200, 201, 202, 203, 207, 219, 222, 223, 224, 225, 228, 229, 230, 258, 259, 260, 261, 262, 264, 265.
Justification, 20, 29, 41, 43, 44, 61, 65, 70, 71, 101, 102, 104, 105, 109, 114, 115, 116, 139, 233, 242.
Justifying grace, 130, 143, 166, 175, 179, 244.
Justifying forgiveness, 166.

K
Karp, David, 110, 112, 294.
Kolb, Robert, xi, 173, 194.
Koppe, Leonhard, 63.

L
Leroux, Neil, 30, 81.
Lewis, Gwyneth, 105, 107.
Lißkirchen, Barbara, vi, 14, 29, 38, 69, 70, 71, 72, 74, 88, 139, 140, 141, 151, 162, 165, 182, 208, 269.
Liturgy, the, 134, 135, 212, 219, 231, 236, 237.
Luther, Martin, passim
Lutheran, 9, 41, 55, 60, 65, 66, 70, 78, 130, 134, 138, 160, 173, 174, 185, 195, 196, 200, 213, 217, 231, 292, 296, 297, 298.

M
Madness, xxi, xxii, 2, 3, 5, 6, 7, 65, 104, 109, 111, 114, 187, 232, 292, 295, 299.
Melancholia, 4, 21, 46, 62, 69, 130, 140, 143, 165, 166, 168, 169, 170, 171, 172, 173, 174, 175, 176, 177, 179, 180, 208, 248.
Melancholy, xiii, xv, xvi, xvii, xviii, xix, xx, xxiii 1, 3, 5, 7, 18, 27, 38, 40, 44, 45, 47, 52, 55, 58, 59, 61, 63, 68, 70, 71, 75, 84, 88, 89, 90, 91, 95, 96, 101, 104, 106, 107, 108, 114, 115, 118, 133, 136, 137, 138, 139, 140, 144, 149, 150, 153, 174, 181, 186, 191, 192, 193, 194, 201, 207, 225, 231, 233, 234, 245, 258, 259, 268, 273, 279, 290, 291, 292, 293, 294, 297, 298, 299.

Melanchthon, xv, 5, 14, 39, 41, 44, 48, 139, 295.
Mennecke-Haustein, Ute, xxiii, 13, 18, 19, 22, 24, 29, 39, 40, 44, 43, 45, 51, 52, 54, 55, 56, 73, 82, 87, 98, 99, 183, 187, 261,
Metacognitive, 141, 172, 173, 208, 244, 251.
Midelfort, HC Erick, xxi, xxii, 3, 5, 6, 7, 114, 295.
Modernity, xix, 1, 2, 110, 111, 154, 181, 232, 292.

N

Narrative, xvi, 11, 28, 34, 39, 55, 102, 106, 107, 120, 121, 123, 124, 152, 153, 157, 159, 160, 161, 173, 174, 190, 191, 207, 209, 212, 214, 215, 219, 220, 221, 233, 244, 245, 248, 251, 252, 298.
Nuremberg, 77.

O

Oberman, Heiko, 151, 152, 153, 155, 164, 295.
Oinotomos, 91, 281.

P

Palmer, Parker, 196, 197, 296.
Pastoral, passim.
Peteet, John, 157, 167, 168, 169, 170, 243, 296.
Pietsch, Stephen, 5, 6, 44, 60, 78, 80, 128, 130, 134, 137, 148, 152, 154, 216, 256, 258, 260, 264, 266, 268, 272, 276, 296.

Postmodernity, xv, 109.
Prayer, 17, 36, 38, 48, 50, 51, 53, 54, 55, 58, 68, 82, 85, 89, 103, 127, 129, 135, 141, 143, 159, 163, 177, 183, 187, 201, 211, 231, 233, 235, 255, 262, 273, 279.

R

Radden, Jennifer, xx, xxii, 106, 118, 119, 297.
Reformation, the, xiv, xv, xviii, 2, 3, 4, 11, 12, 13, 21, 24, 27, 28, 30, 31, 33, 38, 40, 41, 42, 46, 60, 61, 62, 64, 66, 68, 75, 77, 78, 82, 114, 165, 174, 181, 223, 246, 295, 297, 298.
Renaissance, xix, xx, xxi, xxii, xxiii, 2, 3, 8, 9, 11, 15, 37, 38, 66, 101, 104, 109, 114, 191, 242, 243, 246, 289, 292, 298.

S

Saarinen, Risto, xviii, 32.
Saxony, xxiii, 21, 23, 40, 49, 62, 63, 74, 75, 77, 78, 88, 96, 264.
Scripture, 12, 37, 38, 40, 58, 68, 69, 70, 71, 72, 80, 89, 133, 141, 154, 179, 181, 200, 207, 208, 209, 210, 211, 212, 213, 214, 215, 216, 217, 218, 219, 220, 251, 252, 257, 268, 269, 274, 277, 280, 287.
Spalatin, George, xix, 13, 14, 55, 77, 78, 79, 80, 139, 141, 143, 150, 172, 173, 219, 273, 275, 297.

Spirituality, ix, xvi, 15, 42, 45, 46, 102, 108, 118, 125, 126, 127, 128, 129, 130, 133, 134, 142, 145, 155, 157, 162, 166, 167, 168, 169, 170, 175, 177, 178, 188, 194, 198, 202, 206, 219, 223, 227, 237, 291, 294, 299.

Stolt, Birgit, 1, 2, 7, 8, 13, 21, 30, 31, 46, 55, 151, 179, 221, 222, 223, 232, 250, 298.

Suffering, 181, 189, 190, 193, 200, 249.

Swinton, John, 118, 128, 129, 134, 168, 170, 177, 178, 188, 191, 192, 194, 198, 202, 203, 204, 219, 237, 238, 299.

T

Tappert, Theodore, xii, xiii, 12, 33, 37, 65, 69, 74, 75, 76, 82, 84, 89, 99, 294.

Theology, x, xii, xiv, xv, xix, xx, xxi, 4 15, 17, 20, 24, 30, 48, 53, 56, 68, 69, 70, 72, 77, 79, 86, 99, 115, 127, 129, 130, 134, 135, 137, 138, 139, 146, 154, 158, 160, 164, 165, 166, 168, 171, 172, 173, 174, 175, 176, 179, 181, 183, 185, 186, 187, 190, 193, 194, 195, 198, 199, 200, 202, 203, 204, 206, 207, 209, 211, 214, 215, 216, 221, 224, 225, 226, 229, 234, 235, 237, 239, 240, 245, 246, 247, 248, 249, 252, 253.

Therapy, 37, 58, 98, 103, 106, 107, 118, 120, 121, 122, 123, 124, 141, 144, 145, 146, 147, 148, 156, 158, 160, 170, 172, 173, 174, 188, 190, 209, 212, 213, 214, 215, 225, 228, 229, 230, 231, 236, 241, 245, 246, 250, 292.

V

Visualisation,

von Canitz, Elsa, 62, 63, 64, 162, 183, 254, 256, 266.

von Stockhausen, Jonas, 11, 18, 28, 32, 71, 81, 82, 83, 84, 85, 86, 139, 160, 162, 186, 209, 276, 277.

W

Weller, Jerome, xvi, xxiii, 16, 18, 24, 28, 54, 69, 74, 86, 87, 88, 89, 91, 92, 94, 139, 14, 150, 151, 152, 153, 154, 183, 186, 201, 207, 223, 224, 269, 271, 279, 280, 282, 284,

Weller, Matthias, 7, 11, 20, 69, 96, 97, 139, 150, 151, 186, 209, 223, 225, 286.

Wittenberg, 12, 22, 33, 34, 36, 37, 39, 40, 41, 43, 44, 47, 48, 49, 52, 54, 61, 63, 64, 65, 69, 79, 86, 87, 91, 95, 183, 194, 256, 259, 264, 279, 282.

Worship, 33, 40, 75, 134, 149, 215, 218, 219, 231, 236, 237, 246, 285, 299.

Y

Yahnke, Beverley, 132, 134, 135, 171, 187, 199, 299.

Milton Keynes UK
Ingram Content Group UK Ltd.
UKHW021046120524
442393UK00004B/83